CADOGAN GU

Other titles in the Cadogan Guide series:

IRELAND
TURKEY
THE SOUTH OF FRANCE
ITALIAN ISLANDS
GREEK ISLANDS
SPAIN
INDIA
SCOTLAND

ABOUT THE AUTHOR

FRANK BELLAMY has worked in the travel business since 1970. He is an expert in transatlantic travel and has written and researched several travel books. At the moment he is a director of Transatlantic Wings, a company specializing in arranging inexpensive travel to the Americas and holidays to the Caribbean. In the past six months he has updated and substantially revised this guide to the Caribbean with the help of many of the Caribbean Tourist authorities.

CADOGAN GUIDES

THE CARIBBEAN

FRANK BELLAMY

Illustrations by Pauline Pears

Series Editors: Janey Morris and Rachel Fielding

The Globe Pequot Press

Chester, Connecticut

First published as *Caribbean Island Hopping*

Manufactured in the United Kingdom

ISBN 0–87106–832–X

For Valerie and Hilary for bringing
a little sunshine into my life.

ACKNOWLEDGMENTS

The Publishers gratefully acknowledge the assistance of the following:

United States Virgin Islands Division of Tourism; Antigua and Barbados Tourist Office; British Virgin Islands Information Office; Grenada National Tourist Office; Cayman Islands Department of Tourism; Jamaica Tourist Board; St. Vincent and the Grenadines Tourist Office; Bahamas Tourist Office; The West India Committee; Turks and Caicos Tourist Board; Hill and Knowlton; French Government Tourist Office; Barbados Board of Tourism; High Commission for Eastern Caribbean States; and Windotel.

Our special thanks also go to Simon Calder and First Edition, Cambridge.

Every effort has been made to ensure the accuracy of the information in this book at the time of going to press. However, practical details such as opening hours, travel information, standards in hotels and restaurants and, in particular, prices are liable to change.

We intend to keep this book as up-to-date as possible in the coming years. Please write to us if there is anything you feel should be included in future editions.

PLEASE NOTE
Since this edition was first printed, Caribbean Airways has closed down.

CONTENTS

LIST OF MAPS

INTRODUCTION

Boy on donkey

What is 'The Caribbean Dream'? The popular image is of a tiny island with deserted, fine white sand beaches fringed with palms and sea grapes set in a still, turquoise sea. There are coral reefs nearby to be explored, and all manner of watersports. Temperatures are always in the 70s and 80s. Delicious meals are devised from local fruits and vegetables, with a strong accent on seafood.

All this is true, but it hardly begins to tell the full story. Every island is different and each country has its own personality and identity, its own character, which has been forged principally by history, which itself was largely dictated by topography, climatic conditions, natural catastrophes and other circumstances outside the control of man.

The Caribbean is a region of great diversity in a very small land area. If you regard it merely as a holiday resort, you will miss much of what it has to offer. As a traveller you are more likely to notice the differences than the similarities. Perhaps these differences even enhance the Caribbean's claim to be a continent. I only know that there is no easy way to define or describe the Caribbean, so profound and varied is its personality.

As each country's character has been determined largely by its colonial history, the best way to give a background is to divide the Caribbean into language groupings corresponding to the European powers which settled and developed the area: the British, French, Spanish and Dutch. This classifi-

1

U.S.A. (Florida)

Miami

ABACO

Nassau

THE BAHAMAS

ELEUTHERA

ANDROS

SAN SALVA

Havana

EXUMA

CROOKED IS

ISLA DE PINOS

CUBA

MAYAGUANA

THE CAYMANS   Jardines de la Reina

GREAT INA

Guantanamo

Montego Bay

Negril   Ocho Rios

JAMAICA   Kingston

CARIBBEAN SEA

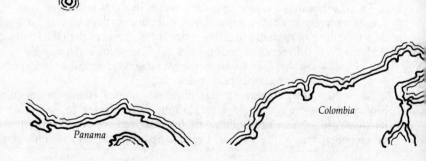

Colombia

Panama

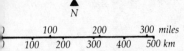

N

	100	200		300 *miles*

| | 100 | 200 | 300 | 400 | 500 *km* |

THE CARIBBEAN

S & CAICOS ISLANDS · ATLANTIC OCEAN

Puerto Plata
DOMINICAN REPUBLIC

Santo Domingo · San Juan · VIRGIN ISLANDS
PUERTO RICO · ANGUILLA
SINT MAARTEN
SAINT BARTHELEMY · BARBUDA
ST CROIX
SAINT KITTS-NEVIS · ANTIGUA
MONTSERRAT
GUADELOUPE
DOMINICA
MARTINIQUE
SAINT LUCIA
BARBADOS
ARUBA · SAINT VINCENT
CURAÇAO · THE GRENADINES
BONAIRE · GRENADA
ezuela · TOBAGO
TRINIDAD

cation is not perfect: there are six languages, English, French, Dutch, Spanish, Creole and Papiamento, and several local dialects, and it ignores the later, yet very evident, American colonisation for example. Yet I think it is the clearest way to give an impression of the Caribbean as a whole.

The People

To understand fully the complex web of people who inhabit the Caribbean, it helps to know a little about their origins.

The first recorded natives of the Caribbean were the Indian tribes who prospered on the Bahamas and elsewhere. Where they—and indeed the Indians who found their way to the Latin American continent—actually came from is still a matter of discussion among historians. A prevailing view is that they were making their way from Asia across the oceans and land masses of the world to Antarctica. In this epic journey they managed to remain isolated from the rest of the human world; so unlike the Arabs or the Chinese, whose civilisations progressed through contacts with other ethnic groupings, the Indians remained isolated from the world until the arrival of Columbus. He was searching for a western route to India, and his conviction that he had at least found some islands lying off the sub-continent persists even today in the name 'West Indies'.

Columbus' travels late in the fifteenth century shattered the lives of these first-known Caribbean dwellers. Although he revered the islanders he encountered, almost all of them perished through newly-acquired diseases against which they had no immunity, and the ravages of those who followed Columbus. Colonialism was all the rage in Europe, and virtually every nation from Sweden to Spain acquired a few jewels in the Caribbean crown. The impact of these various cultures remains as vivid today: the English understatement of Antigua, the Gallic charm of Guadeloupe and Martinique (which are full *départements* of France with the same status as the Pas de Calais and the Île de France), and the Spanish fervour of Puerto Rico. Even when islands were divided in an arbitrary fashion between nations—such as the French/Dutch Sint Maarten—each half retains the character of its motherland.

None of these European powers showed any reticence about becoming involved in the slave trade. Colonialists soon realised the agricultural potential of large tracts of the Caribbean. They were spurred on by the rapid growth in trade between Europe and its empires, and by the increased wealth of Europeans that this trade helped to generate.

The native population of the Caribbean was by now very scarce. The idea of recruiting Europeans to work on tropical islands for a pittance—albeit under the same Caribbean sun that so many Europeans now enjoy—was not practical. The newly-colonised regions of West Africa were densely populated but lacked agricultural potential. What better way to maximise revenue from the Caribbean than to relocate Africans to the island plantations? Thus the infamous slave triangle was conceived. The wishes of those enslaved were not remotely regarded as paramount.

This solution was all the more elegant for the use that it made of the merchant fleets. Black slaves were taken to the Caribbean in the ships that had taken goods from Europe to Africa, and these same vessels were subsequently used to take produce from the islands to Europe. This vicious triangle persisted until slavery was outlawed. The racial consequence is visible everywhere in the Caribbean: black faces characterise the islands, both in popular image and in reality. Yet few regions could claim to be such a melting pot. Every shade from palest white to jet black is represented, and for the most part the concept of racial conflict is utterly alien. Idyllic beaches are most enjoyable, but can be found outside the Caribbean. The charm and diversity of the people cannot.

The English-speaking Caribbean

This comprises the Bahamas, Jamaica, the Turks and Caicos Islands, the Cayman Islands, the Virgin Islands, Saint Kitts-Nevis, Anguilla, Antigua, Montserrat, Dominica, Saint Lucia, Saint Vincent, Trinidad and Tobago, Grenada and Barbados, in addition to many other smaller islands. There are far more countries and islands in this group than in any other, perhaps due to the pre-eminence of the Royal Navy in the 17th, 18th and 19th centuries.

With the exception of the United States' Virgin Islands, all of these countries are members of the Commonwealth, and many have colonial or associated status with Britain. Queen Elizabeth II is the Head of State (except in Trinidad and Tobago, where she is, however, recognised as Head of the Commonwealth). As one would expect, British institutions are well established here and traditions held in respect. Those countries which are independent have a political system based on that of Britain, though the right to sit in the Upper House is not hereditary. Those countries which nominally have colonial status are in fact largely self-governing.

Traditional uniforms are worn by police and other officials, particularly in the Bahamas, Jamaica and Barbados. These tend to make officialdom more human and approachable than is the case in those countries where uniforms are less colourful and more functional. The English sport of cricket is not only fanatically followed in the English-speaking Caribbean; the West Indies fields the world's best all-round cricket team. Soccer is followed and played, though less enthusiastically.

Generally there are economic ties with Britain, though these are declining in the area as the dollar is eagerly sought. Yet travel between Britain and Jamaica and the Eastern Caribbean in particular is still much undertaken, considering the distances involved. You will notice, however, that this traditional influence is not constant; whereas Barbados—christened 'Little England' in the Caribbean—is proud of its heritage, the Bahamas are becoming increasingly Americanised, due perhaps to their proximity to Florida.

Most islands in the English-speaking Caribbean are small, perhaps because they were selected for their strategic locations and harbours rather than their agricultural or other development potential. Their lack of size does not prevent them from having some of the best beaches you have ever seen (Antigua has 365) and some spectacular scenery and seascapes—Jamaica and Saint Lucia are good examples. This has led to the development of a substantial tourist industry, particularly over the past two or three decades. In many cases tourism has become the main industry; this is particularly the case in the Bahamas and prices have risen alarmingly. In addition, there has been little encouragement to establish other industries until now. The tourist industry, and the export earnings of those Caribbean countries dependent upon it, was reduced substantially with the onset of world recession.

Apart from Jamaica, Trinidad and Tobago, Barbados and the US Virgin Islands, all the countries are heavily dependent on imported manufactured goods and foodstuffs. The US Virgin Islands are classed as part of the United States, and the people reap the economic benefits which accrue from this. Jamaica, Trinidad and Tobago and Barbados are just large enough, in terms of population, to support some local manufacturing and food processing industries. The other islands do not have a population large enough to consume manufactured articles or processed foods in the quantity to make production economic. The Bahamas in particular are also faced with sobering transport problems. Thus prices are often high for the native as well as for the visitor (although it is true that in many, if not most, countries the difference is substantial).

The US Virgin Islands apart, these countries have had a similar history, being settled by British adventurers who introduced indentured labourers and African slaves as cheap labour. To a greater or lesser extent almost all of them were involved in the wars between the European powers which extended to the Caribbean. Independence has been recent, beginning with Jamaica in 1962. Yet the differences between these countries are remarkable. Of course the Caribbean is not an homogenous unit; but neither is the English-speaking group.

The French-speaking Caribbean

Again our definition should be handled with care, but in this group I include Haiti, Guadeloupe, Saint Martin, Saint Barthélemy, Marie-Galante and Martinique. Straight away one can argue that Haiti does not belong to this group as it has been independent for a century and a half, thus having developed its own personality, and the people speak Creole (although the official language is French; but then the countryfolk of Saint Lucia speak a kind of Creole which they call 'broken French', yet the official language is English). Following that argument, Haiti should have a group to itself; it is unique.

All the other islands are administratively part of France. You can buy the same goods and food you can get in France and at the same price (if you know where to go, but it is not difficult). When you enter you are entering France, and the people have complete freedom of movement between the French Antilles and France. Because they are French. Legally.

The Spanish-speaking Caribbean

In this group are Cuba, the Dominican Republic, Puerto Rico, San Andrés and some Venezuelan islands. San Andrés and the Venezuelan territories are not dealt with herein. Cuba is difficult and expensive to visit in the way the independent traveller would like. So this grouping really comprises the Dominican Republic and Puerto Rico.

The Dominican Republic shares Hispaniola with Haiti but has little else in common. Independence was won in the 19th century, and since then the country has been hard at work trying to develop its own personality and culture in preference to that of Spain. This has largely been successful, the language now being the main link with colonial days. But no significant personality has yet emerged to replace the colonial one, and Santo Domingo in particular is in many ways characterless.

Puerto Rico has been an American Commonwealth since the Spanish-American War. Here strong efforts have been made to preserve the cultural heritage, which means Old San Juan features some beautifully restored Spanish-colonial buildings. The first language is very definitely Spanish, though of course much English is spoken.

The Dutch-speaking Caribbean

Dutch is not a major language in the same sense as English, French or Spanish, so that most of these islands are nowadays multilingual. This rather scattered group comprises the ABC islands—Aruba, Bonaire and Curaçao—just north of the South American coast, and Sint Maarten, Saba and Sint Eustatius much further north in the Eastern Caribbean.

These islands have continually adapted to the times. Aruba and Bonaire benefited hugely from the oil price increases of the mid 1970s whilst Sint Maarten became a duty-free haven, thus providing a beacon for North American tourists. In much earlier times Sint Maarten and Bonaire had profited from sea salt production. Now tourism seems set to be the main currency earner for some years to come.

Part I

GENERAL INFORMATION

Woman carrying fruit

The Caribbean is expensive for the tourist, and should be. Unless your idea of a good time is trooping round museums, a Caribbean holiday—if selected carefully so that your choice properly reflects your requirements and budget—represents the dream vacation. You can do almost anything you would want to do on holiday with the exception of skiing (snow skiing that is!).

Getting to the Caribbean

To get the best deal on flights you may have to trade off convenience against price savings. We would all like to fly first class on good airlines non-stop to our holiday destination, and to do this for US$10. This is not possible. So you either pay a very high price or make concessions in terms of comfort. In my experience most people fall into the latter category when arranging their vacation travel, so this section aims to give some hints.

Season of travel
High season in the Caribbean is the winter, approximately 15 December to 15 April (though this can be different for individual hotels). Accommodation rates, and often extras such as car hire, reflect this. Many airfares, particularly from North America, are higher therefore in the winter season than in the

summer. In addition, holiday periods such as midsummer also attract a premium. The basic rule is that airline fares will be high when most people want to travel and ridiculously low when business is slack. So if you are leaving from North America you can expect high-season fares from 15 December to 15 April and during July and August.

From the UK, though, patterns differ slightly. There are many West Indians living in the UK and they usually have families. When they go home they want to take their children with them. In addition, British families using the cheaper Caribbean accommodation often need to travel during recognised holiday periods. High-season airfares from the UK thus coincide with school holiday periods; this is not only true of published airfares, but also of the tour-based fares used by the holiday companies. Thus, broadly speaking, the highest airfares are during July, August and September and from mid December to Christmas Eve. The highest fares of all are reserved for the joint British Airways/Air Jamaica Concorde service from Heathrow to Montego Bay via New York. There are supersonic flights every Saturday from late December to early March, and the return fare is over £3,000.

Duration of the trip
Most of the cheaper fares from the USA are valid for a maximum of three weeks. If you are staying longer, therefore, you will need to do some extensive shopping around. From the UK the maximum stay on the cheapest fares is usually four weeks. These fares normally need to be purchased as part of an inclusive holiday arrangement.

Sea travel
Travelling by sea from the UK may be too time-consuming for some, but it is possible to cruise to the Caribbean from various points in the US or find a package that combines both a flight and some cruising. See *Getting Around* for island hopping by ship.

There are regular cruises to the Bahamas and Bermuda and other island ports from Florida, San Juan, West Coast and New York, taking from three nights to sixteen days.

See your travel agent or the list of useful addresses on page 21 and at the end of each island section.

Tour operators
In theory you should make savings by booking with a tour operator although, oddly, this is not invariably the case. The tour operator has access to the lowest fares, gets a wholesaler's commission from the hotels, and often includes 'extras' in the package. From the USA these extras usually comprise special discounts on car hire, excursions and at shops, restaurants, etc. From the UK

operators you can expect free watersports offers, honeymoon offers and a third week free. Besides the cost savings you should be able to make by arranging a package, there is the convenience factor: you will not be involved in long distance telephone calls, airport transfers are usually included, and the tour operator generally has a representative on site to assist with any problems. Also, when you calculate the cost on a do-it-yourself basis, working from the lowest air fares you can find, added to the accommodation cost, you tend to forget the extras that add up and which European tour operators include: hotel service charge and government tax, taxi fares and overseas phone calls, for example. I have often been horrified, when travelling in the Caribbean, to meet people who have not properly researched their trip and have ended up paying hundreds of dollars more than they needed to.

Tourist information services for the Caribbean can be found in London and major cities of the US and Canada by looking in the phone book under the name of the island to be visited. See also addresses sections in this volume.

Travel agents

Make the effort to find a good travel agent. It's not just a question of saving money: a good agent, particularly one who has travelled to the Caribbean, will be able to give sound advice on planning your trip. For some years now I have been a director of a company—which is both a tour operator and a travel agent—which specialises in the Caribbean. This is **TransAtlantic Wings** of 70 Pembroke Road, Kensington, London W8 6NX (01–602 4021).

To safeguard your interests it is best to find a travel agent who is a member of ABTA, ACTA, or ASTA. These are the Association of British Travel Agents, the Alliance of Canada Travel Associations and the American Society of Travel Agents. Their addresses are at the end of this chapter.

Discounts

Discounts for students and older travellers are not as common in the Caribbean as in Europe and the US. Nevertheless, it is well worth making sure you hold a student or senior citizen identity card if you qualify, and asking your travel agent or hotel chain if a discount is available.

The route

Sometimes large distances can be covered at low cost, for a variety of reasons. For example, New York to San Juan is a low fare because of Puerto Rico's association with the States and the large numbers of Puerto Ricans living in New York. Similarly there are low fares available from the United Kingdom to those West Indian countries which were British colonies. (New York–Barbados has often been more expensive than London–Barbados).

Island hopping

If you intend visiting more than one island you will certainly need to do your homework thoroughly. What you should *not* do is buy a return ticket to one destination and then buy the rest as you go along. Airfare regulations, as well as airfares themselves, are volatile, so it is impossible for me to give accurate up-to-date information in a book such as this. There are some basic types which are likely to remain current for the lifespan of this book: **Open jaw tickets.** If you were contemplating, for example, a trip down the islands from Antigua to Barbados, you would be unwise to purchase a return ticket to Antigua. You could buy a ticket to Antigua and back from Barbados with a one-way ticket between the two islands which allows you stopovers on the way. From the UK or Europe this would certainly be cheaper (and more convenient) and may also prove to be so from North America. **Flyaround tickets.** Eastern used to have a ticket that allowed you to visit a number of Caribbean islands for an inclusive fare. At the time of writing LIAT certainly has two such tickets, the Explorer and SuperExplorer ('Super' means it is vastly more expensive). Dominicana has a Caribpass that allows you to visit various destinations at very reasonable cost (more details in the section on the Dominican Republic) and BWIA has a deal too.

Entry Regulations

Citizens of the USA, Canada, the UK and Western Europe will find that in most cases they will not require a visa. Variations to this are shown in the individual country sections, but if you are in any doubt whatsoever you should check with the relevant embassy or consulate. US citizens are welcomed almost everywhere, as are Canadians. UK citizens require a visa for the US territories (Puerto Rico and the US Virgin Islands) and Cuba, but that's about it. Most Commonwealth nationalities are accepted without a visa by most of those islands which are also members of the Commonwealth, plus some others. Whilst Western Europeans are usually able to visit these islands without a visa (the primary exceptions again being the US territories and Cuba) this is by no means universally the case and French citizens in particular should always check first.

Note that possession of a valid passport (and visa, if appropriate) does not automatically entitle you to admittance. Most immigration officials will want to see your onward or return ticket, to indicate that you are unlikely to become a drain upon the local economy. They will also be anxious to satisfy themselves that you have sufficient funds for the proposed duration of you visit. Sometimes you will be asked where you intend to stay. If you have no definite plans,

12

simply quote a hotel listed in the appropriate *Where to Stay* section in this book.

Climate

Everywhere is sub-tropical with normal northern hemispherical seasons, although the seasons are less marked owing to the proximity of the Equator. Islands close to South America (such as the ABC Islands) will be hotter in January than islands closer to Florida; thus in the summer the latter will be more comfortable. Smaller and flatter islands have less local variation than islands (such as Jamaica) with extensive mountains. Heaviest rainfall tends to be from June to November, but this too is not uniform.

Currency

Although the US dollar is accepted almost everywhere, it is not always in your interest to use this currency. Countries where it is advisable, or theoretically compulsory, to use the local currency are Trinidad and Tobago, Barbados and most other Eastern Caribbean islands, Jamaica and Cuba. Local currencies other than the US dollar are as follows (I have omitted here countries such as the Bahamas where the local currency is genuinely at par with the US dollar):
Trinidad and Tobago dollar: Trinidad and Tobago.
Barbados dollar: Barbados.
Eastern Caribbean dollar: Grenada, Saint Vincent, Saint Lucia, Dominica, Antigua, Montserrat, Saint Kitts and Nevis, Anguilla.
French franc: Martinique, Guadeloupe, Saint Martin/Sint Maarten, Saint Barthélemy.
Netherlands Antilles guilder (or florin): Sint Maarten/Saint Martin, Saba, Sint Eustatius, Aruba, Bonaire, Curaçao.
Dominican peso: Dominican Republic.
Gourde: Haiti.
Jamaican dollar: Jamaica.
Cuban peso: Cuba.
Where exchange rates are volatile I have not quoted them. Check with your bank shortly before departure. Where a currency has a fixed rate of exchange against the US dollar I have indicated this in the relevant country sections.

Credit and charge cards are now widely accepted. Major tourist destinations take them (though not usually in the small guesthouses, local restaurants, etc.) and you are only likely to experience problems in those destinations which are still off the beaten track. American Express and Visa are best and can often be used to obtain cash in an emergency.

Getting Around

Island hopping

Lengthy island-hopping journeys, popular a few years ago, are now rarely undertaken. Those who have the time don't have the money, and those who have the money can't afford the time. Consequently this book assumes that most readers will be visiting one island only. Local excursions to another nearby island are becoming increasingly popular, however, as are 'mini' island-hopping trips taking in perhaps four islands in three or four weeks. For these reasons the islands are grouped geographically and details of inter-island connections are included in the relevant country sections. However, as already explained in the section *Getting to the Caribbean*, you will normally find it more economical and convenient to arrange your inter-island travel when planning your trip. This is, of course, if such travel is to be undertaken on scheduled air services. In practice, you will need to fly more than you might wish as inter-island boat services are infrequent and often unreliable.

Ships and boats

Cruise and passenger ships are generally much more expensive than planes, largely because they provide sumptuous meals and accommodation and are very expensive to operate. You also have the disadvantage of being among tourists. Some cargo boats take passengers, but these are becoming rarer and may not be as cheap as you expect. To book and ascertain sailings you should visit agents in the centre of town and/or the harbourmaster's office at the port. Obviously sailings are much more frequent between those countries which trade extensively with each other.

Logically, private yachts are more common in those areas where sailing among the islands is a joy; this means the smaller islands, and principally the Eastern Caribbean and Virgin Islands. It is a good idea to plan beforehand which areas you will visit by this means, if possible, so that you can allow time to make arrangements. Notable areas best visited by cruising yacht are the Exuma Cays in the Bahamas and the Grenadines, between Saint Vincent and Grenada. To get passage on a yacht you should go down to the marina and put up a notice on the noticeboard stating where you want to go and when. Check back and you may find an offer attached. Many owners often need an extra hand and for a few dollars will be glad to take you. Your personal appearance and articulateness can make a difference here. Alternatively, you can seek out the social centre patronised by the yachting fraternity and make a personal approach, but you should note that prices of drinks, etc. will be very high.

14

Land transport

Not all countries have a bus service. Only two Bahamas islands, for example—New Providence and Grand Bahama—have buses, and schedules are limited. The British Virgin Islands and some others have no buses at all. Of course regular services exist in the Greater Antilles, and usually at reasonable cost. Jamaica has country buses and minibuses, Haiti the amazing 'tap-taps', República Dominicana comfortable and inexpensive coaches and Puerto Rico has city buses (in San Juan) and one cross-island route. Many of the smaller islands—for example Barbados, Saint Lucia, Antigua and Guadeloupe—have various kinds of services at a wide range of prices (Guadeloupe is exceptionally expensive).

Car rental can usually be arranged easily. You could book in advance through multinational car rental firms such as Hertz or Avis (advisable in high season), or try your luck finding a vehicle upon arrival: at the airport, through your hotel reception desk or with the help of the local tourist office. Note, however, that automatic transmission is the norm. You can sometimes find manual (stick-shift) cars for hire, but often you will have to pay a supplement for the privilege. Various other conveyances, from jeeps to scooters, are rented out on some islands; details are given in the relevant sections.

Taxis are of course available everywhere, but often you can also find public taxis ('publiques' or 'públicos') which are a cheap alternative to taxis or an expensive alternative to buses.

Trains are more rare, as you would expect, but there is an extensive network in Cuba, two principal routes in Jamaica, a very limited service in the Dominican Republic and a route round most of the coast in Puerto Rico.

Where to Stay

I have tried to give details on the full range of accommodation from luxury hotels to the most primitive guesthouses. Obviously I have not visited every establishment in the Caribbean—but I have tried to concentrate on giving a cross-section so that you should find something to suit your requirements and budget. In some cases, where a destination is particularly suited to a particular type of visitor, I have laid the emphasis on accommodation particularly suitable for that type.

Accommodation prices may or may not include meals. Often a hotel will never give a room rate including meals even when it has a restaurant of which it is proud. Conversely, in the winter sometimes, hotels insist on your taking a room with breakfast and dinner included (the west coast hotels in Barbados are examples of this) to guarantee that you will use their restaurant facilities. Abbreviations used in the later text to describe different accommodation arrangements are as follows:

EP: European Plan—room only.
CP: Continental Plan—room and breakfast.
MAP: Modified American Plan—room, breakfast and dinner.
AP: American Plan—usually room, breakfast, lunch and dinner.
FAP: Full American Plan—usually room and all meals (including afternoon tea).

With all the different cultural influences in the Caribbean you would expect accommodation to differ widely, and it does. Guesthouses and apartments show less variation, however.

Luxury hotels
Those usually considered the best are small, usually but not always on a beach, and with a swimming pool. (Those that are not on a fine beach have a pool). Often they are tucked away somewhere and thus provide a welcome retreat for the high-powered tycoon (those in the British Virgin Islands, Nevis and Anguilla spring readily to mind) and sometimes many of them share an accepted resort area (such as the west coast of Barbados). If 300-bed international hotels with all facilities (sometimes even including a casino) are to your taste, then you may like to include these in this category. They can certainly be included on grounds of price.

Tourist hotels
This category shows the greatest differences in hotel type, from small establishments saturated with atmosphere (such as The Admiral's Inn in Antigua) to depressing, characterless barrack-like places (such as can readily be found in Martinique).

Self-catering
This category has expanded in recent years as the Caribbean has ceased to be the exclusive preserve of the rich. The usual form is in apartment blocks, with studios (efficiencies, or efficiency units), one-bedroom or two-bedroom apartments of anything from six to thirty apartments per block. Sometimes they are featureless, sometimes they are tastefully designed and furnished. There is also a fair selection of cottage and duplex accommodation. Your travel agent or the relevant Tourist Board may have the names of rental agencies.

Guesthouses
These are usually pretty basic, to say the least. By and large they are not designed for tourists but for West Indians travelling in the islands. Thus they

16

generally do not cater for the tourist but for the traveller who really wants to experience the Caribbean. Exceptions to this that spring readily to mind are Julie's in Bequia (Saint Vincent, Grenadines) and the recommended guesthouses in Haiti. Other guesthouses which do understand the tourist's needs can be found elsewhere, but don't depend on it.

Food and Drink

Again there are cultural variations: for example, the best gourmet cuisine is likely to be on the French islands, international cuisine will be commonly available in major tourist destinations, and tiny islands with little tourism will provide only West Indian food. There are some constants however: seafood, including conch, shrimp and lobster (or crayfish) is universally strongly featured, chicken is a great favourite, rice is more common as a source of carbohydrate than you might normally be used to, and meals are usually more spicy than your regular diet. As a generalisation, wine is drunk far less here than in the colder climates and is expensive (though usually obtainable); rum is the most common national drink. Every island that produces rum in the Caribbean produces 'the best rum in the Caribbean'. Any island with a population large enough to warrant it produces a local beer (though imported beers are also widely available). Many of these local beers—such as 'Banks' in Barbados—have an international reputation.

Sporting Activities

The modern fashion for exercise and sport is increasingly evident in the Caribbean. Sophisticated societies such as Barbados and Martinique are providing facilities for their own citizens similar to those available in North America and Western Europe (for example, both have an organised marathon), but, in addition, the tourist authorities in most countries realise that the visitor will often want to engage in sport as part of his holiday. Watersports are a natural. The excellent sea conditions and pleasant temperatures mean that boating, yachting, windsurfing, scuba diving, snorkelling and waterskiing are becoming increasingly popular, and are often included in the price of accommodation. In addition, land-based sports such as golf, tennis and even squash are becoming readily available in the major resorts. If you are particularly interested in sports you will find, as a generalisation, that the larger, international, hotels have the most comprehensive range of facilities.

Other Practical Concerns

Insurance
This is very strongly recommended. It is particularly important that you are covered against any medical expenses, which are likely to be high if incurred. You should also insure your baggage against loss or theft.

Medical matters
The Caribbean is an area to which the worst infectious diseases are alien. You need no inoculations to protect you from disease, though you should be able to produce an international certificate of inoculation against yellow fever if required.

Generally the Caribbean area can be regarded as being healthy and clean, particularly the eastern part, but there are times when you should be careful. You should not drink the water in Haiti and the Dominican Republic, for instance; in other countries—such as the Bahamas—the water is safe but undrinkable as it is brackish and rust-coloured. Many people travel with a small bottle of chlorine tablets for water purification purposes.

The only place where malaria is possible—though unlikely—is Hispaniola (northern Haiti). You will encounter mosquitoes throughout, however, so it is advisable to take some mosquito coils with you. These are also available locally. As the mosquito menace is not severe these burning coils give adequate protection. You may experience a stomach upset or mild diarrhoea, caused by the change of diet or whatever, so you would be wise to take one of the preparations which rectify this.

You can get sunburnt driving around in an open car. If you come from a cold northern climate, spend a couple of hours on the beach on your first day, and then find the rest of your holiday ruined as a consequence, then that's your fault. Take a suntan lotion with an effective sunscreen—protection factor 5 at least—and build up your sunbathing gradually.

Beware of *machineel* trees. These trees, distinguished by smallish curling leaves and fruit in the form of little green apples, are often found near beaches and provide shade. Do not sit under them; the sap will blister your skin and if you are foolish enough to eat the fruit immediate medical care will be required.

Luggage, clothing, etc.
Keep this to a minimum—remember that you have to carry it with you when travelling. Temperatures are generally high throughout the Caribbean year-round. The 'coolest' months are January and February, yet even then you may well find daily temperatures over 80°F (27°C). The rainy season is not constant for the area as a whole but is generally in the period August through November. Evenings can be cool, especially in the mountainous areas.

18

Take at least one sweater, an anorak (windbreaker) or jacket and a light plastic raincoat. Additional clothes, sunglasses, etc. can be more expensive than in your local store, so make sure you are well-equipped before departure.

A cheap watch is a good idea. In many parts of the Caribbean, watches are scarce and regarded as a sign of wealth. There may well be a definite link between being hustled and showing off an expensive-looking timepiece.

Take a camera and plenty of film. The signs at airport security checks proclaiming 'X-rays will not harm film' are not entirely accurate. If a film passes through several scanners (as it might well do if you are island hopping), the dose builds up and can cause blurred photographs. To be safe, always ask for a manual examination of your camera and films.

Documentation
It is a good idea to take any documentation that might be useful: for example, you should take your driving licence even if you don't intend hiring a car or scooter when you leave home. If you haven't got credit cards get them before you go and take them with you. They will be invaluable if you run out of money.

Restaurants and nightlife
There is always some form of nightlife, even if it is only a bar with a jukebox; and there are restaurants everywhere, even if these only comprise a wooden shack serving rotis and chicken with peas 'n' rice. However, if you are looking for restaurants and nightlife comparable with those you have at home you should only expect to find them at major tourist resorts.

National festivals and holidays
National holidays will usually coincide with the Christian calendar and the particular island's Independence Day. Trinidad's Carnival is on the Monday and Tuesday preceding Ash Wednesday, a traditional date based on Christianity (it precedes Lent) whilst other islands hold their main festival or carnival to commemorate their independence or another such event. Sometimes festivities or events such as a regatta are held in the off-season in order to stimulate tourism.

Customs
It is advisable to take receipts for valuables to avoid delay and unnecessary duty. It is normally acceptable to take to the islands anything for personal use with the exception, of course, of drugs. Marijuana, opiates, barbiturates and hallucinogens are illegal throughout the Caribbean. The more sensitive governments will jail tourists for smuggling and look hard and suspiciously at hippy types. In Jamaica be particularly careful not to smoke or trade in grass.

Tipping
Usually service is included in hotel bills. If not 10–15% would be acceptable.
Restaurants and bars 12–15% if service not included.
Taxis usually 15%.
Porters and bellhops 50c (US) per bag.   Maids US$1.

Electricity
The mains electricity supply on most islands is 110/120 volts at 60 cycles,
which corresponds to the US supply. A variety of round and flat two- and
three-pin sockets are used. A good plan is to take dual-voltage equipment and
a suitable adaptor, or to check in advance and buy a transformer/adaptor if
required. Failing this, your hotel reception desk may be able to help.

Traffic
Normally traffic drives on the right unless stated otherwise in the individual
island section.

Time zones
In such a diverse group of islands, it is hardly surprising that there is no standard time zone. The main zones are as follows; those marked D employ daylight saving time in summer, when the clocks are moved an hour ahead.

GMT −5 (noon on island = 5pm in UK, noon Eastern Time):
    Bahamas   D
    Cuba   D
    Haiti   D
    Jamaica
    Puerto Rico   D

GMT −4 (noon on island = 4pm in UK, 11am Eastern Time):
    Barbados
    British Virgin Islands
    Dominican Republic
    Guadeloupe
    Leeward Islands
    Martinique
    Netherlands Antilles
    Saint Vincent/Grenadines
    Trinidad and Tobago
    US Virgin Islands
    Windward Islands

Useful Addresses

Sea travel
Caribbean Tourism Association, 20 East 46th Street, New York, NY 10017.
Cruise Lines International Association, Pier 35, Suite 200, San Francisco, CA
94133 or 17 Battery Place, Suite 631, New York, NY 10004.

Travel agents
ABTA, 55–57 Newman Street, London W1 4AH (01–637 2444).
ACTA, 130 Albert Street, Ottawa, Ontario, K1P 5G4.
ASTA, 4400 MacArthur Blvd, Washington DC 20007.
United States Tour Operators Association, 211 East 51st Street, New York,
NY 10022.

Tourist information
British Virgin Islands Tourist Board, 801 York Mills Road, Suite 201, Don
Mills, Ontario, M3B 1X7 (416–283 2239).
Caribbean Tourism Association, address as above (212–682 0435).
Eastern Caribbean Tourism Association, 220 East 42nd Street, New York, NY
10017 (212–986 9370) or Place de Ville, Suite 1701, 112 Kent Street,
Ottawa, Ontario, K1P 5P2 (416–236 8952).
French West Indies Tourist Board, 610 Fifth Avenue, New York, NY 10020
(212–757 1125).
French Government Tourist Offices in Chicago, Beverly Hills, Toronto,
Montreal and London.
US Virgin Islands Tourist Information Office, 1270 Avenue of the Americas,
New York, NY 10020 (212–582 4520) or 25 Bedford Square, London
WC1 (01–637 8481).
West India Committee (for UK Virgin Islands, Saint Kitts and Nevis, Turks
and Caicos), 48 Albemarle Street, London W1 (01–629 6353).
Most islands have a tourist office in the main cities of the US, UK and Canada.

Insurance
Europ Assistance, 252 High Street, Croydon CR0 1NF (01–680 1234). Not
for Haiti or Dominican Republic.

Discounts
Council on International Education Exchange, 205 East 42nd Street, New
York, NY 10017; 312 Sutter Street, San Francisco, CA 94108.
Association of Student Councils, 44 St George Street, Toronto, Ontario,
M5S QE4.

Handicapped travel

Society for the Advancement of Travel for the Handicapped, 26 Court Street, Brooklyn, NY 11242.

The Royal Association for Disability and Rehabilitation, 25 Mortimor Street, London W1 (01–637 5400) produces *Holidays for the Physically Handicapped*.

Facts on File, 460 Park Avenue South, New York, NY 10016 publishes *Access to the World: a Travel Guide for the Handicapped* by Louise Weiss, $14.95, plus $2 postage.

Part II

LESSER ANTILLES

Schoolgirls

This is the area of greatest diversity. Here are islands which are legally part of France, Dutch islands, former British possessions, and countries which remain colonies. The underdeveloped islands lie cheek-by-jowl with the relatively prosperous. Revolution and invasion are a short plane ride away from enviable stability.

This is also the area where regular scheduled airline services make island hopping very much a practical possibility; there is opportunity to travel by local ferry or private yacht and even a proposal to link many of the islands with a jetfoil service.

Windward Islands

BARBADOS

Not normally considered the most beautiful of the Caribbean islands, Barbados has nonetheless established itself as the Caribbean's Number One holi-

23

day destination. Why? It is only 21 miles long and 14 miles wide, and seems to have no more natural resources than, say, Saint Lucia or Saint Vincent.

The secret probably lies in the island's three distinct advantages: seemingly endless miles of superb white sand beaches, often sheltered by coral reefs; cooling trade winds that keep the humidity low; and a reputation for having an unexcitable and friendly people.

There is, too, probably more accommodation in all categories and price ranges than will be found in any other holiday destination, yet Barbados is without the disadvantages of packed beaches and a raucous atmosphere. High-rise hotels are few and there are long stretches of the coast which have only solitary hotels dotted about, or none at all.

All this means that in Barbados you can have the best of both worlds: uncrowded beaches and countryside by day, and a hectic and varied nightlife in the evening.

Barbados can be regarded as the best introduction to the Caribbean. Whilst tourism is the major industry here, and has been for years, it doesn't appear to have imposed itself artificially on the island. A large indigenous population, very politically aware and literate, with a sizeable and very evident middle class, has created a consumer society along the lines of Europe or North America.

Many of the supermarkets, stores and shops are patronised by both residents and tourists, as are, to a lesser extent, restaurants and beaches (particularly at weekends). The telephones work very efficiently and are much used. Tap water is drinkable, there are no water shortages, and power cuts are unknown. The roads, though narrow and often winding, are on the whole adequate and well-surfaced, though there may sometimes be traffic congestion.

The island is very regional, different parts attracting different types of tourist. The west coast—the parish of Saint James and part of the parish of Saint Peter—is generally regarded as having the finest beaches. Consequently most of the top hotels are built along this stretch, strung out along seven miles of coastline from Cobblers Cove down to Coconut Creek (although, of course, there are good hotels elsewhere in Barbados, and some moderately-priced accommodation on this coast).

The south coast lies to the southeast of Bridgetown and comprises Hastings, Rockley, Worthing, Saint Lawrence and Maxwell. This four-mile stretch of coastline is known for its inexpensive accommodation, mainly self-catering but with some hotels and guesthouses too. There are many good beaches on this stretch, most out-of-town shopping facilities and most of the nightlife.

These main tourist areas roughly coincide with the main residential areas of Barbados, recorded in an official publication as follows:

'The 1980 census showed that because of the pattern of settlement development along the coast, the main urban centre extends into an urban contin-

24

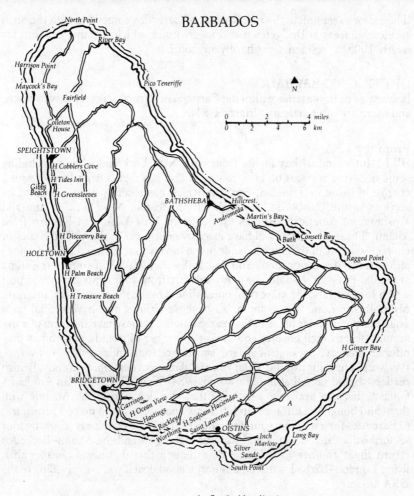

BARBADOS

North Point
River Bay
Harrison Point
Maycock's Bay
Pico Teneriffe
Fairfield

N

0   2   4 miles
0   2   4   6 km

Colleton
House
SPEIGHTSTOWN
H Cobblers Cove
H Tides Inn
Gibbs
Beach
H Greensleeves
BATHSHEBA
Hillcrest
Andromeda
Martin's Bay
H Discovery Bay
Bath
Consett Bay
HOLETOWN
Ragged Point
H Palm Beach
H Treasure Beach

H Ginger Bay

BRIDGETOWN
Garrison
H Ocean View
Hastings
Rockley
H Seafoam Haciendas
Worthing
Saint Lawrence
A
OISTINS
Inch
Marlow
Long Bay
Silver
Sands
South Point

A = Grantley Adams Airport
H = Hotel

uum reaching Speightstown to the north, Oistins to the south and, most recently, St Philip to the east. The total population living in this urban belt was about 152,000 or 62% of the national population.'

The major exception to the tourist areas of Barbados coinciding with the main residential areas is Bridgetown and its environs, which together account for nearly 100,000 residents, yet hardly any tourists.

GETTING TO BARBADOS

Because of its importance within the Caribbean, Barbados is very easy to reach, and there are often bargain airfares available.

From the USA

BWIA International has flights from both New York and Miami, including some non-stop services on both routes. It also has flights from Boston with a change of plane in Trinidad. Pan Am, which has recently been extending its services to the Caribbean, has flights from Boston, New York, Miami and Washington. American Airlines flies in from New York, and Eastern from Miami. These US airlines all have extensive networks in the United States of course, so if any of them serves your home town you may find there is a same-airline same-day connection. And do not discount BWIA; if you are travelling at regular fares there should be a through fare from your nearest major airport which is often valid for more than one airline. On the matter of fares, there are two points to note: firstly, any or all of these airlines may have special fares available at particular times of the year. Sometimes these take the form of a fly-around ticket which enables you to visit a number of islands; sometimes they offer an inclusive package of airfare, accommodation and, perhaps, car rental. It is worth checking around when you are planning your trip. Secondly, British readers should note that in both winter 1984/85 and 1985/86 Pan Am had a fantastic bargain available: assuming that you flew across the Atlantic with them and bought an ultra-cheap USA travelpass, you could make a return trip to Barbados for a nominal sum. In winter 1985/86 the travelpass (allowing four sectors within the USA) would have cost you £88 and the Miami–Barbados return flight another £75. Please note though that this is *not* cheaper than flying London–Barbados direct; it is only a good deal if you are travelling to the USA anyway.

From Canada

Wardair has probably done more for tourism in Barbados than any other airline in Canada. A super airline, with reasonable fares and excellent inflight service, it also functions as a tour operator, so if you are travelling this way you will probably get a better deal by booking an inclusive tour with Wardair. It is predominantly a charter airline, so check schedules with your travel agent. BWIA flies non-stop from Toronto twice a week. Air Canada flies from Montreal and Toronto.

From London
Barbados is very well served from London. Caribbean Airways (the national airline of Barbados) currently serves Barbados from London on Saturdays and Sundays; both of the outward flights and the Sunday return flight are direct. BWIA also flies twice a week, with outward flights on Thursdays and Saturdays and return flights on Wednesdays and Saturdays, all of them non-stop. British Airways flies out and back on Tuesdays, Wednesdays, Saturdays and Sundays. Some of these flights are direct and some are routed via Antigua or Saint Lucia. At peak periods such as Christmas, Caribbean Airways and British Airways often add extra flights (BWIA, as a carrier from a third country, is not allowed to do this).

At the time of writing the cheapest official return air fares from London are the APEX fares, currently £405 low season and £475 high season, bookable at least three weeks in advance. If you are unable to book in advance there is now a PEX fare which requires no advance booking; this is pitched at £455 low season and £525 high season. The low season periods are 1 October to 6 December and 25 December to 30 June; high season periods are 1 July to 30 September and 7 December to 24 December. There is also a little-known return fare of £711 which requires no advance booking and allows one stopover, which must be Toronto, New York or Miami. All these compare with a regular return fare of £1,082 (£541 one way).

In practice, however, few people pay these fares. London is well-known throughout the world as a centre for cheap tickets, and agents specialising in these—often called 'bucket shops'—advertise in the press. As this is a book about the Caribbean and not about the travel business, it is not the place here to evaluate all the pros and cons of using a bucket shop, but with care and caution you'll often find cheap ticket deals available from reputable agencies.

Of course you'll only need an airfare alone either if you have accommodation already provided (for instance if you are visiting friends or relatives) or if you are visiting more than one island and don't want to commit yourself to a fixed itinerary beforehand. In most cases you will arrange your flights and accommodation at the same time. The best way to do this is to book a package holiday, which is not as restricting as it sounds. Tour operators buy airline seats at prices significantly lower than those shown above, and also acquire accommodation at lower rates than you would pay if booking direct with the hotel. Some of the savings are lost in travel agents' commission and the tour operator's profit of course, but nevertheless in almost every case you will save money by making your arrangements in this way. There are over 40 UK-based companies offering package holidays to Barbados. Some tour operators which feature Barbados strongly in their programmes are Caribbean Connection, Kuoni, Trade Winds and TransAtlantic Wings. If you fly via the USA you will need a visa.

From Europe

There are four European cities from which it is possible to fly to Barbados without changing aircraft: Brussels, Frankfurt, Milan and Zurich. All are served by Caribbean Airways. It is certainly possible to fly from almost anywhere else to Barbados, changing in one of these cities or in London, but fares are high. It is usually best to book a package with a local tour operator and let them worry about the best way to route you. There is a substantial flow of tourists to Barbados from Germany and Scandinavia, and local travel companies (e.g. Air Charter Market in Frankfurt and Nouvelles Frontières in Paris) should be able to help you.

Within the Caribbean

You can get to Barbados easily from almost anywhere in the Caribbean—there is even a fortnightly flight from Cuba. Here are a few very general notes to give you an idea.

BWIA (the national airline of Trinidad and Tobago) operates from Barbados to Trinidad, Tobago (sometimes), Saint Lucia, Antigua, Puerto Rico and Jamaica. These are generally jet services, either Tristars or DC9s. Caribbean Airways currently operates a DC10 into Saint Lucia and a small propellor plane into Saint Vincent and Grenada (these flights are timed to connect with the London flights). LIAT, and its subsidiaries Inter Island Air and Four Island Air, operates throughout the Eastern Caribbean from as far south as Caracas in Venezuela to as far north as Puerto Rico. These are small turboprop or piston-engined aircraft however, so if you are travelling any great distance you will find the journey slow and uncomfortable. They are best for short hops. British Airways serves Antigua and Saint Lucia, Pan Am flies on to Trinidad (as does American Airlines), whilst Eastern operates to Saint Lucia.

ENTRY REGULATIONS

Technically, citizens of the USA, UK and Canada can enter without passports, as long as they have other proofs of identity. To attempt such entry in any circumstances other than an emergency is foolish, however, as it is likely to make life unnecessarily complicated and will almost certainly preclude you from visiting some of the nearby islands if you suddenly take it into your head to do so. Citizens of the following countries do not, at the time of writing, require a visa: Australia, Austria, Bahamas, Belgium, Canada, Cyprus, Denmark, Finland, German Federal Republic, Ghana, Greece, Irish Republic, Israel, Italy, Liechtenstein, Luxembourg, Malta, Netherlands, New Zealand, Norway, Spain, Sweden, Switzerland, USA, United Kingdom and colonies, Venezuela and citizens of Caricom countries (and there are many more exceptions). French passport holders *do* need a visa. Holders of South African passports need to apply for a visa and will probably not be given one.

You may be required to show that you have sufficient funds to maintain you for your expected stay in Barbados and will have to show onward and/or return tickets.

You will need to show vaccination certificates (for yellow fever or cholera) only if you have recently arrived from an endemic or infected area.

Customs allowances are fairly strict: 200 cigarettes or ½lb tobacco, one bottle (26oz) of alcoholic beverage (don't take rum, which is very cheap in Barbados) and 150 grams of perfume. In theory the system of red (something to declare) and green (nothing to declare) channels is used, but in practice there is often a row of chairs across the entrance to the green channel, forcing everyone to use the red.

There is a departure tax of 16 Barbados dollars payable by everyone except those who have been on the island for less than 24 hours.

ELECTRICITY
The supply is 110 volts at 60 cycles, as in the USA.

CLIMATE
Barbados is blessed with perhaps the best climate in the West Indies. Being quite far south it is never cold, even in January, with temperatures in the range 72°F to 82°F. Rainfall is less than on some of the other islands, the rainy season running from July to November—though this is by no means guaranteed.

CURRENCY
The Barbados dollar is tied to the US dollar at a rate of US$1 = BD$2, although you must expect to lose a couple of cents when changing money. Accommodation rates are almost always quoted in US dollars, and other prices in BD dollars. Credit and charge cards are widely accepted.

Notes are produced in the following denominations: $100, $20, $10, $5, $2 and $1. There is also a $1 coin. Other coins are 25, 10, 5 and 1 cent.

POPULATION
Most Bajans (inhabitants of Barbados) are black, although there is a sizeable number (over 5%) of white Bajans and immigrants. Most of the white Bajans, certainly those you are likely to meet, enjoy a high standard of living and very many of them are involved in the tourist industry. The tourist infrastructure is

29

far more developed here than in almost any other Caribbean island and is still largely controlled by this group. The white Bajans are also involved in construction, manufacturing and other industries.

In contrast to this, many of Barbados' poorer citizens are white. Living in some of the more remote parts of the island, the Redlegs (as they are called) are rarely written about and almost a forgotten people. They are still largely engaged in traditional agricultural work and are probably descendants of the 'indentured labourers' shipped out at about the time of the abolition of slavery, whereas the more wealthy white people of Barbados are very often descended from more recent immigrants. It is only in recent years that emigration to Barbados has slowed down substantially.

The Bajans are an easy-going people and have been described as the friendliest in the Caribbean. They are highly articulate and literate (the literacy rate is about 98%) with an interest in affairs outside their own backyard.

LANGUAGE

English has been the official language of Barbados since the arrival of the British settlers in 1627.

HISTORY

One of the few islands missed by Columbus, Barbados was actually 'discovered'—in European terms—in 1536 by Pedro a Campos, a Portuguese who was on his way to Brazil. He reputedly christened the island 'Los Barbados' (The Bearded Ones) after the bearded fig trees which grew there then. In 1627 the first British settlers established a community at Holetown in what is now St James' Parish. From this date, right up to independence in 1966, Barbados remained British. British traditions are so strong (a love of cricket being perhaps the best example) that other Caribbean countries often used to allude to Barbados as 'Little England'. British place names abound: the hilly area is known as Scotland, and the island can also boast a Brighton, Windsor, Worthing, Hastings, Yorkshire and Whitehaven, to name just a few.

GETTING AROUND

There is a bus service from Bridgetown to all parts of the island. This is certainly cheap, but it may not be regular. The service from Bridgetown to the airport is downright bad. If you are leaving the island by air you would be ill-advised to rely on this method of transport. This is the only time, however, when waiting for a bus should prove a great inconvenience. Normally the bus service provides a perfectly adequate means of seeing the island.

Barbados is an island where car rental is definitely recommended—to be precise, a moke. Besides the ubiquitous minimoke (minicar) there is the Caribbean Cub (for those who prefer rear-wheel drive, and it has a lockable boot/trunk), Hustler and others. Cars, including automatics, are available but less fun and more expensive. Hertz and Avis are represented at the airport and in Bridgetown. It's best to use credit cards, to avoid paying a hefty deposit.

Mokes (minicars) are still available at BD$270 a week (e.g. Courtesy Car Rental), but nowadays will generally cost more—up to BD$350 a week. The price you pay seems to bear little relation to the quality of service or car you get. These prices generally include unlimited mileage. Bring your domestic licence with you. A local driving permit, obtainable sometimes from the car rental company but otherwise from any police station, costs BD$30 and is valid for a year.

Scooters can also be hired but value is not so good; expect to pay BD$150 to BD$200 per week. Although Barbados is relatively safe for those venturing on two wheels, a moke or something similar is better.

There is a more than adequate supply of taxis. Examples of fares, all in Barbados dollars, are as follows:

Airport to Speightstown	42
Airport to Gibbs (Greensleeves, etc.)	33
Airport to Holetown	30
Airport to Bridgetown	23–26
Airport to Hilton/Holiday Inn	20
Airport to Worthing	18
Airport to Saint Lawrence	16
Airport to Crane	18
Bridgetown to Speightstown	35
Bridgetown to Gibbs	25
Bridgetown to Holetown	20
Bridgetown to Hilton/Holiday Inn	7
Bridgetown to Worthing	12
Bridgetown to Saint Lawrence	13
Bridgetown to Crane	33

WHAT TO SEE

Barbados is far larger in its reputation than its actual size of 166 square miles. With one-third of the population spread over two-thirds of the island, car hire should be compulsory. A leisurely drive around Barbados will reward you with some lovely views, from agricultural vistas of waving sugar cane to spectacular seas and the rugged coastline of the east coast. Rural life is generally seen in the form of picturesque settlements or isolated plantation houses. Workers in the fields are still likely to wave to you.

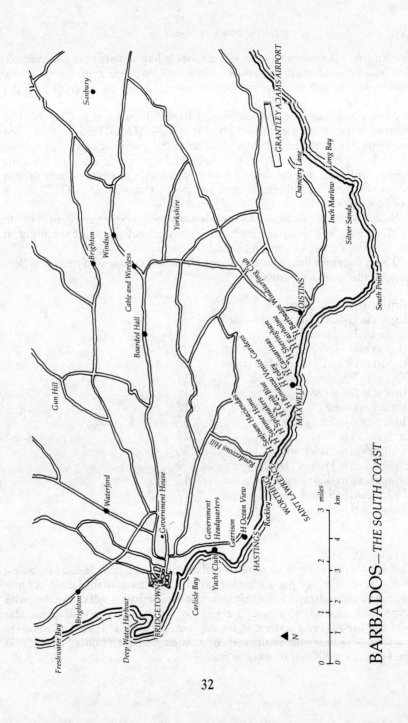

BARBADOS — THE SOUTH COAST

Bridgetown

The central point of Bridgetown is Trafalgar Square, complete with statue of Admiral Nelson, named not so much after London's Trafalgar Square, as before it—in 1813. Nowadays Lord Nelson presides over rush-hour traffic jams. In Barbados all roads lead to Bridgetown, eventually, only to become entangled in a mass of one-way streets. Broad Street is the main shopping thoroughfare and offers in-bond (i.e. duty-free) shopping provided goods are delivered straight to your plane or ship.

Other areas of interest in Bridgetown are the Careenage (the old harbour), Saint Michael's Anglican Cathedral, the Barbados Museum and Washington House, where perhaps George Washington and his brother Lawrence stayed—or perhaps not, depending on who tells you the story.

The Tourist Board is to be found on Harbour Road, at the Hastings end of Bridgetown.

The south coast

An imaginary trip around the coast of Barbados is perhaps the best way to get the feel of the place.

Leaving Grantley Adams Airport you turn left onto Highway 7, heading for the beach areas and Bridgetown. The roads are narrow and winding, though well-surfaced, bordered with small wooden buildings. Every settlement is heralded by the sight of people walking by the road (there are few footpaths).

The first landmark you'll notice is probably the fishing village of **Oistins** with its small, brightly painted fishing boats pulled up on the beach contrasting with its modern shopping centre. Almost immediately afterwards you reach the first tourist area, **Maxwell**. Here there are a few hotels and apartments and a couple of restaurants. It is on this fairly quiet stretch of coast that you'll find Sheringham Beach Apartments, Fairholme Hotel and the Barbados Windsurfing Club. Barbados is known to be one of the best places for windsurfing, and this is an excellent place for proficient sailors. Highway 7 leaves the coast at this point, rejoining it about two miles further on at Saint Lawrence Gap. Now it begins to get busier: from here to Hastings (about a mile before Bridgetown) runs the 'South Coast Strip', the highest concentration of hotels, guesthouses and apartments on the island.

But let's pause here awhile. Along part of that coastline studiously avoided by the architects of Highway 7 is an area which is currently the most popular in Barbados. If you turn off the main road at Saint Lawrence Gap and travel southwards along the minor (but well-maintained) coast road you'll pass through the Saint Lawrence/Dover area. Here hotels, apartments and guest-houses proliferate. First you pass two restaurants, The Witchdoctor and Pisces, then The Ship Inn, then Josef's—at the time of writing one of the very

33

best restaurants on the island—before the road winds through an area of apartments, hotels, minimarkets, a bank and more restaurants until it reaches Casuarinas Beach Club.

For an area with so much happening it has a surprisingly calm and detached air. There is very little through traffic, which makes it a perfect spot for those without a car. Wherever one stays in this area it is possible to walk to nightspots and restaurants easily, and nowhere is far from a beach.

Return to Highway 7 for the journey into town. From Saint Lawrence, through Worthing and Rockley to Hastings, all types of accommodation can be found along the road, most on the beachside, but some on the landward side. Yet, incredibly, the beaches (with the exception of Rockley) remain uncrowded. They look just like the brochure illustrations.

You'll soon see why these beaches remain idyllic: there are few high-rise hotels. You'll also notice, not too far from the silver sands, swaying palms and flower-bedecked roadsides, modern shopping centres and banks. Thus, if you're staying on the south coast, most of your holiday requirements are within easy walking distance of your hotel.

From Hastings continue around Carlisle Bay, past the Garrison Racecourse and into Bridgetown by way of Bay Street. Passing along the Careenage, skirt Bridgetown by way of the Deep Water Harbour Estate until you meet Spring Garden Highway. This excellent wide new road is the best and fastest stretch in Barbados—speeds of up to 55 mph may be legally attained.

The west coast

Highway 1 is as narrow as Highway 7 and just as busy, with minor settlements and the towns of Holetown and Speightstown straddling the road. Many of the hotels are not visible from the road, as they are hidden from view by driveways of luxuriant foliage. At other times the road runs right alongside the beach, affording vistas of turquoise sea and perhaps a glimpse of the 'pirate ship' *The Jolly Roger.*

The majority of the top hotels are situated between the southern border of Saint James' parish and a little to the north of Holetown. Continuing north you will note that the hotels tend to be interspersed more sparsely among the luxury villas and houses which are built on some of the finest beaches. **Gibbs Beach**—generally considered one of the very best—has no hotels on it at all (although Greensleeves and Tides Inn are situated across the road).

After passing Cobblers Cove—a very well-run hotel in a romantic setting on a lovely bay—you find yourself in **Speightstown** (unless you've taken the new road, built to improve access to Heywoods Resort, which bypasses the settlement). Speightstown can be busy, yet is full of character. There are still many traditional wooden buildings intermingled with modern structures and it can be an interesting stop on an island tour.

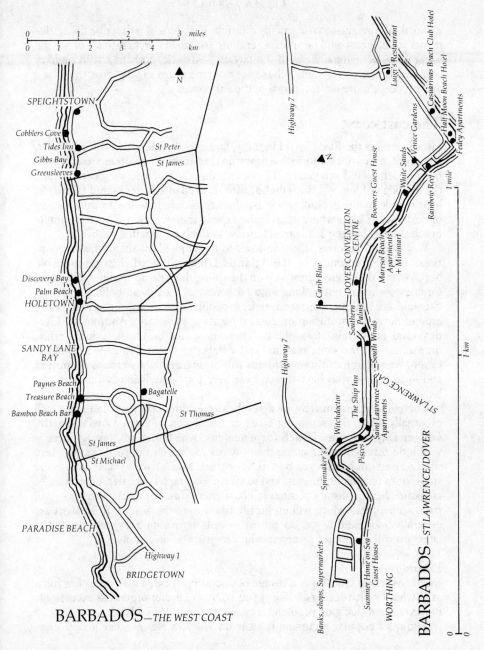

BARBADOS—*THE WEST COAST*

Scale:
0 1 2 3 *miles*
0 1 2 3 4 *km*

N

SPEIGHTSTOWN

Cobblers Cove
Tides Inn
Gibbs Bay
Greensleeves

St Peter

St James

Discovery Bay
Palm Beach
HOLETOWN

SANDY LANE
BAY

Paynes Beach
Treasure Beach
Bamboo Beach Bar

Bagatelle

St Thomas

St James

St Michael

PARADISE BEACH

Highway 1

BRIDGETOWN

BARBADOS—*ST LAWRENCE/DOVER*

Highway 7

N

Lucy's Restaurant
Casuarinas Beach Club Hotel
Venice Gardens
Half Moon Beach Hotel
White Sands
Fedey Apartments
Rainbow Reef
1 mile

Boomers Guest House

DOVER CONVENTION
CENTRE

Maresol Beach
Apartments
+ Minimart

Carib Blue

Southern
Palms

South Winds

1 km

Highway 7

Witchdoctor

The Ship Inn

Saint Lawrence
Apartments

ST LAWRENCE GAP

Pisces

Spinnaker's

Banks, shops, Supermarkets

Summer Home on Sea
Guest House

WORTHING

0
0

35

North of Speightstown is a vastly different Barbados. To describe the settlements as villages would be an exaggeration. Isolated churches, fields of waving sugar cane, occasional views of the far-away Atlantic, perhaps a wild monkey scampering across the path—these are now the norm as you cross the island and proceed, more or less, down to the east coast.

The east coast

Here you meet the East Coast Highway, formerly the island's best road, wider, straighter, more open and with less traffic than most of the other roads. Here, on your left, you'll see young Bajans with their homemade surfboards riding the breakers. Then it's **Bathsheba,** with its eroded stag rocks and tall palms bent double by the prevailing winds, often considered the most beautiful part of Barbados. This is where many Bajans spend their vacation. There are ample beaches here, but the sea is treacherous, so don't be tempted to dive in.

You should, however, allow yourself to be tempted by one of the excellent Bajan buffets presented by the **Atlantis Hotel.** Situated right on a pebble beach with fishing boats drawn up on the shore, the Atlantis traditionally caters for guests who are not looking for a conventional Caribbean holiday. Its main clientele are middle-aged and retired people who enjoy the scenic walks around here, the profusion of tropical plants at the nearby Andromeda Gardens and the family atmosphere. There may also be the occasional artist, drawn here for the same reasons, and a Bajan or two taking their annual vacation. At lunchtimes these residents will be augmented by groups of tourists and local people who have driven over here for the deliciously varied buffet lunch.

Travelling approximately in a southeasterly direction from here you will eventually strike the southeast coast in the region of **Sam Lord's Castle, Ginger Bay** or **Crane Beach** (depending on which road you take). There is very little through traffic going this way, so you'll find the roads empty, very winding and often bordered by shrubs or trees. You'll have to make occasional stops, both to consult the map and to take photographs—a splendid avenue of tall palms here, a distant plantation house there. Just before the coast you will meet a main road which will eventually take you to the airport. Road signs are generally good, and if you do get lost—well, there's no hurry and sooner or later you will encounter someone who can give you directions.

Excursions
Barbados is best enjoyed as a voyage of discovery. A car, a map and a few hints as to what's worth seeing and away you go. If you prefer organised excursions, however, then that's no problem. Try Safari Tours (427 5100).

The most popular excursion is a trip on *The Jolly Roger.* Some people consider this the highlight of their holiday. For BD$55 you get a four-hour coastal cruise (west coast), transfers to and from the hotel, buffet lunch, unlimited drinking (mainly of potent hooch), snorkelling, rope swinging and 'walking the plank'. There is also an evening cruise with a band. A more recent addition to the local cruise fleet is *The Bajan Queen*, a Mississippi-style riverboat. Drinks, barbecue, watersports and live music (on the Sunset Cruise) are included.

Organised excursions are made to **Harrison's Cave,** and this should be booked a few days in advance in high season. You are conveyed by a special little train through formations of stalagmites and stalactites well illuminated to catch the plunging waters at their most attractive (432 8048, or arrange with your hotel or tour representative).

On your driving tour try to visit **Andromeda Gardens** at Bathsheba if you enjoy cultivated shrubs and flowers. A special bonus, if you choose the right day and time, is an excellent buffet lunch at the **Atlantis Hotel** (see above), five minutes away. **Welchman's Hall Gully** in Saint Thomas, now part of the National Trust, has been developed into a botanical garden with many fine specimens of exotic fruit and spice trees.

At **Richmond Plantation,** an old sugar plantation in Scotland, is a new **Flower Forest**. This is one of the most scenic areas of Barbados, so if you lose your way it will still be a lovely drive.

There are many spots like those mentioned above, scattered through the sparsely-inhabited two-thirds of the island. Some you may come across by accident, others you will find with the help of locals.

CALENDAR

The Holetown Festival is the first main event of the year. In February, it celebrates the landing of the first settlers in 1627 and includes concerts, sports and religious services.

The Oistins Fish Festival is in early April, but the main event of the calendar is the Crop Over Festival, beginning in June with a street procession and climaxing on Kadooment Day, the first Monday in July.

All the festivals characteristically include much folk dancing, calypso and steel band music.

WHERE TO STAY

As previously noted, Barbados has an abundance of accommodation of all types and in all price brackets. It is not possible to list them all, but the following is a list of places which are recommended. A full list is available from any office of the excellent Tourist Board.

Cobblers Cove, it is said, is for honeymooners. The most northerly of the west coast hotels until Heywoods was built, and the only one on its reef-protected crescent-shaped white sandy beach, it is smaller than most with only

38 rooms. The suites, which comprise bedroom, bathroom, kitchen, lounge and balcony or patio, are housed in blocks of four. These form a horseshoe, the two ends of which are on the beachfront. Tucked between the two open ends of the horseshoe, along the beach, are the kidney-shaped swimming pool, the pink-painted castle (main building), restaurant and bar. The whole is situated in its own gardens and surrounded by tropical foliage. The manager, Richard Williams, was voted Caribbean Hotel Manager of the Year in 1985.

A little further south is the highly recommended **Greensleeves** hotel and restaurant, across the road from Gibbs Beach. The spacious suites have been designed and built apparently with no expense spared. There are a dozen apartments, two two-bedroomed and ten one-bedroomed, housed in blocks of two or four and set in spacious and pleasant gardens. The effect of this is to give almost the seclusion of a private villa, yet with the hotel facilities of bar and restaurant close at hand. Solid construction and sturdy materials are evident throughout, with marble floors and a marble-topped dining table in a lounge/dining room easily capable of entertaining six.

Each one-bedroom apartment comprises a dining-/sitting-room measuring perhaps 14ft by 18ft and furnished with dining table, six straight-backed chairs, a sofa, easy chairs and occasional tables, leading out onto a semi-circular balcony or patio of similarly generous proportions; a bedroom measuring about 14ft square; ample storage space; spacious bathroom with bath and shower, twin washbasins set into a marble top, bidet, etc; and a kitchen. The kitchen is only intended for snacks and drinks of course. It is not envisaged that guests would want to prepare their own meals when breakfast and dinner are served in Greensleeves' excellent restaurant. Service is old-fashioned but not stodgy or pretentious. But be warned: although the hotel room rates can be extremely good (if you book through one of the UK operators featuring this hotel, or even, at certain off-peak times of the year, by negotiation with the manager, Edmund Manning) the restaurant is very expensive.

It is not really possible to say that any particular hotel is the best in Barbados. Personal tastes must be taken into account. But one which is certainly a candidate for this accolade is **Treasure Beach**. Rather newer than both of the above hotels, it is managed by its owners, the Ward family. Situated on the beach at Holetown in the parish of Saint James, it comprises 24 suites and 3 studios clustered around the swimming pool, restaurant and bar, and is set in well-tended gardens leading on to an excellent beach. If one can judge status by price, then Treasure Beach is in the running for the top hotel title; winter 1985/86 rates showed a significant increase over the previous year and are more than double the summer rates. Occupancy levels are very high too, the hotel being able to boast high levels of repeat business.

Unfortunately restaurant standards in Barbados tend to be mediocre, a criticism which applies to most of the hotels. Fortunately this criticism does not apply to Treasure Beach; the restaurant there is wholeheartedly recommended.

Still on the west coast, another hotel worthy of mention is **Discovery Bay**. Recently purchased by the tour operator Kuoni, this hotel provides an acceptable 'west coast' standard at a more attractive price. The 'rack rates' for this property are as high as you would expect, but there are good rates to tour operators, so if you are making the booking through a tour operator you will get very good value.

The last 'top hotel' listed here is **Ginger Bay,** which can be described as a 'honeymoon hotel'. Situated in an isolated position on the southeast coast, on its own picturesque beach, it comprises a lovely cluster of ginger-pink buildings housing spacious suites. There is a swimming pool and tennis court, and an outstanding restaurant. It would be a first choice for a romantic Barbados holiday, but will not suit everyone because of its isolation from other activities.

There are two particularly good hotels in the middle price range, both of which are fully fledged apartment hotels, allowing you to prepare your own meals should you feel so inclined. **Palm Beach,** situated at Holetown next to Discovery Bay, is often classed in the apartment category. Accommodation comprises studios housed in a four-storey block behind a row of two-storey one-bedroom apartments running down to the beach. A restaurant, the Steak House, is adjacent to the property. In the winter some watersports activities are included in the price.

Casuarinas Beach Club, at Dover on the south coast, is probably the best-value middle-range hotel (it can be classed as a good three-star hotel). Since it opened at the end of 1981, many of its visitors have booked a second holiday. Accommodation comprises 64 studio apartments in two four-storey blocks set in 7½ acres of landscaped grounds leading to a 900-ft long beach. There is a sizeable swimming pool designed for those who take their swimming seriously, and a children's pool. There are tennis and squash courts, a bar and a restaurant. The bar is to be recommended, featuring a wide range of cocktails and all drinks at reasonable prices (considering the category of hotel). Unfortunately the restaurant is not so good, however; although its open-air ambience is pleasant, the food is less satisfactory. However, Casuarinas is very popular and is often difficult to get a room, particularly in the winter.

Among Caribbean destinations Barbados has become well known for its proliferation of self-catering accommodation. When the growth of this sector mushroomed, in the 1970s, it was aimed particularly at British tourists who couldn't afford a traditional Caribbean holiday but who wanted something better than the Mediterranean sunspots. A combination of low accommodation rates and the cost-saving facility of self-catering suddenly brought a Caribbean holiday within the scope of tens of thousands who would otherwise have not been able to afford it.

Most of these apartment hotels are situated on the 'South Coast Strip' from Hastings to Maxwell, though there are others scattered about the island. They range in size from establishments with fewer than ten rooms to the sprawling Sunset Crest development, but most have between eight and thirty apartments.

Many of the apartment hotels at the bottom end of the price scale have suffered from the recession. The decrease in tourist numbers, coupled with an overabundance in this category of accommodation, has meant that prices have stayed the same over the last few years—or even dropped. These low rates have not prevented low occupancy levels. As a consequence many proprietors have been unable to spend the necessary money on renovations.

Carib Blue, which is one of the best of the inexpensive apartment hotels, has only suffered in that as yet it has been unable to build a restaurant. The fifteen apartments are attractively furnished and in immaculate condition, all with balconies overlooking the recreation ground at Dover. The owners, Mr and Mrs Maxwell, are delightful people and the staff very friendly. Carib Blue is 130 yards from Dover Beach.

Another apartment hotel to be recommended is **Fedey,** situated in a little enclave near Casuarinas Beach Club. The dozen apartments themselves are rather basic, though air-conditioned and with Rediffusion radio. What makes them so pleasant to stay in is the management style of the owners: the attitude of Janet, who is responsible for the day-to-day running, is one of genuine concern for the guests who thus settle in and relax right from the start. There is a restaurant on the ground floor which serves quite acceptable local food at reasonable prices.

In the same area is another reasonably priced establishment, **Bonanza/ Venice Gardens.** Bonanza is a fairly old twin block of one- and two-bedroom apartments which are adequate and cheap. Venice Gardens is a newer block of ten studios, almost adjacent, which, again, can be described as adequate. The advantage here is the helpfulness and good service of the staff and very reasonable rates.

Good, friendly management in an average hotel will usually ensure a happier stay than an off-hand or an uncaring attitude in a well-appointed place. For this reason, **Spinnaker's** must be mentioned. It has a pleasant seaside ambience, and the food and service can be recommended. Spinnaker's is set right on the sea, by a tiny beach, at Saint Lawrence Gap. There are eighteen apartments, mainly studios, all facing the sea, which have been refurbished recently. Its location, backing onto the main road, makes communication with other parts of the island easy by bus, and restaurants and nightlife—such as Pisces, The Witchdoctor, Josef's, The Melting Pot and The Ship Inn—are all within about three minutes' walk. The new management team also operates a small diving operation.

If there are four or five of you travelling you may prefer a two-bedroom apartment. **Sea Foam Haciendas** at Worthing has very well-furnished and excellently maintained spacious apartments, situated right on the beach. All rooms face the sea. Both bedrooms in each unit are air-conditioned.

Cricketers

Nestling among palm trees at Maxwell on a fairly quiet part of the south coast are the **Sheringham Beach Apartments**. Ten standard apartments are housed in the century-old seaside home of one of Barbados' plantation owners. Eighteen superior apartments, all with a sea view, have been added alongside. All are air-conditioned. Sheringham's situation means its fine beach is never crowded, and it is only a few steps from the sand to the beach-side bar and café. There is also an air-conditioned cellar bar here, with occasional evening entertainment.

Sheringham is owned and managed by the same people who run the **Fairholme**, about four minutes' walk away. Fairholme Hotel is a converted plantation house which was part of the old Maxwell Plantation. It is managed by Mrs Joyce Noble, a very lovely English lady, and has a restaurant, bar and gardens with swimming pool. It is good value for money (it is only a little more than guesthouse prices). Twenty studio apartments, each with balcony or patio, have been added alongside.

Barbados has a number of guesthouses, but most do not provide bathroom en suite, and some are a fair distance from the beach. **Summer Home/ Summer Place on Sea** has seven rooms, each with a private bathroom, and it is situated right on the beach at Worthing. Although it might be described as 'a shack on the beach', it is a little more than that. The owner, George de Mattos, is friendly and helpful, and the standard of dinner provided by Selwyn, the cook, is excellent by guesthouse standards.

41

Overnighters often try the **Shonlan Guest House,** as it is about the closest place to stay to the airport. It is on the main road in the middle of nowhere. Forget the beach—you'd have to walk miles. Accommodation seemed clean and reasonable; many rooms have their own bathrooms.

Accommodation in Barbados
Daily summer rates in US$

	Single	Double	Triple
Hotels			
Casuarinas Beach Club, Dover, St Lawrence, Christ Church (tel. (428) 3600)	EP 50	EP 50	EP 60
Cobblers Cove, Road View, St Peter (near Speightstown) (tel. (422) 2291)	EP 50–100	EP 72–122	EP 92–142
Colony Club, Porters, St James (tel. (432) 2335)	EP 50	EP 65	EP 80
Coral Reef, St James (tel. (422) 2372)	MAP 76–88	MAP 128–175	MAP 178–241
Discovery Bay, Holetown, St James (tel. (432) 1301)	EP 60–90	EP 70–100	EP 85–115
Ginger Bay, St Philip (tel. (423) 5810)	EP 71	EP 99	EP 127
Glitter Bay, Porters, St James (tel. (422) 4111)	EP 66–85	EP 94–132	EP 114–167
Greensleeves, Gibbs, St Peter (tel. (422) 2275)		EP 80	EP 100
Palm Beach, Holetown, St James (tel. (432) 1384)	EP 30	EP 30–45	EP 45–55
Sandy Lane, St James (tel. (432) 1311)	EP 104	EP 120	EP 180
Tamarind Cove, Paynes Bay, St James (tel. (432) 1332)	EP 45–75	EP 60–90	EP 75–105
Treasure Beach, Paynes Bay, St James (tel. (432) 1346)		EP 72–110	EP 87–125

The management of **Tides Inn,** up on the west coast on the border of Saint James and Saint Peter, would not really consider it a guesthouse, though it is currently listed by the Tourist Board as such. Accommodation consists of a seven-room hotel and a two-bedroom villa set in well-tended gardens. Mr and Mrs Terry, the proprietors, keep the place extremely clean and tidy and have carved out a niche for themselves, providing good meals at extremely reasonable prices and with a very pleasant atmosphere.

Barbados has more than fifty hotels. The list given here is just a selection. The summer season runs approximately from 15 April to 15 December, though there are variants. Rates in the winter season will be at least double, often more, and you will find that most of the west coast hotels will insist that you take MAP, which increases the cost further. Booking these hotels through a tour operator should show significant savings.

	Studio (2 or 3 sharing)		1-bedroom apt		2-bedroom apt	
	1 or 2	3	2	3	4	5
Apartments						
Bonanza/Venice Gardens, Dover, Christ Church (tel. (428) 9097)	20	23	20	23	40	45
Carib Blue, Dover, Christ Church (tel. (428) 2290)	30	35				

	Studio (2 or 3 sharing)		1-bedroom apt		2-bedroom apt	
	1 or 2	3	2	3	4	5
Apartments						
Fairholme, Maxwell, Christ Church (tel. (428) 9425)	35	43				
Fedey, Dover, Christ Church (tel. (428) 4051)	20	25				
Monterey, St Lawrence, Christ Church (tel. (428) 9152)	35	40				
Paradise Villas, Black Rock, St Michael (tel. (424) 4581)			42	47	65	70
Rockley Resort, Golf Club Road, Christ Church (tel. (427) 5890)	50	55	70	80	90	100
Salt Ash, St Lawrence, Christ Church	22	27				
Sea Foam Haciendas, Worthing, Christ Church (tel. (428) 5362)					55	60
Sheringham Beach Apartments, Maxwell, Christ Church (tel. (428) 9339)	45	55				
Spinnaker's, St Lawrence Gap, Christ Church (tel. (428) 7308)	25	30			35	

This is just a selection from the very extensive apartment accommodation available in Barbados. The summer season is the standard 15 April to 15 December. Winter rates will be about 50% higher than the above.

	Single	Double	Triple
Guesthouses			
Berwyn, Rockley, Christ Church	8	15	20
Fortitude, Lower Wellington Street, Bridgetown (tel. (426) 4210)	25	45	60
Pegwell Inn, Welches	9	17	
Shonlan, Coverley Terrace, Christ Church	15	22	27
Summer Home on Sea, Worthing, Christ Church (tel. (428) 6620)	10	18	23
Tides Inn, Gibbs, St Peter (tel. (422) 2403)	33	38	41

Summer season dates as above. Winter season rates are typically 50% higher. Most of these guesthouses also provide meals on request.

8% Government tax should be added to all the rates listed above, and usually 10% service charge.

EATING OUT

Restaurants are a problem in Barbados. Presumably because in colonial days the island was always British, general standards of cuisine have never aspired to the levels found on some of the islands which received more diverse influences during this period. Not that food is bad; it just tends to be mediocre. To complicate the situation further, a restaurant can be excellent one year and average the next. Here, however, are some suggestions of the restaurants which currently enjoy a good reputation.

Josef's, at Saint Lawrence Gap, Christ Church, has been consistently good since it opened in 1984. A favourite with tourists and locals alike, regularly attracting diners from as far away as Heywoods and from the west coast generally, the menu is varied, the decor smart and prices reasonable. During the peak season it is usually necessary to make a reservation several days in advance.

Reid's, opposite Coconut Creek Hotel, is also well-favoured, although it is expensive, as is **Greensleeves,** up at Saint Peter. Perhaps the greatest allure of Greensleeves is the elegance of its poolside dining. With the comfortable open-sided lounge and bar this restaurant provides the most pleasant dining ambience on the island. Service is traditional and courteous and the food is always up to standard. Also included in this category, which can loosely be termed 'gourmet cuisine', is **La Cage Aux Folles,** near Paynes Bay in Saint James.

Most restaurants feature 'Bajan cuisine' to a greater or lesser extent, and those specifically offering this are in the majority. Individual preferences come into play to a much greater extent in this category, so the following are just suggestions. **The Witchdoctor** at Saint Lawrence Gap has a tropical feeling with much use of plants and natural wood. The menu is based on West Indian food designed to appeal to the tourist. Prices are reasonable. **The Ocean View,** Barbados' oldest hotel, at Hastings, is remarkable for its old-world elegance. Dining is on the terrace overlooking the beach and sea, with excellent food and attentive service. There is also a cabaret downstairs on some nights, and The Crystal Room, which is geared to formal dining for parties.

A complete contrast is **The Tourist Trap** on the Maxwell Coast Road in Christ Church. The style here is relaxed and friendly, with native dishes the staples—Bajan chicken, flying fish, dolphin, prawns, peas 'n' rice. If you like to eat and see a show at the same time, you could try **The Plantation** on the main road at Saint Lawrence. On Wednesday nights the Tropical Spectacular is staged here, a popular tourist attraction.

Reasonably priced restaurants, often offering large portions, include **The Tamarind Tree** at the Sea View Hotel, Hastings (lunch only); **The Melting Pot** on the main road at Saint Lawrence, popular with local people and budget-conscious tourists alike; **Pebbles** at Carlisle Bay; and **Dover Express** under Fedey Apartments at Dover, Saint Lawrence.

Most of the specialist restaurants are to be found on the south coast. **Da Luciano** is generally considered the best Italian restaurant, housed in an old Barbadian home and serving meticulously prepared fine meals—with prices to match. **Pisces** has been considered for years one of the island's top restaurants. As the name suggests, the menu is entirely seafood. The general ambience is excellent, the setting is open-air and right on the sea at Saint Lawrence Gap. Over the years opinions have differed as to the quality of food and service, though there is general agreement on the prices (it's considered expensive). More recently the service was not so good.

It is generally held that the best pub is **The Ship Inn** at Saint Lawrence Gap. Expect it to be crowded. The restaurant here is **The Captain's Carvery,** which offers hot roasts in unlimited portions. If you've a healthy appetite and fancy a gregarious evening, stop here.

A last specialist restaurant worthy of mention is **Suzie Yong,** currently situated at the Bresmay Apartments, again in Saint Lawrence. Normally, Chinese food in this part of the world shows strong signs of Trinidadian or Guyanese influences, but this restaurant is described as 'authentic Chinese' (presumably Cantonese), and is well spoken of by Bajans and tourists alike.

NIGHTLIFE
You could probably go to a different show every night of the week in season. Monday night is perhaps the longest established as Show Night, when the **Island Inn** at Garrison, Saint Michael, stages its open-air presentation. This features steel band music, limbo, calypso dancing, fire eating, etc. Dinner beforehand is optional. **Barbados Barbados** at Balls Estate, Christ Church, takes the Tuesday slot. The show here 'explores the many and varied features of the rich history, customs and habits of the Barbadian people'. Dinner, drinks and transport are included.

On Wednesday night **The Plantation** hosts the 'Tropical Spectacular', already mentioned. This has a cast of thousands (well, thirty anyway) and takes you through the island's history in a show of dance and music. '1627 and All That', staged at the Barbados Museum, lays claim to Thursday and Sunday nights. This evening comprises a blend of a walk through history—literally, in the sense of viewing artefacts and being attended by girls in period costume— and history set to dance routines. Dinner is included, at the halfway stage.

This leaves Friday and Saturday nights, but you will not be forced to retire early at the weekends either, as many of the hotels have their own entertainment. There is the Friday night cabaret at the Ocean View and, in season, entertainment at hotels such as Southern Palms, Heywoods, South Winds and other large hotels.

Nightclubs include **The Carlisle,** set appropriately on Carlisle Bay, a fairly large beach bar with open-air disco and dance floor; the **Belair,** a packed jazz club on Bay Street in Bridgetown, best in the early hours; **After Dark,** a plush and packed disco in Saint Lawrence; and **The Stables,** which caters for a very young clientele.

Pubs proliferate. Besides **The Ship Inn** there are **The Windsor Arms** at Hastings, the 'most English' of them; **The Coach House** at Paynes Bay, Saint James; and **Friends** at Saint Lawrence Gap, just to name a few. There are evening cruises on *The Jolly Roger* and *The Bajan Queen*. And if you are still awake and peckish in the early hours, take a trip to Baxter's Road for some of Enid's chicken.

45

SHOPPING

Bridgetown and the west coast offer sophisticated goods for the serious shopper. Bone china and tweed from Britain, jewellery from Brazil, silver from Denmark, watches from Switzerland, and every kind of handicraft made on the island, including custom-made tailoring, shellcraft, dolls, placemats and rugs, pottery, sculpture and embroidery. At Pelican Village you can watch the artisans at work.

Many hotels have boutiques to cater for the ultra fashion-conscious.

SPORT

A comprehensive range of watersports is a fairly new development in Barbados. Many of the west coast hotels—Paradise Beach, Cobblers Cove, Discovery Bay and Heywoods spring readily to mind—provide complimentary watersports for their guests. This usually means windsurfers, sunfish, snorkel gear, etc; you usually have to pay for waterskiing and scuba diving. Waterskiing is good on this coast as the sea is usually calm and there are protected bays. Scuba diving is improving all the time, and there are now several operations and two wrecks, in addition to reef dives. The west coast is not so good for windsurfing, which is best undertaken at the **Windsurfing Club** at Maxwell (intermediate standard), Worthing (beginners) or Silver Sands/Round Rock (wave jumping).

There is some yachting, although it is not so good here as in the Grenadines, and deep-sea fishing is also possible. There are three golf courses, one of 18 holes at **Sandy Lane** and 9-hole courses at **Rockley Resort** and at **Heywoods**. Many of the hotels have tennis courts where non-guests can play (try Casuarinas or Rockley Resort). Both these hotels also have squash courts, as does Heywoods.

Cricket is the first love of Bajans and the major spectator game. If you want to participate and can take a team out there, some of the British tour operators can probably help you: Kestours, Budjet Travel, Caribbean Connections, Sunwing Travel and Gulliver's Travels.

Horse racing, riding and polo are popular inland, and are inexpensive.

GRENADA

Grenada was catapulted into the public consciousness as a result of the US invasion in 1983, and more recent political events have introduced this island to a still wider public. However, in spite of events, Grenada today appears very much as it did four or five years ago. There are the same warm, friendly people, a lush, fertile hinterland, and fine beaches lapped by a gentle sea.

GETTING TO GRENADA

With the completion of the new airport at Point Salines, Grenada has become far more accessible overnight. This is partly because the new airport is able to handle jet aircraft right up to the largest jumbos, thus cutting out the overnight stay in Barbados or Trinidad that used to be necessary, and partly because the new airport is sited close to the tourist areas and the capital, thus eliminating the need for what was, to many tourists, a hair-raising drive over the mountains.

From the USA
Both BWIA and the newly-formed Grenada Airways fly twice-weekly from New York to Grenada. BWIA has a daily service from Miami (which stops twice) and Grenada Airways has a weekly non-stop flight.

From Canada
There are still no flights from Canada direct, so you should use either the traditional route via Barbados or Trinidad, or fly to New York and pick up one of the services mentioned above. There should be a through fare, however.

From London
At the moment no airline flies the same aircraft from London through to Grenada, though British Airways is on the verge of doing so and will presumably commence operations when likely passenger loads permit. Same-airline services are available on BWIA. At the moment Caribbean Airways is the best airline to use as the tiny plane it operates from Barbados to Grenada (a Britten Norman Islander) waits in Barbados for the incoming London flight. Consequently if your transatlantic flight is late you will not miss your connection. BWIA operates with a change of plane in Trinidad, but its schedules are not necessarily convenient and are notoriously subject to change.

From Europe
Brussels, Frankfurt, Milan and Zurich are linked with Grenada by the same Caribbean Airways schedules noted above. It's a long journey but can be done in a day with one change of aircraft (in Barbados).

Within the Caribbean
There is a surprising range of Caribbean islands which can be reached from Grenada on a same-plane service. LIAT flies south to Trinidad and north to

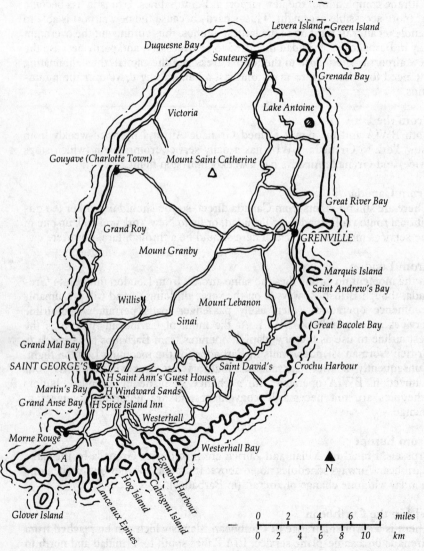

GRENADA

PETIT MARTINIQUE

CARRIACOU

Hillsborough

Grand Bay

Saline Island

Large Island

Frigate Island

Levera Island

Green Island

Duquesne Bay

Sauteurs

Grenada Bay

Victoria

Lake Antoine

Gouyave (Charlotte Town)

Mount Saint Catherine

Great River Bay

Grand Roy

Mount Granby

GRENVILLE

Willis

Mount Lebanon

Marquis Island

Saint Andrew's Bay

Sinai

Great Bacolet Bay

Grand Mal Bay

SAINT GEORGE'S

H Saint Ann's Guest House

Saint David's

Crochu Harbour

Martin's Bay

H Windward Sands

Grand Anse Bay

H Spice Island Inn

Westerhall

Morne Rouge

A

Westerhall Bay

N

Egmont Harbour

Calvigny Island

Hog Island

Lance aux Epines

Glover Island

0	2	4	6	8	miles
0	2	4	6	8	10	km

A = Airport   H = Hotel

Barbados, Saint Vincent, Saint Lucia, Dominica and Antigua. Its subsidiary, Inter Island Air, operates tiny planes to Carriacou, Union, Mustique, Saint Vincent and Saint Lucia (both airports). BWIA serves both Trinidad and Tobago direct, and flies northwards to Saint Lucia, Martinique, Antigua and Sint Maarten.

ENTRY REGULATIONS
Passports are not normally required of visitors from the USA, Canada and the United Kingdom, though onward and/or return air tickets are.

Visas seem to be required in remarkably few cases, even French citizens being allowed entry without them. Most nationalities can transit without a visa, providing they have ongoing reservations and tickets, for up to fourteen days. There is a departure tax of EC$20.

ELECTRICITY
The supply is 220 volts at 50 cycles, about the same as in the UK.

CLIMATE
The dry season is from January to May, and the rainy season from June to December. Grenada gets a fair amount of rain for the same reasons as Saint Lucia and Saint Vincent, namely its mountainous aspect. Rain usually comes in heavy showers which rarely last more than an hour or so. Most people welcome them as they relieve the heat which can become oppressive in summer.

CURRENCY
The Eastern Caribbean dollar is the local currency, approximately equal to US$0.40. US$1 = EC$2.70.

POPULATION
The total population is in the region of 120,000 with the greatest concentration in the Saint George's/Grand Anse area. To a large extent, though, life is still very rural; in addition to the second town of Grenville on the east coast, near the old Pearls Airport, there are large and small settlements scattered over the island. Agriculture is still the main industry.

Although the people are poor (there is a high rate of unemployment, and the island has recently been adversely affected by the economic recession), there is little trace of anti-tourist or anti-white feeling. The people here are among the friendliest in the Caribbean.

LANGUAGE
English with some patois is spoken amongst the islanders, a legacy of French colonisation and African slavery.

49

HISTORY

Columbus arrived here on 15 August 1498 and, after pausing briefly to name the Island Conception, he foolishly sailed on. Subsequently other Spaniards called and changed the name to Granada, presumably because the topography reminded them of that part of Spain. The French later termed it 'Grenade', and the British dubbed it Grenada (Gren-ay-da) as we know it today. Those not familiar with the island often pronounce 'Grenada' as 'Granada'. The Amerindian name was Camaliogue.

As elsewhere in the eastern Caribbean, the peaceful Arawaks were forced out by the warlike Caribs who were in turn supplanted by the French. Morne des Sauteurs in the north was the last retreat of the Carib warriors, some 40 plunging down onto the rocks rather than surrendering.

The French were the first European colonisers, founding plantations of cotton, tobacco and sugar, which became a target of British attacks during a turbulent 18th century. In 1753 the island was ceded to Britain, reoccupied by the French in 1779, returned to Britain in 1783 and suffered a French Revolution-inspired revolt by the French and some slaves in 1795. This was put down the following year.

During the 19th century, first slave trading then slavery itself were abolished, but the planters adapted by planting new crops. Spices, particularly nutmeg and cocoa, became very important.

Full independence was achieved in 1974 under the now notorious Sir Eric Gairey. He still has his supporters, and apparently did much good work as a union leader in his early years, and his activities have ensured that Grenada's 'history' continues to the present day.

In March 1979 the New Jewel Movement, led by Maurice Bishop and Bernard Coard, seized power whilst Gairey was away discussing UFOs in the USA. Initially the revolution was a popular one, though not among those who had grown rich under Gairey. Slowly, however, hard-line socialism was introduced: opposition newspapers were closed down, political dissenters imprisoned and the security forces strengthened.

At the end of 1983 relations between Maurice Bishop and the Coard faction were at their lowest ebb and Bishop was placed under house arrest, ultimately to be released by a large crowd of supporters who bore him to the Fort overlooking Saint George's. This was when the military faction led by Hudson Austin attacked the unarmed crowd with the help of an armoured car, causing much loss of life and injury. Bishop and his supporters from the Cabinet surrendered and were immediately murdered.

After four days of the island's subjugation under an iron fist, the Americans, with token forces from other Caribbean islands, invaded. Elections were held in November 1984 and a moderate coalition under Herbert Blaize won fourteen of the fifteen seats.

The greatest lasting benefit of the socialist years is the fine new airport at Point Salines. Built by the Cubans, allegedly for military purposes, it will undoubtedly be a great boon to the island's economy.

GETTING AROUND

The basis of Grenada's transport system is the cheap truck bus, similar to that of Saint Vincent and Saint Lucia. Slightly more expensive, and more comfortable, are the minibuses of various makes, which carry about sixteen passengers. Please note, however, that Sunday and evening services are few. An even greater degree of comfort can be found in shared taxis, which take up to six passengers. All the transport leaves from the market square in Saint George's (Halifax and Granby Streets). The fare to Grenville by minibus or shared taxi is EC$3.50; truck bus is slightly cheaper. Normal taxi rates are EC$2 for the first mile and EC$1 thereafter.

Should you want to arrange an excursion or hire a car, Grenada has an excellent travel agency, **Grenada Tours and Travel.** It is to be found at Huggins Travel, on the corner of Young Street and the Carenage. Note that Grenadians drive on the left.

WHAT TO SEE

Grenada has an area of 133 square miles, most of which is covered by lush vegetation. The scenery is generally described as 'unparalleled' and the state claims to be 'the most beautiful island in the Caribbean'. This reputation is well founded: Grenada really is very beautiful, and the views are sometimes spectacular. The drive across the mountains from Grenville to the capital, Saint George's, is quite an experience. The road itself is narrow, winding and at times very steep (buses and trucks are unable to use it)—an asphalt switchback snaking through the lush greenery. Reaching the crown of a hill on the way into Saint George's, you can look down and see the soft white body of Grand Anse Beach, basking in the sun. The mellowed bricks, red tiles and wrought-iron balconies of the Georgian-colonial buildings in town and around the Carenage present some splendid man-made views.

Grand Anse Beach, about four miles south of Saint George's, is reputed to be one of the best in the Caribbean. This reputation is based largely on its size (it is broadly sweeping and shallow, and excellent for swimming). It is thus very popular and less attractive to those seeking seclusion.

Grenada's reputation as the 'Isle of Spice' is attributed to its being the only spice-producing island in the western hemisphere. In 1843 Frank Gurney introduced nutmeg from the Dutch East Indies. It was an important development as it was at about this time that the sugar-cane industry began to decline, owing to both falling prices and emancipation. Agriculture remains the island's

51

chief industry, the principal products now being cocoa, nutmegs, mace and bananas. You can see spice-processing at Dougaldston House at **Gouyave**, north of Saint George's.

Tourism is the island's second industry. Although the revolution of 1979 caused a sharp decline in visitor numbers, tourism has increased steadily since the democratically-elected New National Party took control in 1984. From that time, considerable improvements have been made to roads and water and electricity supplies, as well as to overall conditions in Grenada.

Saint George's, the capital, is a lovely little town. Its focus is the Carenage, a looping promenade with schooners at anchor. The tourist office is situated here. Walk to the end, turn right, go up the hill and down the other side and you will come to the market.

Most sightseeing on Grenada is looking at the scenery in general, but you can take a trip to the **Botanical Gardens,** just three miles from Saint George's. Here the trees, shrubs, flowers and all the spices of Grenada grow against a background of ponds and an old sugar mill. **Concord Falls,** in Saint John's parish, is worth a day trip, with much else of interest to see in the surrounding area.

St. George's Harbour, Grenada

CALENDAR

The new year and mid January bring visitors to the yacht race and fishing tournament. The Easter Regatta also celebrates the sea-going traditions of the island.

52

WHERE TO STAY

In the past there have been complaints of a lack of hotel beds in Grenada. Although this may once have been true, a comprehensive expansion programme is in operation, and already the island can provide comfortable accommodation in different styles—hotels, cottages, apartments—and at a range of prices to suit most budgets.

Throughout the last few revolutionary years **Spice Island Inn** has managed to keep up its standards. Situated directly on the lovely Grand Anse beach, accommodation consists of 20 beach cottages and 10 private pool suites behind, each with its own plunge pool. The main building, which houses the restaurant, bar, reception, dance floor, etc. is centrally situated among the beach cottages. Spice Island Inn has been a perennial feature in tour operators' brochures, and if only one Grenadian hotel is featured, this is usually it. It has the small hotel atmosphere appropriate to Grenada, an excellent location on one of the Caribbean's best beaches, and privacy of accommodation.

The most spectacular hotel is **Secret Harbour** at Mount Hartman Bay on the south coast. Sweeping red-brick arches dominate the spacious, cool public areas which make great use of natural materials. The rooms are magnificent—gigantic bed-living rooms with twin antique, double four-poster beds and large Italian-tiled bathrooms. The 20 suites are designed and built to ensure privacy and lovely views of the bay dominated by two headlands. More recently Secret Harbour was showing the effects of political turmoil, but it's worth making inquiries, as Barbara Stevens, the owner, has probably got everything running smoothly again (swimming-pool, tennis court and a small beach nearby down the hill).

The **Calabash,** situated at L'Anse aux Epines in a quiet beach setting among 8 acres of lovely grounds, has 22 suites. A speciality here is the breakfast, which is prepared and served in your own suite. It is a good alternative to Spice Island Inn if you prefer a quieter location, and an alternative to Secret Harbour if you'd rather have all facilities on one level (sea level).

There was once a Holiday Inn in Grenada, which, to put it succinctly, evolved into The Grenada Beach Hotel. It never really began functioning as a hotel, and was used from December 1983 as a billet for American troops. Now, completely gutted, rebuilt where necessary and expanded, it has risen like a phoenix from the ashes as the **Ramada Renaissance Hotel.** Situated right in the middle of Grand Anse Beach, with 186 rooms, swimming pool, watersports (windsurfing, snorkelling, scuba diving, waterskiing), two restaurants, two bars and gift shops, it offers all you expect from a large hotel. Rooms are air-conditioned with radio, TV and in-house movies.

Medium-priced accommodation of a good standard is represented by two properties near Grand Anse Beach. **Blue Horizons Cottage Hotel** is some 300 yards from the beach in beautifully landscaped gardens. Accommodation is in sixteen semi-detached cottages set around a swimming pool and bar. All are air-conditioned and have kitchenettes and a verandah. A short walk up the hill is the restaurant which has a limited but everchanging and delicious menu.

Flamboyant Cottages are scattered among trees, shrubs and flowers at one end of Grand Anse Beach, up a small hill. Most panoramic shots of the beach are taken from here. The spacious cottages, with living-room, kitchen and verandah, are either one-bedroom one-bathroom or two-bedroom two-bathroom units. There is a beach bar at the foot of the property.

Guesthouses abound in Grenada, ranging from the most basic standards to extremely well-run hostelries. Particularly recommended is **Windward Sands Inn,** situated on the main road some 400 yards from Grand Anse Beach. The character of the proprietor, Johnny Philip, permeates every part of this small, friendly inn. Dinners comprise excellently prepared local dishes of native in-

Accommodation in Grenada
Daily summer rates in US$

		Single		Double		Triple	
Hotels							
Blue Horizons Cottage Hotel, Grand Anse	Standard	EP	50	EP	55		
(tel. 4316)	Superior	EP	55	EP	60	EP	70
	Deluxe	EP	60	EP	65	EP	75
Calabash, L'Anse aux Epines	Standard	MAP	90	MAP	130		185
(tel. 4234/4334)	Pool suite			MAP	160		
Ramada Renaissance Hotel, Grand Anse		EP	85	EP	95	EP	105
(tel. 4371/5)							
Secret Harbour, Hartman Bay		EP	55	EP	95		
(tel. 4439/4548)							
Spice Island Inn, Grand Anse	Beach	MAP	97	MAP	115		131
(tel. 4258/4423)	Pool	MAP	110	MAP	135		151
Apartments and cottages							
Flamboyant Cottages, Grand Anse Beach	1 bed			EP	35–45		
(tel. 4247)	2 bed					EP	80
Maffiken Apartments, Grand Anse				EP	25–40		
(tel. 4522)							
South Winds Holiday Cottages, near	1 bed			EP	30–35		
Grand Anse (tel. 2351)	2 bed					EP	45
Guesthouses							
Roydon's Guest House, near Grand Anse		MAP	30	MAP	40		
(tel. 4476)							
St Ann's Guest House, near Yacht Lagoon	Private	CP	20	CP	27		
(tel. 2717)	bathroom	MAP	26	MAP	39		
	Shared	CP	16	CP	23		
	bathroom	MAP	22	MAP	35		
Windward Sands Inn, near		MAP	35	MAP	50		
Grand Anse (tel. 4238)							

gredients, served with more style, and in more atmospheric surroundings, than you would normally expect in a guesthouse. Johnny struggled through with three rooms for years, but has been quick to capitalise on the island's newly acquired political stability; he has recently built another four rooms.

If you find Windward Sands full, try **Roydon's** next door.

For really cheap guesthouse accommodation you will find it hard to beat **St Ann's Guest House**. This fifteen-room establishment is situated on the road between Saint George's and Grand Anse, near the Yacht Lagoon. The best description is perhaps a recommendation from a former guest: 'The way we were treated at St Ann's Guest House set the pattern for our stay: nothing was too much trouble, and the service at breakfast and evening mealtime was quaintly polite without being at all cold or formal, and mealtime conversation amongst the other visitors was very interesting. The atmosphere was just like an old-fashioned English seaside boarding-house with the warm intimacy of a family dining-table, and touches of colonial "correctness".'

Hotel and cottage rates will show an increase of at least 50% in the winter season, but in some cases rates are nearly double. Expect an increase of 20% on guesthouse rates in the winter. You will need to add 10% service charge and 7½% tax to these rates.

EATING OUT

In keeping with Grenada's low tourist profile there are few restaurants, but fortunately plenty of variety and a reasonable standard. On the Carenage in Saint George's there are **Rudolf's** (West Indian food with an 'international' bias), **The Nutmeg,** (upstairs dining of no particular style serving local food), **The Turtle Back** (a rather rickety wooden structure whose main benefit is a fine panoramic view of Saint George's), **Ristorante Italia** (fairly new, of good reputation), and **Pebbles** (a very cheap and well-run snack bar). There are others in town. Outside Saint George's, near the beaches, you'll find **The Red Crab** near L'Anse Aux Epines, a haunt of medical students, tourists and locals alike.

NIGHTLIFE

Some of the hotels (Spice Island Inn and Ramada Renaissance, for example) provide either a band or a cabaret, particularly in season, but you'll have more fun mixing with the local people. **Sugar Mill** is the best known haunt, over towards the airport, but **The Love Boat** near Grand Anse has acquired the best reputation in recent years. Others are **BBC Club, Coconut Grove** and **Cubby Hole.**

SHOPPING

There are three main shopping areas in Saint George's—around the Market

Square, the Carenage and Young Street, and the Grand Anse shopping centre near to the hotels. All the big brand names are here at almost duty-free prices as well as fresh spices grown on the island bought from the market or direct at the factories.

SPORT
Sports lovers will find the emphasis in Grenada on sea and shore-based activities: fishing, sailing, diving, snorkelling, swimming and surfing. It is possible to get a game of tennis or golf, though serious golfers are more likely to be found in Tobago.

Carriacou

Normally pronounced 'Karrykoo', Carriacou is the largest of the Grenadine Islands with an area of 13 square miles, but is generally regarded as being part of Grenada. It is connected to Grenada by a boat service and by a daily Inter Island Air Services flight.

The population is about 7,000. The people are mainly of African descent, though there is also a Scottish influence.

The 'capital' of Carriacou is the small town of **Hillsborough**, where the Parliamentary Secretary has his office. There is still a small cotton gin in the town too, though only a little cotton is grown. The main industries are boat-building, lime growing and processing, fishing and tourism, although there isn't much of any of these.

Carriacou's relative inaccessibility makes it ideal for studies of tropical sea birds and marine biology, both of which have remained free from pollution. And the oysters here 'grow on trees' (actually on mangrove roots).

Try to catch the August Regatta.

WHERE TO STAY
There are currently just two places to stay here, both of which are on a good beach. The **Mermaid Beach Hotel** represents the best accommodation on Carriacou—but that doesn't mean luxurious: rooms are spartan, though full of character, and there may at times be a lack of hot water in the shower. Meals are excellent though—large portions of excellently produced local food. Service is courteous and prompt and there are fine views of Sandy Island and Onion Island.

It would be fair to say that **Silver Beach Cottages** has seen better days. There are eight spacious apartments in duplexes and an open-fronted main building with restaurant and bar right on the beach. It lies just to the north of

Hillsborough, five minutes' walk from Mermaid Beach Hotel. Daily rates do not give particularly good value, but there is a special weekly rate (equivalent to about five days) which is good value.

Accommodation in Carriacou
Daily summer rates in US$

	Single	Double	Triple
Mermaid Beach Hotel, Hillsborough	EP 23	EP 30	
	MAP 35	MAP 50	
Silver Beach Cottages, Hillsborough	EP 30	EP 35	

Again, a 10% service charge and 7½% tax will probably be added to all bills. The rates for the Efficiency Units (or Housekeeping Units, as they are called) at Silver Beach include electricity, gas, linen, cutlery and crockery.

SAINT VINCENT AND THE GRENADINES

Saint Vincent has a reputation for the friendliness of its people, although it is also rich in history, scenery and has some of the Caribbean's most fertile soil in its valleys.

The area of the island is around 133 square miles and the population in the region of 120,000. There is a volcano, called Soufrière (like several other places in the Caribbean), which has caused trouble in the past. In 1902 it erupted, a day before its namesake in Martinique, killing 2,000 people and ruining crops for miles around. In 1971 it became active again, but although the area was evacuated there was, fortunately, no eruption. Both the activity and the evacuation were repeated in April 1979.

Saint Vincent has not escaped the economic recession affecting the Caribbean and the rest of the world, and this has perpetuated unemployment among the young and fostered general poverty.

The economy is largely based on agriculture. Few tourists come here, largely because there is only a small airstrip served by LIAT and charter flights. The airport is thus not dissimilar to Castries in Saint Lucia. The runway runs inland from the sea so that the aircraft approach low over the rocky coastline, whatever the wind direction, with the wheels only a few feet above the water.

GETTING TO SAINT VINCENT AND
THE GRENADINES

The tiny airport at Arnos Vale can only handle small aircraft up to about the size of LIAT's 48-seater Hawker Siddeley 748 turboprops, not jet aircraft. Consequently there are no direct links from here except to a handful of Caribbean destinations.

From the USA

Travel to Barbados with BWIA (from New York and Miami), Pan Am (Boston, New York, Miami and Washington), American (New York) or Eastern (Miami) Airlines (please see page 26 for details). From Barbados you take a connection on LIAT. Currently it is possible to arrange a same-day connection, but LIAT schedules are notoriously 'subject to revision', and when you come to make your reservations you may find there is no LIAT connection late enough in the day to make an efficient transfer. It is also possible that you may be able to make such a reservation but find the schedule changed after you have booked.

From Canada

Wardair does not appear to operate a holiday programme to Saint Vincent and the Grenadines, but it is worth your while to check. Flights will be via Barbados in any case. BWIA flies Toronto–Barbados twice a week, and Air Canada flies Toronto–Barbados and Montreal–Barbados. From Barbados you should take a LIAT connection as above.

From London

Traditionally travellers from London were resigned to an overnight stay in Barbados, but two recent developments have changed that. In the first instance, there are now landing lights at Arnos Vale airport, so aircraft can take off and land in the hours of darkness; secondly, Caribbean Airways has a small aircraft which is provided purely for through traffic from the UK and Europe. This means that if the incoming transatlantic flight is late the small aircraft is held until its arrival, so there is no fear of a missed connection. It is possible to use a combination of British Airways, BWIA and LIAT flights based on the through APEX fare, with possibly a same-day connection, as the airlines will be responsible if you are stranded in Barbados through a delay on the transatlantic flight. If, however, you are forced to overnight in Barbados through a change in the LIAT schedule subsequent to booking, then BWIA will not accept responsibility. Thus Caribbean Airways is the best bet.

Through fares to Saint Vincent from London, as officially quoted, are the same whether you fly Caribbean Airways or BWIA/LIAT: Caribbean Airways charges the London–Barbados fare plus £50, whilst BWIA charges the

London–Port of Spain fare (which at the time of writing is just £50 more than London–Barbados). Small discounts can be obtained on both airlines' fares.

From Europe

Caribbean Airways offers the same connection facility, mentioned above, from London, from Brussels, Frankfurt, Milan and Zurich. Through flights are only once a week from each point. This should be the cheapest way to get there, particularly bearing in mind that a same-day arrival in Saint Vincent is almost assured. From Paris it is worth while checking Air France fares to Martinique, as currently there is a fairly late LIAT flight Fort de France–Saint Vincent. Nouvelles Frontières should have some charter services to Fort de France at attractive rates.

Within the Caribbean

LIAT is the major airline operating to or from Saint Vincent, with services to Antigua, Barbados, Dominica, Grenada, Saint Lucia and Trinidad. Its subsidiary, Inter Island Air Services, operates tiny planes to Saint Lucia (both airports), Union, Carriacou and Grenada. Air Martinique flies north to Saint Lucia and Martinique and south to Mustique and Union. Winlink operates from Saint Lucia. It is now possible to fly direct to some of the tiny Grenadine Islands from major airports in the region. Mustique can be reached from Barbados, Grenada and Saint Lucia using LIAT services; Carriacou and Union are linked with Saint Lucia and Fort de France courtesy of Air Martinique, with LIAT providing direct connections from Barbados, Grenada and Saint Lucia to Union.

ENTRY REGULATIONS

Everyone requires a passport, and most nationalities require a visa. Those not requiring a visa are British subjects who are 'citizens of the United Kingdom and colonies', Canadian and US citizens, nationals of Belgium, Denmark, Finland, France, Greece, Iceland, Italy, Liechtenstein, Luxembourg, Netherlands, Norway, San Marino, Spain, Sweden, Switzerland, Tunisia, Turkey and Uruguay.

Certificates proving vaccination against yellow fever are required if you arrive within fourteen days of being in an infected area.

ELECTRICITY

The supply is 220–240 volts at 50 cycles, as in the UK.

CLIMATE

Rainfall varies from 150in per year in the mountains to as low as 60in per year

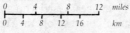

SAINT VINCENT
& THE GRENADINES

0   4   8   12   miles
0 4 8 12 16   km

KEY
1 Villa Lodge Hotel
  Indian Bay Hotel
2 Mariners Inn
3 Julies Guest House
4 Frangipani
5 Sunny Caribbee
6 Palm Island Beach Club
7 Sunny Grenadines

60

on the south coast (where most of the hotels are). The rainy season is from May to November (in theory). The average temperature is 80°F.

CURRENCY
This is the Eastern Caribbean dollar (EC$), which is approximately equal to US$0.40. US$1 = EC$2.70.

POPULATION
The total population of Saint Vincent and the Grenadines is around 127,000, the great majority of whom live on the island of Saint Vincent itself. The Grenadines are sparsely populated, the most populous being the two largest islands of Bequia and Union.

LANGUAGE
English.

HISTORY
Saint Vincent shares with Dominica the distinction of being settled rather late by the Europeans owing to the opposition of the indigenous Caribs. Thus it was not until 1773 that the British could claim to control the island, and then only because of a treaty with the Caribs. The French briefly occupied the island during the American Revolution. Then in 1795 they fostered a rebellion with the support of the slaves and Caribs.

GETTING AROUND
The brightly painted truck buses and pickups, similar to those seen in Saint Lucia and Haiti, have largely been replaced by Japanese minibuses, but the decorative tradition persists to some extent. Fares are quite low, perhaps as little as EC$10 from Kingstown to Georgetown, the second town on the east coast.

Currently there are more taxis available than potential passengers. The service is regulated quite well at the airport, with a despatcher directing you to the next car in line. The fare should be EC$14 from the airport to Grenadine Pier, slightly less into the centre of Kingstown.

Car hire firms operate in Kingstown. A temporary driving licence can be issued for a small charge if you don't have an international licence. Remember to drive on the left.

WHAT TO SEE
Saint Vincent is scenically spectacular. Unfolding vistas of ever-changing scenery are the reward of a day spent driving around the island, as you pass from the fertile Mesopotamia Valley to the area of Soufrière.

The east coast has broad black sand beaches lashed by the Atlantic surf, whilst the west coast and its settlements can be reached by a winding hilly road or by chartering a yacht for the day.

Kingstown, the capital, is situated in a shallow bay surrounded by higher ground. Fine views of the Grenadines can be seen from here. Of some interest are the ruins of **Fort Charlotte**, which is now used partly as a prison, but still houses historical artefacts. Other places of interest are Bay Street with its arcaded buildings and market, the 'Wedding Cake' Saint Mary's Church, and Saint George's Cathedral. The tourist office is in Halifax Street (457 1502).

Saturday morning is market day in this normally sleepy port, and it bustles then with busloads of people from the outlying villages. The **Botanic Gardens** are also of interest, with various species including a breadfruit tree from the original plant brought to the island by Captain Bligh of *Mutiny on the Bounty* fame.

Soufrière, which is in the north, is perhaps the island's main attraction. A visit to the crater ridge is recommended. Looking inside you should see the cone of lava formed in 1971, surrounded by a lake of almost a mile in diameter.

BEACHES
The best beaches are on the south of the island as the volcanic north has black sand. Consequently most sea and beach activity is in the south. The waters on the windward (Atlantic) side of the island can be tricky so swimming is more popular on the western side and in the lagoons.

CALENDAR
The main event, the Saint Vincent Carnival, is held in late June/early July climaxing on Carnival Tuesday, the first Tuesday in July. Later in the year the big day is 27 October, Independence Day, followed in November by Tourism Week and the Petit Saint Vincent boat race around the Grenadines. The timing of this is usually just before Thanksgiving.

WHERE TO STAY
Saint Vincent is the island that many tourists bypass. This may be because of the volcano—it last erupted in 1979; it may be because of inherent difficulty in getting here; more likely it is the relative scarcity of beaches.

Consequently there are few hotels geared to tourists. The prices are a little on the high side, for what you get. Prices remained stable in Grenada because of the troubles; in Barbados hotel rates went up in the late 1970s and early 80s as a result of demand, then plummeted again in 1983/84 when tourist demands declined. In Saint Vincent prices have in many cases remained the same for years, which now makes them, by the standards of the immediate area, fractionally too high.

A favourite hotel here is **Mariners Inn** on Villa Beach, opposite Young Island. Rustic simplicity is the keynote; wood predominates in the construction, including the main building and the four rooms on the beach. There is an open-air restaurant and an open-air bar (constructed from a boat), and the effect of the hotel's design is to give fine views of the bay and Young Island.

Young Island Resort is the most expensive Saint Vincent accommodation and perhaps can be regarded as the best. Accommodation is cottage-style and it has the advantage of being an island retreat yet is within close proximity of Saint Vincent (it operates its own regular shuttle service).

Villa Lodge is situated at Indian Bay, about 100 yards from the beach, with lovely views of the coastline. Recent refurbishment includes a pleasant restaurant, guest rooms of a reasonable standard, and much attention has been paid to the gardens. There is a swimming pool.

Down on the beach at Indian Bay you will find **Indian Bay Beach Hotel**.

Accommodation in Saint Vincent
Daily summer rates in US$

		Single	Double	Triple
Hotels				
Coconut Beach Hotel, Indian Bay (tel. 84231)		EP 25	EP 35	
Grand View, Villa Point (tel. 84811)		EP 48	EP 66	EP 90
		MAP 75	MAP 120	MAP 171
Indian Bay Beach Hotel, Indian Bay (tel. 84001)	1 bedroom	EP 30	EP 35	
		MAP 45	MAP 64	
	2 bedroom			EP 45
				MAP 90
Mariners Inn, Villa Beach (tel. 84459)	Standard	EP 25	EP 35	EP 47
	Superior	MAP 35	MAP 50	MAP 70
Sunset Shores, Villa Beach (tel. 84411)		EP 45–56	EP 55–66	EP 75
		MAP 70–81	MAP 105–116	MAP 150
Villa Lodge, Indian Bay (tel. 84641)		EP 50	EP 60	EP 70
		MAP 80	MAP 120	MAP 160
Young Island Resort, Young Island (tel. 84826)			EP 40	
			MAP 60	
	Cottage	MAP 135	MAP 160	
Guesthouses				
Cobblestone Inn, Kingstown (tel. 61937)		CP 32	CP 45	
Chubbys Inn/New Haven, Kingstown (tel. 71719)		EP 12–18	EP 18–22	
		CP 15–22	CP 25–30	
Haddon Hotel, Kingstown (tel. 61897)		EP 20–25	EP 27–35	
Heron Hotel, Kingstown (tel. 71631)		MAP 29	MAP 52	
Kingstown Park Guest House, Kingstown (tel. 61532)		MAP 15–20	MAP 30–40	

You should allow extra for tax, etc. in the high season.

Though meals are available here, this largely scores as apartment accommodation. The general atmosphere is very much that of a guesthouse.

A little way along the beach is **Coconut Beach Hotel**. Prices are reasonable; it has recently come under new management. There are 20 rooms, and it's probably worth a try.

Grand View, up on Villa Point, lives up to its name. Very much an old-style hotel, though with such conveniences as a swimming pool, it is quiet, light and airy. A path leads down to the beach. However, the prices are rather too high for what you get.

Sunset Shores is a 'modern' hotel not far from Mariners Inn. The rooms are pleasant, the pool and sundeck good, and its situation on the beach at Villa is perhaps the best.

The **Haddon Hotel** is on the road into town from the airport. It can be seen from afar as it has its name emblazoned in white paint across its red roof. The differences in price relate to the size of the room and whether or not it is air-conditioned. It has twelve rooms, a good bar with large dance floor (there is sometimes a band on Saturday nights), friendly staff and a homely atmosphere.

The **Kingstown Park Guest House** is a century-old plantation house with 20 guest rooms. It is situated a little further from the airport and town. The **Heron Hotel** is a white building well situated on Bay Street and popular with businessmen.

EATING OUT

The Dolphin is near Young Island Dock at Villa (reasonable prices and walking distance from Mariners Inn). In the same area is **Aquatic Club** and **The French Restaurant**. **Mariners Inn** should soon begin to serve good food, as there has been a recent change of management. **Villa Lodge Hotel** is good, and **Grand View** might be worth a try. In the case of these hotels you should book in advance—particularly in the high season—if you're not staying there.

SHOPPING

Locally made clothes can be acquired in a very short time in Saint Vincent and craftsmen specialising in straw-work, ceramics and jewellery—including black coral—are at Saint Vincent's Craftsmen Centre. There are other craft centres around the island and on Bequia visitors may watch material being silk-screened for making up into clothes.

SPORT

Sea activities form the major sports—swimming, snorkelling, diving, windsurfing, fishing and sailing. Instruction is available from various sources. Inland are golf at the Aqueduct Golf Course and riding in Saint Vincent and Mustique. Tennis is available at the Kingstown Tennis Club and elsewhere, and for spec-

The Grenadine Islands

tators there is cricket in Kingstown, and football, basketball and netball at Arnos Vale Playing Field (near the airport).

The Grenadines are one of the finest locations in the world for yacht cruising. The waters are generally fairly calm, there is no great distance between anchorages (which makes short journeys not only a practical proposition but the norm, and also means that you are always in sight of land, which is far more interesting than the open sea) and complete flexibility in chartering. You can take a bareboat or a crewed yacht, and can charter for as little as a day or for as long as several weeks. There is a large variety of vessels available within the sizes 33ft to 47ft, accommodating between two and eight persons.

The Grenadines also provide an excellent location for the concept of 'barefoot cruises'. There are now a number of these operating locally, from tall sailing ships organised by the **Windjammer** organisation (based in Miami) to smaller motor vessels such as *The Carib Islander* and *Vela Star*. Both of these last two operate from Saint Lucia. *The Carib Islander* includes Saint Lucia and Martinique in its itinerary and full details are given in the Saint Lucia section (page 78).

THE GRENADINES

This string of islands running from Saint Vincent to Grenada is best visited by cruising yacht. To sail from Kingstown, Saint Vincent, to Grenada, calling in at the islands, has to be one of the most visually beautiful experiences in the Caribbean. A stay on any or some of the islands will relax even the most stressed city dweller's nervous system, although landlubbers should note that the voyage can lose some of its romance if the weather is inclement.

Politically all but two of the inhabited islands are administered by Saint Vincent. Grenada looks after the interests of Carriacou and Petit Martinique. You can thus expect to leave Saint Vincent immigration at the island of Union and enter Grenada's domain at the next major island, Carriacou.

Saint Vincent and Bequia are linked by three vessels: *Friendship Rose*, which

Boat timetable

My Edwina (motor vessel)

	Depart		Arrive	
Mon.–Sat.	Bequia	06.30	St Vincent	07.30
	St Vincent	12.30	Bequia	13.30

Friendship Rose (island schooner)

	Depart		Arrive	
Mon.–Fri.	Bequia	06.30	St Vincent	07.45
	St Vincent	12.30	Bequia	13.45

Grenadines Star (motor vessel)

	Depart		Arrive	
Mon.	St Vincent	10.00	Bequia	11.00
	Bequia	11.15	Canouan	13.15
	Canouan	13.30	Mayreau	14.30
	Mayreau	14.45	Union Island	15.05
Tues.	Union Island	07.00	Mayreau	07.20
	Mayreau	07.30	Canouan	08.30
	Canouan	08.45	Bequia	10.45
	Bequia	11.00	St Vincent	12.00
Thurs.	St Vincent	10.00	Bequia	11.00
	Bequia	11.15	Canouan	13.15
	Canouan	13.30	Mayreau	14.30
	Mayreau	14.45	Union Island	15.05
Fri.	Union Island	07.00	Mayreau	07.20
	Mayreau	07.30	Canouan	08.30
	Canouan	08.45	Bequia	10.45
	Bequia	11.00	St Vincent	12.00
Sat.	St Vincent	12.00	Bequia	13.00

(approximate times only)

Currently fares are as follows:
St Vincent–Bequia EC$5; St Vincent–Canouan EC$10;
St Vincent–Mayreau EC$12; St Vincent–Union EC$15;
Union–Carriacou EC$10.

operates both ways Mondays to Fridays; *My Edwina*, which operates both ways Mondays to Saturdays on the same schedule; and the government boat *Grenadines Star*, which travels down the islands as far as Union on Mondays and Thursdays and back up on Tuesdays and Fridays. There is no boat service on Sundays, although there are occasional day excursions which visit Bequia and Mustique. Another boat, the *Obedient*, shuttles between Union and Carriacou on Mondays and Thursdays (it doesn't connect with the *Grenadines Star*).

Bequia

Pronounced 'Bekwee', Bequia is a tropical paradise of lush scenery, friendly local people and few tourists. The best word to describe it is 'charming'. Many, if not most, of the visitors come from the yachts that throng the splendid natural harbour of Port Elizabeth, particularly in the winter months. An island of some seven square miles, it offers fine walks and good beaches. Here it is a pleasure, rather than an inconvenience, to walk to a beach.

WHAT TO SEE
To say that there are few tourists in Bequia may be misleading; for an island of only seven square miles there is a fair amount of tourism, probably more than in Saint Vincent. Over Christmas and New Year there are quite a few visitors. Yachts throng Admiralty Bay and cruise liners occasionally call in the winter months—even Queen Elizabeth made sure she called in on her recent Caribbean tour. But in the summer most of the hotels are half empty or closed and the yachts are absent.

Bequia has some beautiful beaches and lovely walks. The two beaches which seem to be most popular are **Princess Margaret** and **Lower Beach Bay**, both on the south side of Admiralty Bay. You can walk there or get a local boy to ferry you across for a dollar or two. There is a little restaurant/bar on Lower Beach.

Lovely walks can be taken through the woods to **Spring**, **Industry Bay** and, for the real enthusiast, **Hope**. At the end of each walk there is a beach. **Friendship Bay** is reached by road, so the walk is not so picturesque, although the Friendship Bay area itself is very pretty. Boatbuilding in the traditional style is still undertaken and there is, in theory at least, a small whaling station. Technology here has yet to progress from the days of Moby Dick so, happily, it poses no threat to the whale's survival.

An oddity in Bequia is **Moon Hole**, literally a hole that goes right through the island near its rocky southern tip. You can only see it if you are in a yacht and exactly alongside. An expatriate community, jealous of its privacy, lives a somewhat reclusive life here.

WHERE TO STAY
A favourite place to stay here is **Julie's Guest House**. This is the best value accommodation to be found anywhere in the Caribbean. There are old buildings, tucked away behind trees and shrubs and the police station, and a new building which faces onto the harbour about 50 yards from the jetty. The old building is exceptionally well designed to be both functional and pleasing in appearance and atmosphere. Natural wood is used throughout, and a balcony runs right around the building, preventing rain from entering the bedrooms as well as providing a nice cool place to sit. The design is such that air-conditioning is unnecessary. All of the ten rooms are well furnished with private facilities. The new building has been constructed in a completely different style. Painted white, with 'antique' lamps from Barbados, the floors are tiled and here the balcony faces the sea (excellent for sunset photography). The water is heated by solar energy panels in the roof. The owner is the island's foremost building contractor, and a man who would be a success at his trade anywhere in the world. Julie's wife, Isola, actually runs the guesthouse. The excellent meals are taken in the old building and standards of service cannot be faulted.

Sunny Caribbee, the main building of which is the island's oldest hotel, has for the last few years been the main abode for package tourists. Most accommodation is provided by seventeen wooden cabanas, some with kitchenette facilities, scattered in the shade of palm trees in the hotel's 10 acres of grounds. There is a small beach, swimming pool, beach bar and tennis court. Watersports, including windsurfing, waterskiing, scuba diving and snorkelling, are organised here. Additional accommodation is provided in the main hotel building, where meals are taken, but these rooms do not have a bathroom en suite. Entertainment—usually a steel band or something similar—is arranged in the winter season once or twice a week. If you are looking for hotel rather than guesthouse accommodation, and need to be on a beach, Sunny Caribbee is to be recommended. But book on EP; the meals, reputedly, are not good here and there are many good restaurants on Bequia in the Port Elizabeth area.

Frangipani is the other recommended hotel in Bequia. More of an inn than a hotel, it caters largely for the yachting fraternity who come ashore here to eat and drink and who can usually be found clustered around the bar in the evenings. The older rooms in the original wood-frame building do not have private facilities, but the new stone-built rooms behind, each with a balcony, are excellent.

Other hotels on Bequia include **Spring Hotel**, across the island at Spring on a hill, notable mainly for its Sunday curry lunch (which is recommended), **Friendship Bay** and **Bequia Beach Club**.

Accommodation in Bequia
Daily summer rates in US$

		Single	Double
Frangipani, Port Elizabeth (tel. 83255)	Old rooms	EP 15	EP 25
	New rooms	EP 30	EP 45
Friendship Bay Hotel, Friendship Bay (tel. 83222)		MAP 50	MAP 100
Julie and Isola's Guest House, Port	Old building	MAP 15	MAP 25
Elizabeth (tel. 83304)	New building	MAP 19	MAP 30
(strongly recommended)			
Spring Hotel, Spring (tel. 83414)		MAP 60	MAP 100
Sunny Caribbee, Belmont (tel. 83425/83448)	Hotel room	EP 15	EP 20
(prices May to November)		MAP 35	MAP 50
	Cabana	EP 20	EP 40
		MAP 35	MAP 80

Add 10% service and 5% tax to all prices. Winter rates are about 20% higher at Julie's and around 50% higher for the others.

Mustique

This is the next island along, travelling southwards. It seems to be the favourite of Princess Margaret, but for the rest of us lacks reasonably priced accommodation, which is a pity, as it appears to be the most beautiful island—gorgeous white sandy beaches fringed with palms and dotted with brightly painted fishing boats. The sea here is the most incredible shade of blue. There is little sign of habitation except on the rickety wooden pier. Sometimes there are excursions (usually on Sundays) from Saint Vincent and Bequia to Mustique, so if you are in Bequia over a weekend you should have the opportunity to make a visit. Otherwise you may like to charter a yacht for a day. The current rate is about US$150 for up to six people, and a barbecue lunch is often included.

Of some interest is the wreck of the *Antilles*. The waters around Mustique are shallower than those surrounding Bequia, and the *Antilles* was a French cruise liner which found out the hard way. Its rusting hulk can still be seen off Mustique's windward (east) coast.

The one hotel is **Cotton House**, which has had a chequered career. It has not always been well managed in the past, though the latest reports are that things have improved. Expect to pay at least US$110 for a single room and US$150 for a double in the summer, and up to twice that in the winter.

Most visitors to Mustique rent a house; contact Errol Agard on Saint Vincent (tel. 84621; telex 7549). These villas are quite expensive but are fully staffed and a car or moke (minicar) is usually included in the price.

Canouan

This is a 'Bacardi ad' type of island. Almost entirely unspoilt, and with a population of less than 1,000, it boasts beautiful beaches, enticing lagoons and some lovely, leisurely walks. Tourist development is recent. The **Crystal Sands Beach Hotel** has apartments and cottages, and its own white-sand beach. A new hotel, **Canouan Beach Hotel**, is situated on a fine beach with accommodation in cottages of stone and wood. Expect to pay about US$130 per night for a double room on the American Plan basis (all meals included).

Union

Union is a major port of entry and departure for Saint Vincent. The government boat terminates here, and there is a small airstrip (owned by the Anchorage Yacht Club and Hotel) which handles small planes, both charter flights and the increasingly regular scheduled services. Officially the best accommodation is provided at **The Anchorage**, although there are mixed reports on this. Try staying at **Sunny Grenadines Beach Hotel**, or—if you are on a budget—**Sunny Grenadines Guest House** above Mitchell's Hardware Store. Both are under the same ownership, but the former is primarily intended for local people travelling through the islands, and the latter is for tourists. All of this accommodation is set around the port of entry, Clifton. This is the largest settlement, though there are enclaves elsewhere on the island and the best beaches are on the other side (and usually deserted).

Union is perhaps the driest of all the islands, and not worth a long visit. Its main importance is as a centre, or transit point, for the beautiful islands around. Tourists in Saint Lucia and Barbados are able to take excursions which bring them to Union and then give them a chartered yacht for the day. This will either take them to the **Tobago Cays**, a tiny group of pinprick islands surrounded by coral, for some superb snorkelling, or alternatively be a leisurely cruise taking in **Palm Island, Petit Saint Vincent (PSV)** and a sandy shoal.

Both Palm and PSV are privately owned and should really be considered as 'hideaway hotels', though you may consider they are not really hidden away if they are visited by day-trippers on yachts and even cruise liners (in the winter)! Each provides cottage accommodation along its beaches, full watersports facilities which may even include a private yacht, four meals daily, etc. Palm is quite flat and has, in theory at least, a small airstrip and tennis court. PSV is more undulating and provides room service by minimoke (minicar).

Accommodation in Union, Palm and PSV
Daily summer rates in US$

	Single	Double	Triple
Anchorage Yacht Club, Clifton, Union (tel. 88244)	CP 50	CP 50–100	
Palm Island Beach Club, Palm Island (tel. 84804)	AP 125	AP 175	AP 245
Petit Saint Vincent Resort, Petit Saint Vincent (tel. 84801)	AP 160	AP 212	
Sunny Grenadines Beach Hotel, Clifton, Union (tel. 88327)	CP 22 MAP 30	CP 33 MAP 48	
Sunny Grenadines Guest House, Clifton, Union	EP 15	EP 20	

Mayreau

Mayreau is so tiny (one-and-a-half square miles) that it has no need of any roads, just pathways. It has only about 150 inhabitants and one hotel, the **Salt Whistle Bay**, which can arrange transport for you from Union. With a safe, picture-book beach and no traffic it makes an ideal holiday for families with children. The hotel offers watersporting facilities and boating trips.

SAINT LUCIA

Saint Lucia has to be the most beautiful island in the Caribbean. It has a natural beauty which explains why the British and French fought so long over it. Of volcanic origin, not only is it mountainous—as indeed are the other islands formed in this way—but it can truly be described as spectacular. Along the coast, mountains push steeply up from the sea, yet still leave room for nearby beaches of great natural beauty. Most of them are deserted.

The best known peaks are The Pitons. These are two extinct volcanic cones which rise precipitously from the sea, guarding Soufrière, a dormant yet bubbling volcano. This is known as 'the drive-in volcano' because of its ease of access. Although full of bubbling sulphur springs and continually emitting steam, we are assured that it is unlikely to erupt. (That's what they said about Soufrière in Guadeloupe until 1976!)

The mountainous interior, particularly around and south of Castries, is thickly covered with lush vegetation, much of which is cultivated. Saint Lucia

71

has a great deal of rain, usually in the form of brief yet heavy showers which cascade down whilst the sun continues to shine. If it didn't have so many other things to choose from, Saint Lucia's national symbol could be the rainbow!

GETTING TO SAINT LUCIA

Although about the same size as Grenada and Saint Vincent, with a similar topography and population, Saint Lucia has more tourism. This is primarily because there has been an airport capable of handling large jet aircraft here for many years.

Saint Lucia in fact has two airports, both of which are in regular use. Vigie, just to the north of the capital, Castries, is only capable of handling small aircraft up to the size of LIAT's 48-seater turboprops. Hewanorra, at the southern tip of the island, was built specifically for the big jets. Intercontinental flights arrive and depart from here, as do BWIA's jet Caribbean services. The tiny island-hopping flights of LIAT's Inter Island Air subsidiary serve both airports, so if travelling with them be sure to specify which airport you require.

Although Vigie is the smaller of the two airports, activity here is constant as travel connections are always available; it is more convenient for the capital and places in the north and even parts as far south at Marigot Bay. Activity at Hewanorra comes in fits and starts; the total number of jets per week is understandably limited, although terminal facilities are of necessity constructed to handle hundreds of people at a time.

From the USA

Saint Lucia is easily accessible from the States on direct services. BWIA operates from Miami and New York, Pan Am and Eastern from Miami. The last two airlines have through services from other major cities in the USA. In recent years Saint Lucia has seen many tourists from the USA, and this means a wide range of inclusive holidays is available.

From Canada

Air Canada operates from Toronto and there may also be Wardair charters. There is certainly a comprehensive choice of inclusive holidays.

From London

There are no non-stop services from London at the time of writing, though British Airways operates a same-plane service with one stop in Barbados. If you intend staying in a hotel, apartment or villa it will almost always be cheaper to book a package. Pegasus operated whole-plane charters here for years (for a long time Saint Lucia was its only Caribbean destination) and established a tradition of bulk-buying hotel rooms at large discounts on the normal hotel rates.

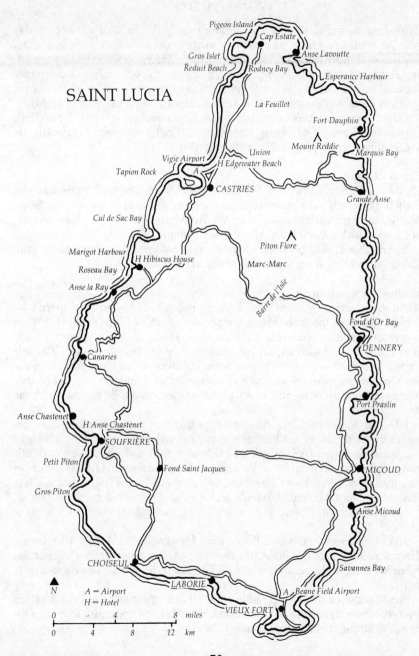

SAINT LUCIA

Pigeon Island
Cap Estate
Anse Lavoutte
Gros Islet
Reduit Beach
Rodney Bay
Esperance Harbour
La Feuillet
Fort Dauphin
Mount Reddie
Union
Vigie Airport
A
H Edgewater Beach
Marquis Bay
Tapion Rock
CASTRIES
Grande Anse
Cul de Sac Bay
Piton Flore
Marigot Harbour
H Hibiscus House
Marc-Marc
Roseau Bay
Anse la Ray
Barre de l'Isle
Fond d'Or Bay
Canaries
DENNERY
Port Praslin
Anse Chastenet
H Anse Chastenet
SOUFRIÈRE
Petit Piton
Fond Saint Jacques
MICOUD
Gros Piton
Anse Micoud
CHOISEUL
Savannes Bay
N
LABORIE
A = Airport
A
Beane Field Airport
H = Hotel
VIEUX FORT

0   4   8   miles
0   4   8   12   km

Part of the saving thus achieved is passed on in the form of a lower holiday price, a tradition which now applies to many of the other tour operators. Pegasus no longer uses charters; tour operators' rates on wide-bodied aircraft are about the same as the seat cost on a less efficient 707, and consumer demand is in favour of the larger aircraft and a greater flexibility of departures which is possible with a smaller commitment on a larger number of flights.

Other tour operators featuring Saint Lucia include Kuoni, Speedbird, Hayes and Jarvis, Caribbean Connection, Tradewinds and TransAtlantic Wings (just a small programme at the moment).

From Europe

Caribbean Airways operates a direct service from Brussels, Frankfurt and Zurich. If Paris is your most convenient airport it should be possible to fly via Martinique with a connection on LIAT, Air Martinique or BWIA; or connect at London with a Caribbean Airways or BA flight.

There should also be some charters from Europe either straight to Saint Lucia (most likely from Germany) or via Martinique.

Within the Caribbean

All of the flights mentioned thus far fly in and out of Hewanorra airport, with the exception of the Martinique connection which is from Vigie. But when taking an inter-Caribbean flight you could get in a muddle if you haven't made sure you know at which airport you are supposed to present yourself. The following information attempts to give some guidance, though you must remember that this information was correct at the time of writing; it may not be true when you are travelling, and all travel information should be checked with the tour operator.

LIAT and its subsidiary, IAS, both appear in international airline schedules under the designator LI. The only way you can tell which is which is by checking the airline type. IAS operates southbound only, a service which currently runs Vigie–Hewanorra, Saint Vincent, Union, Carriacou, Grenada, Port of Spain and vice versa. LIAT, however, operates only from Vigie; it flies south to Barbados, Saint Vincent, Grenada and Port of Spain, and north to Fort de France, Dominica, Pointe-à-Pitre and Antigua (and onwards with a plane change).

BWIA operates jets, which have to use Hewanorra, to Antigua, Barbados, Grenada and Tobago. Winlink, the domestic carrier, flies from both airports to Saint Vincent, and operates, with LIAT, a domestic service *between* both airports.

Air Martinique makes life a little easier; it only operates from Vigie and flies from there north to Fort de France and Sint Maarten and south to Saint Vincent, Mustique, Union and Trinidad.

Interconnecting services by North American airlines have to use Hewanorra of course; Eastern flies to Barbados, and Air Canada to Trinidad.

ENTRY REGULATIONS

Visas are not required by US citizens and nationals of almost all Commonwealth and West European countries. In addition, all except citizens of Cuba or communist bloc countries are allowed to visit Saint Lucia in transit to a third country for up to fourteen days. But if you think that might apply to you, please check.

If you have arrived within six days of being in a yellow fever infected area you will need a vaccination certificate.

ELECTRICITY

The supply is 220–240 volts at 50 cycles, as in the UK.

CLIMATE

Rainfall varies considerably both in seasonal terms and within the island, the mountains receiving heavier rainfall than the coastal areas. February to May is normally considered the driest period and July through September the wettest, but don't bank on it. The temperature range is 80°F–90°F.

CURRENCY

This is the Eastern Caribbean dollar (EC$) which is approximately equal to US$0.40. US$1 = EC$2.70.

POPULATION

Although Saint Lucia and her people have a distinct character which is all their own, there are minor similarities with Haiti. For example, many of the old houses in Castries, at the back of town on or near Brazil Street are adorned with latticework, balconies and other points of architecture which are very reminiscent of the old houses in Port-au-Prince. Perhaps this can be attributed to the fact that Saint Lucia finally became British at about the same time that Haiti achieved independence. As both are poor countries, many of the old houses of this style remain in each.

Another obvious similarity is in the form of transport. There are 'tap-taps' here, both the small, Japanese pick-up trucks converted to a local public service, and also the large, long-distance trucks with wooden coachwork and bench seating. The craftsmanship is much cruder here than in Haiti, and the decoration shabbier and less ornate, but the basic idea is the same.

As elsewhere these 'tap-taps' are being phased out in favour of more comfortable, modern Japanese minibuses. Fares are still low.

LANGUAGE
English is the official language, and all but some of the old countryfolk speak it. But the real national language, called 'broken French' by the people, is very close to Creole.

HISTORY
The island was inhabited for hundreds of years by the Carib Indians, until early in the sixteenth century, although the exact date of European settlement is a matter of debate. 13 December 1502 is celebrated as Discovery Day—the anniversary of the arrival of Columbus—but the French claim to have arrived at around the same time. A group of English settlers arrived a century later, and in the next 200 years the island changed hands a dozen times between the English and the French. In 1967 St Lucia became independent, joining the Commonwealth in 1979.

GETTING AROUND
It is essential that you travel around Saint Lucia. If you get up early enough you can make some day excursions, but for long trips you may need to stop overnight. The first point to remember, as already noted, is that there are two international airports. So you should plan your travel within the island according to your arrival and departure points. If you arrive by boat you will probably come to Castries or Marigot, although other marinas—such as Rodney's Harbour—are possible too.

If you arrive in Vieux Fort and travel north from there, get up early to take the truck bus. The cost is EC$2.50 to Castries. This may take the new highway on the eastern side of the island, so take the opportunity of visiting The Pitons and Soufrière on a day trip before leaving the south. Alternatively you could stop overnight in the Soufrière area and continue north the next day.

The country areas and the small settlement life of Saint Lucia are of very great interest. Bananas, the chief export, are more in evidence here than anywhere else in the Caribbean, and one can see them being harvested almost by accident. Wages are low, however, and unemployment high; the people are very poor.

The only real problem is the *means* of transport. The local trucks and buses mentioned above usually either operate at inconvenient times or only travel short distances; and as they are intended as transport for the local people, they will not be making for sites of natural beauty which you may wish to see. It is possible to hire a little 'fun-bike' with a 50cc engine for about EC$30 a day; the mobility this affords is well worth the money. The 'fun-bike' is a particularly good investment for a couple, although those unused to motorcycling and wary of Saint Lucia's generally bad roads may prefer a Toyota jeep, which is the only practical solution for groups of three or more. These motorbikes and cars can be hired at the reception desks of the larger hotels. Be sure to take your domestic driving licence. A temporary driving licence may then be obtained for three months—for the over 25s. Saint Lucians drive *on the left*.

WHAT TO SEE

Castries

The port of Castries in the northwest is the capital of Saint Lucia, a town which displays its mixed French and British heritage in those buildings and architectural features which have survived the devastations of fire and hurricanes over the last few centuries. However, the main result of this damage has been that new buildings have risen in steel and concrete.

In the town the main sights are the Cathedral of the Immaculate Conception and, rising behind the city, Fort Charlotte, built in stone by the French in the 18th century. The view is spectacular from the top.

Local farmers and smallholders come to the market on the corner of Jeremie and Peynier Streets on Saturdays to sell the fruits of their labours—fresh meat, vegetables, fruits, baskets, rugs and hardware, and at the harbour—a flooded volcano crater—can be found fishermen selling the day's catch.

The Tourist Board head office is in Sans Souci Street in Castries.

Around the island

Saint Lucia has one good road running from north to south. From Pigeon Point (once an island but now joined to the mainland by a causeway) to Castries the road is entirely satisfactory; coming out of the town and travelling south the road twists steeply up the Morne, then runs downhill for a little way before crossing over to the eastern side of the island; it then runs along the coast, continually ascending, descending and curving through the lush vegetation bordering the rain forest until it reaches the jet airport at Vieux Fort. On the route empty beaches pounded by the Atlantic breakers can be glimpsed. It should be noted that although Saint Lucia is only some 24 miles in length, the road journey from Castries to Vieux Fort is about 40 miles. Unless you are crazy, motorcycling at night is not advisable as even this good road is not without its share of potholes and roadworks.

The other road between Castries and Vieux Fort is slower, in a far worse state of repair and consequently more hazardous. You will want to use it, however, as many of the places worth visiting are on or near it. Many of the views are astounding, even in the rain, and **Soufrière** volcano itself is very interesting. The suphur springs emit strong-smelling fumes with their steam; usually there are a number of young people here selling handicrafts, and 'guides' willing to lead tourists along safe routes. Just south of the sulphur springs are **The Pitons** which are breathtakingly spectacular, and along the coast are fishing villages and banana plantations. Continuing north to Castries you can visit Marigot Bay, certainly one of the prettiest natural harbours in the Caribbean

Two volcanic peaks on St. Lucia

Because it is so beautiful, Saint Lucia is probably the best island of all for sightseeing. It would be a crime to spend every day here on the beach. The main attractions have already been mentioned, but so has the difficulty of reaching them by public transport or driving yourself. If you enjoy driving, then definitely hire a car, jeep or motorcycle. The road from Castries to Rodney Bay and points north is excellent by any standard, the east coast road is fairly good and makes an enjoyable drive through beautiful rain forest, whilst parts of the west coast road are very bad indeed (particularly the stretch from Soufrière to Anse la Raye). If you don't particularly enjoy driving you should avoid doing so on that coast but take an organised excursion instead. **Barnards Travel** in Bridge Street, Castries (tel. 22214) organises a full range of excursions including a full-day island tour, a tour to Soufrière which involves travelling one way by road and the other by sea, a rain forest walk, a two-day trip by yacht to Martinique, and a Grenadines excursion.

Probably the best way to see the Grenadines (apart from chartering your own yacht) is to travel on *The Carib Islander.* This 120-ft motor yacht operates most weeks of the year from Marigot Bay, sailing south to Bequia, Mustique, the Tobago Cays, Palm Island and Union, then returning north to Mayreau, Saint Vincent, Castries, Martinique and back to Marigot Bay. The full tour takes just under a week (departing Sunday night and returning Sunday morning) but it is possible to book a five-night trip (originating in Marigot Bay, terminating in Castries and not including Martinique). There are sixteen air-conditioned cabins in two-, three- and four-berth configurations; the total number of passengers carried is 40. Prices, which include breakfast and dinner, start at $295 for a five-night cruise in low season ranging up to $695 for a seven-night cruise in high season.

A combination of a one-week stay in Saint Lucia and a one-week cruise on *The Carib Islander* can make a superbly rounded Caribbean holiday. It is possible to book such a passage before you leave home; general sales agents are as follows:

USA: Copeland and Cutler, Suite 1107, 183 Madison Avenue, New York, NY 10016 (212–683 0400);
Copeland and Cutler, 409 N Camden Drive, Beverly Hills, CA 90210 (800–821 4749).
Canada: Unitours Canada Ltd, Suite 4000, 3080 Yonge Street, Toronto, Ontario, M4N 3N1 (416–484 8855).
UK and Europe: TransAtlantic Wings Ltd, 70 Pembroke Road, Kensington, London W8 6NX (01–602 4021).

CALENDAR
In Castries the new year is celebrated on 1 and 2 January in Columbus Square with Le Jour de l'An festival, and parties throughout the island. But the biggest event is Independence Day, 22 February, which more or less coincides with the pre-Lent festivities, depending on when Easter occurs.

WHERE TO STAY
Most of the hotels here, particularly the large ones, are geared to the package-plan holiday tourist and get most of their custom from that source.

Couples, formerly The Malabar, is extremely choosy about its guests: only couples are accepted, no singles, groups or children. Once you are in the only thing you can spend money on is telephone calls—everything else is included: accommodation, meals, drinks, sports and other activities, entertainment, sightseeing and even cigarettes. Tipping is not allowed.

The hotel, which comprises 68 double rooms, is situated right on the beach about two miles north of Castries. Rooms are air-conditioned, there is a swimming pool and tennis courts, and the activities extend to horse riding and a day cruise on a schooner. The concept may not be to everyone's taste but the people who go there love it.

A favourite hotel on Saint Lucia is **Anse Chastanet,** near Soufrière. This is a hotel for romantics. Built on a hillside which drops down to an excellent beach, the cluster of buildings peeps out from among luxuriant tropical foliage. Construction is from traditional materials, and in the traditional style with peaked ceilings and wooden balconies. Views—of The Pitons, the beach, the reef and the sunsets—are the essence of dreams.

It is not a hotel for the elderly or infirm, however. There are 123 steps from the restaurant to the beach, where you will find facilities geared to the young and fit—a superb scuba-diving operation, minisailing, windsurfing and snorkelling.

The 'package tour' hotels include **La Toc,** a Cunard-owned hotel of 54 double rooms and 60 villas a little to the south of Castries, the **St Lucian** (formerly the Holiday Inn), located on Reduit Beach at Rodney Bay, and the **Steigenberger Cariblue** right at the north of the island. The St Lucian is the biggest of these with 192 rooms; the beach is good, the area fine, and many people enjoy their stay here. The staff are very courteous and friendly.

The Halcyon tradition is maintained mainly by the **Halcyon Beach Club** at Choc Beach about three miles north of Castries. This is exclusive to Pegasus among UK tour operators, and significant savings can be made by booking with them. They also feature **Halcyon 2** on Vigie Beach, close to the airport.

Their flagship hotel used to be Halcyon Days, right on the southern end of the island within walking distance of Hewanorra airport. Affectionately known in the business as 'Butlins', it was particularly suitable for families, with a very wide range of activities from a well-equipped 'Aqua Centre' to archery and go-carts. Now, after a period of closure and several months housing the cast and crew of a feature film, it has had a rebirth as a **Club Méditerranée,** the original 'all-inclusive hotel' idea—but you buy your own drinks.

Smaller hotels include **East Winds Inn** and **The Islander.** The first of these is situated on the beach at the end of rugged land five miles north of Castries. It comprises ten hexagon-shaped cottages and a rather rustic restaurant.

The Islander is not quite on the beach, but close to the St Lucian at Rodney Bay. Accommodation is a combination of apartments and rooms and its restaurant enjoys a good reputation.

Another small hotel with a good reputation for its food—in fact it has some of the best food on the island—is **The Green Parrot** on the Morne overlooking Castries. This means that it is miles from any beach. All is not lost however; there is a swimming pool and excellent views to compensate.

Dasheene, at Soufrière, has some very nice villa and apartment accommodation, again some distance from the sea and again with excellent views. There are one-, two- and three-bedroom units.

If you are looking for villa accommodation you need go no further than the lovely **Marigot Bay Resort.** The atmosphere in this sheltered anchorage is magical. It is not a normal beach resort (though there is a small beach), but a lovely enclosed bay protected by thickly-forested lush hillsides reaching right down to the water.

Perhaps this is the best of both worlds—your private house set just above a small resort with all the facilities that term implies. There are sunfish, windsurfers and yachts for hire, a restaurant, **Doolittle's,** bars, a hotel **(Hurricane Hole)** with a swimming pool, and transport between them by water taxi. The film *Dr Doolittle* was made here.

The cottages, which are scattered on one of the hillsides and can be reached by a small cable railway (though this is not really necessary and often not working), are one-, two- and three-bedroom units built and furnished mainly with wood.

Accommodation in Saint Lucia
Daily winter rates in US$

		Single	Double	Triple
Hotels				
Anse Chastanet, Soufrière (tel. 47354)	Gazebo	EP 96–104	EP 108–132	EP 120–150
	Deluxe	EP 140–180	EP 160–200	EP 180–240
		(MAP supplement $28 per person)		
		(excellent-value weekly packages available)		
Couples, Malabar Beach (tel. 24211)		(All inclusive:		
		$1,720 to $1,890 per couple per week)		
Cunard La Toc, La Toc	Standard	EP 125	EP 150	
	Superior	EP 150	EP 175	
	Deluxe	EP 175	EP 200	
East Winds Inn, La Brelotte Bay		EP 70	EP 80	
The Green Parrot, The Morne		EP 55	EP 85	
(tel. 23399)		(MAP supplement $18 per person)		
Halcyon Beach Club, Choc Beach	Standard	EP 70	EP 90	
	Superior	EP 90	EP 120	
Halcyon 2, Vigie Beach		EP 40–60	EP 90–120	
		(MAP supplement $19 per person)		
The Islander, Rodney Bay (tel. 20255)	Apartments	EP 65	EP 75	
	Superior rooms	EP 55	EP 65	
		(MAP supplement $18 per person)		
St Lucian, Reduit Beach, Rodney Bay	Standard	EP 90	EP 120	
(tel. 28351)	Superior	EP 110	EP 145	
		(MAP supplement $25 per person)		
Steigenberger Cariblue, Cap Estate		EP 74–100	EP 135–175	
(tel. 58551)				
Apartments and cottages				
Dasheene, Soufrière	Standard suite	EP 130		
	Deluxe suite	EP 155		
	Honeymoon suite	EP 165		
	Villa	EP 175		
Harmony Apartel, Rodney Bay Lagoon	Studio	EP 46		
(tel. 28756)	2-bedroom/1-bathroom	EP 66		
	2-bedroom/2-bathroom	EP 74		
Kimatrai, Vieux Fort (near Hewanorra)	Double room	EP 30		
	Apartment	EP 40		

81

	Single	Double	Triple
Marigot Bay Resort, Marigot Bay	Studio cottage	EP 75	
	1-bedroom villa	EP 90	
	2-bedroom villa	EP 110–130	
	3-bedroom villa	EP 160	
Smugglers Village, Cap Estate (tel. 20551)	1-bedroom apt.	EP 80	
	2-bedroom apt.	EP 120	

Guesthouses	Single	Double
Boots Guest House, 36 Micoud Street,	EP 11–17	EP 21–33
Castries	CP 14–20	CP 27–39
	MAP 19–25	MAP 37–49
Cloud's Nest, Vieux Fort (near	MAP 20–25	MAP 40–50
Hewanorra)		
Creole Inn, Vide Bouteicle, Castries	EP 10–12	EP 18–20
	CP 12–14	CP 22–24
Home Guest House, Soufrière	EP 10	EP 16
Lee's Guest House, Leslie Land, Castries	EP 8–9	EP 16–18
Matthew's Guest House, 13 High Street,	EP 11	EP 22
Castries		
Sundale, Choc	CP 18	CP 32
Twin Palm Inn, Victoria Road, The	EP 12	EP 20
Morne	CP 15	CP 28

You should add 10% service charge and 8% tax to all rates. Summer rates at most hotels and apartments should show a discount of at least a third on these prices, but guesthouse rates are normally the same all year round.

EATING OUT

There are a number of worthwhile restaurants in Saint Lucia, but, like the tourist sights and hotels, they are spread all round the island. Castries, of course, has the greatest concentration. **Rain** is probably the best known: a curious name, almost as though the island's relatively high rainfall is a tourist attraction in itself. Rain is situated in Brazil Street, in the same block as the LIAT office, so if you are experiencing LIAT trouble, and the queues are too long or the office shut, you could pop along to Rain for a light lunch. Besides local dishes, you can get snacks such as hamburgers, and there is an interesting cocktail list with items such as 'The Reverend's Downfall' (which is actually a Pina Colada); you can sit inside or outside with water cascading beside you. The restaurant with perhaps the highest reputation on the island for the excellence of its cuisine is **The Green Parrot,** up on the Morne. **The Coal Pot,** in Vigie Marina, besides being a restaurant, is the departure point for the *Brig Unicorn,* a facsimile of a pirate brigantine which makes day excursions down the coast.

In the Vieux Fort area, **Cloud's Nest Hotel** has a reputation for excellent local food with friendly, fast service. There is even a restaurant out in the wilds of Soufrière—**The Still**—for those taking a day over their volcano excursion. A new restaurant up on the Morne is **St Antoine's**. This comes highly recommended with cuisine in the gourmet class and lovely surroundings. Yachtsmen find **The Chart House** at Rodney Bay to their taste. Clientele tend to be the yachting fraternity, both expatriates working in the area and the charterers who are collecting or returning a yacht. Also in the same area, in fact opposite the St Lucian hotel entrance, is a shack called **Caribbean Kitchen** or some such name. The pepperpot soup and local fish dishes are good—and cheap. It also serves an acceptable wine.

Going back south again a stop at **Edgewater Beach Hotel,** about two miles north of Castries (next door to Couples) can be recommended. There is a restaurant here that does excellent pizzas, and a regular West Indian-style restaurant that is also good. The staff are very friendly and courteous, and it is right on a good beach. There are also seven rooms here at little more than guesthouse prices (US$25 and US$31 year round EP).

In Castries it is worth while checking out the **Banana Split,** particularly for lunch, and **Rosie's** stall in the market (a full lunch can cost as little as EC$27).

NIGHTLIFE
On a Friday night anybody looking for a good time and staying in the north of the island goes to **Gros Islet**. This sleepy fishing village wakes up on payday and the streets fill with people and little food stalls. Definitely head for **Hector's Conch,** reputedly the best, and of the many little bars, **Scottie's** and **Village Gate** are strongly recommended. This is the best nightlife on a Friday night. With your joints well-lubricated with copious quantities of rum you should find little difficulty joining in the dancing and general bonhomie.

Other nightlife tends to be centred around the hotels. **Lucifer's** at the St Lucian has a mixed reputation; it certainly used to be good with much calypso, soca and reggae, but latest reports are that it has declined a little. Maybe they changed the disc jockey.

The **Halcyon Beach Club** is worth a visit, but otherwise organised nightlife is a little restricted. The local nightlife is more fun anyway.

SHOPPING
Castries is the main shopping district of the island with department stores to browse through and boutiques specialising in batik and silk-screen printing. The Saint Lucia Perfumery is worth a visit and in Soufrière try the pottery shop.

SPORT
Swimming—and beaches—are best on the western coast, away from the wild Atlantic. (Soufrière in the southwest has a black volcanic sand beach.) Water-

sports and fishing are well catered for with instruction where needed. The island is growing in popularity with yachtsmen and it is possible to charter boats, at a price.

Inland, the island can be explored on horseback or on foot, and golfers have two courses to choose from. Cricket and football are played in season at Marchand, east of Castries.

DOMINICA

The island of Dominica, with Guadeloupe to the north and Martinique to the south, covers an area of 300 square miles. It is a region of astonishing natural beauty. The unexplored rain forests with their unique flora and fauna are hard to equal anywhere. The island is also the site of the only Carib Indian reservation in the world.

Dominica was devastated in 1979 by Hurricane David. However, against all predictions, the islanders' determination has ensured that homes have been rebuilt and agricultural programmes restored.

GETTING TO DOMINICA

Like Saint Lucia, Dominica has two airports. Neither, however, is capable of handling any aircraft larger than the LIAT 48-seater; Melville Hall is the longer established and can take these larger (by Dominica's standards) aircraft. Cane Field was opened a few years ago because Melville Hall is a long way from the capital (35 miles) thus necessitating long journeys over difficult roads. Cane Field is near the capital, Roseau, and takes aircraft up to the size of Twin Otters.

From the USA

There are no flights direct from the USA for the reason stated above; it is doubtful, in any case, whether there would be enough traffic to justify such a service. Thus a change of plane and airline is necessary. There are four 'gateways' or routes by which you can reach Dominica from the USA: Antigua, Saint Croix, Saint Thomas and San Juan. Saint Lucia is not satisfactory unless you intend spending a few days there in each direction, as you would need to change airports. Of the four routes mentioned the best one for you will depend on the following criteria:

(a) Can it be reached by a direct flight from your nearest major US airport?

(b) Which combination of a flight from the USA to a Caribbean airport plus connection offers the most convenient flying arrangement?

(c) Which routes offer a through fare all the way to Dominica?

(d) If no through fares are available, which final segment to Dominica offers the lowest add-on fare?

(e) Which route has the lowest fares from the USA?

It sounds very complicated—and it is. Add-on fares for your Caribbean sector are liable to be lowest for Antigua and highest for San Juan because the flying distances are greater. Conversely, the fares for the jet part of the trip are liable to be lowest for San Juan, Saint Thomas or Saint Croix because these are US territories. San Juan and Saint Thomas are probably your best routes, but get a good travel agent to work it all out for you when you are ready to book.

Details of flights from the USA are as follows:

To Antigua. Flights to Antigua are possible with BWIA from New York and Miami, with Eastern from Miami and Atlanta, and with American from New York. Flights are generally early enough in the day to allow a same-day connection to Dominica.

To Saint Thomas and Saint Croix. These points are served from a wider range of US departure airports. Services from New York are operated by Pan Am and American, whilst Pan Am, Eastern and Midway Airlines fly down from Miami. Midway Airlines also flies from Chicago whilst American has flights from Dallas.

To San Juan, Puerto Rico. This is the widest choice of all, and the route most likely to offer bargain fares. The following is a list of departure points in alphabetical order with carriers which operate a service:

Atlanta: Eastern and Delta; *Baltimore/Washington International:* Eastern and World; *Boston:* Eastern, American and World; *Chicago:* Eastern, Delta, TWA and American; *Dallas:* American; *Los Angeles:* Eastern and World; *Miami:* Eastern, American and TWA; *New York:* Eastern, American, TWA and World; *Orlando:* Eastern; *Philadelphia:* Eastern; *St Louis:* TWA; *San Francisco:* Eastern; *Tulsa:* American.

For information on which airlines operate connections along your chosen route, and which airport they fly into in Dominica, please see the *Within the Caribbean* section below.

From Canada

Like people flying from the USA, you will need to change aircraft and airline to get to Dominica. This you should do either at Antigua or San Juan. There may be through fares available; otherwise you will want the best combination of fare from Canada to your entry point in the Caribbean, and from there to Dominica.

From Toronto BWIA or Air Canada can fly you to Antigua. Check with a local travel agent not just the best fare combination but also the best connections.

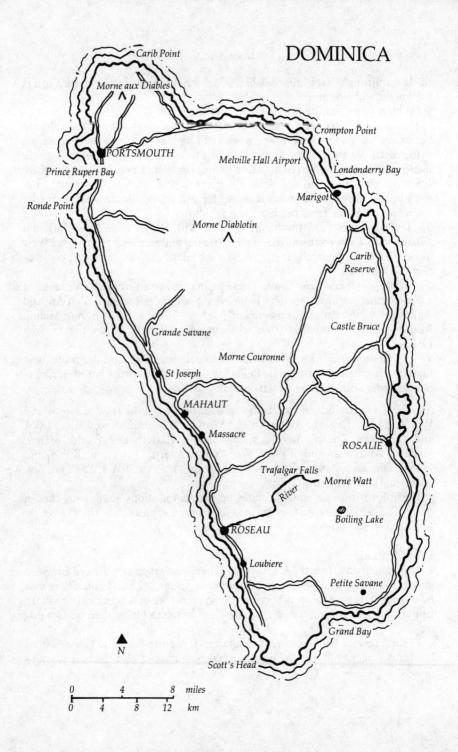

DOMINICA

Carib Point

Morne aux Diables
∧

PORTSMOUTH

Prince Rupert Bay

Ronde Point

Crompton Point

Melville Hall Airport

Londonderry Bay

Marigot

Morne Diablotin
∧

Carib
Reserve

Grande Savane

Castle Bruce

Morne Couronne

St Joseph

MAHAUT

Massacre

ROSALIE

Trafalgar Falls

River

Morne Watt

Boiling Lake

ROSEAU

Loubiere

Petite Savane

Grand Bay

N

Scott's Head

| 0 | | 4 | | 8 | miles |
| 0 | 4 | 8 | | 12 | km |

From London

Traditionally, the best route from London is via Antigua. This is partly because the Antigua–Dominica fare is less than the Barbados–Dominica fare (the other gateway used) and partly because connections are better: sometimes an overnight stay is necessary, but this is not always the case. If you are intending to spend some time in Saint Lucia both outward and back this route can produce the lowest fares (with the small discounts available in the UK) but it is not otherwise recommended, as you would need to change airports in Saint Lucia. For onward flight information from Antigua please see the *Within the Caribbean* section below.

From Europe

Dominica is best reached from Europe by way of Antigua, Guadeloupe or Martinique. It may be possible, depending on flight connections when you are travelling, to make the journey without having to stop overnight. Nouvelles Frontières operates some charters from Brussels to Guadeloupe and Martinique at attractive fares, and Air France flies from Paris to both those points. Often a same-day connection is possible through Pointe-à-Pitre and sometimes through Fort-de-France.

Within the Caribbean

Dominica's two airports may cause some confusion but no major problems unless you go to the wrong one when leaving the island. Briefly, LIAT operates to both, but all other airlines operate only in and out of Cane Field (which is near the capital). Some people prefer Melville Hall, even though it is a long way from town, as it is less hazardous. LIAT operates services from Antigua and Barbados to both airports, and from Trinidad to Melville Hall only. From Fort de France (Martinique) LIAT and Air Martinique both fly into Cane Field, which is the airport used by LIAT and Air Guadeloupe from Pointe-à-Pitre. Saint Thomas, Saint Croix and San Juan are all linked to Cane Field by Puerto Rican-based Air Caribe International. Air Martinique flies into Cane Field from Union, Saint Vincent and Saint Lucia (Vigie). LIAT flies into both airports from Saint Lucia (Vigie) and into Melville Hall only from Saint Vincent. .

ENTRY REGULATIONS

Passports but not visas are required for most nationalities, together with return and/or onward tickets.

ELECTRICITY

The supply is 220–240 volts at 50 cycles, as in the UK.

CLIMATE

You will find temperatures 'typically Caribbean', although Dominica has a higher rainfall than average because of its mountains.

CURRENCY

The Eastern Caribbean or Bee Wee dollar is approximately equal to US$0.40. US$1 = EC$2.70.

LANGUAGE

Officially English, but most islanders speak a French-Creole patois.

POPULATION

Most of the population of 76,000 is concentrated around the coast, with about a quarter of them living in the capital.

HISTORY

Perhaps it is the wildness and inaccessibility of Dominica which ensured the survival of the Caribs. For this is the only island in the Caribbean which has a substantial Carib population. Some 7,000 of its inhabitants have Carib blood, while about 400 are of predominantly Carib descent.

Back in the 17th century, and even as late as the 18th, both the British and French were unable to dislodge the Caribs or even gain a foothold themselves. However, midway through the 18th century the French managed to establish a settlement. The island then changed hands once or twice in the normal eastern Caribbean fashion until finally becoming British in 1782. Thus it stayed until the island was given independence in 1967 as an associated state. It attained full independence in 1978.

WHAT TO SEE

Arriving by air in Dominica is something of an experience. The aspect of the approaching island is mountainous, with ridge after ridge of hills covered in lush and seemingly impenetrable forest. After a shower of rain the foliage glistens in myriad hues of green. Here and there a red-brown muddy track, seemingly fit only for pedestrian use, can be seen winding into the wilderness.

It is difficult to imagine where there can be an airport here, but a runway and a few buildings have been carved out of a landscape which is still very much the preserve of nature. The impression is that nature is simply biding her time; a little neglect on man's part and the forest will reclaim its own.

This impression of wilderness barely curbed by man is probably stronger in Dominica than anywhere else in the Caribbean. The Tourist Board is perhaps justified in calling it the 'Getaway Place'. The island is dominated by a heavily wooded mountain range which runs along its entire length. The highest point is **Morne Diablotin** (4,750 ft), whilst **Morne au Diable** in the far north and **Morne Watt** in the south are also noteworthy peaks.

Although the name of the island is actually Spanish (it is one of the few to keep the name Columbus gave it), French place names abound including the capital, **Roseau**. While it is not one of the finest towns in the Caribbean, it does have a good market, and its Botanic Gardens are reputed to be among the best in the Caribbean.

But it is that splendid wild scenery which beckons. Tourists are told that there are 365 rivers cascading down from the mountains. In the south are the spectacular **Trafalgar Falls,** sulphur springs (at Wotton Waven) and beaches. Then there is the **Boiling Lake,** a mass of volatile and steaming water which periodically throws up geysers, and the apparently bottomless and certainly tranquil **Freshwater Lake.** It is said that a Carib leader dived in here and was next seen swimming out at sea. You should certainly see the Carib reserve, which is near the airport.

Waterfall in Dominica

CALENDAR

The best time to catch the islanders at play is the period just before Lent when the Carnival is in full swing with band competitions, dancing in the streets and the inevitable street procession.

National Day on 3 November is the climax of the autumn festivities commemorating independence, a very colourful spectacle when everyone wears national dress, speaks in patois, and remembers their cultural roots.

WHERE TO STAY

All of the settlements are on the coast, fairly evenly distributed around the island's perimeter. Petit Marigot is nearest the airport, which is diametrically opposite Roseau, the capital. Most of the hotels take advantage of the splendid scenery, and are located in the hills. Dominica is not the first choice for a beach holiday. Nevertheless, there are a handful of hotels situated on or near beaches and equipped with the appropriate facilities.

The Anchorage is probably the best-known hotel, situated on a pebbly beach about half a mile south of Roseau. There are 26 air-conditioned rooms (each with two double beds), swimming pool and restaurant (which serves French and native cuisine). This hotel has a subsidiary (Anchorage Tours) which organises a wide range of safari excursions, car rental, boating, fishing and waterskiing. Summer rates are around US$35 single, US$45 double EP. MAP supplement is another US$15 per person.

A somewhat larger hotel (48 air-conditioned rooms), The Layou River Hotel, is situated some 10 miles north of Roseau slightly inland along the Layou River. This is like staying in a botanical garden which itself is within a jungle. There is a pool, restaurant and ample organised activities and excursions. MAP rates in the summer are about US$58 single and US$88 double.

Guesthouses are most likely to be found in Roseau, which is the port of call for the banana boats, and perhaps Petit Marigot. You can expect prices to be reasonable. Inquire at the airport or, if you have arrived by banana boat, down by the waterfront in Roseau.

MARTINIQUE

About 385 square miles in area, Martinique is roughly 50 miles long by 15 wide. Mountains and tropical forest in the north become fertile plains in the centre; the south is arid, cacti being the most prolific vegetation.

GETTING TO MARTINIQUE

Martinique, as the most important French island in the Caribbean, has excellent communications with metropolitan France as well as a reasonable network of connections within the Caribbean. North America is reasonably served too.

From the USA

As you would expect, services are most frequent from Miami. Air France and Eastern both fly this route, with Eastern also having a flight from Atlanta. American Airlines flies down from New York. Some reasonably priced package tours are available in the USA; in early December 1985 it was possible to book a one-week package staying at the Club Méditerranée and including meals and all its sports facilities, etc. for as little as US$800. That included flights and, even allowing for price increases which must since have been imposed owing to the weakening of the dollar and strengthening of the franc, it must represent good value.

From Canada
The French connection means that Air Canada operates from Montreal as well as from Toronto. Check Wardair and Unitours; there may be charters.

From London
Ah, a problem! The only European scheduled flights seem to be from France, and through fares on Air France ex London have always been expensive. Using this route, Air France Vacances holiday prices *begin* at over £700 (compared with £400-plus for a Barbados holiday possible with most UK operators). The UK operators tend to route you via Barbados. However, there are charters available from Paris and Brussels; try Nouvelles Frontières, which now has an office in London. Otherwise get a cheap return fare to Barbados or Saint Lucia (the Saint Lucia route is cheaper but involves an airport change).

From Europe
French citizens have a wide choice of departure airport; they can fly from Bordeaux, Lyon, Marseille, Mulhouse and Paris. All these services are operated by Air France and special fares are sometimes available. Also check out the situation with regard to charters, some of which operate from Brussels.

Within the Caribbean
The local airline Air Martinique operates fairly small planes as far north as Sint Maarten and southwards to Saint Lucia, Saint Vincent, Mustique, Union, Barbados and Trinidad. Eastern flies in from Sint Maarten. BWIA operates jet services from Sint Maarten, Antigua, Grenada and Trinidad and turboprops from Saint Lucia and Trinidad. Air France flies northwards to Guadeloupe, Puerto Rico and Haiti and also has some connecting services from South America (Caracas, Bogotá and Cayenne, for example). LIAT services Martinique from Antigua, Dominica, Saint Lucia, Saint Vincent, Barbados and Grenada.

ENTRY REGULATIONS
Visas are not required by citizens of the USA and Canada if staying for less than three months. This exemption also covers nationals of Australia, New Zealand, most non-EEC West European countries and certain African countries. Citizens of EEC countries and some former French possessions in

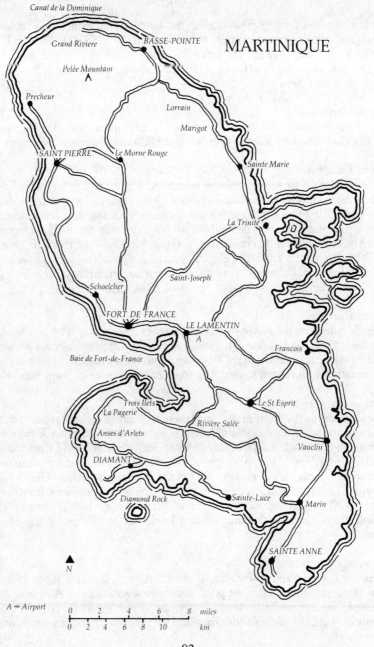

Canal de la Dominique

Grand Riviere

BASSE-POINTE

MARTINIQUE

Pelée Mountain
∧

Precheur

Lorrain

Marigot

SAINT PIERRE

Le Morne Rouge

Sainte Marie

La Trinité

Saint-Joseph

Schoelcher

FORT DE FRANCE

LE LAMENTIN
A

Francois

Baie de Fort-de-France

Trois Ilets
La Pagerie

Le St Esprit

Anses d'Arlets

Rivière Salée

DIAMANT

Vauclin

Diamond Rock

Sainte-Luce

Marin

SAINTE ANNE

▲
N

A = Airport

| 0 | 2 | 4 | 6 | 8 | miles |
| 0 | 2 | 4 | 6 | 8 | 10 | km |

Africa are allowed entry without visas for an unlimited stay. Most West Indian nationals need a visa. You should have an ongoing or return ticket.

Proof of inoculation against yellow fever is required if you have travelled from or via an infected area.

ELECTRICITY

The supply is 220 volts, 50 cycles, about the same as in the UK.

CLIMATE

It is tropical, but quite varied. The average temperature is 83°F. Rainfall can be as low as 40in per year or as high as 140in in the mountains. The rainy season is May to November and the humidity is particularly high then. Most rain falls in the north; there is adequate rainfall in the fertile centre and very little in the south.

CURRENCY

This is the French franc, which is divided into 100 centimes. The US dollar is approximately equal to FFR 7.50 but this is very variable.

POPULATION

The population is 350,000.

LANGUAGE

French.

HISTORY

Martinique has all the attributes of the French Antilles—Creole cuisine, duty-free French goods—and more than its fair share of history. The most memorable incident was the eruption of Mount Pelée in 1902. Up to then it overlooked the town of Saint Pierre, known as the 'Little Paris of the West Indies', the cultural and economic capital of Martinique. The eruption had been forecast, as Mount Pelée had been smouldering for several days (there had even been a two-hour-long fall of ash). This was disregarded by the inhabitants, who took heed of the reassurances of the governor. At least one ship tried to leave but was refused permission.

At this time the population, including temporary visitors, of Saint Pierre numbered some 40,000. Of this number there were only two known survivors when, on 8 May, the side of Mount Pelée split from top to bottom and a huge jet of fire poured out over the town and bay. The steamer *Roddam*, which had tried to leave that day, had dropped only one anchor. Most of the crew were immediately roasted alive on deck whilst the others jumped into what must have been the boiling sea. Only the captain survived, badly burnt, and was able to

93

struggle with his boat to Saint Lucia. The other survivor was a convict awaiting the death penalty in a solidly built dungeon. The thick walls ensured that when he was discovered four days later he had suffered only some burns and was able to walk the four miles home. Ruins of the church, theatre and some other buildings survive, and there is a museum (the **Musée Volcanologique**) which displays relics and photographs.

GETTING AROUND
The roads on Martinique are very good indeed and by and large the standard of driving is excellent. Car rental rates seem cheap at first glance—but actually they are not; the cheap rates do not include mileage, which can really increase the price if you do a lot of driving. Cars are normally French and if you are looking for a small car, and have a choice, the new Renault 5, which seems to outperform the Peugeot on the roads, is to be recommended. Fuel is expensive. Avis, Hertz, Budget and National are on the island.

There is a comprehensive and reasonably priced bus service, although there do not seem to be many of them.

WHAT TO SEE
Saint Pierre and Mount Pelée are by no means the only places worth a visit. **Vauclin,** on the southeast coast, is a pre-Columbian fishing port and market. There is also an 18th-century chapel here. Nearby is Mount Vauclin, the highest point in the south of the island, which affords fine views as far as Saint Lucia.

On the south coast, opposite Diamant Beach, is **Diamond Rock.** During the Napoleonic Wars (in 1804) a British expeditionary force loaded cannon, supplies and some 110 men onto the top of this rock and held it, obstructing the passage between it and the island, for a year and a half. The rock was actually commissioned as a sloop, the *HMS Diamond Rock.*

Also of interest is the small settlement of **Les Trois-Ilets** where Marie-Joseph Rose Tascher de la Pagerie, who later married Napoleon and became Empress Joséphine, was born. The ruins of the Pagerie sugar mill and the local church have been partially restored. The museum here has some items of interest to culture vultures. Les Trois-Ilets is inland, across the bay from Fort de France.

There is much else of interest in Martinique, including the small fishing village of **Prêcheur,** where Madame de Maintenon, the second wife of Louis XIV, spent part of her youth.

Fort-de-France

This is the administrative, commercial and cultural capital of Martinique. A town of some 96,000 people, it is situated on the bay, surrounded by foliage-covered hills. Here you will see, on the opposite side of town to Fort Saint Louis, pastel buildings and roadside cafés. In the centre is a park, La Savane. There are a number of buildings of interest, yet the town also displays much of the soulless architecture to be found in Pointe-à-Pitre. Many of the hotels seem to be in or near Fort de France, although the beaches are some distance away. Start a city tour at the tourist office on the waterfront in central Fort de France.

CALENDAR

The two main events of the year are the Carnival before Lent with parades, masquerades, dancing and singing in the streets culminating in a 'funeral pyre' on Ash Wednesday; and the evening Fête Nautique de Robert—the sea festival at **Robert** in September.

WHERE TO STAY

Purely in terms of Caribbean holidays, Martinique enjoys the same relationship with metropolitan France as Barbados enjoys with Britain. Thus resorts and hotels are geared around what the French like to do. Most of the top hotels, in theory at least and if you believe the tourist guide, are at Les Trois-Ilets. Here you will find a sleepy little settlement with a few boats on the beach and a lively harbour bar—but no hotels. Go back to the main road, turn right at what seems like a major junction, and you will find yourself in Pointe du Bout. Situated here are the four-star **Bakoua** and **Méridien,** three-star hotels like the **Frantel** and **PLM Etap** and other establishments. One thing they all have in common: a lack of sympathy with their Caribbean environment. All are quite large (Bakoua has 100 rooms, Méridien 303, Frantel 215 and PLM 98) and it seems nonsensical to cram them all into such a tiny space when Martinique is so big. It is not as though the area is particularly rich in beautiful beaches; the beaches are all right—but that's all—and the beach at Bakoua which looks so nice in photographs can be seen, on close inspection, to be man-made.

Sainte Anne is almost, but not quite, as far south as you can go. Here is the two-star **Dunette Hotel** which at first sight is unimpressive—southern European seaside architecture, in a small town—but this hotel is a good choice. It is right on the seafront beside a scrappy beach on a little bay opposite the Club Méditerranée. The rooms (with bathroom) are sizeable, adequately furnished, with air-conditioning (necessary), a balcony (facing the town) and internal telephone. Breakfast, which is included, is French-style but adequate. The only snag: if you arrive back after midnight when it is locked up, dark and silent, it will take some time and a lot of noise to wake the night porter from his (presumably) deep slumbers.

As for the **Club Méditerranée** ... one is tempted by the enticing advertising, but when you get there … To be fair, the facilities (comprehensive watersports, tennis, large communal areas, spacious grounds, good beaches) are more than adequate. The fact that there is an American staff is a strong point in its favour. If you can book a week's holiday including flights, meals, accommodation, transfers and all the facilities for less than US$900, then it's worth it. All the American staff are pleasant and helpful, as are some of the Martiniquais (for example, the lady manning the telephone exchange) and the French (the gentleman running the little travel agency).

Behind Sainte Anne is 'Savane des Pétrifications'—the petrified forest. The trees are as hard as iron. **Manoir de Beauregard** is nearby, a converted 18th-century mansion of 27 rooms. If you continue down the main road, bypassing Sainte Anne, you come to Les Salines, a wide beach pounded by crashing surf, at the southernmost point of the island.

Accommodation in Martinique
Daily summer rates in French francs
All of the prices below should be treated with discretion. Though these rates are as officially published, they should be increased by about 50% to indicate the actual rate the hotels are charging.

	Single	Double	Triple
Auberge de l'Anse-Mitan, Pointe du Bout, Les Trois-Ilets (tel. 660112)	CP 180	CP 220	
Auberge du Vare, Case-Piote (tel. 778056)	CP 135	CP 190	CP 252
	MAP 195	MAP 310	MAP 432
Bakoua, Pointe du Bout, Les Trois-Ilets (tel. 660202)	CP 500–570	CP 680–780	CP 900
Bristol, Rue Martin Luther King, Fort de France (tel. 713180)	CP 180	CP 250	CP 300
Chez Anna, 26 Rue Perrinon, Fort de France (tel. 715562)	EP 105	EP 160	EP 215
Chez Julot, Vauclin (tel. 744093)	CP 130	CP 175	CP 210
	MAP 180	MAP 285	MAP 380
Un Coin de Paris, 54 Rue Lazare-Carnot, Fort de France (tel. 700852)	CP 110	CP 160	CP 210
	MAP 155	MAP 250	MAP 345
Délices de la Mer, Sainte Luce (tel. 765012)	CP 125	CP 180	CP 215
	MAP 180	MAP 290	MAP 380
Dunette, Sainte Anne (tel. 767390)	CP 150–180	CP 200–300	CP 350
Frantel, Pointe du Bout, Les Trois-Ilets (tel. 660404)	EP 317–381	EP 422–486	EP 545–609
Madiana, Schoelcher (tel. 724878)	EP 220	EP 250	
Le Madras, Tartare-Trinité (tel. 582144)	EP 131	EP 179	EP 215
Manoir de Beauregard, Sainte Anne (tel. 767340)	CP 259	CP 308	CP 387
Méridien, Pointe du Bout, Les Trois-Ilets (tel. 660000)	EP 510–610	EP 620–740	EP 840–940
La Nouvelle Vague, Saint Pierre (tel. 771434)		CP 100–150	
Novotel, Diamant (tel. 764242)	EP 426	EP 543	EP 703
PLM Etap, Pointe du Bout, Les Trois-Ilets (tel. 660530)	EP 218	EP 270	

EATING OUT
Most cuisine is Creole and French and very good, as you would expect. Don't make the mistake of assuming all restaurants are good, as it is possible to find

mediocre ones. The main tourist area of Pointe du Bout/Les Trois-Ilets is at its best at night; hotels such as the **Bakoua** and the **Méridien** serve good food (expect it to be a little overpriced by restaurant standards) and have a show *tous les soirs* (every evening). Sometimes it is a steel band, sometimes a local dance troupe, sometimes a Biguine band. The Méridien has limbo dancing some nights, some jazz, a discotheque and a casino. There is a Chinese restaurant at Pointe du Bout, **Le Cantonnais** (tel. 660233) and another, **Le Jardin de Jade** (tel. 611550), a little to the north of Fort de France at Schoelcher. There is a Vietnamese restaurant, **La Muraille d'Asie** (tel. 501382), in Lamentin (the town closest to the airport). The **Hotel Bristol** specialises in couscous and does a paella on Fridays.

Otherwise most of the restaurants are in Fort de France. Some of the better (and more expensive) ones are **La Grande Voile** at Pointe-Simon (tel. 702929), **La Biguine** at 11 Route de la Folie (tel. 714007), **Le d'Esnambuc** at 1 Rue de la Liberté (tel. 714651; near La Savane) and **New Brummel's,** which features a piano bar, at 1 Rue Schoelcher (tel. 605329). Telephone reservations in advance, as they do not have the same closing days (although Sunday is the most popular).

What appears to be the entrance of the **Parasol,** outside the Club Méditerranée, is guarded by a fierce-sounding large dog, presumably stationed there to prevent patrons attempting to gain entrance by that door. (A tasteful sign in French and English directing potential diners to the real, hidden, entrance might have been a better idea!) It is situated on a nice beach, very suitable for sea bathing, with the open-air ambience one expects in the Caribbean. The food and wine are good—the accent is on seafood—but prices seem to be about 25% more than they should be. It's about the best place in the area, though.

NIGHTLIFE
Besides the nightclubs in hotels there are a number in Fort de France. These include **Le Manoir** on Route des Religieuses (Fridays and Saturdays only), **Hippo-Club** at 26 Boulevard Allègre (every night except Sunday), **Club des Iles** at 180 Avenue Maurice Bishop (Sainte-Thérèse on some maps) and **Le Must** at 20 Boulevard Allègre, which is open every night.

There are two casinos on the island, at the Méridien and Casino Hotels. No slot machines. Dress well and take proof of identity.

SHOPPING
Its French heritage is reflected in the island's shops and boutiques, with French perfumes and chic fashions for sale as well as luxury items and local handicrafts. In Fort de France try the Rue Victor Hugo, Rue Schoelcher, and

the area near Rue de la République. A local speciality is the island's rum. So try the rum shops on Rue Victor Hugo and Rue de la Liberté.

SPORT

Sea- and shore-based sports thrive on Martinique, though the beaches are not as spectacular as some, having a greyish, volcanic hue or even having imported sand. Topless sunbathing may make up for this, and the variety of activities available, which include snorkelling, diving, sailing, spinnaker flying, water-skiing, windsurfing, and sea angling. Your hotel or the tourist office will be able to supply details.

Inland you can explore the island on foot, horse or scooter, watch football or sailing matches, and play golf and tennis.

Leeward Islands

GUADELOUPE

The Carib Indian name for Guadeloupe was *Caloucaera* or *Karukera*, which means 'Beautiful Waters'. Christopher Columbus, on his second trip in 1493, named the island in honour of 'Our Lady of Guadeloupe de Extremadura' to thank her for protecting him during a storm. In its turn the Spanish 'Guada-lupe' derives from an Arab word meaning 'River of Love', *Oued-el-Houb*.

GETTING TO GUADELOUPE
The main differences between Guadeloupe and Martinique in terms of getting there are regional. Guadeloupe has better connections in its immediate area with some of the tiny islands and none at all with many of the southern Carib-bean points. Long-haul services are very similar to Fort de France; in many cases the same aircraft serves both islands.

From the USA
Eastern flies from Atlanta and Miami, Air France also from Miami, and American from New York.

From Canada
Air Canada flies in from both Toronto and Montreal.

From London
The advice here is exactly the same as in the section on Martinique, as there

are no flights here from London. Alternatively you can fly to Antigua (Barbados is too far away) and take a connection from there, although an overnight stop may be necessary.

From Europe

Connections with France are excellent. There are flights from Bordeaux, Lyon, Marseille, Mulhouse and Paris. There should be charters and reasonably priced packages and sometimes special fares. Brussels is often linked with Guadeloupe by charter; check with Nouvelles Frontières.

Within the Caribbean

The nearby islands of Marie-Galante, La Désirade and Les Saintes and the more distant territories of Saint Barthélemy and Saint Martin belong to the same French department as Guadeloupe and are administered from Basse-Terre, Guadeloupe's capital. They are all linked to Pointe-à-Pitre by the tiny planes of Air Guadeloupe which fly to both airports in Saint Martin/Sint Maarten (Grand Case in the French part and Juliana, the major, jet, airport in the Dutch sector). Air Guadeloupe also flies, in partnership with LIAT, to Cane Field in Dominica. LIAT operates Twin Otters to Montserrat and turboprops to Antigua, Saint Lucia (Vigie) and Barbados. Air France flies jets to Fort de France and Eastern flies to Sint Maarten.

ENTRY REGULATIONS
These are the same as for Martinique.

ELECTRICITY
The supply is 220 volts at 50 cycles, about the same as in the UK.

CLIMATE
The average daytime temperature is around 83°F and humidity is relatively high in the summer. Rainfall is heavier on the island of Basse-Terre than on Grande-Terre.

CURRENCY
As in Martinique, the French franc is used.

LANGUAGE
French, with little else spoken in remote areas.

POPULATION
Guadeloupe's 315,000 inhabitants are mainly descendants of slaves. They are citizens of France.

HISTORY

Columbus discovered the island in 1493. In keeping with a promise, he made Guadeloupe over to the Spanish King and Queen, Ferdinand and Isabella. The Spanish abandoned it one hundred years later. Apart from two brief periods of British occupation, it has been under French control ever since.

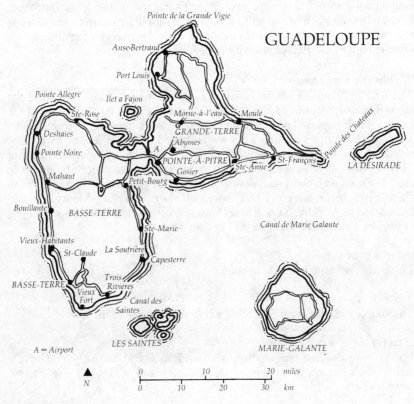

GETTING AROUND

All the 'big name' car rental companies and some local ones are represented at the airport, and take most major credit cards. Please note however, that credit cards and US dollar traveller's cheques are often not accepted at petrol stations. Make sure you always have an adequate supply of French francs in folding money on your person. If you don't use a credit card when hiring the car you will need to leave a large cash deposit.

Rates start at FFR1,000 per week for a small car; an automatic with air-conditioning will be about double. CDW (Collision Damage Waiver) is

FFR30–40 per day. It is possible to hire bicycles and motorbikes.
There are bus services connecting the main towns. Fares are rather high by
Caribbean standards.

WHAT TO SEE
Guadeloupe is really two islands, Grande-Terre and Basse-Terre, separated
by a narrow channel, La Rivière Salée (Salt River). The terms Grande-Terre
and Basse-Terre should not be translated literally. Grande-Terre means
'Windward', and Basse-Terre 'Leeward'.

These two parts of Guadeloupe are roughly equal in area, but quite different
in character and topography. Whilst Basse-Terre is quite mountainous, and
includes the volcano of Soufrière in the national park, Grande-Terre is flat
with chalky soil and most of the agriculture.

The commercial capital of Guadeloupe is in Grande-Terre. This is **Pointe-
à-Pitre,** the largest town (the population is either 50,000 or 82,500, depending which information source you refer to—the latter is the official figure). Its
commercial importance is such that much of its Caribbean flavour has been
lost. Now the town is proud of its bustling port, shopping arcades, modern
buildings and important international airport. The most noticeable characteristic, clearly distinguishable from the incoming aircraft, is the spread of
medium-rise housing developments. Ostensibly these are a benefit as they provide decent housing for the poor. Perhaps they damage the community spirit,
as has proved the case in Europe and North America; they certainly destroy
any character the town may have had. Some side streets near the centre of
town, and Place du Victoire, have a little character. Otherwise Pointe-à-Pitre
is grey, soulless, overtly and materially French yet without the spirit of France.

Travelling southeast from Pointe-à-Pitre you soon come to the village of
Gosier. It is in this area that most of the plush hotels, restaurants and nightclubs are situated. Continuing along this coast road you pass the villages of
Sainte Anne and **Saint François,** and miles of superb, empty beaches. If you
take the road northwest from Saint François you will come to **Moule**; it is now
renowned for its splendid beach, but before its destruction by tidal wave in
1928 it was the main harbour of Guadeloupe. There is a good road across the
island which connects Moule with Pointe-à-Pitre.

The mountains of Basse-Terre can be seen clearly from Pointe-à-Pitre, as
the distance over the bay is not great. An iron bridge spans La Rivière Salée
and the road then continues down the coast of Basse-Terre towards the capital, also called Basse-Terre. Perhaps the greatest point of interest on the way to
the capital is the site of engraved rocks at **Trois Rivières.** It is thought that
these engravings were made by the Arawak Indians, the first known inhabitants
of these islands. They are set in an area rich in the foliage and vegetation which
is thought to have been important to the Arawaks and Caribs. On the way there

you will have passed the **Carbet Falls,** waterfalls which require some walking to reach but are worth the effort.

The capital, **Basse-Terre,** has a population of 38,000 (official figure). It has retained much of its charm, being a small town with narrow streets lined with balconied houses. Its position at the foot of the 'dormant' volcano of Soufrière makes it susceptible to eventual catastrophe. Much of the written tourist information refers to **Soufrière** as 'dormant', and one booklet on the National Park stresses the safety of walking to the crater. All of this literature was obviously prepared before the eruption of 1976 which threatened great damage and loss of life. In the event, no full-scale eruption developed (apparently the molten lava found an outlet elsewhere in the world's crust) so that it is still possible to climb the peak and walk across the National Park. There are colour-coded trails to assist you to do this. If this is a serious intention, visit the tourist office in Place du Victoire which will be pleased to give you information on how best to accomplish the walk.

Les Saintes

These two islands, **Terre de Haut** and **Terre de Bas,** lie to the south of Basse-Terre. The main commercial activity undertaken by these people of Breton descent is fishing. The airfare is FFR 180 each way, but there are boats from Basse-Terre and Trois Rivières.

Marie-Galante

Apparently named by Columbus after his own ship, this is the largest of Guadeloupe's dependencies. There are some beautiful beaches here and a lovely coastal road linking **Grand Bourg** and **Saint Louis.** Cheap accommodation is available. The airfare is again FFR 180 each way and there is a boat service which takes two hours.

La Désirade

A very quiet and arid island, Désirade can again be reached by air and boat. It is an attractive spot for an excursion, offering peace and calm to anyone who wants to get away from it all. Fishing is the main occupation, and the island boasts some excellent seafood restaurants.

FOOD AND DRINK

This (and the people) is what makes the French Antilles so pleasant. So many of the Caribbean islands are without staple items of the European diet that one takes for granted at home. Here fresh milk is always available. There is an easy

Soufrière, Guadeloupe

availability of the world's best food and drink in supermarkets, stores and markets, and there are also many superb restaurants. French and Creole dishes are featured most strongly, but you will also find touches of Africa and Asia, and there is plenty of seafood.

Some of the best known and most representative Creole dishes are *accras* (cod fritters), stuffed crabs and *ouassous* (crawfish). But perhaps it is the use of the indigenous vegetables which most characterises the Creole cuisine—*taro* (Caribbean cauliflower), sweet potato, *chow-chow* (potato), red bean and *berengene* (egg plant).

Here is a recipe for Creole punch: one-fifth sugar-cane syrup, four-fifths white rum, ice cubes and lemon peel. (Don't drink it all at once.)

Pointe-à-Pitre has some snack bars, and Gosier has one or two. There are numerous picturesque, small restaurants, especially in Pointe-à-Pitre and the main resorts. Eating *à la carte* can be very expensive, though there are a fair number of places offering at least one menu *à prix fixe*—usually a three-course meal and far better value. The price (from 60F up) sometimes includes a quarter litre of wine per person.

Reasonable value is offered by both of the small semi-outdoor restaurants situated side by side opposite the Callinago Beach Hotel just outside the village of Gosier (but be wary of the fries in the one on the left: not exactly classic *frites*).

The French Antilles is subsidised by mainland France. Although there is some tourism, particularly French, the economy is mainly based on agriculture. The principal products are sugar-cane, rum and bananas.

Supermarkets and grocery stores are as common and well-stocked as those in France, with luxury goods for sale to the local people, not just to the tourists. This is just one sign of the French policy which maintains that the French Antilles are part of mainland France, separated by a mere 4,000 miles of sea. It's not surprising that French butter, cheese, juice, wine and the rest should cost more here; what's surprising is that it should cost *so much more*. Sample prices 1985/86: local mineral water, 8F; baguette of French bread, about 5F; milk, 1.5 litres (the only size readily available), 15F. The last especially is a puzzle: in UK terms the price would be 55p per pint. Yet there are plenty of cows on the island, and in fact the dairy industry in Port Louis is a point of Guadeloupian pride. (Even more puzzling, prices for many of these self-caterers' items are markedly lower in Saint Barthélemy, a dependency of Guadeloupe which receives most of its European imports through the bigger island.)

It's worth trying the market in Pointe-à-Pitre for fresh fruit and vegetables if you are self-catering. There are always those *boulangeries*, too, for fresh French bread, pastries and other goodies.

CALENDAR
The first event of the year is the pre-Lent carnival, which lasts for weeks of revelling and street dancing, climaxing in a torch-lit parade and the burning of 'King Carnival' on Ash Wednesday.

Special to Guadeloupe is the Cooks' Festival in early August, when an offering is made to Saint Laurent, the patron saint of cooks, at Pointe-à-Pitre Cathedral. The women carry baskets of food to the Cathedral followed by mass and a feast with singing and dancing. Tickets may be available from your hotel or the tourist office. In Pointe-à-Pitre this is at 5 Square de la Banque.

WHERE TO STAY
In Gosier, about five miles east of Pointe-à-Pitre or the airport, you will find the main cluster of this resort's hotels by taking the first signposted turning off the main dual carriageway. Just west of the village itself is **Ecotel,** among the cheapest of this group at FFR340/480 for CP single/double in winter, but otherwise not particularly recommended. It offers rooms only, and piped music plays relentlessly.

Probably best in this group if you can afford it is the 80-room **Auberge de la Vieille Tour.** It has most comforts and is an attractive place. It is easy to find because it has a tower, as the name suggests. Winter rates are from FFR 655/920 CP single/double. The beach is three minutes' walk away.

Of the more affordable places, **PLM Callinago Village** and **PLM Callinago Beach** (with direct access to a private stretch of beach) are well situated and popular, and there is a clutch of three-star establishments (**Salako, PLM Arawak, Novotel Fleur d'Epée** and **Frantel Marissol** being just a few of them). At the other end of the scale there is the fourteen-room **Les Flamboyants** and sixteen-room **Bungalow Village**.

For an economical place to stay in Gosier—actually just the other side of the village, but only a few minutes' walk from the shops and restaurants—you couldn't do better than **Serge's Guest House**. A complex of buildings connected by red-tiled walkways and screened from the road by dense greenery and hibiscus, this is a place of some character. In Caribbean terms it is not really a guesthouse, more a simple hotel, nor is there anyone called Serge in evidence. It is not luxurious, but adequate and clean, and good value at about FFR 180/240 for CP all year (some studio units with kitchenettes, by the week only). There are no extras for service, government taxes or energy. Breakfast is liberal. Some rooms share a bathroom; others have a private bath. The air-conditioning is very effective. Note that some French is essential here. It is perhaps ten minutes' walk to Gosier's beach.

Farther along the coast, at **Saint Félix** (not much village here) there's **Carmelita's Village Caraïbe** offering reasonably priced units with kitchenettes next to a rather rocky sea shore—there is very little real beach. The restaurant here is popular. Winter rate: CP about FFR 360 double.

In the **Sainte Anne** area the first of the listed hotels you encounter, coming from the west, is **La Toubana**, a group of spacious bungalows, each with its own patio. The rooms have solid mahogany beds and furniture. The kitchenette has a large fridge, double hotplate and the bare minimum of pans and plates. There's a large central building with a terrace and a small pool and sundeck. The food is passable, but service is often slow. The management are friendly and speak English. The son's Alsatian dogs, though docile, may bother some people. This place has one of the nicest situations on the island—spread out on the hillside, with a steep path down to a small sandy beach and jetty. At night the chorus of cicadas and frogs will ensure you don't forget you're still in only partly tamed tropical terrain. One of the best beaches on the island is a few minutes east, at Sainte Anne itself. There are a couple of general stores not far away. Rates start at FFR 500 in winter for double occupancy with breakfast.

Nearer the village, you could try **Le Rotabas,** at somewhat lower rates (hotel rooms only). It's right on one end of Sainte Anne's superb beach and has a reasonable restaurant.

For a more rural but very pleasant experience, continue east for about four miles beyond Sainte Anne to **Relais du Moulin** at Chateaubrun. Look for the sign and the old sugar mill tower off to the right in the bright green undergrowth. It is a neat development: compact bungalows cluster around the old mill tower which now houses the reception. Next to it is an outdoor bar surrounded by tropical vegetation, and a pool with sundeck. Tennis, archery and horse riding are available. The Tap Tap Restaurant is spacious, with beamed ceiling and stylish decor; the food is good and reasonably priced. The bungalows, nestling among flowers and greenery (and their concomitant insect life), are labelled with the names of flowers. In each there's a bedroom and a living-room, both small. Altogether it is a very pleasant place for a quiet stay, although insects could be a problem. It claims a private beach, but that's a good ten minutes' walk across the fields. Rates are about FFR 450 in winter, CP, with MAP available.

Saint François, some 25 miles from the airport and almost as far east as you can go, is probably the most exclusive resort. Here you will find the **Méridien, Hamak** and **Trois Mats** hotels. There are other hotels sprinkled around Guadeloupe and her dependencies.

Le Moule, an old sugar town and the former capital, on the northeast coast of Grande-Terre, has several resort hotels. Despite the sheltering breakwaters, the surf can be rough. Only the **Hotel de la Rade,** a bit of a bargain, is listed by the Tourist Board (about FFR 240 for two in winter, CP). Here is pastoral countryside with cows grazing just inland—most attractive, restful and unusual for the Caribbean (Marie-Galante has some similar landscapes).

If you have to make an overnight stop before an early flight, or just want to stay in Pointe-à-Pitre for a while, **La Bougainvillée** is as good a place as any. It's central—not far from the quay and the Place de la Victoire. English is spoken, Amex and Visa accepted. There are comfortable rooms with well-equipped bathrooms and effective air-conditioning. The restaurant is unprepossessing but the food is quite good and reasonably priced.

There are two **Club Méditerranée,** one at Sainte Anne on Grande-Terre's south coast, about 14 miles east of Pointe-à-Pitre (the **Caravelle**) and the other at Deshaies on the lee shores of Basse-Terre equidistant from Pointe-à-Pitre and the capital (about 23 miles). This is the **Fort Royal.** Bookings for both have to be made before arrival in Guadeloupe.

There's plenty of choice of accommodation, but try to arrive early in the day if you have no reservations and want to be in the popular area—the stretch of Grande-Terre's south coast from Gosier to Saint François. Almost alone among Caribbean 'holiday' islands, Guadeloupe does good tourist business as early as October/November, and most hotels along this stretch can be full by late afternoon each day.

Basse-Terre

The **Hotel du Rocroy** at Vieux Habitants is right on a beach of fairly good, though not white, sand. This could be ideal for a quieter beach holiday. Winter rates, CP, are about FFR 300/330, single/double, with air-conditioning and fridge. The location is good, the people seem friendly, and there's a *menu touristique* for FFR 60 and a better menu for FFR 85. The beach is clean and has showers and toilets.

Near Trois Rivières on the spectacular east coast is the well-regarded **Grand' Anse** hotel. The address is Trois Rivières but it is actually a few miles south on the road to Vieux Fort. Rooms are comfortably furnished, with kitchenettes and air-conditioning. There's a restaurant and a pool. It is an attractive but rocky stretch of coast, more suitable for the visitor interested in walking and scenery than in lying on the beach. It is conveniently situated for the ferries to Les Saintes.

Accommodation in Guadeloupe, Marie-Galante, Les Saintes and La Désirade

Quoted below are official rates given on a daily basis in French francs for the summer season. Treat them with caution: experience shows you should expect increases of up to 50% on these. Winter rates are up to double.

	Single	*Double*
Guadeloupe		
Grande-Terre		
Auberge de la Vieille Tour, Gosier, Grande-Terre (tel. 841204)	CP 410–518	CP 554–706
Auberge du Grand Large, Ste Anne, Grande-Terre (tel. 882006)		CP 270
Bungalow Village, Gosier, Grande-Terre (tel. 840447)		EP 160
Le Canibis, Gosier, Grande-Terre (tel. 841183)	CP 140	CP 175
Ecotel, Gosier, Grande-Terre (tel. 841566)	EP 177	EP 228
	CP 205	CP 284
	MAP 310	MAP 494
	EP 208	EP 268
Les Flamboyants, Gosier, Grande-Terre (tel. 841411)	CP 140	CP 175
Frantel Marissol, Gosier, Grande-Terre (tel. 836444)	EP 297–378	CP 389–485
Hamak, St François, Grande-Terre (tel. 844180)	CP 720–780	CP 890–950
Honoré's Hotel, St François, Grande-Terre (tel. 844061)	CP 130	CP 180
	MAP 185	MAP 300
Hotel de la Rade, Le Moule, Grande-Terre (tel. 845092)	CP 95	CP 166
Méridien, St François, Grande-Terre (tel. 844100)	EP 510–610	EP 620–740
Novotel Fleur d'Epée, Gosier, Grande-Terre (tel. 834949)	CP 324	CP 428
PLM Arawak, Gosier, Grande-Terre (tel. 841274)	CP 290–405	CP 340–480
PLM Callinago Beach, Gosier, Grande-Terre (tel. 841293)	CP 250	CP 344
PLM Callinago Village, Gosier, Grande-Terre (tel. 841293)	EP 208	EP 268
PLM Village Soleil, Gosier, Grande-Terre (tel. 830576)	EP 211–245	EP 220–280
Relais du Moulin, Ste Anne, Grande-Terre (tel. 882396)	CP 217	CP 294
	MAP 300	MAP 460
Le Rotabas, Ste Anne, Grande-Terre (tel. 882560)	CP 270	CP 290
	MAP 350	MAP 450
Salako, Gosier, Grande-Terre (tel. 841490)	CP 297	CP 424
Trois Mats, St François, Grande-Terre (tel. 844290)	EP 330	EP 430
Village Viva, Gosier, Grande-Terre (tel. 830666)	EP 300	EP 400
Basse-Terre		
Auberge de la Distillerie, Petit Bourg, Basse-Terre (tel. 942591)	EP 145	EP 160
	CP 165	CP 200
	MAP 235	MAP 360
Grand' Anse, Trois Rivières, Basse-Terre (tel. 861047)	CP 225	CP 270
Hotel de Basse-Terre, Basse-Terre (tel. 811978)	EP 50	EP 75–85
Hotel du Rocroy, Vieux Habitants, Basse-Terre (tel. 984225)	EP 220	EP 220

	Single	Double
Marie-Galante		
Auberge de Soledad, Grand Bourg (tel. 979224)	EP 150	EP 200
Le Salut, St Louis (tel. 979167)	EP 105	EP 145
Les Saintes		
Hotel Bois Joli, Terre de Haut (tel. 995038)	MAP 285–305	MAP 405
Hotel Jeanne d'Arc, Terre de Haut (tel. 995041)	CP 140	CP 190
	MAP 190	MAP 290
La Désirade		
La Guitoune, Désirade (tel. 829408)	Not available	

NIGHTLIFE

This is the island to Begin the Beguine, and every other kind of dancing from calypso to disco, all night if you can stand the pace. There are also casinos—which need proof of identity with a photograph. They don't have slot machines and are not cheap. Dress smartly.

SHOPPING

Shopping is not as sophisticated here as it is in Martinique, but then it isn't as tourist-orientated. This also means that some French may be needed. There are good shopping areas in Pointe-à-Pitre (Rues Frébault, Nozières and Schoelcher) and Bas du Fort (Mammoth Shopping Center and the Marina). Saint François has a marina shopping centre and there are some interesting shops in Gosier.

SPORT

Guadeloupe is the place for windsurfers and international competitions are held here. Lessons can be obtained and boards hired from beach hotels. As with all the islands there is an emphasis on sea-based sports—sailing, fishing and diving, but enthusiasts for inland sports are not forgotten. There is an 18-hole golf course in **Saint François** and many tennis courts. Stables can offer beach riding and picnics as part of their programmes and spectators can watch the racing at **Bellecourt** and **Anse Bertrand**.

ANTIGUA AND BARBUDA

Antigua's coastline is so magnificent that it provides some of the best locations for tourist hotels anywhere in the world. There are so many beaches, and so much beauty, that these hotels are distributed all over the island. Many of them include watersports and other facilities in the price so that the tourist does not have to leave the hotel. When he does, besides the two main beacons to attract him—namely Saint John's, the capital, and Nelson's Dockyard, a tourist sight—there are a host of other things to see.

GETTING TO ANTIGUA AND BARBUDA

Antigua is one of the major hubs in the Caribbean, with long-haul flights from North America and Europe calling in here, and regional routes spraying out in all directions.

From the USA
Same-plane services currently operate to Antigua from four US cities. New York offers the choice of BWIA and American, whilst Miami departures are split between BWIA and Eastern. Eastern operates a service from Atlanta whilst American flies down from Boston. Antigua's current popularity as a holiday resort means that there are plenty of package plans available.

From Canada
The only scheduled service direct from Canada is the Toronto route served by BWIA and Air Canada. Unitours has packages and it is worth checking whether Wardair has any charters.

From London
British Airways has a non-stop service three times a week, and there are two or three Concorde charters each year. Most of the larger Caribbean tour operators feature Antigua in their brochures; try Kuoni, Caribbean Connection or Tradewinds. Two-centre holidays combining Antigua and Barbados are readily available.

From Europe
Travel via London or the USA (visa required), unless you are travelling from a major French city or Brussels; in this case you may find convenient and economical services via Guadeloupe, both scheduled and charter.

Within the Caribbean
LIAT is the closest thing Antigua has to its own airline. Owned jointly by many of the English-speaking eastern Caribbean governments, LIAT's main hub is Antigua. Services from the south terminate here, whilst routes in the area are regularly serviced. LIAT's 'island hopper' comes up from Trinidad, Grenada,

Barbados, Saint Vincent, Saint Lucia (Vigie), Dominica (both airports), Martinique and Guadeloupe. Around and to the north of Antigua LIAT serves Anguilla, Tortola (also linked by Air BVI), Montserrat, Nevis, Saint Kitts, Sint Maarten, Saint Croix, Saint Thomas and San Juan. BWIA should be given due credit for providing comprehensive services through Antigua. In addition to the long-haul services already mentioned, it operates Tristar and DC9 jets to Antigua from Trinidad, Grenada, Barbados, Saint Lucia (Hewanorra), Martinique, Sint Maarten, San Juan and Jamaica. Large jet services link Antigua with Trinidad (British Airways, Eastern and Pan Am), Barbados (Air Canada and British Airways), Sint Maarten and San Juan (both American Airlines).

The domestic link to **Barbuda** is serviced twice daily by a tiny plane of LIAT's fleet. There are also charters using piston-engined, and sometimes elderly, aircraft to many of the islands around Antigua.

ENTRY REGULATIONS

Visas are not required by US, Canadian, British and Commonwealth citizens. Nationals of most Western European countries may also enter without a visa.

The immigration officials here are particularly keen that you have a reservation for your accommodation or at least somewhere to go. The easiest thing of course is to give them the name of one of the hotels named in this book. Otherwise you simply go to the tourist information counter, get a name, and take it back to immigration.

If you have arrived within six days of being in a yellow fever infected area, you will be required to show a certificate of vaccination.

ELECTRICITY

The supply is not standardised; both 110 volts and 230 volts are used, sometimes in the same hotel. So check with reception before plugging anything in.

CLIMATE

As you will find in most of the eastern Caribbean islands, conditions are perfect. Temperatures are usually in the 80s(°F) year round, with the cooling trade winds preventing the heat from becoming oppressive, and enough rainfall to make water shortages a rarity.

CURRENCY

The legal tender is the Eastern Caribbean dollar (EC$), which is approximately equal to US$0.40. US$1 = EC$2.70. American dollars are accepted everywhere. There are seven banks in Saint John's.

LANGUAGE

English, but spoken with a very strong island accent in some places.

110

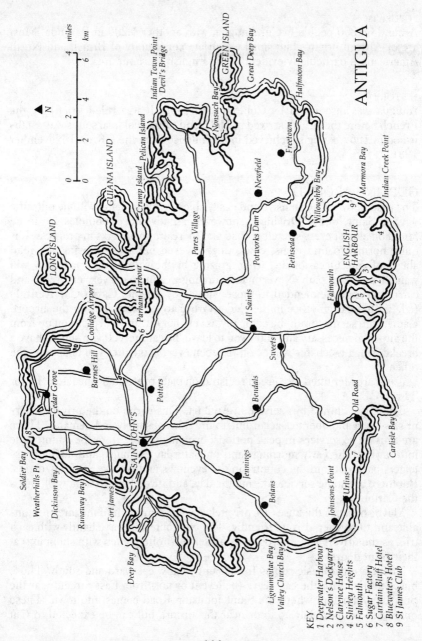

ANTIGUA

KEY
1 Deepwater Harbour
2 Nelson's Dockyard
3 Clarence House
4 Shirley Heights
5 Falmouth
6 Sugar Factory
7 Curtain Bluff Hotel
8 Bluewaters Hotel
9 St James Club

LONG ISLAND

GUIANA ISLAND

Crump Island

Pelican Island

Indian Town Point
Devil's Bridge

Nonsuch Bay

GREEN ISLAND

Great Deep Bay

Halfmoon Bay

Freetown

Newfield

Marmora Bay

Indian Creek Point

Willoughby Bay

Potworks Dam

Bethseda

Pares Village

Parham Harbour

Coolidge Airport

Barnes Hill

Cedar Grove

Potters

All Saints

Sweets

Bendals

Old Road

ENGLISH HARBOUR

Falmouth

Carlisle Bay

SAINT JOHN'S

Fort James

Deep Bay

Runaway Bay

Dickinson Bay

Weatherhills Pt

Soldier Bay

Jennings

Bolans

Johnsons Point

Urlins

Lignumvitae Bay

Valley Church Bay

N

miles
km

111

POPULATION
Around 80,000 people live in Antigua, with another 1,200 in Barbuda. Most are of African origin. The small expatriate community of British and North Americans is particularly evident in the English Harbour area

HISTORY
Antigua was discovered by Columbus in 1493. It was ruled briefly by the French before the British arrived in 1632, and formal colonial status was established in 1667. Antigua achieved independence from the UK on 1 November 1981.

GETTING AROUND
The road network is extensive and easily able to cope with the volume of traffic outside Saint John's. Driving is, however, an adventure: potholes are to be found on almost every stretch of road and there are roadworks in progress. It is quite normal to find goats, cows, dogs or even herons occupying the road ahead of you. Occasionally, when grazing by the side of the road, they will wander into your path. Nevertheless, driving in Antigua is very enjoyable and car rental is recommended to those who enjoy driving. **Carib Car Rentals** (tel. 22062) has an office in the Cedar Grove area, convenient for the airport. Cathy, who seems to run the company, is very helpful and will pick you up from the airport if necessary and allow you to leave the car there. If you should have a breakdown, a mechanic will be on the scene very soon after you telephone the office.

Taxis are identified by a green registration plate prefixed by the letter 'H' for 'Hire'.

There is a limited bus service in Antigua. This is run on the private enterprise system and operates according to the rules of supply and demand. There are thus more services in peak periods, bringing people from the countryside into town in the early mornings and on Saturday evenings, and taking passengers back out into the country in the evenings and late on Saturday nights. But there are some services during the day, and if you have to wait, well, that's the Caribbean.

Maybe because the buses are privately owned, you will find the fares reasonable and the owner-drivers friendly. The bus route will vary slightly with each trip, as the drivers like to drop their passengers (often laden with shopping) at their front doors.

There are two basic routes from Saint John's, eastward and south. Those buses destined for the east leave (believe it or not) from East Street, near the Spanish Main Inn, where the Saint Johnston Road comes into town. These buses will not normally go to or near the airport, but can be expected to visit

Saint Johnston, the Sugar Factory, Pares Village and other destinations in the east.

Southbound buses for English Harbour and Nelson's Dockyard leave from the market in Saint John's (see map). The fare is EC $0.70–0.80. Descending from the hills you will be treated to superlative views of the bay known as Falmouth Harbour before the bus drops you in the town or near the entrance to the Dockyard.

WHAT TO SEE

Antigua is a very beautiful island, and the Antiguans a very friendly and courteous people. Over the years the island has progressively become busier, both in terms of tourism and also with local activity.

The island offers hills that plunge into the sea then change their minds and rise up again, a coastline that undulates more than a belly dancer's midriff, and still finds time to unveil 365 beaches, and the feeling—if not always the sight and sound—that wherever you go you are not far from the sea.

Antigua is uncrowded. You won't find here the sardine-packed buses of Jamaica, the impassable sidewalks and blaring car horns of Port-au-Prince, or the native bustle and tourist shuffle of San Juan and Saint Thomas. Leisurely walks, even in the town's centre on Saturday afternoons, are the rule. There is always a bus seat available and the towns are so small that only a short walk will take you into the countryside.

The sights worth seeing are those which are examples of Antigua's great natural beauty. You will find the tourist office eager to supply details. You may not be able to see everything by bus, but at least you can make a start this way.

Nelson's Dockyard, Antigua's best known tourist sight, is situated in one of the world's safest natural harbours. It was used by the Napoleonic Royal Navy as the headquarters of the Caribbean fleet during the Napoleonic Wars. The Dockyard had fallen into disrepair but was recently rescued and restored to some of its former glory. An admission charge of EC$2 or US$1 is the main source of revenue for its upkeep.

Clarence House overlooks Nelson's Dockyard. It was built of stone for the Duke of Clarence (who was Prince William Henry at the time, and King William IV later) around 1787. It is now the country home of the Governor-General and is sometimes open to visitors.

In the same area you will find **Shirley Heights,** named after General Shirley who fortified these hills to protect English Harbour and the Dockyard. There is a little pub at Shirley Heights (The Lookout) which puts on a Sunday afternoon barbecue with fried chicken, hamburgers, etc. and a steel band. Entrance appears to be free, the food is fine and prices are reasonable, and the band excellent for dancing to. There are fine views of English Harbour.

Potworks Dam is usually regarded as one of Antigua's most beautiful

113

inland spots. It is the island's largest man-made lake, and besides serving a most useful purpose affords beautiful views and imparts a feeling of serenity and peace. Also with a reputation for natural beauty is **Fig Tree Drive** on the southwest coast where a winding road takes you through lush tropical scenery and picturesque villages. Antigua even has megaliths; these stones, allegedly set up by human hands for the purposes of sun-worship, can be found at the end of a walk up **Green Castle Hill**. And although it is difficult to select just one from the many incredibly beautiful seascapes, you will find a visit to **Indian Town Point** worth making if you have transport. This is the northeast point of the island; Devil's Bridge is one of the rugged rock formations caused by thousands of years of Atlantic surf breaking over this coast.

Saint John's

Possibly the best time to visit Saint John's, if you're exploring rather than buying, is on a Sunday. Both pedestrian and vehicular traffic is a little more than the small town can cope with, making progress slow. In addition, although the old wooden buildings predominate, the skyline is high enough to restrict the beautiful cooling breezes that otherwise make Antigua's climate ideal. Fortunately it is the only part of Antigua that is crowded.

There is a cathedral here, which was badly damaged in the earthquake of 1974. Down by the waterfront there is a tasteful new development: a pedestrian precinct of boutiques, shops and restaurants garnished with historical artefacts.

For the traveller, however, the only deficiency is in native restaurants. Snack bars abound, but these are usually of the type which also offer a limited range of groceries. As often as not you stand at the counter to consume your beverage and cheese roll or hamburger. The **Cozy Nook** on Saint Mary Street offers light snacks but service can be abrupt. Very close to the suggested accommodation on Ottos Main Road is the **Soul Inn Snack Bar** run by a couple of 'hip guys' and decorated with some clever posters. The limited menu and prices are well displayed. The clientele are young and very friendly.

Restaurants do exist, however, and here are some suggestions. **Maurice's** on Market Street serves excellent lobster and native food and is centrally located. The **Spanish Main** may tend towards the touristy, but should not be obviously so; **Brother B's** is quite definitely native fare. Two Chinese restaurants are worth mentioning: the **China Garden** on Newgate Street and the **Sea Dragon** in Fort Road.

Market lovers should note that the best time to savour Antigua's is on Saturday mornings. You will find it—in Saint John's—at the beginning of Ottos Main Road, from where the southbound buses leave.

Excursions

Antigua seems to have a wider choice of boat trips than anywhere else. Besides the *Jolly Roger* (462 2064), which seems to operate from the Dickenson Bay area, there is a range of boats operated by Basil Hill Tours (462 4882) including motor yachts and a tall ship that takes you to Barbuda (sail one way, fly the other). Prices range from US$45 to US$65. *Servabo* is a converted trawler which is supposed to do all its cruising under sail (462 1581).

CALENDAR

Sailing enthusiasts should make a note of Sailing Week in April, ocean racing during the day and merry-making in the evenings with Lord Nelson's Ball on the final night when awards are presented.

The summer carnival is at the end of July, early August with its usual quota of Caribbean *joie de vivre* and calypso.

WHERE TO STAY

With 365 beaches to choose from, it is hardly surprising that most major hotels are on a beach. And with these beaches fairly evenly distributed round the island, the result is that Antigua has no real resort area as such. The nearest thing to it is the English Harbour-Nelson's Dockyard-Falmouth area, in the southeast corner of the island. This superb natural harbour and compulsory tourist excursion is host to six hotels. **The Admiral's Inn** is perhaps the most appropriate of these, being drenched with the aura of history that the visitors come here to see. This fourteen-room hotel with its weathered brick, hand-hewn beams and four-poster beds seems to be the favourite of the yachting set, which is usually able to cope without swimming pools and casinos. Not to be confused with it is **The Inn,** a collection of more modern buildings set on the beach at Freeman's Bay and also on the hillside overlooking Nelson's Dock-yard. Cottage accommodation is available both on the beach and on the hill-side, and The Inn has its own sailfish, waterskiing and yachting facilities. This area is also geared up for self-catering, with the 18th-century converted **Copper and Lumber Store** in the Dockyard itself and **Falmouth Harbour Beach Apartments** just on the other side of the headland.

Saint James Club has excellent staff—courteous, friendly and well-trained. In a previous life this was the Halcyon Reef, and before that Mamora Bay Holiday Inn. The rooms, in barrack-like blocks, show this, though extensive refurbishment has been undertaken, and architecturally the hotel has been somewhat remodelled.

There is a casino, boutiques and salons, marina, watersports facilities, seven tennis courts, stables, etc. The Club is built on a small peninsula with one beach tucked inside the sheltered Mamora Bay; on this are the yacht club and marina, 'Docksider' restaurant and bar and watersports facilities. Coco Bay

115

Beach, with its own beach bar, is on the other, east, side of the peninsula, facing the Atlantic but sheltered to some extent by barrier reefs. There is, apparently, excellent snorkelling over here. There are glass-bottomed boat trips and organised hotel boats to take you out to the farther reefs.

There has been recent development work on the **Saint James Village**. These villas and town houses are built on the apex of the bay as a development running down from the hill to the beach. The village will be bisected by the entrance road to the Club; all houseowners automatically become Club members.

Curtain Bluff is still considered by many to be the top hotel in Antigua. Its location is dramatic, with a beach either side of the bluff (on which some suites are being constructed). The accommodation is mainly in slightly barrack-like blocks (a style which is common in Antigua) on the beach at Grace Bay. The watersports facilities, beach bar and jetty are on the other, more sheltered, beach. Watersports include scuba-diving, waterskiing, sunfish, windsurfers, yachting and deep-sea fishing. There are four tennis courts. Generally open only in the winter months, Curtain Bluff is usually full with a high ratio of regular clientele.

The **Half Moon Bay** has good-sized rooms with large patios, and is nicely, though simply, furnished. All of the 99 rooms, housed in three two-storey blocks, face the beach. There are five tennis courts, a 9-hole golf course (par 34), a large swimming pool, windsurfers, minisailing and snorkelling.

The **Blue Waters Hotel** is up on the northwestern tip of the island. There are 75 rooms (standard, superior and deluxe) and some recently added villa-type accommodation. This is a very well-maintained property, some 25 years old, with two small beaches in its own secluded cove with beautifully landscaped grounds. It has been renovated recently. Watersports facilities include sailboards, minifish, hobicats and a motor launch. Most of the air-conditioned rooms are housed in two two-storey blocks, facing the sea. There is some entertainment in season and a gift shop in the lobby, and a wide choice of sunbathing spots—on the beaches, around the pool, on the landscaped breakwater or on the wide lawns. There is a tennis court, archery and shuffleboard. Rates are under review and may be increased if the renovations result in a substantially upgraded hotel.

In the same area is **Sandpiper Reef Resort,** formerly the Atlantic Beach Hotel but closed for about three years. This is on the beach with a fine reef offshore. Recently it has been totally refurbished, remodelled and upgraded.

The **Blue Heron,** at Johnson's Point down on the southwestern corner of Antigua, is a new hotel and looks it. Perhaps because it is so new, it is not usually fully booked; you could probably describe it as 'undiscovered Antigua'. There are 40 rooms in all, 10 standard and 30 superior, all very close to the beautiful white-sand beach. There is a beach bar, watersports facility, regular entertainment and two tennis courts.

Galley Bay Surf Club, at the west end of the island and two miles from the capital, combines excellent gourmet cuisine with rustic informality. For accommodation you can choose one of the beach houses or stay in the Gaugin Village, 24 thatched mock-Polynesian villas 50 yards from the beach. Activities here include horse riding, sailing in the hotel's 35-ft sloop, tennis and snorkelling.

On the same coast, a little further south, you will find **Hawksbill Beach Hotel.** Its location is this hotel's strong point, as it has four lovely beaches to itself. Just offshore is the rock which gives its name to the hotel, and on one of its headlands is an old sugar mill, now seeing out its days as a souvenir shop. Watersports facilities include windsurfing, sailfish, pedaloes (pedal boats) and waterskiing, and there is also a tennis court.

The major hotel resort area is the Dickenson Bay/Runaway Bay region on the west coast north of Saint John's. The largest hotel here is **Halcyon Cove,** with 153 air-conditioned rooms. This is perhaps the best beach on the island, and this hotel has the nicest part of it. A restaurant is built in the sea (Warri Pier) and more formal dining is available in the main part of the hotel. There is a casino, nightclub, extensive shopping facilities, a large pool and watersports.

Further down Dickenson Bay beach you will find **Antigua Village.** This high-density development, which is quite pleasant, is based on condominium/timeshare ownership, so the rooms and villas differ according to the owners' wishes. Some of the older apartments are showing signs of wear. The whole, exterior and interior, is nicely designed though, particularly the studios (and especially those on the beach).

Siboney is next door. As this hotel is fond of stating in its tourist literature, it has 'no rooms, only suites': twelve in fact, in a three-storey building. Each suite comprises a well-furnished lounge leading to a balcony or patio, bedroom (with kingsize or twin beds and bathroom and overlooking the swimming pool—barely discernible through the palm fronds and bougainvillea). Some suites have a kitchenette and some are air-conditioned (all have a refrigerator). Siboney is on the beach, and has a small restaurant/beach bar. The suites are very tastefully furnished and the owners, Ann and Tony Johnson, are very pleasant, managing a well-maintained property which looks as good as new.

Runaway Beach is a stone's throw away as the crow flies, but to reach it by road you have to drive down to the Barrymore and then take a rough road back north again. **Runaway Beach Club** has its good and bad points. For some reason the brochure sports a massive picture of English Harbour (taken from Shirley Heights) which is on the other side of the island! Most of the accommodation—the superior rooms and the old standard rooms—is uninspiring, and the same can be said of the public areas. The new villa accommodation is pleasant, though, and there is a pool.

Callaloo is a small establishment (approximately 12 rooms) adjacent to Curtain Bluff. It is run by Mr Fuller, an American ex-military gentleman. If you are looking for a quiet spot this may be it. Callaloo is on the beach and has a nice little bar.

A Mrs Fuller runs the **Lord Nelson Club** over by the airport. The newer rooms are spacious with lovely tiled floors and the stiff breezes which whip through the windows render air-conditioning quite unnecessary (this bay is probably the best spot in Antigua for windsurfing); the restaurant has some character.

The **Cortsland Hotel** near Saint John's is considered good for businessmen, and **Le Gourmet,** on Fort Road, which comprises nine rooms attached to a Swiss restaurant, is also recommended.

Accommodation in Antigua
Daily summer rates in US$

	Single	Double	Triple
Hotels and apartments			
The Admiral's Inn, Nelson's Dockyard (tel. 31027)	EP 40–46	EP 44–52	
	MAP 70–76	MAP 104–112	
Antigua Village, Dickenson Bay (tel. 22930)	Studio	EP 65–90	
	1-bedroom apt.	EP 85–115	EP 95–125
Barrymore Hotel, Fort Road (tel. 21055)	EP 38–46	EP 52–60	EP 67
Blue Heron, Johnson's Point (tel. 20407)	EP 60–85	EP 70–95	EP 95–100
	MAP 90–115	MAP 130–155	MAP 185–190
Blue Waters Hotel, Cedar Grove (tel. 20290)	EP 54–74	EP 60–86	EP 75–116
Callaloo, Callaloo Beach (tel. 31110)	EP 65	EP 65	EP 65
Cortsland Hotel, Upper Gambles (tel. 21395)	MAP 45–50	MAP 60–65	MAP 84–89
Curtain Bluff, Carlisle Beach (tel. 31115)	MAP 175–600	MAP 220–700	MAP 300–780
	(open only 15 October to 31 May)		
Falmouth Harbour Beach Apartments, English Harbour (tel. 31094)	EP 46	EP 56	EP 81
Galleon Beach Club, English Harbour (tel. 31450)	EP 75–100	EP 75–100	EP 120–170
Galley Bay Surf Club, Fort Barrington (tel. 20302)	EP 80–100	EP 85–100	EP 115–130
Le Gourmet, Fort Road (tel. 22977)	EP 20	EP 25	
Halcyon Cove, Dickenson Bay (tel. 20256)	EP 85–105	EP 85–105	EP 110–130
	MAP 120–140	MAP 155–175	MAP 215–235
Half Moon Bay, Half Moon Bay (tel. 32101)	MAP 100	MAP 170	MAP 200
Hawksbill Beach Hotel, Five Islands (tel. 21515)	EP 30–55	EP 45–75	
	MAP 55–80	MAP 95–125	
The Inn, English Harbour (tel. 31014)	EP 40–85	EP 40–85	EP 100
Lord Nelson Club, near the airport (tel. 23094)	EP 40	EP 45	EP 60
Runaway Beach Club, Runaway Bay (tel. 21318)	EP 58–120	EP 58–120	EP 90–120
Saint James Club, Mamora Bay (tel. 31113)	EP 165–515	EP 200–550	EP 235–585
Siboney, Dickenson Bay (tel. 23356)	EP 70–90	EP 75–100	EP 90–120

10% service charge and 6% tax should normally be added. Increases in rates for the winter (high season) vary greatly, but approximate increases for particular establishments are as follows: 25% Barrymore Hotel; 40% Admiral's Inn, Blue Heron, Curtain Bluff, Falmouth Harbour Beach Apartments, Runaway Beach Club, Siboney; 80% Galleon Beach Club, Half Moon Bay, Saint James Club; 90% Antigua Village; Double—Blue Waters, Halcyon Cove.

	Single	Double	Triple
Guesthouses			
Central Hotel, Ottos Main Road, St John's (tel. 20489)	EP 15	EP 20	
Christian Villas, Gambles Terrace (tel. 22619)	EP 12	EP 24	
Montgomery, Radio Range, St John's	EP 18	EP 36	
Montgomery Guest House, Tindale Road, St John's (tel. 21827)	EP 6	EP 12	
Piggotsville Hotel, Clare Hall (tel. 20592)	EP 11	EP 19	EP 26
Roslyns, Fort Road (tel. 20762)	EP 12–18	EP 22–34	
St John's Motel, Fort Road (tel. 21448)	EP 13–16	EP 17–20	
Saint Mary's Court, Saint Mary's Street, St John's (tel. 24770)	EP 35	EP 45	
Skyline Guest House, Airport Road (tel. 20869)	EP 12	EP 21	EP 30
Spanish Main, Independence Avenue, St John's (tel. 20660)	EP 25	EP 30	

10% service charge and 6% tax will normally be added. Often guest rates are year-round, though some may show a small increase in the winter.

St Mary's Court guesthouse in Saint Mary's Street is a recently renovated property. It comprises six rooms on two floors, a restaurant and a bar. There is a boutique downstairs. It is not near the beach.

EATING OUT
There is nowhere considered to be consistently outstanding except perhaps **The Bistro**, or you could try **The Gourmet** and **Jean-Michel**. There are also hotels like **Curtain Bluff** at the top end of the range. The **Barrymore** at the hotel of the same name is recommended. For a pizza in a fun atmosphere at English Harbour try **Pizzas in Paradise** (which also has a branch in Saint John's). Nightlife and sports are largely hotel-based.

There are two hotel casinos open to the public with slot machines.

Barbuda

Many would say that Antigua's most beautiful scenery is 28 miles to the north. Here lies the island of Barbuda, formerly known as Dulcina, a dependency of Antigua. It is 62 square miles in area—about two-thirds the size of Antigua—and has a population of only 1,500, all of whom live in the village of Codrington.

Like Antigua, Barbuda is a coral island. Its beaches stretch for miles, unbroken and deserted, on both the leeward and windward coasts. The island is heavily wooded and abounds in birdlife, wild pig and deer, while the waters surrounding it are rich in seafood.

There are no customs and immigration facilities on Barbuda, as entry to the island must be made through Antigua. There are two airports: one is at Coco Point, completely isolated from the principal settlement of Codrington, where the second, main airport is situated. LIAT flies five times a week (Monday to Friday) early in the morning, using nine-seater Britten Norman Islander planes. The fare is US$14 (EC$38) each way. Or you may be lucky and get a passage in a fishing boat or other vessel from Saint John's.

You can stay at **Coco Point Hotel**, the **Cockleshell**—with eight rooms on the beach—and a new hotel near Codrington. Your travel agent will have the latest information on these. There is also a guesthouse in Codrington at reasonable rates.

SHOPPING
Local specialities include Antigua rum, basketwork and pottery. Good areas to look for bargains are Redcliffe Quay, and the shops along the High Street, Saint Mary's Street and Long Street. Head for the shops the locals go to, as many are aimed at ripping off the unwary tourist.

SPORT
Sailing is very popular in the waters around Antigua, and you can charter yachts or deep-sea fishing boats by the day or the week. These operate from English Harbour, Nelson's Dockyard and Falmouth Harbour. Scuba diving and snorkelling can be arranged through most of the hotels.

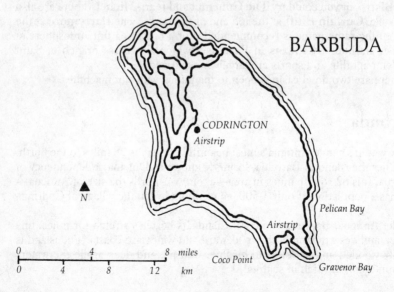

BARBUDA

CODRINGTON
Airstrip

N

Pelican Bay

Airstrip

0   4   8   miles   Coco Point
0   4   8   12   km   Gravenor Bay

SAINT KITTS AND NEVIS

When Christopher Columbus spotted Saint Kitts in 1493 he gave it the name of his patron saint, Saint Christopher. The English under the leadership of Sir Thomas Warner arrived in 1623, when they founded what was to become the first successful British colony in the West Indies. Five years later they established a settlement on Nevis, and in succeeding years parties left here to settle other Caribbean islands. Thus to this day Saint Kitts is described as the 'cradle of the Caribbean' or 'mother colony'.

Within two years of Sir Thomas Warner's arrival the French landed. At first relations between the original settlers and the newcomers were cordial, and the island was shared. However, the 18th-century wars between England and France had their repercussions, and the islands often changed hands until the English gained full possession in 1783 by the Treaty of Versailles. It gained independence in 1983.

Saint Kitts is about 20 miles long and has an area of 68 square miles; Nevis has an area of 36 square miles and is a more regular shape, being roughly oval.

GETTING TO SAINT KITTS AND NEVIS

Although Saint Kitts has an airport capable of handling large jet aircraft (Golden Rock, about two miles from Basseterre), there are relatively few jet services here. This is partly because the population is so meagre, and partly because tourists are so few. The scarcity of beaches means that Saint Kitts is never likely to suffer from touristic overdevelopment and should remain, as the Tourist Board likes to style it, 'The Secret Caribbean'.

Women carrying baskets

121

From the USA
Although services are infrequent, you can fly in directly from Miami with Pan Am (currently four flights a week) and from New York with BWIA (one a week). Otherwise take a connection through San Juan, Saint Croix or Saint Thomas. There are occasional charters too.

From Canada
BWIA calls in here on its way from Toronto through the islands. There may be charters, but don't bank on it. Otherwise you may find something cheap via San Juan from both Toronto and Montreal with Arrow.

From London
The normal route is via Antigua with a connection on LIAT, particularly as there are now no direct services from London to San Juan.

From Europe
You could try travelling via New York or Miami, although connections will be a problem. Alternatively, travel via London to Antigua, where you can take a connection on LIAT. There are also direct services from Paris and Madrid to San Juan from where you can take a connection on LIAT or Dorado Wings.

Within the Caribbean
BWIA flies here, on its way to North America, from Trinidad and Barbados. The only other jet service is operated by Pan Am from Sint Maarten, which is also linked by the services of Windward Island Airways and LIAT. Windward Island Airways also operates a service to Sint Eustatius. LIAT is thus the major carrier here with services from Anguilla, Antigua, Tortola, Montserrat, Saint Croix, Saint Thomas, San Juan and, of course, Nevis. Air BVI has a service to Antigua and Dorado Wings to San Juan.

There are also some flights from Nevis to other islands which do not involve a change of plane in Saint Kitts: LIAT serves Antigua and Saint Croix (also linked by Coastal Air Transport) and Windward Island Airways flies to Sint Maarten and Sint Eustatius.

ENTRY REGULATIONS
Visas are not normally required for citizens from the USA, Canada, the United Kingdom, the Commonwealth or Western European states. Any visitor not in possession of a return ticket may be required to deposit a sum of money sufficient to provide for his repatriation.

Passengers arriving within six days of being in a yellow fever infected area need a certificate of vaccination.

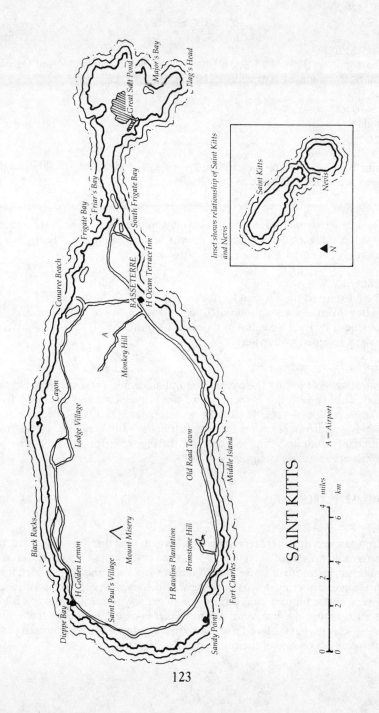

SAINT KITTS

Major's Bay

Flag's Head

Great Salt Pond

South Frigate Bay

Frigate Bay

Friar's Bay

Conaree Beach

BASSETERRE

H Ocean Terrace Inn

A

Monkey Hill

Cayon

Lodge Village

Black Rocks

Old Road Town

Middle Island

H Golden Lemon

Mount Misery

Saint Paul's Village

H Rawlins Plantation

Brimstone Hill

Dieppe Bay

Sandy Point

Fort Charles

A = Airport

Inset shows relationship of Saint Kitts and Nevis

Saint Kitts

Nevis

N

miles

km

123

ELECTRICITY
The supply is 220–240 volts, as in the UK. Some hotels catering for North American visitors also provide a 110-volt supply.

LANGUAGE
English.

POPULATION
Saint Kitts' 45,000 inhabitants are known as Kittitians; the 15,000 people of Nevis are called Nevisians.

CLIMATE
The average temperature is 78°F. As you would expect, it is warmer round the coast but can get quite cool up on Mount Misery. Humidity is fairly low, with rainfall between 50 and 80in. Nevis is usually drier.

CURRENCY
The currency is the Eastern Caribbean dollar (EC$), known as EeCee dollars or Bee Wee dollars (abbreviated from British West Indian dollar). The exchange rate is variable, but in approximate terms US$1 = EC$2.70. US dollars are accepted everywhere.

FOOD AND DRINK
You can expect to find the usual West Indian dishes, roast suckling pig, turtle steak, chicken with rice 'n' peas, pepperpot soup, etc. In addition to the Caribbean vegetables—yam, breadfruit, sweet potato, plantain—European vegetables are grown. Fresh meat and fish are readily available. Fresh fruit is abundant. Rum and rum cocktails are the predominant alcoholic beverages. Spirits are relatively cheap.

Saint Kitts

GETTING AROUND
Hiring a car is definitely recommended here, though there are only three major roads. The main road is, in plan, a squashed oval running around the coast but not venturing south of Basseterre. Another road is specifically provided for this purpose, meandering down to Frigate Bay (this one is very popular with learner drivers under tuition), and a third wends its way towards Monkey Hill, just about reaching the hamlet of Bayfords. Of course, this means that you can cover every part of surfaced road easily in a day, but if you feel cheated you can always set off on one of the tracks into the hinterland.

Once out of town you will find the road excellent and almost devoid of traffic. There are lovely views, both natural and of the quaint settlements you pass through. Brimstone Hill is easily reached and well worth two or three hours of your time. It covers quite an area and is by no means as forbidding as its title: the fortifications are surrounded by, and sometimes covered with, beautiful emerald foliage (now largely manicured, as restoration is progressing well). The imposing and unfortunately named Mount Misery (now called Mount Liamigua) provides a splendid backdrop. If you've made a reservation you can stop at Rawlins Plantation for lunch, and make a short stop at Golden Lemon on the way back. Be sure to get a map or you'll miss Black Rocks. It is all a lovely day's excursion, probably better taken as a self-drive than as an excursion.

You may need a local driving licence, obtainable from the police station in Basseterre, and remember to drive *on the left*. Not all local car hire firms accept credit cards.

Daily/weekly rates in US$ from:

	Manual	Automatic
Caines, Princes Street, Basseterre	28–168	33–198
Sunshine, Cayon Street, Basseterre	28–168	36–216
TDC, Fort Street, Basseterre (tel. 2991)	28–168	33–198

Taxis are reasonably priced: the airport to Basseterre is EC$10 and the airport to Frigate Bay is EC$18. There is also a limited bus service.

WHAT TO SEE

There is a road around the perimeter of the island (the interior is quite hilly with Mount Misery as its highest point), along which are most of the villages. A jeep is needed to drive to the southeastern part of the island. Taking the good road west from Basseterre you will come to **Brimstone Hill** after a drive of eight to ten miles. Brimstone Hill was fortified in order to repel the French and any other troublemakers, its natural hilly aspect earning it the title of the 'Gibraltar of the West Indies'. It was badly damaged by a hurricane in 1834 and in 1852 was evacuated and partly dismantled. Parts of it, notably the Prince of Wales Bastion, have been restored and the cannon remounted.

Gibraltar has its baboons, and Saint Kitts has its monkeys. Apparently the early French colonists brought pet monkeys with them. When the French were driven from the island the monkeys escaped and ran wild, breeding to such an extent that when the French returned seven years later the monkeys had become a pest, and 'periodic monkey shoots' had to be undertaken to reduce their numbers.

If you enjoy a good climb then the prospect of ascending the volcanic cone of **Mount Misery** may appeal. You will need to arrange transport from Belmot or Harris Estate in advance. This is not a normal tourist route, so your climb will be through wild undergrowth, orchids and forest. If you are fit it is possible to make a descent into the crater.

Spectacular scenery is also provided by the black rocks (lava rocks tossed down to the sea during prehistoric eruptions) and the salt ponds area, which is still worked. Carib and Amerindian remains can also be viewed on the island.

The original industry of Saint Kitts is still the island's most important—sugar. After emancipation the former slaves were prepared to continue working the sugar estates, and so the plantations have continued to be worked to the present day. There is a modern sugar processing plant on Saint Kitts which can be visited and a train that encircles the island collecting the cut cane. The industry suffered a recession following emancipation, and both Saint Kitts and Nevis were soon deserted by most of the whites; both islands still have derelict and deserted plantation houses (although some have been converted to hotels).

The best beaches are at the southeastern tip of Saint Kitts and cannot be reached by road (they are reached by boat, frequently from Nevis as a day excursion with barbecue). One of them, **Cockleshell Bay**, has (theoretically at least) two hotels on it, Cockleshell Hotel and Banana Bay Hotel. The principal white-sand beaches that can be reached by road (a very fine road in fact) are the two at **Frigate Bay**. Most tourist development is based on the one on the north shore with the large Jack Tar Village Hotel and the Sun 'n' Sand Beach Village being the major properties. The sea can be very rough here. A fairly short walk or a very short drive takes you over to **South Frigate Bay**, which is a better beach, with a calmer sea and some fine views. There are no hotels at all on this beach (Frigate Bay Beach Hotel is actually on a hill overlooking the beach and some distance away if you are on foot) but there is a watersports facility and restaurant.

Basseterre

Like the rest of the island, the capital is notable for its cleanliness and tidiness. There is an undertone of discipline, if not regimentation, apparent as soon as you land at the airport and present yourself to immigration.

Traffic around the town is orderly and there is no congestion. Buildings are by and large undistinguished, but around **The Circus** (as in Piccadilly Circus) there are some architectural gems. **Independence Square** has a pleasant grassy park as its centrepiece, and around its perimeter are colourful, varied wooden or stone and wood buildings. Many have a solid ground floor supporting elegant wooden storeys with latticed balconies, well-proportioned pitched roofs and cosy gables. They are painted in bright, pastel colours, and are very clean. The Tourist Board is in Church Street.

CALENDAR
Christmas time is carnival time in Saint Kitts and festivities run right through to the new year. British bank holidays are observed and an extra fête day is on 19 September, Independence Day.

WHERE TO STAY
There are very few tourist hotels for reasons already explained, yet the range is extraordinary: it's almost as if there had been a deliberate decision to build one in each category. **Golden Lemon**, up at Dieppe Bay, about as far from Basseterre as you can get, would probably be regarded as the best hotel. Situated at the sea's edge (though at a spot unsuitable for swimming) it manages to convey an atmosphere of olde worlde exclusivity without appearing pretentious.

A favourite is **Rawlins Plantation**, which is situated miles from the sea along a basic track through a working sugar plantation. Really this a place to unwind, through pleasant conversation with the managers (Philip and Frances Walwyn), relaxing by or in the pool, enjoying fine views out to sea, the cooling breezes ('too breezy', according to Philip) and some excellent food (the hotel is a popular stop for lunch on round-island tours). Accommodation is excellent: either large rooms and suites, elegantly furnished in buildings of a wooden rustic simplicity, or the 'honeymoon suite', a converted sugar mill (recommended).

Frigate Bay Beach Hotel is a misnomer, being a stiff climb from the beach, but there are some fine views from here. It is a condominium development of whitewashed buildings with many attractive architectural features including a pool with swim-up bar.

The **Sun 'n' Sand** nearby has 16 cottages, all single-storey, and detached as two-bedroom units (though they are available in the summer as semi-detached one-bedroom units as well). All amenities are on site—a bar and restaurant, minimart, a few small shops, swimming pool and children's pool. It should be cool here (you get the full benefit of the prevailing winds), and there are some fine walks in the area, not to mention the 18-hole golf course nearby. It is, however, a little overpriced, but does feature in tour operators' brochures, so you would get good value if you booked it as part of a package, especially off season.

Fairview Inn is an 18th-century French Great House surrounded by flowering plants and trees about three miles to the west of Basseterre. Accommodation is in cottages with a rustic air. For a place with a plantation-house feel it's not in the same class as Rawlins, but then it's a fair bit cheaper.

For a hotel in town which caters splendidly for businessmen, it's surprising that **Ocean Terrace Inn** features in so many tour programmes. But then, why not? You wouldn't come to Saint Kitts to lie on the beach, but to explore a lovely unspoilt island. On the whole, OTI (as it is known by its management and devotees alike) is very well-managed. There is an immediate and abiding impression that the management is trying very hard to please everybody all of the time. All rooms are air-conditioned, from the standards in the annexe (which are quite adequate) to the luxury apartments overlooking the sea. Rooms are large, well—though not opulently—furnished with lots of brochures useful to the tourist and the businessman. The staff are both courteous and efficient.

OTI's name is appropriate. Its facilities are terraced from reception and restaurant, down a few steps to the bar, down some more steps to another bar, sundeck and swimming pool (and more rooms), finally ending up down by the sea with the fairly new Fisherman's Wharf restaurant. It is landscaped too, so you don't necessarily feel that you are on the outskirts of town. Some nights there is entertainment, for example a steel band.

Meals are always described as excellent and this is undoubtedly one of the best restaurants in Basseterre. The hotel is very well run, excellent value for money, definitely a recommendation for your stay in Saint Kitts (along with Rawlins)—but it does lack that extra touch of magic.

As for guesthouses in Basseterre, **On The Square** has five air-conditioned rooms, all with bathroom en suite and tastefully furnished with fitted carpets. Two of the larger double rooms overlook the square (it's a little park really, sur-

Accommodation in Saint Kitts
Daily summer rates in US$

	Single	Double
Fairview Inn, Boyds (tel. 2472)	EP 40–50	EP 50–60
	MAP 66–76	MAP 102–112
Frigate Bay Beach Hotel, Frigate Bay (tel. 3253)	EP 50	EP 50–125
	MAP 80	MAP 110–185
Golden Lemon, Dieppe Bay (tel. 7260)	AP 140	AP 175–475
Ocean Terrace Inn, Basseterre (tel. 2754)	EP 54–85	EP 78–130
	MAP 80–110	MAP 130–165
On The Square, 14 Independence Square West, Basseterre (tel. 2485)	EP 20	EP 35
Park View, Victoria/Lozac Road, Basseterre	EP 15	EP 35
Rawlins Plantation, St Pauls (tel. 6221)	MAP 120	MAP 180
Sun 'n' Sand, Frigate Bay (tel. 8037)		EP 55
Windsor Guest House, Cayon Street, Basseterre	EP 12	EP 20

10% service charge and 7% tax should be added to these prices. Most establishments will charge 40–50% more in the winter; Frigate Bay Beach Hotel will be about double.

rounded by colourful and elegant wooden buildings) and have kitchenettes. The other two are more basic and marginally overpriced for what you are getting. **Park View** (it doesn't really have one) has nine rooms, some of which are air-conditioned. The double rooms have bathroom en suite, the single doesn't. The **Windsor** is above a hardware store in the middle of town and has nine rooms and two bathrooms.

NIGHTLIFE
Nightlife, as in most of the smaller islands, is centred on the hotels. There is a casino at the Jack Tar Village Hotel which has slot machines, and casual dress is acceptable.

SHOPPING
The local speciality is batik, wall hangings as well as clothes, to be seen and bought at Caribelle Batik, Romney Manor. They are all made here and exported throughout the Caribbean. All designs are originals.

Nevis

In the 18th century this island was known as 'The Queen of the Caribbean Islands' because of its spectacular and beautiful scenery. The capital is Charlestown, linked by a regular boat service to Basseterre, Saint Kitts. There is a boatbuilding industry south of the town. The sugar industry is less developed and less important here, as it declined significantly after emancipation.

South of Charlestown is Bath Village, famous for its supposedly beneficial mineral springs. There are five hot baths with naturally hot water. In the past rich hypochondriacs came here to be cured.

Nevis' other claim to fame is as the birthplace of Alexander Hamilton. One of his friends, Lord Nelson, has a museum dedicated to him at Morning Star. Nelson was actually married here (at Montpelier Great House) and the records remain in the register of Saint John's Church in Fig Tree village.

Ferry between Saint Kitts and Nevis
Schedule of MV Caribe Queen

	Depart		*Arrive*	
Monday	Charlestown	07.00	Basseterre	07.40
	Basseterre	08.00	Charlestown	08.40
	Charlestown	15.00	Basseterre	15.45
	Basseterre	16.00	Charlestown	16.45
Tuesday	Charlestown	07.30	Basseterre	08.15
	Basseterre	14.00	Charlestown	14.45
	Charlestown	18.00	Basseterre	18.45

	Depart		Arrive	
Wednesday	Basseterre	07.00	Charlestown	07.45
	Charlestown	08.00	Basseterre	08.45
	Basseterre	16.00	Charlestown	16.45
	Charlestown	18.00	Basseterre	18.45
	Basseterre	19.00	Charlestown	19.45
Thursday	No service			
Friday	Charlestown	07.30	Basseterre	08.15
	Basseterre	08.30	Charlestown	09.15
	Charlestown	15.00	Basseterre	15.45
	Basseterre	16.00	Charlestown	16.45
Saturday	Charlestown	07.30	Basseterre	08.15
	Basseterre	08.30	Charlestown	09.15
	Charlestown	14.00	Basseterre	14.45
	Basseterre	15.00	Charlestown	15.45

Confirm departure times with Ministry of Communications at Government Headquarters.

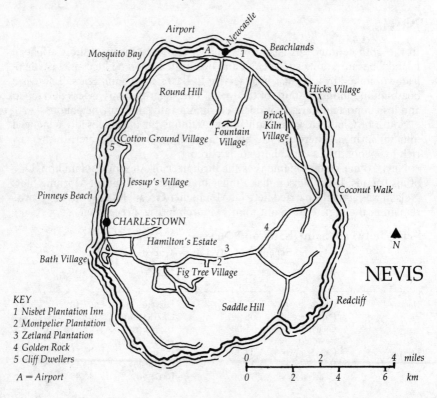

KEY
1 Nisbet Plantation Inn
2 Montpelier Plantation
3 Zetland Plantation
4 Golden Rock
5 Cliff Dwellers

A = Airport

NEVIS

WHERE TO STAY

Nisbet Plantation Inn is generally regarded as the top hotel on Nevis. (The summer rate shows a considerable discount on the high season price.) Situated on the site of an 18th-century plantation house, the main building is built in the traditional style of wood and stone. Sitting on the terrace over a full and delicious breakfast, you look down through an avenue of palm trees to the beach. It is not a brilliant beach, but you can sunbathe and swim here and there is a small restaurant for lunches, and a bar. Accommodation (20 rooms) is in the form of duplexes scattered under the palm trees. When you feel the need for an excellent beach, perhaps for some windsurfing, minisailing, waterskiing, etc., then you'll find Oualie Beach a five-minute drive away. Dinner is at 8 pm sharp, and you'll find yourself dining with strangers in true country house style. A very acceptable wine is served with the meal. At the time of writing the Inn does not accept credit cards.

Nisbet is just one of six inn-type hotels on Nevis, the highest concentration anywhere, and accounting for all but one of the hotels. This is appropriate, as their ambience is totally in keeping with the spirit of the island. The others are not on the beach and thus generally are equipped with swimming pools and usually a beach facility on Pinneys Beach (one of the island's best).

Zetland Plantation is reminiscent of Rawlins on Saint Kitts: a hillside situation in undulating, open country affording fine cooling breezes. This plantation of 750 acres on the slopes of Mount Nevis feels very open with fine views, particularly to the south. It is a lovely spot for walking, riding horses, discovering orchids or just relaxing with a rum punch. There is a swimming pool and a beach facility. There are fifteen spacious and nicely furnished suites and a converted sugar mill, another favourite as at Rawlins.

Another inn which has put its sugar mill to the same good use (and this is the best adaptation of the lot) is **Golden Rock**, in the same area. This hotel has the best brochure to be seen anywhere, so even if you don't stay here you should at least call in to collect a brochure! Again views are wonderful, and there will be no more than 30 guests to sample them. Here the accent is on lush, semi-wild tropical vegetation rather than the wide open spaces, with open-air dining to take full advantage of it. Probably the most romantic of the inns, Golden Rock nevertheless has a large swimming pool, tennis court and beach facility.

Montpelier Plantation Inn is a favourite in the tour operators' brochures and on any other island would be an outstanding hotel. Although obviously quite as good as those already mentioned, it is a little claustrophobic. There is just a little too much vegetation. Here too is a pool and an arrangement to take you to the beach.

The finest views of Saint Kitts are probably those from **Cliff Dwellers**. Built on a steep hill complete with its cable railway close to the sea, Cliff Dwellers is a favourite spot for a sunset cocktail.

Accommodation in Nevis
Daily rates in US$ for summer and winter

	Single		Double	
	Summer	Winter	Summer	Winter
Cliff Dwellers, Tamarind Bay (tel. 5262)	MAP 80	MAP 140	MAP 120	180
Golden Rock, Zetlands (tel. 5346)	MAP 100	MAP 125	MAP 125	190
Montpelier Plantation Inn, Morning Star (tel. 5462)	MAP 70	MAP 90	MAP 95	120–160
Nisbet Plantation Inn, Newcastle (tel. 5325)	EP 35–60		EP 60–90	
	MAP 70–95	MAP 150	MAP 130–160	215–260
Zetland Plantation, Zetlands (tel. 5454)	MAP 95	MAP 145	MAP 120–200	170–220

All accommodation in an adapted sugar mill attracts a supplement and, obviously, is subject to availability. Add 10% service charge and 7% tax to all rates.

There are a handful of guesthouses on Nevis, mainly around Charlestown. Try **Walwyn's**, on the road into town from the airport, or **Donna's** and **Evelyn's**, not too far from where the boat from Saint Kitts docks.

MONTSERRAT

'The Emerald Isle in the Caribbean', Montserrat was one of the few islands in the British West Indies which chose to remain a British colony, rather than become an associated independent state, when presented with the alternatives. The choice was perhaps a wise one, as the island is small (in area 39½ square miles with a population of 12,809) and would quite possibly have otherwise been incorporated in a federation with Saint Kitts-Nevis or Antigua-Barbuda.

The capital, Plymouth, is a settlement of some 12,000 souls on the south-western side of the island. This is the busiest part of the island, as the commercial centre, harbour and most of the limited accommodation are all here. George Martin, the erstwhile producer of the Beatles, recently opened a recording studio in Montserrat. The complex includes watersports and other facilities for wives and girlfriends and relaxing pop stars. But do not think that there is a lot of action on the island—there isn't: this is the ideal place for a rest cure. The rest of the population is scattered liberally over the island, which combines rugged beauty with lush vegetation and lovely beaches.

GETTING TO MONTSERRAT
The tiny Blackburne airport, on the opposite side of the island from Plymouth and the hotels, can handle only small aircraft (up to the size of a Twin Otter). There are few services—in fact only to Antigua, Guadeloupe and Saint Kitts—and all are operated by LIAT.

From the USA
Connections are best made through Antigua. In addition to the frequent flights from the USA to Antigua, a very regular shuttle from there to Montserrat should ensure a same-day service. You can fly to Antigua from New York, Miami, Boston and Atlanta.

From Canada
Again the best connection should be through Antigua, using BWIA or Air Canada from Toronto. Alternatively you could try the Air Canada service from Montreal to Pointe-à-Pitre, but as there are only about three flights per week from Guadeloupe to Montserrat (and LIAT in Barbados denies that such a service even exists) connections may be a problem.

From London
Definitely via Antigua. There is always a connection with the thrice-weekly British Airways service.

From Europe
If Paris is your best bet, and flights are going to connect, then Air France to Pointe-à-Pitre may be best: also check out connections via Paris or on charters from various French cities and Brussels. Otherwise change at London for the Antigua flight and Montserrat connection.

ENTRY REGULATIONS
Visas are not normally required and citizens of the USA, Canada and the United Kingdom do not even need passports. All visitors require adequate funds and a return ticket. You may introduce the usual personal allowances through customs.

ELECTRICITY
The supply is 220–240 volts, as in the UK.

CLIMATE
Temperatures are in the 70s and 80s($°F$) as elsewhere in the eastern Caribbean. There is rather more rainfall here, due perhaps to the island's mountainous aspect.

CURRENCY
This is the Eastern Caribbean dollar (EC$) which is worth roughly US$0.40. US$1 = EC$2.70 approximately.

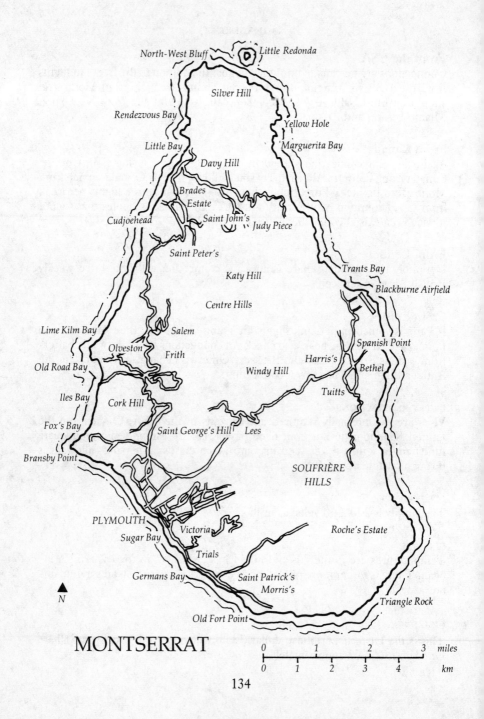

North-West Bluff

Little Redonda

Silver Hill

Rendezvous Bay

Yellow Hole

Little Bay

Marguerita Bay

Davy Hill

Brades
Estate

Cudjoehead

Saint John's

Judy Piece

Saint Peter's

Katy Hill

Trants Bay

Centre Hills

Blackburne Airfield

Lime Kilm Bay

Salem

Olveston

Frith

Spanish Point

Old Road Bay

Harris's

Bethel

Windy Hill

Iles Bay

Tuitts

Cork Hill

Fox's Bay

Saint George's Hill

Lees

Bransby Point

SOUFRIÈRE
HILLS

PLYMOUTH

Victoria

Roche's Estate

Sugar Bay

Trials

▲
N

Germans Bay

Saint Patrick's
Morris's

Triangle Rock

Old Fort Point

MONTSERRAT

| 0 | | 1 | | 2 | | 3 | miles |
| 0 | 1 | 2 | 3 | 4 | | | km |

LANGUAGE
English. This is usually spoken with a lilting brogue, reflecting the Irish ancestry of some of the 12,000 inhabitants.

FOOD AND DRINK
Fertile soil and an industrious people produce some of the best vegetables and fruit in the Caribbean. Tomatoes, carrots and mangoes are specialities. 'Goat water' (a kind of goat curry) is the national dish, but you will also find good Creole dishes and plenty of seafood. As this is the Caribbean, rum-based drinks are the norm.

HISTORY
Montserrat was first settled in modern times around 1633 when a group of mainly Irish Roman Catholic settlers came here from Saint Kitts where they had been unable to live in harmony with their Protestant brothers. A shamrock adorning the Governor's residence and a host of Irish family names still attest to this heritage. The shamrock is the national symbol.

GETTING AROUND
Plymouth is connected by several bus routes to the more remote parts of the island. Fares vary according to the distance travelled but are generally low. Taxi fares for most journeys are standardised; details from the tourist office. This office can also help to arrange car rental.

WHAT TO SEE
Nobody comes to Montserrat for a beach holiday: the beaches on the east coast are regarded as treacherous and, in any event, are too far away once you've found your accommodation on the west side of the island. Those on the Caribbean side show their volcanic origin, being of black sand, but can be safe for swimming and are certainly attractive in a dramatic way. Both of the major hotels sit above such beaches and afford lovely views of same.

Walks, hiking and climbing, discovering the bubbling Soufrière and Great Alps Waterfall, are the main activities here. In between you can relax on a friendly unsophisticated island as untypical of the Caribbean as anything you are likely to imagine. If you hire a car remember to drive on the left and to buy a temporary driving licence at the police station.

CALENDAR
Christmas is the best time to go to Montserrat if you like a lively atmosphere. Festivities start well before Christmas and go on until the new year. 17 March, Saint Patrick's day, also sees some celebrations.

Montserrat Museum

WHERE TO STAY

Vue Pointe Hotel is generally regarded as the top hotel on the island, largely, perhaps, because of the charming old-world courtesy of the owner, Cedric Osbourne, and his wife. Though the accommodation, in cottages dotted on the hillside, is perfectly adequate, it is neither luxurious nor particularly well-furnished. There is a bar down by the sea, two tennis courts and a swimming pool. The hotel seems to capture the essence of Montserrat.

In many ways the accommodation at **Montserrat Springs Hotel** is preferable. There is some cottage type accommodation, originally conceived as a condominium development, in addition to rooms, well-furnished in modern style. There are tennis courts, a swimming pool and mineral baths (next to the beach bar). This is the nearest Montserrat has to a tourist hotel.

Flora Fountain Hotel, centrally situated in Plymouth, is ideal for the businessman, who can walk to his meetings. It is very new and comprises eighteen air-conditioned rooms (a little on the small side) built in a ring around a courtyard with fountain. The restaurant features not only West Indian, but also East Indian food. Unless you are on a very tight budget it is by far the best place if you want to be in town.

A little way out of Plymouth you will find **Coconut Hill Hotel**. An older building, mainly of wood and in the traditional style, it has a guesthouse-feel but lacks the price advantages normally concomitant with that. **Wade Inn**, in

Parliament Street, Plymouth, has seen better days; again it is overpriced. There are three incredibly cheap guesthouses: **Captain's Cabin, Humphrey's** and **Peter's**.

Montserrat is the kind of place you either never visit or which you visit frequently, making your stay as long as possible. For this reason there is extensive villa accommodation.

Accommodation in Montserrat
(Daily rates in US$ for summer and winter)

	Single		Double	
	Summer	Winter	Summer	Winter
Captain's Cabin, Kinsale (tel. 2013)	EP 10	EP 10	EP 15	EP 15
Coconut Hill Hotel, Plymouth (tel. 2144)	MAP 55	MAP 68	MAP 78	MAP 92
Flora Fountain Hotel, Lower Dagenham Road, Plymouth (tel. 3444)	MAP 58	MAP 68	MAP 96	MAP 110
Humphrey's, Kinsale (tel. 2904)	EP 10	EP 10	EP 10	EP 10
		Hotel rooms		
Montserrat Springs Hotel, Richmond Hill (tel. 2481)	EP 55	EP 80	EP 65	EP 90
	MAP 85	MAP 110	MAP 125	MAP 150
		One-bedroom efficiency suites		
	EP 80	EP 125	EP 90	EP 135
Peter's, Kinsale (tel. 2628)	EP 10	EP 10	EP 10	EP 10
		Hotel rooms		
Vue Pointe Hotel, near golf course, Isles Bay (tel. 5210)	EP 40		EP 50	
	MAP 70	MAP 100	MAP 110	MAP 135
			Cottages	
	EP 55		EP 70	
	MAP 85	MAP 125	MAP 130	MAP 165
Wade Inn, Parliament Street, Plymouth (tel. 2881)	EP 25	EP 30	EP 35	EP 40
	MAP 35	MAP 40	MAP 55	MAP 65

Add 10% service charge and 7% tax to these rates.

SAINT MARTIN/SINT MAARTEN

This small island is a free port with three languages (French, Dutch and English), three currencies (French franc, Dutch guilder and American dollar) and two political affiliations. In 1648 the Dutch and French, tired of fighting over supremacy for the island, decided on partition as a means of sharing control. The border was drawn in an unusual way: a Frenchman and a Dutchman set off to walk in opposite directions round the island. A line was then drawn from the point at which they met to the starting point. The Frenchman either walked faster or cheated, as the French part of the island is larger than the Dutch.

The international airport and salt lakes are situated in the Dutch part of Sint Maarten, the capital of which is Philipsburg. There is complete freedom of movement between the Dutch and French areas, with no border controls.

Marigot on the northern coast is the most important French town. Cruising yachts and vessels from other non-French islands call in here to stock up with French wines, cheeses, other Gallic luxuries and duty-free items. There is some trade between Saint Martin and Anguilla (a few miles to the north) and this is the normal transit point for Anguillan-bound travellers.

GETTING TO SAINT MARTIN/SINT MAARTEN
First impressions—hectic. I arrived at the same time as a Pan Am Airbus and an American Airlines DC10. There were a lot of people queuing for half a dozen immigration desks. Fortunately there were none of the interminable delays one often seems to experience in the Caribbean. A couple of questions, a brisk marking with a picturesque stamp, and I was through. As soon as I reached the baggage carousel my luggage hove into sight and a few steps later I was sitting inside a taxi. There was no customs clearance as I recall.

SAINT MARTIN/
SINT MAARTEN

N

A = Airport

From the USA
The lion's share of Sint Maarten's tourism is from the States, so flights are frequent and from five major cities. American Airlines flies in from three of them—New York, Boston and Dallas—Pan Am from New York and Miami, the latter city also being served by Eastern which provides a link with Atlanta. All of these are same-plane services and often non-stop flights. All three airlines should also have connections with other American cities offering same-day connections.

From Canada
At the time of writing there are no scheduled services from Canada, though there may be charters in the winter. Otherwise your best bet is probably to take a flight to Boston, New York or Miami and then a connection from there.

From London
As far as the British are concerned, Sint Maarten is off the beaten track. Consequently there are neither direct flights nor attractive through-fare deals. The nearest island with a reasonable fare from London is Antigua, where a same-day connection can sometimes be made. Otherwise try travelling via Miami. Pan Am would probably be a good bet, even if it proved necessary to overnight in Miami. In winter 1984/85 and 1985/86 it had special fares ex-London with add-ons that could not be purchased in the States.

For example, in early 1986 you could have flown London–New York return for £299, bought a four-flight add-on for £88 (which you would have used to fly New York–Miami–New York) and a further add-on fare of £75 return to Sint Maarten. That would have cost you £462 and would have been the cheapest way to get there (the cheapest fare via Antigua would have been £491). At other times of the year (probably spring or autumn) you may be able to get a cheap charter to New York and find American or Pan Am has a special fare from there. In spring 1986 Virgin had ultra-low fares to Miami. You need a US visa if you plan to transit via a US city.

From Europe
Again, there are no direct flights, not even from Paris or Amsterdam! From Paris you would be expected to fly to Guadeloupe on Air France (or on a charter if there is one) and then take a connection on Air Guadeloupe or Eastern. Guadeloupe would be the best transit point if Brussels is most convenient to you, using one of the Nouvelles Frontières charters.

Within the Caribbean
ALM connects up two of the other Netherlands Antilles islands, Aruba and

139

Curaçao and also flies to San Juan and Santo Domingo. The local airline, Windward Islands Airways (Winair), operates local links to Anguilla, Nevis, Saba, Saint Barthélemy, Sint Eustatius, Saint Kitts and Saint Thomas. BWIA serves Sint Maarten from Trinidad, Grenada, Barbados, Martinique, Antigua and Jamaica. This diversity of services is occasioned by Sint Maarten's liberal aviation policy and its importance within the Caribbean as a free port. The French islands of Martinique and Guadeloupe are linked by Eastern and Air Martinique, and Air Guadeloupe respectively. The former also flies here from Barbados and Saint Lucia (Vigie); Pan Am also comes in from Saint Lucia, but its large jets have to use Hewanorra. Regional airlines flying here also include Air BVI (from Anguilla, Tortola, Virgin Gorda, Saint Thomas and San Juan) and LIAT (from Antigua, Tortola, Saint Croix, Saint Thomas and San Juan). San Juan has the most frequent services; in addition to the airlines already mentioned, American and Dorado Wings come here.

The only airline flying in or out of Sint Eustatius and Saba is Winair; from the former it serves Nevis and Saint Kitts, whilst Saba is linked only with Sint Eustatius and Sint Maarten.

ENTRY REGULATIONS

They are very liberal here. Citizens of the USA, Canada and the United Kingdom may enter without a passport, as may nationals of Belgium, West Germany, Luxembourg, the Netherlands and San Marino amongst others. It is best to have a passport, but if you are determined to travel without, check thoroughly.

Visas are not issued, but in many cases a certificate of admission may be issued on your arrival.

You will require a certificate of inoculation against yellow fever if you have arrived within six days of being in an infected area.

ELECTRICITY

The Dutch side of the island uses the US supply of 110 volts, 60 cycles, and the French side the European supply of 220 volts, 50 cycles. Adaptors will probably be necessary for US visitors to the French side and UK visitors to the Dutch side.

CLIMATE

Temperatures average 80°F to 82°F with most rain in the period September to November.

CURRENCY

Theoretically this is the Netherlands Antilles florin (AFL) on the Dutch side and the French franc (FFR) on the French side, but in practice the US dollar is used, particularly on the Dutch side where prices are generally quoted in both AFL and US$.

POPULATION

Although the Dutch sector is smaller (16 square miles as opposed to the 21 square miles of the French part) most of the population lives here—over 90% in fact. There are 19,000 on the Dutch side as against 1,800 on the French. This is probably partly because of the Dutch 'open door' policy and partly because there is free movement between the two parts.

HISTORY

When Columbus discovered the island he claimed it for the Spanish, who defended it against seventeenth-century French and Dutch settlers but then abandoned it. Legend has it that several settlers—four French and five Dutch, who had hidden on the island—then divided it up among themselves.

GETTING AROUND

Car rental is a good idea here. If you're staying in Philipsburg you will probably need a car for a few days only, to visit other parts of the island for specific activities and that day tour. Everything in Philipsburg is in easy walking distance. If you are staying outside town you will probably need the car for a longer period, perhaps for your entire stay.

I rented a jeep (brand new, it turned out, with only 70 miles on the clock) from **J C Car Rental**. They delivered it to the hotel and I left it at the airport. It was, however, a Suzuki jeep, and one of the worst vehicles I have ever driven on asphalt. Its handling improved considerably off road and on poor road surfaces. You may get a car for US$28–$30 and a jeep for $30–$35, plus insurance and 5% tax. Rental can easily be organised at the airport.

Scooters and motorcyles can be rented from **Carters** near the airport (tel. 2621, 2721 and 4251). Driving tends not to be fast, but it is erratic, so if you watch out for potholes you should be moderately safe on two wheels.

WHAT TO SEE

Dutch Sint Maarten, and Philipsburg in particular, is the most cosmopolitan place I've ever seen. In addition to the local differences—and there are differences between the sectors—there are many people from the 'ABC' islands (Aruba, Bonaire and Curaçao) living here. Add to this an influx of people from all over the world and you have a fabulous melting pot of cultures, languages (there are five commonly spoken on the Dutch side: Dutch, English, French, Spanish and Papiamento—a dialect that emanates from the ABC islands) and colours. Thus you will find Italian, Indian, American, Chinese, French and

141

Indonesian restaurants within walking distance of each other (although French predominate).

I had determined to stay in town (taxi fare US$7) and, knowing nothing of Sint Maarten, had sought advice at the Tourist Board desk. They sent me to the **Seaview. Philipsburg** is the only Caribbean capital I know where you can stay right in the centre of the action and be situated on a superb beach at the same time. Front Street is to Philipsburg what Bay Street is to Nassau, but far better. A conglomeration of old wooden buildings jostles with modern concrete structures, all fairly low-rise. Duty-free shops, jewellery stores, hotels, restaurants, casinos, hi-fi stores, boutiques and banks line both sides of the street. Sometimes there is a pavement, sometimes not. One side of the street is occupied by an almost unbroken line of parked cars. There is room for traffic only in single file, and one drives slowly and patiently, giving precedence to meandering pedestrians. The whole experience, from the airport to Front Street, is of organised anarchy.

Running parallel with Front Street is a superb beach. Broad white sands, uncrowded, are lapped by a tranquil turquoise sea. A few steps from your hotel and you're bathing on a splendid beach; a few steps the other way and you have shopping, gambling and dinner.

Peaceful co-existence is a thread running right through this island. There is an unspoken, unwritten law of courtesy and consideration which seems to infect the tourists as soon as they land. Everything is attended to in a leisurely manner (always excepting the taxi despatcher at the airport) as if to encourage the tourist to slow down.

Outside the town there is some traffic congestion too, but mainly on the road to the airport, particularly around Cole Bay Hill. But it never seems to be any great inconvenience. The roads heading north to the French side which, surprisingly, are not well surfaced, have little traffic. The only indication of a border is a sign telling you you've crossed it.

In spite of an insistence on 'togetherness' on the Dutch side, there is quite a difference between the two sectors. An island tour, which can easily be undertaken in a day, points up these dissimilarities. Once inside Saint Martin you will notice more verdant countryside, more apparent agriculture and a hillier aspect (Paradise Peak rises to 1,500 feet).

Grand Case is the first major settlement you will reach if you've taken **Sucker Garden Road** north from Philipsburg. Although there are more restaurants here than anywhere—relative to its size—and almost half the accommodation available on the French side, there is a very sleepy, undeveloped atmosphere. During the day traffic is light (at night the streets are choc-a-bloc with parked cars, as many of the best restaurants are here). The attraction is a fine beach largely uncluttered by hotels. It's probably the best place to stay on the French side if you want quiet days and fine evening dining.

142

Travelling south you will soon come to **Marigot,** capital of the French part. During my last visit it resembled a building site. Presumably the old buildings are being torn down to build a new town geared to tourism. I was not overjoyed with the harbour front or the tourist-orientated marina. Grand Case still has character, and I much preferred the garlic shrimp lunch I had in a beachside shack there.

The French side has recently suffered an influx from metropolitan France, and I sensed that this was not universally welcomed. French is spoken here to such an extent that many people do not speak English at all—or very little at any rate—in contrast to the Dutch side where English is the main language. Though the Dutch seem to have no desire to leave an indelible imprint, preferring to allow a melting pot of races, cultures, currencies and languages, the French seem keen to show they're still around. Frequently one is addressed in French, then met with beaming smiles when you prove to be an English-speaker.

Sint Maarten is almost certainly the best island in the Caribbean for shopping, combining duty-free facilities with all the best of France. For more details call at the tourist office in De Ruyterplein in Philipsburg.

CALENDAR

As the island is divided into Dutch and French parts it is not surprising that two national holidays are celebrated, the Dutch Coronation Day on 30 April and the French Bastille Day on 14 July. Friendship between the two is celebrated at the border on 11 November, Concordia Day. Carnival is celebrated all over the island: for the French it comes before Lent, and for the Dutch at the end of April.

WHERE TO STAY
Sint Maarten
If Sint Maarten is the only Caribbean island you are visiting, then Philipsburg may be too hectic for you as a place to stay, and it certainly is not 'typically Caribbean' (in the sense of the popular image). Apart from this reservation, I would recommend Philipsburg as the best choice for your lodgings: apart from the practical considerations of the beach on one side and the shopping and nightlife facilities on the other, Philipsburg is the essence of Sint Maarten.

There are ten hotels on Front Street itself. The **Seaview Hotel** is a fairly old hotel, somewhat reminiscent of some of the older properties on Miami Beach. On its ground floor it boasts a casino. I found the reception staff warm and friendly. They had arranged car rental within minutes of my arrival and showed me to a room immediately overlooking the beach. Rooms are of an adequate size, comfortable, with air-conditioning, television and telephone, although sometimes lacking hot water.

Pasanggrahan Royal Guest House, closest to the Head of Town, is a 21-room hotel with a guesthouse character, set in a tropical garden. You will probably need to book in advance. Next along, moving west, is **Holland House Beach Hotel**, a new development and quite expensive. All of these are right on the beach. On the other side of Front Street, more or less opposite Holland House, is **St Maarten Beach Club.** This has a casino (as does Seaview) but is more noted for its **Fandango Restaurant and Bar** which provides a parrot and an adequate breakfast.

There are also a number of guesthouses in Philipsburg (**Beco's, George's, Lucy's, Marcus'** and **Jose's**) but you will find prices a little higher than you might normally want to pay for this class of accommodation.

Outside Philipsburg the main resort area is around the airport, stretching along the coast from Cole Bay to the 'border' at Cupecoy Bay. **Sheraton Mullet Bay Resort** is by far the biggest with nearly 600 rooms—so big that the main road goes through it and has become a feature of the hotel. A 63-room hotel such as **Caravanserai** thus describes itself as 'intimate'. More genuinely intimate, in the sense of being small, is **Mary's Boon,** one of the hotels on Simpson Bay's 3-mile beach which runs parallel with the airport runway. Here there are twelve studios with kitchenettes and the accent is on informality. There is a restaurant and bar.

The most exclusive hotel is the 20-room **Oyster Pond Yacht Club** on the beach at Oyster Pond. It is very elegant, with marina, boating, fishing, watersports and tennis (no children). In the same area is the rambling bungalow-

Steel band in Sint Maarten

144

style **Dawn Beach**, with swimming pool, tennis, entertainment, etc.—and the dawn every morning.

Accommodation in Sint Maarten

There is no pattern to hotel rates in Sint Maarten. Accommodation is expensive, relative to elsewhere, but it is for the local people too. Service charges can be between 5% and 15% and some establishments are still adding 5% energy surcharge! Where charges are known they are indicated below. Government tax is 5%.

Daily summer rates per room in US$ (expect winter rates to be about double)

		Single	Double	Triple
Hotels				
Caravanserai, Airport Road (tel. 2510)		EP 75	EP 88	
		MAP 110	MAP 158	
	Winter	EP 175	EP 175	
	Winter	MAP 320	MAP 245	
			(service charge 15%)	
Caribbean Hotel, Front Street,		EP 30	EP 50	
Philipsburg (tel. 2028)				
Dawn Beach, Oyster Pond (tel. 2929)		EP 55–85	EP 65–95	EP 85–115
		MAP 90–120	MAP 100–165	MAP 190–220
	Winter	EP 173	EP 183	EP 203
	Winter	MAP 210	MAP 257	MAP 314
			(service charge 15%)	
Holland House Beach Hotel, Front Street,		EP 62–73	EP 69–78	EP 79–88
Philipsburg (tel. 2572)				
The Jetty, Kanaalsteeg, Great Bay,		EP 65	EP 65–99	EP 99–109
Philipsburg (tel. 2922)	Winter	EP 130	EP 130–195	EP 195–215
		(1- and 2-bedroom apartments:		
			service charge 15%)	
Mary's Boon, Simpson Bay (tel. 4325)		EP 60	EP 60	EP 75
Oyster Pond Yacht Club, Oyster Pond			EP 130–170	
(Tel. 2206)			MAP 210–250	
	Winter		EP 240–280	
	Winter		MAP 320–360	
			(service charge 15%)	
Pasanggrahan Royal Guest House,		EP 49–59	EP 49–59	EP 59–69
Front Street, Philipsburg (tel. 3588)	Winter	EP 79–95	EP 79–97	EP 89–105
		(service charge 10% and energy surcharge 5%)		
St Maarten Beach Club, Front Street,		EP 66–80	EP 80–100	
Philipsburg (tel. 3434)				
Seaview Hotel, Front Street,		EP 42–50	EP 60–75	EP 85–100
Philipsburg (tel. 2323)			(service charge 10%)	
Sheraton Mullet Bay Resort and Casino,			EP 88	EP 115–155
Mullet Bay (tel. 2801)	Winter		EP 150	EP 210–250
			(service charge 15%)	
Guesthouses				
Beco's, Cannegieter Street, Philipsburg		EP 20	EP 23–30	EP 34–41
(tel. 2294)				
George's, Pondfill and Cole Bay		EP 15	EP 35	EP 45
(tel. 2126)				

145

	Single	Double	Triple
Guesthouses			
Jora's, Backstreet, Philipsburg (tel. 2231)	FP 18–25	FP 24–28	FP 33–37
Lucy's, Backstreet, Philipsburg (tel. 2995)	EP 17	EP 34	EP 51
Marcus, Front Street, Philipsburg (tel. 2419)	EP 22	EP 22–26	
Sea Side Guesthouse, Great Bay Beach, Philipsburg	EP 10	EP 10–55	

Saint Martin

La Samanna, at Baie Longue on the Western side of the island snuggled right up close to the 'frontier' with Sint Maarten, is the best hotel in the French sector: luxurious living with splendid cuisine, a lovely beach, tennis and watersports. Otherwise you are probably best advised to stay at Grand Case, Marigot being somewhat depressing.

Grand Case Beach Club is located at the north end of the fine beach. Surprisingly perhaps, this hotel seems to be pitched at the American tourist. Accommodation is in studios and one- and two-bedroom apartments, and nicely furnished in the modern style. Friendliness is not overtly obvious here. I was to be shown the rooms by a housekeeper and had to find her myself. Someone else at reception was also being curtly dealt with.

Grand Case has a number of small hotels and guesthouses. Some people in Antigua recommended I check out **Hevea**, a Vietnamese restaurant with five rooms. The owners, a Frenchman and his Vietnamese wife, were indeed lovely and very charming. Unfortunately it transpired that they were in the throes of selling up, but nevertheless it is worth checking out. Otherwise try **Chez Martine, Atlantic Guest House, Chances** or **Dimitri**.

If you want to stay in **Marigot** proper there are seven hotels there, but a better bet would be to stay at Sandy Ground, just south of town. Though this beach is very poor compared with its namesake in Anguilla, at least it is a white-sand beach and provides hotels such as you would find in Guadeloupe or Martinique. There is the **PLM St Tropez** and **Le Pirate Guest House**.

There is a naturist hotel, the **Club Orient**, on Orient Beach near Orleans.

Accommodation in Saint Martin

Daily summer rates per room

	Single	Double
Chez Martine, Grand Case (tel. 875159)	CP FFR350	CP FFR450
Club Orient, Orleans (tel. 875385)	EP FFR558–666	EP FFR668–1116

			Single	Double
Grand Case Beach Club, Grand Case			Studio	EP FFR750
(tel. 875187)			Studio	EP US$ 60–75
			1-bedroom	EP US$ 90–110
	Winter		Studio	EP US$160–200
	Winter		1-bedroom	EP US$225–275
			(tax included; no service charge)	
Hevea, Grand Case (tel. 875685)			CP FFR200	CP FFR280
Marina Royale, The Marina, Marigot			EP FFR264	EP FFR352
(tel. 875728)				
PLM St Tropez, Sandy Ground, Marigot			CP FFR275–390	CP FFR325–435
(tel. 875472)				

EATING OUT AND NIGHTLIFE

Besides some excellent French restaurants at Grand Case, there are also those providing Italian, Vietnamese and Indonesian food. Marigot may prove to have some excellent restaurants; the marina would be a pleasant place to dine in the evening.

Philipsburg caters for all tastes; gourmet French restaurants are particularly in evidence on Front Street, with Italian food also prominent. On Backstreet there is a Chinese restaurant that does Cantonese and Szechwan cuisine, **The Dragon Phoenix**. Backstreet seems to be the place for Chinese restaurants, with **China Palace** and **Hong Kong** also here. **Asha's** on Front Street serves 'Nouvelle Indian Cuisine'. American food and fast food snacks are also in evidence.

The West Indian Tavern on Front Street, run by an Irishman, is not as rustic as it sounds. Although dishes are certainly West Indian-influenced, it lacks any real feel, as exemplified by the strolling minstrel strumming and singing 'Island in the Sun' and similar melodies. The food is good, though that too is sanitised. A lovely Muscadet is served here. The Tavern is not cheap, but could be fun if a group of you arrives fairly late.

If you've got more money than sense you'll be welcomed at the island's casinos. There are four in Philipsburg, at the **Seaview (Rouge et Noir), St Maarten Beach Club**—both on Front Street—**Great Bay Beach Hotel** and **Little Bay Beach Hotel**. Others are situated at the **Sheraton Mullet Bay** and **Pelican Resort** in Simpson Bay. Also in Philipsburg you have **Pinocchio's**, which provides late-night music and snacks on the beach.

SPORT

Sea-based sports are popular on the island. Deep-sea angling for exotic species is excellent and there are facilities for snorkelling, scuba diving and windsurfing. Waterskiing and jet-skiing are available on **Simpson Bay**

147

Lagoon, as elsewhere, and for those so inclined a schooner can be chartered to explore the offshore islands.

Inland there is golf and tennis, or you can explore the island by bicycle or on horseback.

Sint Eustatius

Known locally as 'Statia', this island is still very underdeveloped with apparently more goats than people (there are 1,500 residents, but an unknown number of goats). There are a few cars.

In the American War of Independence Sint Eustatius proved a useful ally to the revolutionaries, being used as a transfer point for arms and supplies. The British objected and sent Admiral Rodney along to sack the island.

There are three 20-room hotels, **The Old Gin House, Golden Era** and **La Maison sur la Plage**, all of which are on the beach and of a decent standard.

Saba

This rugged volcanic cone is devoid of beaches. Its 1,000 residents make a living from fishing, subsistence farming and lace-making. Saba can be reached by boat or by tiny planes which fly into the handkerchief-sized airstrip. A steep,

Accommodation in Sint Eustatius and Saba
Daily summer rates per room in US$

	Single	Double	Triple
Sint Eustatius			
Golden Era, Lower Town, St Eustatius (tel. 2345)	EP 70	EP 75	EP 85
La Maison sur la Plage, Zeelandia, St Eustatius (tel. 2256)	CP 55	CP 55	CP 80
The Old Gin House, Oranjestad, St Eustatius (tel. 2319)	EP 70	EP 75	EP 85
	MAP 100	MAP 135	MAP 175
Saba			
Captain's Quarters, Windwardside, Saba (tel. 2201)	EP 55	EP 70	EP 90
	MAP 80	MAP 120	MAP 165
Cranston's Antique Inn, The Bottom, Saba (tel. 3203)	CP 28	CP 38	
Scout's Place, Windwardside, Saba (tel. 2205)	MAP 35	MAP 50	MAP 65

winding road runs across the island from the airstrip via Windwardside and other villages to the pier at Fort Bay.

Accommodation is in tiny inns: **Captain's Quarters** in Windwardside claims excellent views, whilst **Scout's Place** with its open-air dining is probably the best value. **Cranston's Antique Inn** at The Bottom was formerly the government guesthouse.

ANGUILLA

Anguilla was settled by the English in 1650. In 1971 the 6,000 people of Anguilla decided that they did not wish to be governed from Basseterre, Saint Kitts. Their unilateral declaration of independence led to a British frigate being sent to the area and a commando force being landed. As this force met no resistance it was quickly withdrawn and replaced with a number of policemen and a detachment of sappers who set about building roads, bridges, and an airstrip. These good works and a lot of talking failed to persuade the Anguillans that life would be better under the Basseterre administration, and late in 1975 the British Government accepted the inevitable and bowed to the Anguillans' wishes, which were to be reinstated as a British colony.

Anguilla today is still not geared to tourism, and is best that way. Those of its citizens involved in the tourist industry appear blissfully naive; at the airport on departure they don't issue boarding cards and seemed surprised that I had luggage! At the car rental agency they kept waiting for me to tell them what to do next, and when I returned the car they suggested I leave it at the airport with the keys in the ignition. There's no crime, so no one locks anything.

GETTING TO ANGUILLA

The airport is probably the most basic anywhere; only small planes land here, and there appears to be only one immigration officer to deal with the dozen or so arriving passengers. There seem to be no customs officials. The immigration officer also serves as taxi despatcher, telling the taxi driver which car rental company to go to and phoning ahead to advise them of one's imminent arrival.

From the USA

If you are leaving from a major US gateway, such as New York or Miami, connect through Sint Maarten, Saint Croix, Saint Thomas or San Juan. The first of these is most convenient (it's only a short US$13-hop to Anguilla) with Pan Am from New York or Miami, Eastern from Miami and Atlanta, and American from New York, Boston and Dallas. There may be economic advantages, though, in arriving via San Juan or Saint Thomas; Air BVI and Dorado Wings fly in from both these points.

From Canada
Either take Air Canada or BWIA services from Toronto to Antigua and a LIAT connection, or the inexpensive Carib Aviation charter.

From London
Definitely fly by British Airways via Antigua. LIAT's connections are timed to link up with the London flights, or use Carib Aviation from Antigua.

From Europe
Connecting with the BA flight from London to Antigua is one possibility. Avianca flies from Paris and Madrid to San Juan and has a direct connection to Anguilla.

Within the Caribbean
LIAT flies between Anguilla, Sint Maarten, Nevis, Saint Kitts and Antigua. Air BVI covers Saint Thomas, San Juan and Beef Island (Tortola). Dorado Wings charters are available from San Juan and Saint Thomas and Carib Aviation charters throughout the entire area.

A large proportion of visitors to Anguilla arrive via Sint Maarten. The Sint Maarten ferry (about every half hour) takes 15 minutes and costs US$4.

ENTRY REGULATIONS
Passports are required by all. Visas are not required by citizens of the USA, UK, Commonwealth countries and Western Europe. If in any doubt check with your nearest British Embassy or High Commission.

A certificate of inoculation against yellow fever will be required if you have come from or transited an endemic area within the last six days.

ELECTRICITY
The supply is 110 volts at 60 cycles, as in the US.

CLIMATE
It is perfect. The average temperature is 78°F to 80°F and there is less rain here than on the other islands. Anguilla is not arid however, though there are relatively few trees and vegetation consists mainly of shrubs and flowers.

CURRENCY
This is the Eastern Caribbean dollar (EC$) which is approximately equal to US$0.40. US$1 = EC$2.70 approximately. US dollars are accepted readily, though the exchange rate will be nearer EC$2.60.

POPULATION
The population is officially quoted as 7,019. The ancestry is predominantly African, with the usual suggestion of European mixture. The fishing village at

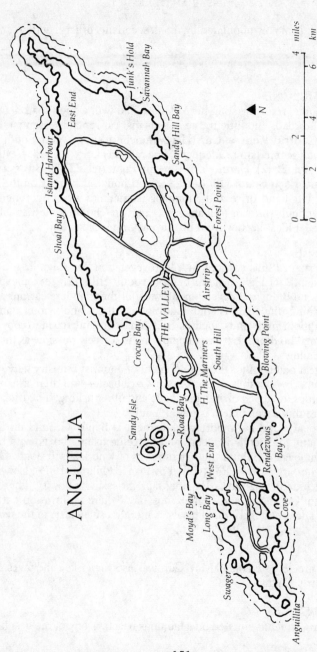

ANGUILLA

Shoal Bay
Island Harbour
East End
Junk's Hold
Savannah Bay
Sandy Hill Bay
Forest Point
Crocus Bay
THE VALLEY
Airstrip
South Hill
Blowing Point
Sandy Isle
Road Bay
H The Mariners
Rendezvous
Bay
Moyd's Bay
Long Bay
West End
Cove
Swager
Anguillita

H = Hotel

N

0   2   2   4   miles
0   2   4   6   km

Island Harbour is mostly populated by the descendants of Irish settlers.

LANGUAGE
English.

GETTING AROUND
There is no public transportation here. This, allied with a good road network of well-surfaced roads and little traffic, means that car rental is essential. I got my car from **Central Rent-a-Car** (Hertz franchisees) of Lower South Hill (tel. 2434) which seemed quite adequate. The rate was US$25 per day. Otherwise try **Apex** (tel. 2642), **Bennie's** at Blowing Point (tel. 2221), **Budget** (tel. 2217) or **Connor's** at South Hill (tel. 2433). Although driving is on the left, most cars are left-hand drive and automatic (sometimes air-conditioned). If you try hard enough you can probably get a non air-conditioned manual vehicle. You need a local licence from the airport or police station.

WHAT TO SEE
There are no rugged hills covered with lush vegetation, for Anguilla is a flat, sandy coral island, its highest point being **Crocus Hill**, 213 feet above sea level. There is no industrial development, most of the islanders earning their living from fishing (the catch is sold in advance to the island's hotels, and to those on neighbouring islands such as Sint Maarten) and raising crops and chickens on smallholdings. Large-scale farming is scarcely possible as the soil is generally shallow.

There is great potential for the development of a tourist industry here. The beaches are superb—possibly the best in the Caribbean—and there are excellent opportunities for scuba diving, big-game and other fishing. The trick is to get here before this development is put in hand.

The main beach and an important settlement is Sandy Ground on Road Bay. It has a jetty for incoming sloops and outgoing fishing boats, with boat-building on the beach. Behind the narrow strip of land is a salt pond. Other splendid beaches are Mead's Bay (visited by Prince Philip in 1964), Long Bay (small and secluded), Maundy's Bay (perhaps the island's finest), The Cove (skin diving and seashells) and Rendezvous Bay (where an invasion party of French met a sticky end in 1796). This list is merely a small taste of the feast in store.

CALENDAR
Anguilla Day is celebrated on 30 May. Carnival lasts for a week and takes place in late July–early August.

WHERE TO STAY
The Mariners, which is situated on a fabulous beach, is one of the best hotels

I've seen, with broad white powdery sands shelving gently into a calm turquoise sea, marred only by a few commercial vessels anchored in the bay. It is built on the same sand, acres of which stretch back to the cliffs behind. It has been landscaped into sandy paths which intersect beds of flowers, plants and grassy verges. The rooms are lovely, built as villa units in the traditional wooden, West Indian-style. Each unit can be offered in four ways: a hotel bedroom; a studio; a suite comprising bedroom, two bathrooms, lounge/living-room and kitchenette; or a two-bedroom/two-bathroom villa. A lovely patio runs along the front of each. Apparently the designs and furnishings are the work of a top British interior designer and it certainly shows. Rattan furniture with subtle pastel shades in the materials is echoed in the tiles. Staying there was a pleasure. Dinner—the menu is a sort of West Indian-based *nouvelle cuisine*—was good. The dining experience is exceptional, the lovely restaurant again being built in traditional style, the tables set on a covered verandah overlooking the beach and sea. The concept is so obvious it's difficult to see why more Caribbean hotels have not adopted the same ideas: it's a traditional colonial beach house updated, and done to perfection.

Anguilla's top hotel—certainly in terms of price—is the **Malliouhana**. This was built at phenomenal expense over four years at Mead's Bay (which seems to have been renamed Maid's Bay). The accent is on the very best in standards of service and appointment that can be found in the Caribbean. There are high vaulted ceilings in the lobby, three swimming pools, gigantic rooms and suites, Jo Rostang and his team from La Bonne Auberge in Antibes, a Schumi hairdressing salon, boutique and jewellery store, three championship tennis courts, all watersports and a staff-to-guest ratio of 2:1. For the ultimate in European- or American-style luxury set in Paradise you will find it difficult, if not impossible, to find a superior.

For real luxury and spacious elegance, with what must surely be one of the most magnificent pools anywhere, splash out at **La Santé**, Barnes Bay. It had only just opened in 1985 and this perhaps explains why so fabulous a place was almost empty in November. It began life as a holiday spa offering everything from facelifts to thigh trimmings. There is now a splendid gym with saunas, jacuzzi and massages as well as a variety of watersports along the beach. It offers detached villas, each with sitting room, patio, bathroom, dressing room and bedroom with two double beds and a sea view.

The **Cinnamon Reef Beach Club**, Little Harbour, is not my favourite but has its devotees. The accommodation is in really vast cottages along the beach: rather Spanish-style and cooled by huge paddle fans. The rates include watersports (the only Anguillan hotel to do this).

Seaview is a guesthouse which is really a set of apartments: two self-contained one-bedroom units with bedroom, bathroom, kitchen and lounge/diner on the ground floor, and a very large two-bedroom two-bathroom apartment on the first floor. The latter boasts a very large kitchen and lounge/diner. The beach—Road Bay—is about 50 to 100 yards away.

Lloyd's Guest House, The Valley (but actually at Crocus Hill, just a five-minute walk down to the beach at Crocus Bay), is perhaps the best place on the whole island to stay for a real Anguillan experience. Mrs Vita Lloyd's welcome is warm, the rooms simple but comfortable, the food more than adequate, and you help yourself to hot or cold drinks whenever you want. If you're around at the right time you'll be offered some lunch, or sometimes a packed picnic snack. Mrs Lloyd, who once made Prince Charles' sandwiches, is the island's Public Health Nurse/Administrator. You are in good hands, and standards of cleanliness are high. Some people who could easily afford the 'top end' places prefer to come here. There are regular comings and goings; you will feel part of the island life here and meet interesting people.

The Lloyds also have a couple of apartments on the beach (Crocus Bay) (US$40 a night, or US$60 with breakfast and dinner in the guesthouse). The two together can be taken as a unit by a family—probably negotiable.

There are many villas and apartments available, often on the beach. Some of the beachside properties are **Sile Bay Apartments**, studio and one-bedroom apartments near the east end of the island facing south, with swimming pool, windsurfers, sunfish and snorkelling equipment; **Shoal Bay Villas** are efficient units on the idyllic beach of the same name; and there are **Seahorse Apartments** at Blowing Point.

Accommodation in Anguilla
Daily rates per room in US$

		Winter		Summer	
		Single	*Double*	*Single*	*Double*
Hotels and guesthouses					
Cinnamon Reef Beach		EP 215	EP 230	EP 110	EP 120
Club, Little Harbour		MAP 250	MAP 300	MAP 145	MAP 190
(tel. 2727)					
Cul de Sac, Blowing Point	Cottage		EP 120		EP 90
(tel. 2461)					
Florencia's, The Valley (tel.		MAP 25	MAP 38	MAP 25	MAP 38
2319)					
La Santé, Barnes Bay			EP 205		EP 150
(tel. 2871)					
Lloyds Guest House, Crocus		MAP 35	MAP 60	MAP 35	MAP 60
Hill (tel. 2351)					
Malliouhana Hotel,	Room		EP 260–300		EP 200
Mead's Bay (tel. 2111)	Suite		EP 600		EP 400
	Villa (6 persons)		EP 1200		EP 800
The Mariners, Sandy	Room	EP 100	EP 125	EP 85	EP 95
Ground, Road Bay	Studio	EP 115	EP 135	EP 90	EP 100
(tel. 2671)	Suite		EP 200		EP 180
	Villa		EP 310		EP 310

(MAP supplement: US$35 per person per day)

	Winter		Summer	
	Single	Double	Single	Double
Mayhern, South Hill (tel. 2350)	MAP 25	MAP 36	MAP 25	MAP 36
Sea View Guest House, Sandy Ground, Road Bay (tel. 2427)		EP 45		EP 40
Apartments, villas and cottages				
Shoal Bay Villas, Shoal Bay		EP 140		EP 75
Sile Bay Apartments, Sile Bay (tel. 2470)	EP 90	EP 90	EP 40	EP 45

10% service charge and 8% tax should normally be added to these rates.

EATING OUT
Most of the hotels have good restaurants, but Anguilla is an excellent island for trying local cuisine. Restaurants are dotted about the island, often on beaches, and are best discovered by car.

SPORTS
Boat racing is a popular spectator sport in Anguilla and major events are on New Year's Day, Easter Monday, Anguilla Day (30 May), and during the summer carnival at the end of July and beginning of August. Watersports with instruction can be found at the Malliouhana. There is also fishing and sailing to be had around the coast, and tennis inland.

SAINT BARTHÉLEMY

This is the island known as 'The Normandy of the Tropics'. There is one town, Gustavia, which has the usual shopping facilities to be found in the French Caribbean, in addition to being a free port.

GETTING TO SAINT BARTHÉLEMY
Saint Barthélemy is ten minutes away from Sint Maarten by air, and an hour's flight from Guadeloupe.

From the USA
Sint Maarten is the best transit point, with American flights from New York,

155

Boston or Dallas, Pan Am from New York or Miami and Eastern from Miami and Atlanta. Connections from Sint Maarten are provided by Winair.

From Canada
You should travel via Boston, New York or Miami to San Juan, then as above via Sint Maarten.

From London
The best route will be by British Airways to Antigua, then connections via Sint Maarten. You may need to overnight in Antigua.

From Europe
The Nouvelles Frontières charters from Brussels to Guadeloupe must be favourite. From there you take an Air Guadeloupe connection. Air France flies from Paris to Guadeloupe.

Within the Caribbean
There are flights from Saint Croix on Coastal Air Transport, from Sint Maarten on Winair and from Guadeloupe on Air Guadeloupe.

If you prefer to go by boat, there's a chance of sailing catamarans and one motor catamaran making the trip from Philipsburg on the south (Dutch) coast of Sint Maarten. The sailing boats are tempting as they look like more of an adventure (one's a racer), but be warned that the crossing time and the state of the sea are both unpredictable, whereas the motor cat makes the trip fairly reliably in 1½ hours or less—it's over before you could begin to feel sick.

These 'ferry' services are really designed for day-trippers, though you can use them for longer visits to Saint Barthélemy. They leave at 9 am most mornings and depart from Gustavia for the return journey at 3.30 pm. Get your ticket (US$22.50 one way) in advance and check in early, as they tend to be

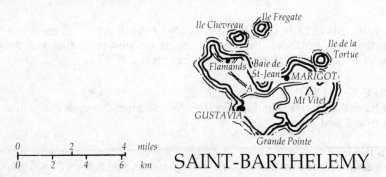

SAINT-BARTHELEMY

156

overbooked to allow for no-shows. Note that the sailing cats leave from the Ruyterplein dock in the centre of Philipsburg, opposite the post office (tickets for all the boats are also sold here), whereas the motor cat leaves from another dock nearly half a mile to the east.

ENTRY REGULATIONS
These are the same as for Guadeloupe, of which Saint Barthélemy is administratively a part.

ELECTRICITY
The supply is 220 volts at 50 cycles, about the same as in the UK.

CLIMATE
Average temperatures are around 80°F year round with relatively light rainfall.

CURRENCY
This is the French franc (FFR), though US dollars are more readily accepted here—at a fair rate—than elsewhere in the French islands.

LANGUAGE
French.

POPULATION
The population of 2,200 is largely descended from Normans who arrived in the latter part of the 17th century. The first thing you notice, perhaps, is that all the taxi drivers are white. In fact the majority of the population is white, but there are some black and mixed-blood families living here too. Everybody, of whatever colour, appears to have the same positive, cheerful attitude. This seems to be a unified society (small-scale though it is) with absolutely no racial undertones evident to a visitor.

HISTORY
Saint Barthélemy was named for Columbus' brother Bartholomew. The island was under French control until they sold it to Sweden, who made it a free port. It remained so even after the French regained the island.

GETTING AROUND
Mokes (minicars) are the most popular form of transport on the island. There are no buses. You either travel in your own car, or hitch a ride in someone else's. Hitching is normal and expected. You never have to wait more than a few minutes during the day. At night you may wait ten or twenty minutes between cars.

Car hire is easy at the airport, or ask for Mathew Aubin at the Sodexa supermarket in Saint Jean—he's the manager and also runs a car rental business. He is very friendly and helpful and speaks good English. Car rental rates run from about FFR150 (US$20) a day for a moke in summer to US$35 in winter. Small cars cost about the same as mokes. You need to be 25 years old with two years' driving experience.

Distances are small and with a hired car you can explore most of the island's roads in a day. The main resort area, Saint Jean, is less than half a mile from the airport and two miles from Gustavia. The best plan, if you're one or two persons and staying in or near Saint Jean, is to rent a moke or car for two or three days (give lifts to others if you have room, to keep the system going) and thereafter join the hitchers—young and old, visitors and locals alike. The system is part of the general friendliness of the island. Of course, there are always the taxis if you prefer, or if the trip is to some remote corner and you want to be sure of getting back. Taxi rates are reasonable.

WHAT TO SEE

Saint Barthélemy (which for a hundred years of its history belonged to Sweden) is certainly very different from anywhere else. Some regard it as the best bit of France—anywhere; and one certainly meets settlers from mainland France who are of that opinion. Saint Barth not only impresses immediately with 'good vibes'—but everything is clean, tidy and well-cared for: the streets of the charming capital, **Gustavia**, the picture-postcard harbour, the beaches, the shops and restaurants, and the tasteful boutiques, are each a gem. Galvanised iron roofs are almost universal all over the island, but you won't see any rusting, dirty or patched-up ones here: they're all painted an attractive pinky-red shade; and what's more they *all* seem to have been painted just yesterday! There's a little icecream-parlour-cum-*crêperie* in Gustavia that's all pink and white, beautiful to behold—almost edible in itself (needless to say, the icecream and *crêpes* are delicious.) Even the pharmacies here have tremendous chic. The tourist information office is in the *Mairie* on the Rue August Nyman. They can supply you with a list of taxi drivers to call (there are no taxi ranks).

Amongst themselves the people speak a baffling patois—nasal French with bits of Swedish and English mixed in. They will also politely speak standard French with you, and many of them speak English. Not the least remarkable thing about this island is the way France and America meet and blend here, or at least co-exist happily. Elsewhere, French and American is often not the happiest of combinations. Here, getting on for half the visitors are American; the islanders take US dollars—at a fair rate—very nearly as readily as they take French francs. There seems to be a very friendly spirit both ways.

Many of the people are descended from early settlers of Norman and Breton stock. But it's a bit misleading to say that the traditional dress is still worn: the truth is that in one area, the hamlet of **Corossol**, *some* of the women *sometimes* wear the starched white bonnets—*quichenottes*—often depicted in Saint Barthélemy publicity; and even then it's probably done for the tourists these days.

Basically the people have moved with the times: Saint Barth is unmistakably a holiday island—with something of the atmosphere of a still-unspoilt Saint Tropez—although it's true that they remain traditional in some ways. The majority are Catholics and celebrate mass at different churches, on Saturday night or Sunday morning, 'serviced' by the one mobile priest.

Fishermen

CALENDAR

As well as celebrating French national holidays Saint Barthélemy has a festival of its own in late August to commemorate its patron saint. For three days the island takes on the air of a French country fair, with stall-lined streets, competitions and wining and dining.

WHERE TO STAY

In Gustavia there's one inexpensive hotel offering very good value. It's **La Presqu'île** near the yacht marina on the far side of the harbour—perhaps seven or eight minutes' walk from the ferry dock. This is fairly basic accommodation, though with air-conditioning. It has a restaurant and offers CP, MAP and AP terms. (Examples: summer MAP single FFR300 (US$39), MAP double FFR400 (US$52); winter CP single FFR 200 (US$26), AP double FFR550 (US$71). Like most hotels here, it charges 10% extra for service. Long-stay discounts are available.

Also in Gustavia, on steeply rising ground just out of the centre, is the very pleasant **L'Hibiscus**, with a superb view over the harbour. The owner is M. Henri Thellin, a former French international soccer star. The manager looked after a prestigious hotel in Saint Tropez for many years. 'Bungalows' are for two, with bathroom, air-conditioning, kitchenette and large terrace. There is indeed lots of hibiscus. The units are well done out and very attractive, as are the rest of the premises. In fact it's very tasteful. Guests are mainly from Saint Tropez and New York. There's a pool, and complimentary transport to a nearby beach. (EP winter US$115. 10% off for stays of more than ten days; rates are halved in summer.)

There's plenty of choice elsewhere on the island. If you want to pay at least US$260 a night (EP) for total luxury among an almost exclusively American clientele, the **Manapany**, towards the western end of the north coast, is for you.

If you just want a place on the popular but seldom crowded beach at Saint Jean, with adequate facilities and comfort, probably the best value is offered by the **Tom Beach Hotel**. It has a good position at the western end of the beach—near the airport. The little planes take off towards the sea and pass perhaps a hundred feet above the heads of swimmers and sunbathers. The proximity of the airport is more of an attraction than a nuisance. The noise of the eight- and fifteen-seaters isn't obtrusive; the airport itself nestles in a green valley, with a short runway that seems to go right into the bay (actually it stops at the beach!). The hotel is run by Joe Lederle and his wife, who speak good English (especially Joe). The accommodation is in 'bungalows'. They're proper efficiency units, with bathroom, kitchenette, effective air-conditioning and everything supplied that sensibly needs to be—tissues, paper towels, matches, salt and pepper, detergents, insect sprays (not that there are any insects in evidence). There's a small beach bar with snacks, and the Chez Francine restaurant next door. The St Barth Windsurfing School operates on the beach here. The hotel rates vary with your distance from the beach. (Summer EP rates about US$40 single, US$50 double, with some special 'package' reductions available up to mid October; winter EP US$85.)

Most other hotels which are actually on a beach cost more. That includes the **Eden Rock**, beautifully situated on the rocky promontory in the middle of Saint Jean Bay. This was the island's first hotel; they'll tell you that Greta Garbo was among its first guests, in 1955. The guest rooms (no fridges or stoves here) are made distinctive by antiques, four-posters and mosquito nets. It has been said that the hot water system is erratic—not generally a problem on the French islands. (CP double about US$80 in summer, US$120 in winter.)

Just up the hill—five minutes to the beach—the **Village St Jean** offers particularly good value out of season, when you might get a comfortable studio for two, with breakfast, for about US$40 a night (package of seven nights or more; winter rates about US$95 per night). Facilities are good, but instead of a pool there is billiards and table tennis.

Described as 'in the mountains', **Hostellerie des 3 Forces** would suit those of 'Aquarian' interests. It faces east, and therefore, as the brochure proclaims,

160

'the sun rises for us first. A magic hour to do some yoga by the pool, between Fire and Water.' And then, the brochure continues, 'at the time the setting sun brings up the tropical fragrances of the garden, the hour is astrologic... You will enjoy sleeping in one of the 12 sign-named cottages ... the Pisces, the Gemini, the Scorpio...' The cottages are rather plainly furnished, in local wood, and there's a pool. (Rates not published, but probably winter CP about US$90.)

Les Noettes, on the beach at Lorient (an unofficial nudist area), is not listed by the Tourist Board. (Simple studios for about US$45 summer, US$75 winter, EP double. As in some other places, an extra bed can be supplied for a third person for a supplementary payment of US$10–$15.)

EATING OUT

There are plenty of bars—the most famous being **Select** in the middle of Gustavia, Mecca of yachtsmen and run by Marius, a well-known and very distinguished-looking local of Swedish descent. There are also some pleasant beach bars/restaurants. **Chez Francine**, at the airport end of Saint Jean Bay, next to the Tom Beach Hotel, is a popular local gathering place for lunch: steak, fish, lobster (spiny lobster or crayfish in European terms), enough to fill you up for the day for between FFR100 and FFR180.

The *menu touristique* at an all-inclusive price is not established here. But there are places offering reasonably priced snacks and light meals (including that **crêperie** in Gustavia).

Most of the hotels have good (but not cheap) restaurants. Especially well regarded, in fact eulogised, is the restaurant at **Autour du Rochet**, at Lorient, half a mile east of Saint Jean.

L'Hibiscus (overlooking Gustavia) has a gourmet restaurant claiming the best cuisine (*nouvelle*) on the island; the chef is Robert Lesenne, formerly of Liège and Monte Carlo, and (it's said) of some culinary fame. (Starters around FFR60–90; entrées FFR 120–150 and up; a full dinner would cost at least FFR300 per head with wine.)

The **Hostellerie des 3 Forces** has a superb restaurant too, as has the **Manapany**, Saint Barth's most expensive hotel (it may well be the most expensive restaurant, too).

In Gustavia itself, **La Crémaillière** offers very good and only moderately expensive food—say FFR240 for a dinner with wine.

The **Beach Club** at Saint Jean has a beautiful position right on the waterfront in the middle of the bay, but the food is average only. Drinks alone, and light snacks, can also be taken here. Nearby is a pizzeria, best avoided.

For fairly cheap snacks try the takeaway counter next to the Sodexa supermarket.

The two supermarkets, both handy if you're staying in the Saint Jean area, are the Sodexa and, in the attractive complex opposite the airport, the Gourmet Shop. **Gourmet Shop** has the wider range of foodstuffs; **Sodexa** is slightly better for stationery, batteries and other sundries. Most imported goods are predictably expensive (though even French imports are mostly cheaper here, for some reason, than in Guadeloupe): table wine from FFR10 a bottle; mineral water from FFR5. Food is imported from Europe and the USA. Meat from the USA is cheaper here than in Europe. The same small bottles of Heineken sold in bars for FFR10 or more work out at less than FFR4 each if bought in six-packs in a supermarket.

The supermarkets sell bread, of course; but worth a visit or two is the bakery run by an old woman in a roadside shack near Lorient. *Baguettes* come hot from the oven—FFR2.80 for the size sold in France as a *demi*.

US VIRGIN ISLANDS

Although if we include every piece of land in the group there are some 50 islands, the name 'US Virgin Islands' usually means the three main ones— Saint Thomas, Saint Croix and Saint John. The islands are an unincorporated Territory under the US Department of the Interior with a non-voting Delegate in the House of Representatives. The Governor is elected every four years. There are fifteen Senators.

One of the greatest attractions of the US Virgins is their position as a free port. US citizens are allowed a duty-free quota of US$800. If you've ever wanted to buy a very good and usually expensive camera this may be the place to get it, but you should check the prices before you leave home so that you have an idea of how much, if anything, you are actually saving. Liquor by the bottle is almost unbelievably cheap.

GETTING TO THE US VIRGIN ISLANDS
The two major islands, Saint Thomas and Saint Croix, have regular services to the USA and within the immediate Caribbean area. Saint John's scheduled services are restricted to seaplane services to these two major islands and San Juan.

From the USA
Saint Thomas and Saint Croix share the same services from the USA. American Airlines flies down from New York (as does Pan Am) and Dallas, whilst

THE VIRGIN ISLANDS

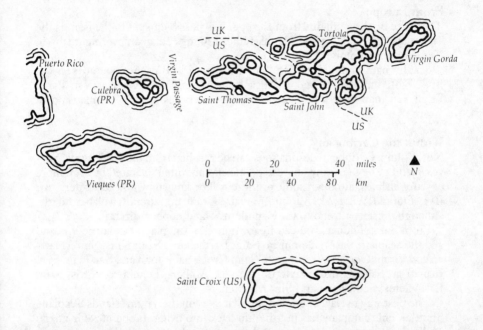

three airlines operate services from Miami: Pan Am, Eastern and Midway. Midway also comes here from Chicago.

From Canada
There are no direct flights from Canada. Travel via one of the cities above.

From London
The most advantageous route from London will depend on the time of year you are travelling, the duration of stay and what special deals are on offer. If travelling in the winter you may find Pan Am repeating the special deal it had in winters 1984/85 and 1985/86: a cheap transatlantic APEX to New York, combined with an ultra-cheap four flight USA flyaround (which you could use to travel to Miami and back) and a Caribbean add-on of £75 return. In the

spring or autumn you may find a good deal out of New York (often including accommodation) which you could combine with a cheap transatlantic charter. In the summer an Iberia APEX to San Juan with a connection might be the answer, or a discounted Avianca ticket to San Juan via Frankfurt, Paris or Madrid. You need a visa if you come through the US.

From Europe
There are no direct flights from Europe. It is possible to get to the islands the same day using Pan Am via Miami. Other routings entail an overnight stop in New York or Miami.

An alternate routing is to San Juan. Lufthansa and Avianca operate services from Frankfurt, Iberia and Avianca from Madrid and Avianca from Paris. From San Juan there are regular commuter services into St Thomas and St Croix.

Within the Caribbean
No far-flung Caribbean destinations can be reached from the US Virgins. Services tend to be to nearby obscure points and are often operated by even more obscure airlines, although some of these will be known by now to readers: Air BVI, Dorado Wings, LIAT and Winair. Often the aircraft will be elderly, although there is a trend towards modern 'island hopper' aircraft.

From Saint Thomas you can fly to Anguilla, Antigua, Tortola (Beef Island and the seaplane base), Dominica, Saint Barthélemy, Saint Kitts, Sint Maarten and Virgin Gorda, in addition to Saint Croix, Saint John and San Juan. Services from Saint Croix operate to Anguilla, Antigua, Dominica, Nevis, Saint Barthélemy, Saint Kitts and Sint Maarten.

The best way to travel between the islands is on the Virgin Islands Seaplane Shuttle. This company has put the fun back into flying. It operates Grumann Mallard seaplanes, still affectionately known as the 'Goose'. The planes take off and land on the water but taxi up a ramp so that you are able to board on dry land. If you have never flown this way before, you should try it just for the experience. The Seaplane offers a regular service between St Thomas, St Croix and San Juan, with infrequent services to St John and Tortola. In San Juan the Seaplane lands on its wheels at the International Airport. It then flies direct to the downtown searamps in St Thomas, St Croix, St John and Tortola.

On checking in, your baggage is weighed. Don't be alarmed if they also ask your weight. Then you can either wait in the newly-built air-conditioned terminal or sit out in the sunshine until the plane arrives.

Besides the fun of take-off and landing, the seaplanes probably provide the best views of the Virgin Islands. Flying at a low altitude and a slow speed gives a truly bird's-eye view of this island group. Most major settlements in the Virgins are built by the sea, quite normal in the Caribbean but here inevitable, owing to

164

the physical nature of the islands. Thus the airboats can fly from the centre of one town to another, and long trips to airports and bus or taxi fares are avoided.

ENTRY REGULATIONS
There are no formalities for US citizens except a return ticket and evidence of sufficient funds. Others require a US visa, of course. If you have just arrived from Puerto Rico there are no formalities at all.

ELECTRICITY
The supply is 110–120 volts at 60 cycles, about the same as in the US.

CLIMATE
Weather conditions are as near perfect as makes no difference.

Average temperatures

January	February	March	April	May	June
77°F	77°F	78°F	78°F	79°F	81°F

July	August	September	October	November	December
82°F	82°F	81°F	80°F	78°F	76°F

CURRENCY
This is the US dollar. Credit cards are accepted more widely here than perhaps anywhere else I know.

Apart from duty-free attractions, the cost of living is the highest I have encountered anywhere. But then, the standard of living is high too. As the local people earn enough to pay the high prices, and the tourists expect them, it is only the traveller who suffers—and he probably won't be here long enough to mind.

POPULATION
The indigenous population is so small in number that nationals of the other islands are welcomed with open arms: they are needed to provide the labour force for the huge tourist trade. Those people that I spoke to were from the British Virgins, Antigua, Saint Lucia, Saint Kitts or some other island. They all come here in search of the dollar and seemed happy to have found it.

HISTORY
Saint Croix was the first of the islands to be settled, by the British and French early in the 17th century. There was the usual squabbling between the British, French and Spanish before the island was eventually purchased by Denmark in 1733. The Danes had already settled Saint Thomas and Saint John in the second half of the 17th century, using the islands—and Saint Croix in

particular—mainly for agricultural purposes. With the decline in importance of sugar the Danes began to lose interest and in 1917 were happy to sell the islands to the United States for $25 million.

Everyone speaks English, and a good many people also speak Spanish, French or Creole.

The US Virgin Islands celebrate the same public holidays as the US mainland, but there are additional island festivities.

Saint Thomas' carnival takes place shortly after Easter in Charlotte Amalie. It features stilt-walkers (*Moko Jumbis*), calypso, steel bands and parades, along with the best of the island's native dishes. The ceremony derived originally from Voodoo but in its present form it bears no relation to Voodoo practices. For a start, it is a party in the streets rather than a religious event. Many of the participants dress as followers of Satan, but it is difficult to say whether they triumph or are routed.

The venue for the annual spectacle in Saint Croix alternates between Frederiksted and Christiansted. It runs from Christmas to 6 January when the Three Kings Day parade is held in the crowd-lined streets. Saint John's week of festivities climaxes with fireworks to mark the Fourth of July. The preceding days are filled with celebratory island meals, dancing and *Moko Jumbis*.

Saint Thomas

Those in search of peace and solitude would consider Saint Thomas to be outrageously touristy. Besides the planeloads arriving for their annual vacation, there are those who come for a few days' break plus day-trippers from San Juan in search of duty-free liquor and other shopping treats. But the people who live here seem to like it, so why quibble?

Charlotte Amalie

What is now the capital of the US Virgin Islands was founded by the Danes in the second half of the seventeenth century. It was named for the consort of King Christian V. The harbour is interesting, host to all kinds of private yachts, cruise ships and cargo vessels, not to mention the seaplanes. Houses painted white or pastel shades dot the hillsides behind the town, whilst between the hills and water lies a shopper's paradise.

There is a bus service within the Charlotte Amalie area and beyond to Red

SAINT THOMAS, US VIRGIN ISLANDS

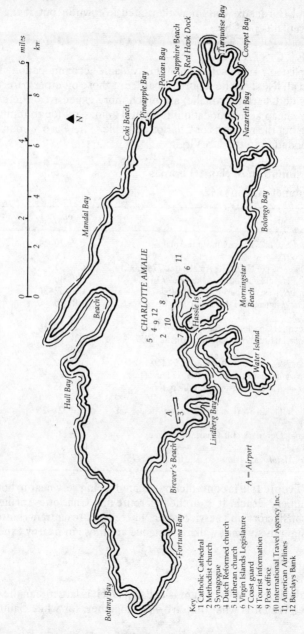

Key
1 Catholic Cathedral
2 Methodist church
3 Synagogue
4 Dutch Reformed church
5 Lutheran church
6 Virgin Islands Legislature
7 Coast guard
8 Tourist information
9 Post office
10 International Travel Agency Inc.
11 American Airlines
12 Barclays Bank

A = Airport

N

Hook and Bordeaux. Cars may be rented in town or out at the airport, and scooter rental is possible.

WHERE TO STAY
Below is listed a small selection of the available accommodation. There are 51 places in all listed by the Tourist Board, but those on other parts of the island (i.e. outside Charlotte Amalie) are much more expensive. There seems to be no really cheap accommodation in Saint Thomas, although it might be worth checking out the outskirts of Charlotte Amalie. There is 6% room tax on hotel accommodation in the US Virgins.

Accommodation in Saint Thomas

Daily summer rates in US$

	Single	Double
Danish Chalet, in hills above Charlotte Amalie (tel. 774 5764)	CP: 20–24	30–36
Estate Thomas, east of Charlotte Amalie (tel. 774 2542)	CP: 31	41
Hotel 1829, central Charlotte Amalie (tel. 774 1829)	EP: 46	54
Maison Greaux, west of Charlotte Amalie (tel. 774 0063)	CP: 32–36	44–48
Michele Motel, Constant 61, Charlotte Amalie (tel. 774 2650)	EP: 30	50
Midtown, central Charlotte Amalie (tel. 774 9157)	EP: 30–46	40–50
Miller Manor, on hill above Charlotte Amalie (tel. 774 1535)	CP: 38	44–54
New Holiday Isles, Charlotte Amalie (tel. 774 9873)	EP: 32	44
Ramsey's, east of Charlotte Amalie (tel. 774 6521)	EP: 28	40
Tropic Isle Hotel, near the airport, Lindberg Bay (tel. 774 1980)	EP: 45	55
Villa Fairview, on hill overlooking Charlotte Amalie (tel. 774 2661)	CP: 22–26	34–40
Villa Santana, Denmark Hill, Charlotte Amalie (tel. 774 1311)	EP: 35	60
West Indian Manner, Charlotte Amalie (tel. 774 2975)	EP: 32	44

The Tropic Isle is conveniently situated, being very near to both the airport and Lindberg Beach. It is on the bus route into Charlotte Amalie. I found the rooms satisfactory and service good. There is no restaurant, however, and the only restaurants within walking distance are those in nearby expensive hotels.

Saint Croix

This is the largest of the Virgin Islands; in fact it is larger than the other two put together. Which is what they are—put together; for while Saint John is only

SAINT CROIX, US VIRGIN ISLANDS

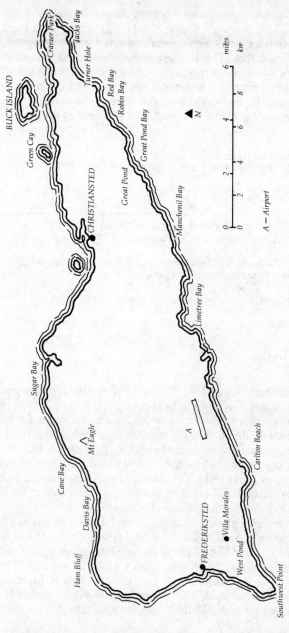

BUCK ISLAND

Green Cay

Crazier Park
Jacks Bay
Turner Hole
Red Bay
Robin Bay
Great Pond Bay

CHRISTIANSTED

Great Pond

Manchenil Bay

Limetree Bay

Sugar Bay

Mt Eagle

Cane Bay

Davis Bay

Ham Bluff

Carlton Beach

FREDERIKSTED

Villa Morales

West Pond

Southwest Point

A

miles
km

N

A = Airport

169

about three miles from Saint Thomas, Saint Croix lies 35 miles south of both of them. There are two towns on Saint Croix, Christiansted and Frederiksted, some 12 miles apart. Christiansted, founded in 1734, was the capital of the Danish West Indies. This is where the seaplanes come in, and this is where you leave from if you take a trip to Buck Island and its underwater National Park. Near to Frederiksted is a tropical rain forest and the restored Whim Great House. A regular bus service connects the two towns, with regular stops, otherwise big name car hire firms operate in town and at the airport.

Accommodation in Saint Croix
Daily winter rates per room in US$

	Single	Double
Island Inn, 29 Prince Street, Christiansted (tel. 773 2418)	EP: 36–40	50–60
The Lodge, 43A Queen Cross Street, Christiansted (tel. 773 1535)	CP: 44	52
Royal Scotia, 43 King Street, Christiansted (tel. 773 2138)	EP: 30–40	44–60
Smithfield, near Fisher and Strand Street junction, Frederiksted (tel. 773 0510)	EP: 30	36
Villa Morales, near Whim Great House, Frederiksted (tel. 772 0556)	EP: 24	30–36

Saint John

This is the smallest and least developed of the island group and is situated between Saint Thomas and the British Virgin Island of Tortola, separated from each by about three miles of water. Much of it is a National Park: 14,500 acres of lush growth, fine beaches and relics from Indian and Danish settlements. Accommodation is available in the park itself, at the Cinnamon Bay Camp, but unfortunately bookings have to be made months in advance. Beach huts, tents and bare sites are available. There are two settlements—Cruz Bay, the larger, and Coral Harbour. There is no bus service, travel around the island generally being by jeep, minimoke (minicar) or taxi.

If you are going on to the British Virgin Islands you may like to take a launch called either the *Bomba Charger* or the *Bomba Cruiser* (for reservations, telephone 774 7920 or 774 3389). If you need help from a travel agent you will be pleased to learn that there is an agency which knows what it is doing (something which is less easy to find in Tortola). This is **International Travel Agency Incorporated,** 32 Dronningens Gade (near Raadets Gade), Charlotte Amalie (tel. 774 8700; ask for Julie Olive).

Accommodation in Saint John
Daily winter rates per room in US$

Cinnamon Bay, Cinnamon Bay (northwest Saint John; tel. 776 6330)	Beach huts 35, tents 20, bare sites 8
Sewer's Guesthouse (near Ferry Dock, Cruz Bay; tel. 776 6814)	EP: S 30, D 40

SHOPPING
Shopping in the Virgin Islands has a US flavour except that the Scandinavian influence is still apparent and you can buy furniture, dinner services and glassware from Denmark and fabrics and fashions from Sweden, as well as the

SAINT JOHN, US VIRGIN ISLANDS

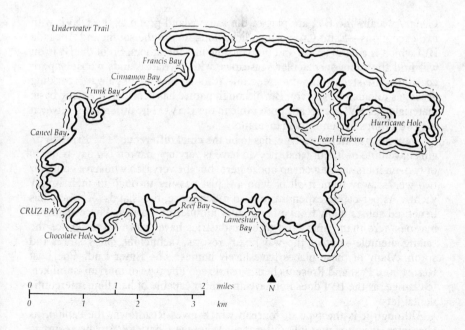

171

usual luxury items calculated to be so easy to carry home as gifts. The paper *Saint Thomas This Week* should help find some items and tell you what's on by way of entertainment. Otherwise call in at the tourist offices in the main towns on each Island.

SPORT
There's something for everyone in the Virgin Islands so it isn't easy to know where to begin. Watersports, fishing and sailing are the most popular, as with most Caribbean islands, and instruction is available in most places.

Some of the most beautiful beaches in the world are on these islands and they are all open to the public by law. On Saint John they are managed by the National Park Service, which inevitably means there are some rules and regulations. Their centre in Cruz Bay will provide details.

Inland can be found tennis and golf in Saint Croix and Saint Thomas while only tennis is available in Saint John.

BRITISH VIRGIN ISLANDS

Geographically the BVI are part of the same island group as the USVI, with two exceptions—Saint Croix which lies a long way to the south, and Anegada BVI which is a coral island and not volcanic like the others. So in the BVI you will find the same spectacular seascapes, with myriad islands whose superb coastlines rise steeply into the green hills (though they are not always sparkling green, as rain can be scarce). But although nature has provided the same basic materials, the BVI are greatly preferable to the USVI. The differences between the two groups are entirely man-made.

Tourism, its extent and type, has to be the chief difference. The British Virgins have little of it, but what they do have is very up-market. No day-trippers or two-nighters seeking cheap booze here, but the very rich who have come for two weeks away from it all or who are just passing through in their luxury yachts. As per capita expenditure is so much more, the islands' economy has benefited substantially from a far smaller number of tourists. There are more marinas here than banks, and whole industries have grown up to service the sailing clientele—out-of-the-way luxury resorts, yacht clubs, ships' stores and so on. Many of these places have lovely names: The Bitter End, The Last Resort, and Past and Presents being just three. The type of tourism is unlikely to change, as the BVI does not have an airport capable of handling intercontinental jets.

Although it is the type of tourism which gives Roadtown, the capital, its character, it is not the only difference. Whereas Charlotte Amalie seems to exist mainly as a huge shopping centre, one gets the impression that Road-town's facilities are primarily meant to serve the needs of the community. Buildings and services in the capital are geared towards local consumers, whilst the expensive hotels and clubs are either out of town, on another part of Tortola, or, as is becoming increasingly usual, on the other islands. All this makes Roadtown a humble—though reserved rather than friendly—settlement, sleeping in the sun.

GETTING TO THE BRITISH VIRGIN ISLANDS

There is no major airport in the British Virgins so that up to now a change of aircraft has been necessary, and in most cases this will continue to be so.

From the USA

A new airline, British Caribbean Airways, has recently been formed to operate jet services from Miami to Tortola (Beef Island) using British Aerospace 146 jet aircraft. No other jet aircraft can operate from the 3,600-ft runway, but this four-engined, new technology plane has been specifically designed for re-gional flights into microscopic airstrips. This service can accommodate up to 80 passengers and the journey takes less than three hours. If this service is full when you want to travel, then take a flight to San Juan or Saint Thomas and a connection on Air BVI, Dorado Wings or LIAT.

From Canada

Your best means of travel will be via Miami to connect with the British Carib-bean Airways service.

From London

Traditionally you would fly on British Airways to Antigua and then take a con-nection from there on Air BVI or LIAT. If your destination is Virgin Gorda then you will find a direct connection on Air BVI from Antigua. These connec-tions are timed to meet the British Airways flights, thus making an overnight stay unnecessary. Now, however, you may be able to travel via Miami using the new British Caribbean Airways service which is operated by staff seconded from British Airways. Check the connections and fares; via Antigua may still prove to be the best route.

From Europe

You should either come to London and take the services via Antigua as out-lined above, travel to Miami and connect with British Caribbean, or take a flight from Frankfurt, Paris or Madrid to San Juan and connect on Dorado Wings, Air BVI or LIAT.

THE BRITISH VIRGIN ISLANDS · TORTOLA AND SURROUNDING ISLANDS

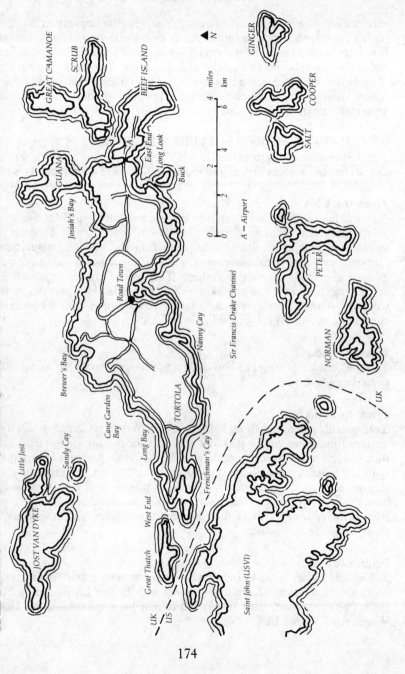

Within the Caribbean

In addition to the seaplane shuttle from West End to Saint Thomas and San Juan there are five airlines operating into the BVI from Caribbean points: Air BVI, British Caribbean Airways, Eastern, LIAT and Dorado Wings. Tortola (Beef Island) has links with Anegada, Anguilla, Antigua, Providenciales, Saint Kitts, Sint Maarten, Saint Thomas, San Juan and Virgin Gorda. Virgin Gorda has direct flights from Anguilla, Antigua, Tortola, Saint Kitts, Sint Maarten, Saint Thomas and San Juan.

ENTRY REGULATIONS

Canadian and British citizens may enter without passports if they can produce other identification. Few other nationalities require a visa. You must have sufficient funds and *a continuous chain of tickets* to your home country. For US citizens that can mean as far as Saint Thomas or Puerto Rico. You are also supposed to have arranged accommodation in advance. There is a $2.50 departure tax. Passengers travelling via the US, Puerto Rico, or US Virgin Islands need US visas.

ELECTRICITY

The supply is 110–120 volts at 60 cycles, about the same as in the US.

CLIMATE

Temperatures are of the same range as elsewhere in the Caribbean, between 77°F and 85°F through the year. It is a little cooler at night, with beneficial effects from the trade winds. There is an annual rainfall of 45 inches.

CURRENCY

The US dollar is the official currency. There are many places which accept credit cards, though personal cheques are not readily acceptable. The islands' independence on imports and the financial status of most visitors means that prices are usually high, especially in those businesses which cater for the tourist trade. However, it is possible to live cheaply if you wish to do so.

POPULATION

The people here are very much more reserved than in most of the Caribbean. This is partly because they all seem to have achieved something, or built something, and have a pride in their work and themselves. It is possibly also partly because the small indigenous population has been accustomed to expatriates for so long. You will never be asked for a handout here.

LANGUAGE

English.

175

HISTORY

Columbus discovered what are now the British and the US Virgin Islands. Nearly 100 years later Sir Francis Drake arrived on the scene and gradually claimed some of the islands, in particular Tortola, which became established as British despite the threat of piracy. The BVI are now ruled by a Governor appointed by the Queen.

GETTING AROUND

There are no buses. Any resident who travels frequently has a car (all number plates are prefixed 'VI' and numbered sequentially, so you can get an idea of the age of a vehicle from its number—an old Land Rover may be VI200 and a new Mercedes VI2000). Thus transport for the visitor is on foot or by taxi. Taxi rates are controlled by the government and have one peculiarity: there are two types of fare, 'single' and 'charter'. A single passenger will be charged the charter fare, while two or more people in the same taxi will be charged the single fare on a per person basis. As the charter fare is three times the single fare, one person will pay more for a taxi than two people travelling together. For example, the single fare to Beef Island from Roadtown is US$2; thus a couple will pay US$4, whilst a single person has to pay the charter fare of US$6. Here are some official fares:

From Roadtown to	Fare in US$		From Roadtown to	Fare in US$	
	Single	Charter		Single	Charter
Long Look	3.00	9.00	Cane Garden Bay	6.00	18.00
Brewer's Bay	3.00	9.00	West End	3.00	9.00
Long Bay	4.00	12.00			

It is possible to hire a car in Tortola and Virgin Gorda. Take your driving licence and drive *on the left*.

WHAT TO SEE

Tortola has the lion's share of the islands' population: some 9,000 live here. The beaches are mainly on the north coast, a long walk, but you may be able to hire a bicycle. The marinas are mainly along the south coast, overlooked by jagged peaks covered with scrub and frangipani. Beef Island, joined to the mainland by Queen Elizabeth Bridge, is important because the international airport is here.

Recent developments, both for the tourist trade and for residential requirements, are tending to favour the many other islands. So Virgin Gorda (the Fat

Virgin) now has a population of 1,000—mainly in and clustered around Spanish Town. The northern half of the island is mountainous, while the southern portion is largely flat apart from a sprinkling of giant boulders. The island is best known for 'The Baths', an unusual rock formation of sea caves. Many of the smaller islands (Peter Island is a good example) are becoming known internationally as away-from-it-all resorts for those who like the good life. Anegada is a coral and limestone island some way from the main group.

CALENDAR
The BVI celebrate with a Spring Regatta in April and a carnival at the beginning of August. In addition Virgin Gorda has a three-day Easter Festival. Not only do the islands recognise British Bank Holidays but they also have a day off for Territory Day (1 July), Saint Ursula's Day (21 October) and the Prince of Wales' birthday (14 November).

WHERE TO STAY
Accommodation in The British Virgin Islands
Daily summer rates per room in US$

	Single	Double
Biras Creek, Virgin Gorda	AP: 200	250
The Bitter End Yacht Club, North Sound, Virgin Gorda	AP: 145–170	195–220
The Castle, Roadtown, Tortola	EP: 34	44
The Last Resort, Bellamy Cay, Beef Island, Tortola	AP: 55	75
Little Dix Bay, northwest Virgin Gorda	AP: S or D 285	
Long Bay Hotel, Long Bay, northwest Tortola	EP: 70	80
Maya Cove Yacht Club (approx 4 miles east of Roadtown)	EP: 30	40
Moorings – Mariner Inn, Roadtown, Tortola	EP: 45	54
Peter Island Hotel and Yacht Harbour, Peter Island	AP: 250	300
Prospect Reef Resort, Roadtown, Tortola	EP: S or D 98–158	
Seaview Hotel, Roadtown, Tortola	EP: 36	42
Sugar Mill Estate, Apple Bay, north Tortola	EP: S or D 70–85	
Village Cay Resort Marina, Roadtown, Tortola	EP: 18–36	20–40
Wayside Inn Guest House (opposite Court House), Roadtown, Tortola	EP: 20–28	

EATING OUT
I found that **The Happy Lion** restaurant under the Central Guest House did a splendid breakfast for about US$2—worth investigation. Besides this there are sufficient native eating places in and around Roadtown and ample fine restaurants of varying prices around the island. The **Fort Burt Hotel** is pricey but does lunches for around US$8 whilst the nearby **Sir Francis Drake Pub** (often known as The Pub) serves snack lunches from US$4.50. The price of non-alcoholic drinks is very expensive here, largely, presumably, because this

is a haunt of the yachting fraternity. This is one of the places to try if you are looking for onward transportation by yacht: getting into casual conversation with yacht owners/captains is straightforward enough. The **Seaview Club** in the same vicinity may be of greater interest as it features West Indian dishes. You can expect prices to be reasonable too. The **Harbour Lights** in the centre of Roadtown serves breakfast, lunch and dinner, and specialises in seafood, pizzas, draught beer and darts. Another place in town is **Cell 5**. Here you can get reasonably priced pizzas and sandwiches. At slightly higher prices, there is the **Poop Deck**, very close to the seaplane terminal. If you are in the region of the Deep Water Harbour (on the east road out of town) you could try **Stonehaven**, which prepares West Indian cuisine at about US$4 per meal.

SHOPPING
Most shops are in Roadtown, Tortola, as is the tourist office, which you can find on a shopping trip at Palm Shopping Centre. Rum, sea salt and small handicraft items can be found, as well as stamps, jewellery made from old island coins, cigars and gems—to name but a few of the more portable gifts for sale. For clothes, there are places specialising in original silk-screen prints and the usual boutiques in hotels and elsewhere.

SPORT
As with the US Virgin Islands the beaches are the main attraction here with restaurants and changing facilities. Don't be put off by the sinisterly named Dead Man's Bay on Peter Island, which in fact looks as if it came straight out of Treasure Island (apart from the picnic tables, that is!)

The watersports enthusiast can dive to see coral or shipwrecks or tame fish. Sailing and windsurfing are also popular, and inland you can find a good game of tennis on Tortola, Peter Island and Virgin Gorda.

TRINIDAD AND TOBAGO

If we take the French islands as separate entities, Trinidad and Tobago is the largest state (in area) in the Eastern Caribbean. It is also the closest to South America, being separated from Venezuela by only two narrow channels.

There are some fundamental differences between Trinidad and Tobago and the other islands with British links. For a start, it is the only country in what was the British West Indies to have become a republic. Queen Elizabeth II is no longer Head of State, although she is still recognised as Head of the Commonwealth, of which Trinidad remains a member. Secondly, tourism has traditionally been an industry of little importance; Tobago theoretically is 'The

178

Holiday Island' but, for reasons amplified below, even here tourism has been negligible. The islands' economy has been founded upon the oil industry, manufacturing and agriculture, and it is only recently, with the decline in oil values, that much time and thought has been given to developing tourism.

A wealth of flora and fauna, a genuinely multiracial society, diversity and tolerance of religions, and the most spectacular carnival are all evidence of Trinidad and Tobago's claim to be unique within the Caribbean.

GETTING TO TRINIDAD AND TOBAGO

Trinidad's national airline, BWIA International (subtitled Trinidad and Tobago Airways Corporation), is the Caribbean's major airline. Within the Caribbean it flies to Barbados, Saint Lucia, Grenada, Martinique, Sint Maarten, Saint Kitts, Antigua, Puerto Rico, Jamaica and Curaçao, and its tentacles spread as far as Miami, New York and Toronto in North America, Caracas and Georgetown in South America, and London in Europe. Bargains are often available, either in the form of special package deals or as special arrangements for the ethnic market. It also operates a regular 'air bridge' to Tobago.

Trinidad is served regularly by many airlines partly because of its geographical location (it slots into schedules nicely as a last or penultimate stop on long-haul flights) and partly because of its commercial importance.

From the USA

Daily same-plane services are operated from New York by BWIA, Pan Am and American Airlines and from Miami by BWIA, Pan Am and Eastern. The latter two carriers can provide a same-airline service from other major cities with a change of aircraft in New York or Miami.

From Canada

Toronto is the only city linked directly with Trinidad, services being operated by BWIA and Air Canada. Nevertheless there appears to be a high proportion of Canadian visitors to Tobago, so check with the tour operators.

From London

British Airways and BWIA both serve Trinidad three times a week from London, though BWIA exclusively offers a same-airline service to Tobago. BWIA's Sunday flight is non-stop. Small discounts—around 10%—are available in the UK, though if you require any accommodation, in Trinidad or Tobago or both, you are best advised to book a package. Tour operators include Caribtours, Kestours, Kuoni and TransAtlantic Wings.

From Europe

You could fly from Brussels, Frankfurt, Milan or Zurich to Barbados with

179

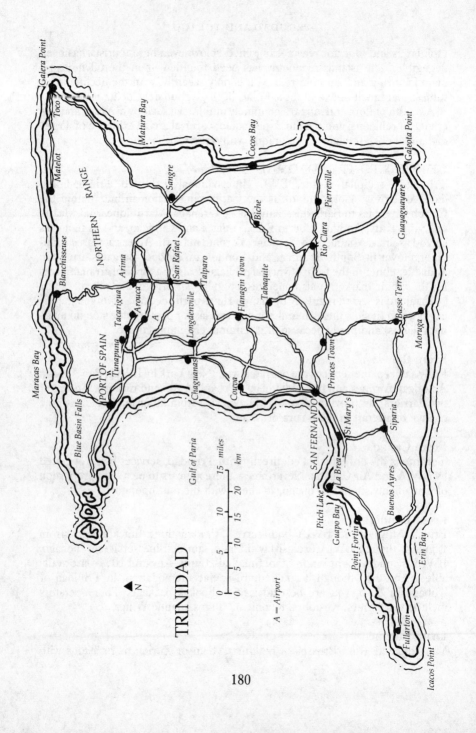

TRINIDAD

N

A = Airport

miles
km

0 5 10 15
0 5 10 15 20

Galera Point
Toco
Matura Bay
Cocos Bay
Galeota Point
Matelot
Sangre
Pierreville
Guayaguayare
Blanchisseuse
NORTHERN RANGE
Biche
Rio Clara
Basse Terre
Arima
San Rafael
Talparo
Flanagin Town
Tabaquite
Moruga
Maracas Bay
Arouca
Tacarigua
Tunapuna
Longdenville
PORT OF SPAIN
Blue Basin Falls
Chaguanas
Couva
Princes Town
Siparia
Gulf of Paria
St Mary's
SAN FERNANDO
La Brea
Buenos Ayres
Pitch Lake
Guapo Bay
Point Fortin
Erin Bay
Fullarton
Icacos Point

Caribbean Airways and take a connection from there, or connect at Amsterdam for the weekly KLM non-stop service.

Within the Caribbean

BWIA's network has already been mentioned. Additionally almost all Eastern Caribbean destinations—including pinpricks like Union in the Grenadines—are linked to Trinidad by LIAT. Air Martinique operates services to Martinique, Saint Lucia and Sint Maarten and ALM flies from Curaçao. Barbados and Antigua are regularly served by large jet aircraft.

ENTRY REGULATIONS

This is one of the few Caribbean countries which require all visitors to show a valid passport. On arrival you will be given an immigration card which you should complete and sign, keeping the carbon copy to surrender on your departure. You will also be required to show onward and/or return tickets.

Visas are not required by most nationalities likely to visit Trinidad and Tobago as tourists. Thus Commonwealth citizens generally need no visa (though there are special rules for citizens of Sri Lanka), neither do Americans, Canadians or most West Europeans (exceptions include nationals of France, Belgium and Greece). Businessmen do require a visa.

A yellow fever vaccination certificate is required if you arrive within a week from an infected area, and it is recommended in any case.

ELECTRICITY

The supply is not standardised; both 110 volts and 230 volts at 60 cycles are used, so check before plugging anything in.

CLIMATE

The tropical warmth is regulated by the trade winds as elsewhere. Average annual temperatures are 74°F at night and 84°F during the day. You can expect lower temperatures (slightly) and more rain in the highlands.

CURRENCY

The Trinidad and Tobago dollar (TTD) is approximately equivalent to US$0.28, having been devalued recently. US$1 = TTD3.60. There used to be a black market in currency, but this may have disappeared with the recent devaluation.

POPULATION

The population numbers about one million, with a greater ethnic and cultural diversity than anywhere else in the Caribbean. The melting pot of Trinidad and Tobago is one of the world's few multiracial societies. After the original

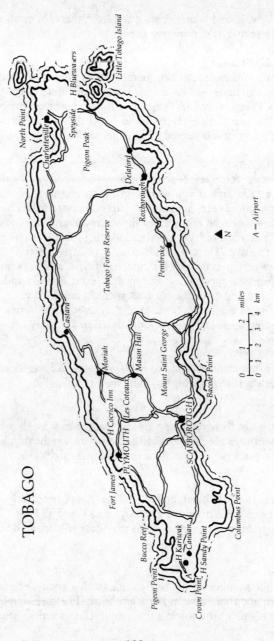

TOBAGO

North Point

Charlotteville

Speyside

H Blue waters

Little Tobago Island

Pigeon Peak

Delaford

Roxborough

Tobago Forest Reserve

Pembroke

N

A = Airport

Castara

Mason Hall

Moriah

Mount Saint George

Les Coteaux

H Coctico Inn

SCARBOROUGH

Bacolet Point

PLYMOUTH

Fort James

Columbus Point

Buco Reef

Pigeon Point

H Kariwak

H Sandy Point

A Canaan

Crown Point

miles

km

0   1   2

0   1   2   3   4

Amerindian inhabitants came the Spanish and their African slaves. Trinidad remained a possession of Spain until as late as 1797 when the British decided it was time for them to go. From the mid 19th century until 1914 the British imported East Indians and Chinese as indentured labourers to solve the contemporary labour shortage.

Thus there is an extremely rich mix of races in Trinidad and Tobago, and a diverse and fascinating cultural heritage. Besides Christians, there are many Hindus and Muslims. Each group celebrates its own religious festivals.

Most visitors to Trinidad tend to restrict their travels to Port of Spain and its environs, which is where the majority of the people live. There are other towns of some importance, however, the chief of these being San Fernando about 30 miles to the south.

LANGUAGE
The official language is English, but there is also some French, Spanish, Chinese and Hindi spoken.

FOOD AND DRINK
As you would expect with such a diversity of cultures, the food is as cosmopolitan as the people. Thus there is Indian and Chinese cuisine, West Indian, American and European, with the expected overlaps. Rum is the national drink, although there is a serviceable local beer—*Carib*. Although actually invented in Venezuela, Angostura Bitters are produced here.

MUSIC
It is said that 'Every day is carnival in Trinidad'. It's not true of course, but it's a comment on the Trinidadian attitude to life. The people find it hard to take anything seriously, which is perhaps why they are struggling a bit now the boom is over. Trinidadians in business always seem to mean well, but never quite get organised. Sometimes you love it, sometimes it drives you mad. But it certainly explains why Trinidad gave the world calypso and the steel band.

The calypso is based on a rather jaunty rhythm and (usually) satirical or 'naughty' lyrics. Although copied by musicians from other islands, none can equal the Trinidadian panache and way with words. Sometimes the lyrics are unambiguously concerned with sexual matters, such as in the classic 'Shame and Scandal in the Family', sometimes heavy use is made of *double entendre*, as in Lord Kitchener's 'Doctor Kitch', and sometimes the message is political—but always a lot of fun.

Trinidad's other great musical gift to the world, the steel band, has become increasingly versatile in recent years. The steel pan has a surprising range and, when augmented with more traditional instruments, can produce calypso, pop and even make a stab at classical tunes.

THE MAS

This is short for 'Masquerade', the carnival. The Trinidadian Mas ranks with Rio's Carnival and New Orleans' Mardi Gras as one of the world's greatest. It originated as a Latin Christian festival and is held around February/March, depending on the Christian calendar. Originally the participants dressed up (hence 'masquerade'). There are fewer costumes nowadays, although costume competitions are still arranged and fantastic designs, usually on a theme, are produced. Today the event has strong musical overtones and, of course, there is still an overwhelming atmosphere of gaiety and joyful abandon—with or without the use of artificial stimulants.

GEOGRAPHY

Trinidad and Tobago's geography is as diverse as the other facets of her character. There are, on Trinidad, the three mountain ranges which inspired the island's name (named after the Holy Trinity). The Northern Range is the highest, whilst the central hills of Montserrat and the southern Trinity Hills rise less spectacularly from the undulating countryside. Besides many small rivers, Trinidad has two big swamps, the Caroni, part of which is a bird sanctuary, and the Nariva.

Trinidad's oil reservoirs are in the south of the island, both underground and offshore. The Pitch Lake is the result of asphaltic oil seeping into a huge mud volcano. Natural gases and movement, and the evaporation of the lighter oils, caused the deposits which are so useful today. In modern times the Pitch Lake was first found in 1595 by that well-known explorer, Sir Walter Raleigh. There are a number of mud volcanoes in Trinidad which periodically erupt—causing little if any damage—but no conventional volcanoes.

Tobago is much smaller (116 square miles) than Trinidad, with its own distinct personality. The only sizeable town is the capital, Scarborough, although there are other settlements dispersed around the island, mainly on the coast. Plymouth, Speyside and Charlotteville are the most important of these. Tobago is the holiday island of the two sisters, not just for foreigners, but for Trinidadians too; they come at weekends and to recover from the Carnival. But Tobago is not a tourist centre; there are less than a dozen functioning hotels and a handful of guesthouses. Most of these are concentrated in the southwestern corner of the island along with the capital, airport and two prime tourist attractions, Bucco Reef (fabulous diving and snorkelling) and Pigeon Point (an idyllic beach). Even in this concentrated quarter there is little sign of an organised tourist infrastructure. The rest of the island, boasting good roads, is yours to discover.

HISTORY

Perhaps history holds the key to the differences between these islands. Trinidad was discovered by Christopher Columbus in 1498 on his third voyage. On spotting the three prominent peaks in the southeast he named it 'Trinidad' after the Holy Trinity. Four years later the first Spanish settlement was established, although the island saw little development at that stage. Eventually, through the intervention of a Frenchman from Grenada, Philippe de St Laurent, other nationals were allowed to settle, and introduced agriculture as the major contributor to the island's economy. Sugar quickly became a boom crop.

After Spain and England declared war, a British naval expedition arrived and took control. Trinidad remained British until independence in 1962. Agriculture had its ups and downs; as on other islands the sugar boom ended with the emancipation of the slaves in 1834, which eventually encouraged the importation of indentured labour (mainly from the Indian subcontinent).

There is no evidence that Tobago was Daniel Defoe's model for *Robinson Crusoe*, or even that the model was in the Caribbean at all. But the island's history is colourful enough. Fought over frequently by the Spanish, British, Dutch and French, they all got themselves in such a tangle that they decided to declare the island neutral. The consequence: a lack of law and order. Reprobates found this attractive and eventually the British had to possess the island. Subsequently sugar made the island prosperous until its decline and eventual union with Trinidad in the 1880s.

Port of Spain

It is not surprising that the capital of Trinidad, Port of Spain, should look towards Venezuela at its nearest point, in the northwest, being the island closest to the coast of South America. The only reasonably sized town on the island, its grander structures betray its colonial history, while bustling Frederick Street is much more redolent of the Caribbean of today with its jumble of little shops and local merchandise. The Tourist Board is in Frederick Street and will guide you to the Angostura Bitters Factory, or the Roman Catholic Cathedral of the Immaculate Conception, whichever takes your fancy.

The biggest open space in the city is the Savannah, a 200-acre plot with a racecourse in the centre, the Hyde Park of the island—or Central Park for New Yorkers—where stall-holders sell popcorn or bananas, and where Trinidadians and visitors can jog, ride, picnic or listen to the band. Not a place, however, where women should walk alone after dark.

FLORA AND FAUNA

The flora, fauna and bird life of Trinidad and Tobago form a complete contrast to that found anywhere else in the Caribbean. This is because the islands were once part of South America, and are still close enough to retain the same

Hummingbird feeding its young

botanical and zoological make-up. The Botanic Gardens north of Port of Spain display the native flowers and shrubs, whilst the indigenous wildlife is housed in the Emperor Valley Zoo.

Trinidad's national bird is the scarlet ibis which is protected in the Caroni Bird Sanctuary. There are also nineteen different species of hummingbird in Trinidad and seven in Tobago. Frigate birds, herons, kingfishers, toucans and kiskadees are just some of the 400 species of birdlife to be found on these two islands.

CALENDAR
Although the Mas is the main festival on the islands, several others are celebrated. The most important of these are *Hosein*, a Muslim festival taking place in the autumn and lasting three days, and *Diwali*, the Hindu festival of light in October/November.

GETTING AROUND
The fact that petrol is cheap means that people are not afraid to use it. The people's comparative wealth means that there are many motor vehicles of all types. Those without their own transport tend to use *públicos* and taxis to a great extent. Although there are government-operated bus services, taxi fares are comparatively low. *Público* or *point* (shared) taxi rides cost about 50 cents a trip within Port of Spain. These are identified by the prefix 'H' on their licence plates and their route is displayed on the windshield. Two useful pick-up points for taxis are Independence Square and the corner of Park Street.

Port of Spain has too many traffic jams to make it worthwhile hiring a car. If you do you may find a large deposit is payable, and an international driving licence is required. Booking in advance is advisable and charges are dearer than on other Caribbean islands. Drive *on the left* in Trinidad and Tobago.

WHERE TO STAY IN TRINIDAD

From a tour operator's point of view accommodation in Trinidad and Tobago is something of a disaster area. Trinidad—which means, effectively, Port of Spain—is geared to the businessman, with high prices not necessarily allied to high standards.

If money is no object and you are staying in Port of Spain, there is either the **Hilton** or the **Holiday Inn.** They are well-sited, comfortable and have a full range of facilities. Otherwise try the **Kapok,** a little way off the Savannah. All these have a swimming pool and air-conditioning. If you have to stay in Port of Spain and have to do so cheaply, try one of the guesthouses. They're only a little more than guesthouses of a similar standard elsewhere in the region, though not normally central. **Monique's** seems to be satisfactory.

Accommodation in Trinidad
Daily summer rates in US$EP

	Single	Double
Hotels		
Bel Air, Piarco International Airport (tel. (664) 4771)	45–52	60–70
Chaconia Inn, 106 Saddle Road, Maraval, Port of Spain (tel. (629) 2101)	70–80	85–95
Hilton, Port of Spain (tel. (624) 3211)	105–132	120–143
Holiday Inn, Wrightson Road, Port of Spain (tel. (625) 3361)	79–90	89–100
Kapok, 16/18 Cotton Hill, St Clair, Port of Spain (tel. (622) 6441)	60–80	72–92
Guesthouses		
Central Guesthouse, 45 Murray Street, Woodbrook, Port of Spain (tel. (622) 7137)	33	33
Fabienne's, 15 Belle Smythe Street, Woodbrook, Port of Spain (tel. (622) 2773)	15–20	30
Hillcrest Haven Guesthouse, 7a Hillcrest Avenue, Cascade, Port of Spain (tel. (624) 1344)	10–12	15–18
Monique's, 114 Saddle Road, Maraval, Port of Spain (tel. (629) 2233)	22	28

EATING OUT

If you are determined to sample the local specialities you could try armadillo stew or fried iguana. Otherwise there are excellent menus from all over the world to be found in Port of Spain, not only in the best hotels but in tiny restaurants dotted around the town. But be warned that not everyone accepts credit cards and imported wines are very expensive.

187

NIGHTLIFE
There is something every night for lovers of live (and lively) music. Start your search at the **Hilton** or **Holiday Inn**. Tobago is quieter altogether, and more romantic.

SPORT
The beaches in the north and east are best, where surfing is possible, especially in winter months. Sea fishing for exotic catches can be arranged, along with hunting and sailing. The Tourist Board or your hotel reception can give up-to-date information. Tennis can be found at the **Hilton Hotel** and local clubs, and at the public courts in the town. Golf is at **Moka Golf Club** in Maraval, near Port of Spain. Cricket enthusiasts will already know Trinidad's reputation for the game. Matches are held in Port of Spain from January to June.

WHERE TO STAY IN TOBAGO
From an international standpoint many of Tobago's hotels are not worthy even of mention. Many of the others undergo regular management changes. The island has for many years sustained a reputation for slow and surly service which, however, is unjustified. Although some hotels do display these symptoms, others are good.

Kariwak is the hotel which challenges the allegations of hotel mismanagement in Tobago. As well-managed a small hotel as any in the Caribbean, it is talked about as the best hotel on the island, irrespective of price. There are twenty air-conditioned rooms in ten duplexes set around a swimming pool among lush tropical foliage. Food is excellently prepared 'Caribbean cuisine'—delicious! Service can't be faulted. It's about five minutes from the beach (at Crown Reef) and five minutes from the airport.

Sandy Point is also recommended. It is rather bigger, and on the beach with a pool. Accommodation (which, being on the condominium basis, offers self-catering facilities) comprises studios or spacious split-level suites. Restaurant service is ultra-quick (so that the Trinidadian guests can retire to their television sets) and the food is tasty, though not quite up to Kariwak's standard.

Arnos Vale is officially a contender for the title of the island's top hotel. Set in a fantastic 40 acres of thickly vegetated grounds displaying much of Tobago's prized flora and birdlife, it certainly has the most atmosphere. Accommodation is in cottages scattered about, rooms in the main building, or rooms down by the beach. Although the food is not brilliant, there have been recent management changes.

Mount Irvine Bay was, long years ago, the island's top hotel, but it could not be considered for that title nowadays. At the end of 1985, however, the hotel was taken over by Taj Hotels, a very good Indian hotel group. If the new management imbues the property with the style and management quality normally practised by this group, then perhaps Mount Irvine will regain its former status. The spacious grounds include an 18-hole golf course.

The success of **Bluewaters Inn** will depend largely on its management. This place is a real hideaway, situated on the beach in a quiet little bay at the far end of the island opposite Bird of Paradise Island. Accommodation is limited to a few cabanas. There is a tennis court. The food is excellent. During a recent visit the managers were a mildly eccentric couple doing a second stint and under their control one could have a fantastically relaxing, almost hermit-like two weeks (or two years). Write your first novel here. One thing to watch—the rather high prices are not justified by the quality of the accommodation (although, to be fair, renovations are planned in the near future, and may already be in progress).

Accommodation in Tobago
Daily summer rates in US$

	Single	Double
Hotels		
Arnos Vale, Culloden Bay, near Plymouth (tel. (639) 2881)	MAP 86	MAP 105
Bluewaters Inn, Batteaux Bay, Speyside (tel. (639) 4341)	MAP 60	MAP 105
Cocrico Inn, Plymouth (tel. (639) 2961)	EP 30–35	EP 36–44
Crown Reef, Store Bay (tel. (639) 8571)	EP 80	EP 121
Kariwak Village, Crown Point (tel. (639) 8545)	EP 36	EP 50
	MAP 50	MAP 76
Mount Irvine Bay, Black Rock (tel. (639) 8871)	EP 50–70	EP 50–70
Sandy Point Beach Club, Crown Point (tel. (639) 8533)	EP 50–60	EP 60–70
	MAP 65–76	MAP 90–100
Turtle Beach, Turtle Beach, near Plymouth (tel. (639) 2851)	EP 48–75	EP 56–83
Guesthouses		
Coral Reef, Milford Road (tel. (639) 2536)	MAP 33	MAP 50
Della Mira, Windward Road, Scarborough (tel. (639) 2531)	EP 24	EP 40

Expect prices at Arnos Vale and Mount Irvine Bay to be about double in the winter months. Rates at Kariwak and Sandy Point will be about 25% more.

(Tax and service to be added.)

SHOPPING
If you are looking for sophisticated shopping facilities, you will be disappointed with Trinidad and Tobago. In Port of Spain the best shops are to be found around Independence Square and in Frederick Street, with its bustling little stores full of local jewellery and wood carvings, while in Tobago the hotel arcades, particularly those at the **Mount Irvine** and the **Crown Reef**, are the best hunting grounds.

189

SPORT

Tobago is the place to visit for snorkelling, especially at Buccoo Reef at low tide to see the coral gardens just under the water. The clear water round Tobago makes it popular with divers as well and there are several clubs offering this facility with instruction. Bird watchers will find much to keep them occupied here as well as on Trinidad, and the Mount Irvine Golf Club at Scarborough is famous throughout the world.

Netherlands Antilles

Known sometimes as 'The ABC Islands', Aruba, Bonaire and Curaçao form, with Sint Maarten, Saba and Sint Eustatius, the Netherlands Antilles. The Dutch influence is noticeable here, particularly in the architecture and cleanliness.

GETTING TO THE NETHERLANDS ANTILLES

Flight patterns are based both on commercial links and the requirements of the tourist industry. Thus connections with South America are more common than those with other Caribbean islands, and there are direct flights from the United States to all three islands.

From the USA

ALM, the national airline, serves all three islands from Miami and New York. Eastern flies to Curaçao and Aruba from Miami and Philadelphia, and American connects New York with the same two islands.

From Canada

Connect through New York or Miami as above.

From London

It is certainly worth checking whether there are any reasonable fares from or via Amsterdam, the only European point with direct flights to Aruba and Curaçao. Otherwise look at travelling via Miami, particularly if there are bargains available on that route (British Airways, Pan Am and Virgin Atlantic). You will need a visa if travelling via the US.

From Europe

If it's convenient to you, flights from Amsterdam should be your best bet. Otherwise you can fly via Miami from Berlin, Hamburg, Madrid and Paris (all on Pan Am), Oslo (Northwest Orient) and Madrid (Iberia and Aeromexico). Aeromexico and Delta fly to Miami from Paris and Lufthansa operates from Düsseldorf and Frankfurt.

Within the Caribbean

The three islands are linked together by ALM services; ALM also flies from Curaçao and Aruba up to Sint Maarten, San Juan and Santo Domingo (Santo Domingo is also served from Curaçao by Viasa and Dominicana). Curaçao is also linked with Haiti, Kingston (both services operated by ALM) and Trinidad (ALM and BWIA). The only other services are with Latin American countries. You can fly into both Curaçao and Aruba from Barranquilla, Bogotá, Medellín, Caracas and Panama; Aruba has links with Guayaquil, Quito and Lima, whilst there are services into Curaçao from Guatemala and San José.

ENTRY REGULATIONS

Visas are not normally required for stays of less than fourteen days. Some nationalities, if staying longer, may need a Certificate of Temporary Admission. If you have recently come from, or transited, a yellow fever endemic zone (which includes large areas of South America) you will need to show proof of inoculation.

ELECTRICITY

The supply varies between 110 and 130 volts (127 volts in Bonaire), roughly the same as in the US.

CLIMATE

It can become very hot, though there are usually cooling breezes. Temperatures average 75°F to 90°F. There is little rain, but when it does come it tends to be in November and December.

CURRENCY

Official currency is the Netherlands Antilles florin or guilder (AFL) although US dollars will be accepted. The current exchange rate is US$1=AFL1.80.

POPULATION

The total population is around 245,000; about 165,500 of these live in Curaçao, 68,000 in Aruba and 10,000 in Bonaire. Curaçao in particular is very cosmopolitan, with about 40 different nationalities resident and some 16% of the population born off the island.

LANGUAGE

The principal languages are Papiamento and Dutch with English very widely spoken.

191

CURAÇAO

Originally discovered by the Spanish in 1499, Curaçao first became a Dutch possession in 1634. Peter Stuyvesant became Governor in 1642 for a period. From the late 17th to the early 19th centuries both the British and French attempted to take the island; the British were successful in 1800 and 1807, but Curaçao was handed back to the Netherlands in 1815 by the Treaty of Paris.

Its early prosperity was based on the slave trade, so it entered a period of economic decline with the abolition of slavery in 1863. During more recent times oil has been the major industry, though tourism is now an important industry (second in fact) and there is some local manufacturing—from Curaçao liqueur and Amstel beer to soap, cigarettes and batteries.

CALENDAR
The pre-Lent Carnival is the biggest event of the year and hotel accommodation may be scarce, so book well ahead.

WHERE TO STAY
Daily summer rate per room in US$

Name	No. of rooms	Double EP	Double MAP
Avila Beach Hotel (tel. 614377)	45	55	105
Coral Cliff Hotel (tel. 641610)	35	50	86
Curaçao Concorde (tel. 625000)	200	80	150
Curaçao Plaza Hotel (tel. 612500)	254	80	134
Hotel Holland (tel. 81120)	20	41	
Hotel San Marco (tel. 612988)	60	36	
Las Palmas Hotel (tel. 625200)	98		107
Park Hotel (tel. 623112)	81	28	
Princess Beach Hotel (tel. 614944)	140	64	124
Troupial Inn (tel. 78200)	74	38	

There is a 5% government tax and usually a 10% service charge to be added to these rates.

EATING OUT
Many of the hotels feature their own entertainment in the evenings, usually a cabaret or band and dancing. All of those listed above have a restaurant. There are also a number of nightclubs and discos in addition to pubs and bars, many of which feature a band or pianist.

Restaurants in Curaçao reflect the cosmopolitan nature of the island: there's a bistro serving Swiss and French cuisine (**Bistro Le Clochard**), Scandinavian food served in a 200-year-old mansion, Indonesian Rijsttafel, Italian

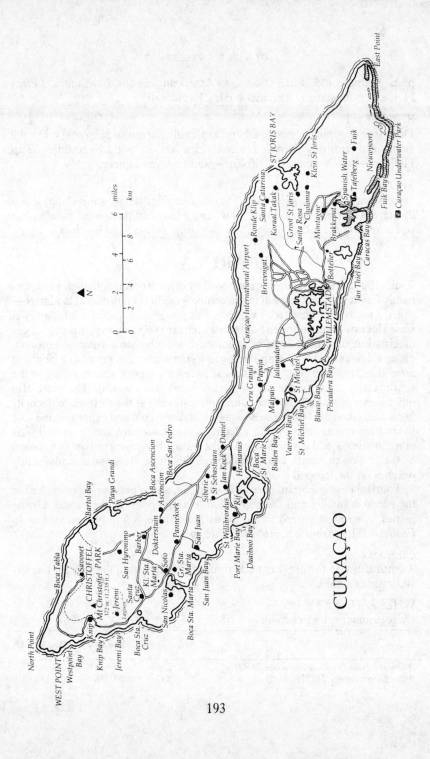

CURAÇAO

East Point

Curaçao Underwater Park

Fuik
Nieuwpoort
Tafelberg
Spanish Water
Caracas Bay
Fuik Bay
Jan Thiel Bay
Brakkeput
Montañu
Klein St Joris
ST JORIS BAY
Groot St Joris
Santa Rosa
Cholorna
Botteller
Koraal Takak
Santa Catarina
WILLEMSTAD
Ronde Klip
Piscadera Bay
Blauwe Bay
Brievengat
Juliandorp
St Michiel Bay
Curaçao International Airport
St Michiel
Vaersen Bay
Papaja
Bullen Bay
Ceru Grandi
St Marie
Malpais
Boca
Daniel
St Marie
Jan Kock
Hermanus
Siberie
St Sebastiaan
Rif
Kip
Port Marie Bay
St Willibrordus
Daaibooi Bay
Boca San Pedro
San Juan
Boca Ascencion
Pannekoek
Ascencion
Dokterstuin
Playa Grandi
Barber
Gr. Sta.
Marta
Sta.
Bartol Bay
Kl. Sta.
Marta
San Juan Bay
Soto
San Hyronimo
Boca Tabla
Santa
Cruz
San Nicolas
Sacomet
Boca Sta. Marta
CHRISTOFFEL
PARK
Jeremi
Boca Sta.
Cruz
Mt Christoffel
372 m (1,239 ft.)
Knip
Knip Bay
WEST POINT
Jeremi Bay
Westpoint
Bay
North Point

N

miles
0   2   4   6
0 2 4 6 8
km

193

pasta, Chinese and Dutch cuisine, an American 'cowboy' steakhouse, a Pizza Hut, and even some restaurants serving local food!

SHOPPING
Duty-free shopping is possible here, especially for cruise passengers, but the shops can get very crowded when ships are in port. Specialities from Holland—Dutch cheeses, Delftware—and Curaçao liqueur.

SPORT
Watersports—sailing, swimming, sunning, surfing, skiing, snorkelling, scuba diving, sea fishing—are available. To move a little further around the alphabet you have to come inland to golf, tennis, riding, football and baseball.

ARUBA

Aruba is a particularly interesting island to drive around. Although predominantly flat, it has a conical hill in the centre—the best known local landmark—called **Hooiberg** ('Haystack') which is volcanic in origin. Not too far away at **Casi Bari** are some rounded boulders which are supposed to be a puzzle to geologists but then might just be connected with the same volcanic eruption. Other oddities are the **Watapana** (or Divi-Divi) tree; this grows to a height of around eight to ten feet, then takes a horizontal aspect, always facing to the southwest (a result of the prevailing northeast trade winds). There are also other sights of historical or economic interest, such as the disused gold smelting works (almost 3,000 pounds of gold was discovered and exported), the aloe fields (this cactus seems to be effective against sunburn and apparently has other medicinal and cosmetic uses) and a natural bridge, carved out of the coral by the sea, on the north coast. Besides all this there are some splendid sandy beaches on the leeward coast.

Tourism is as important here as in Curaçao, and is perhaps more evident as the island is smaller and the population less. Shopping in the capital, **Oranjestad,** is strongly geared to the tourist, and there is a duty-free zone as in Curaçao. The nightlife is probably better here.

CALENDAR
As with Curaçao the pre-Lent Carnival is the highlight of the year for tourists and residents alike.

WHERE TO STAY
Daily summer rates per room in US$

Name	No. of rooms	Double EP	Double MAP
Americana Aruba Hotel and Casino (tel. 24500)	206	70	
Aruba Beach Club (tel. 24595)	131	56	115

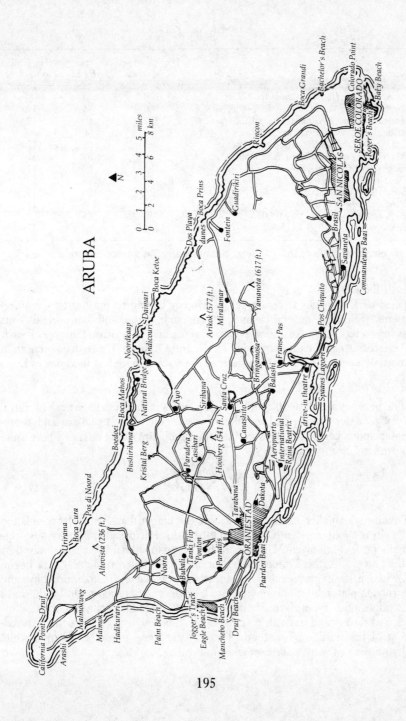

ARUBA

California Point—Druif
Arashi
Malmok
Hadikurari
Palm Beach
Jogger's Track
Eagle Beach
Manchebo Beach
Druif Beach
Paarden Baai
Noord
Bubali
Tanki Flip
Ponton
Paradis
Uriramo
Boca Cura
Pos di Noord
Altovista (236 ft.)
Malmokweg
Bushiribana
Kristal Berg
Paradera
Casibari
Hooiberg (541 ft.)
Canashito
Aeropuerto International Reina Beatrix
Dakota
Tarabana
ORANJESTAD

Boedoei—Boca Mahos
Natural Bridge
Ayo
Siribana
Santa Cruz
Balashi
Franse Pas
Brinsamosa
drive-in theatre
Spaans Lagoen

Noordkaap
Andicouri
Daimari
Boca Ketoe
Arikok (577 ft.)
Miralamar
Yamanota (617 ft.)
Pos Chiquito
Commandeurs Baai
Savaneta
Brasil

Dos Playa
dunes
Boca Prins
Fontein
Guadirikiri

Boca Grandi
Rincon
SAN NICOLAS
SEROE COLORADO
Roger's Beach
Bachelor's Beach
Colorado Point
Baty Beach

N

0 1 2 3 4 5 miles
0 2 4 6 8 km

Name	Daily summer rates per room in US$		
	No. of rooms	Double EP	Double MAP
Aruba Caribbean Hotel and Casino (tel. 22250)	200	85	
Aruba Concorde Hotel and Casino (tel. 24466)	500	85	163
Aruba Palm Beach Hotel and Casino (tel. 23900)	200	60	134
Atlantis Apartahoteles and Villas (tel. 24343)	80	60	
Best Western Manchebo Beach (tel. 23444)	71	65	129
Best Western Talk Of The Town (tel. 23380)	64	60	124
Bushiri Beach Hotel (tel. 25216)	50	60	116
Divi Divi Beach Hotel (tel. 23300)	152	75	139
Dutch Village (tel. 32300)	28	110	174
Holiday Inn Aruba (tel. 23600)	387	66	130
Playa Linda Beach Resort (tel. 31000)	60	85	
Tamarijn Beach Hotel (tel. 24150)	204	60	124

Government tax is again 5% here, but normally the service charge will be 15%.

EATING OUT
After dark activities here are very obviously geared to the tourist's requirements. There are several casinos, a Paris-style revue, and dance bands from
swing to steel pan. Restaurants again are diverse: Mexican, Chinese, Italian,
American steakhouses, Argentine steaks and German. There does seem to be
more of a preponderance of American diners and more fast food places here.

SPORT
The beaches are all public, and are the island's main claim to fame. Visibility is
very good for driving and instruction is available. The usual sea and shore-
based sports can be found as well as tennis, golf and riding inland. There's also
a gym and beauty parlour.

BONAIRE

Bonaire is a smaller island than Curaçao but bigger than Aruba. Its population
density is about one-tenth of each of the others. Historically, Bonaire was originally no less important. Discovered by the Spanish in 1499 and colonised by
them in 1527, the Dutch took over in 1634. Salt production was begun
for which slaves were imported, and there was some livestock breeding and
corn was planted. Conditions dictated, however, that salt would be the most
lucrative industry, the island being somewhat arid. This declined with the abolition of slavery and has only recently been restarted, using a more modern version of the traditional method. The salt-pans and mounds of bright white
drying sea salt will be seen on an island drive.

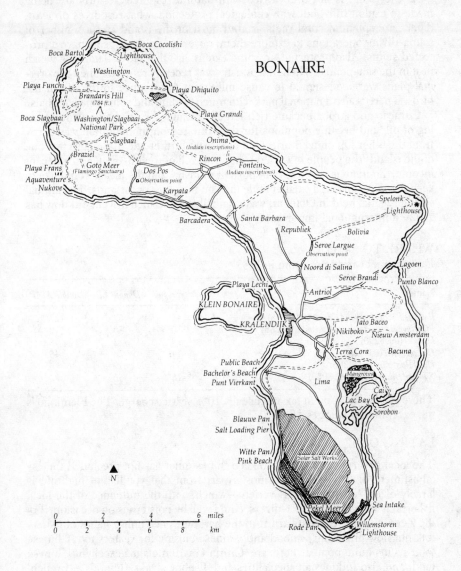

BONAIRE

Boca Cocolishi
Boca Bartol
Lighthouse
Washington
Playa Funchi
Boca Slagbaai
Brandaris Hill
(784 ft.)
Playa Dhiquito
Playa Grandi
Washington/Slagbaai
National Park
Slagbaai
Onima
(Indian inscriptions)
Braziel
Rincon
Fontein
(Indian inscriptions)
Playa Frans
Goto Meer
(Flamingo Sanctuary)
Dos Pos
Aquaventure
Nukove
Observation point
Karpata
Spelonk
Lighthouse
Barcadera
Santa Barbara
Republiek
Bolivia
Seroe Largue
Observation point
Lagoen
Noord di Salina
Seroe Brandi
Punto Blanco
Playa Lechi
Antriol
KLEIN BONAIRE
KRALENDIJK
Jato Baceo
Nikiboko
Nieuw Amsterdam
Terra Cora
Bacuna
Public Beach
Bachelor's Beach
Punt Vierkant
Lima
Mangroves
Cai
Lac Bay
Sorobon
Blauwe Pan
Salt Loading Pier
Witte Pan
Pink Beach
Solar Salt Works
Sea Intake
Pekel Meer
Rode Pan
Willemstoren
Lighthouse

N

| 0 | | 2 | | 4 | | 6 | miles |
| 0 | 2 | 4 | 6 | 8 | | | km |

As the island is not overblessed with natural resources, efforts are being made to exploit fully, but with ecological protection, what resources do exist. There are splendid coral reefs around most of the island and a number of scuba-diving operations to explore them; nevertheless these reefs have a protected status. Also protected, to some extent, are the native flamingos which nest in the salt-ponds. When the industry was recently re-established the original plans were redesigned to cause minimum disturbance to the life of the birds. There is also a national park with much birdlife and some small animals.

Curaçao and Aruba became rich largely through the production and refining of oil, and became populous for the same reason; immigration was partly from the other Dutch territories, but also from further afield. Bonaire was one of the islands the people migrated from in search of wealth, or at least a decent income. Tourism is now a very important industry, but the locals would like to keep it quieter and on a smaller scale than on the other two islands. The annual sailing regatta, held in October, was originally a fishermen's event but now has attained international importance.

WHERE TO STAY
Daily summer rates per room in US$

Name	No. of rooms	Double EP	Double MAP
Bonaire Beach Hotel and Casino (tel. 8448)	145	62	122
Flamingo Beach Hotel and Casino (tel. 8285)	110	50	110
Habitat (tel. 8290)	19	52	96
Hilltop Hotel (tel. 4266)	14	26	45
Hotel Rochaline (tel. 8286)	35		
Sorobon Beach Resort (tel. 8080)	16	50	

There is 5% government tax and usually 10% service charge. The Flamingo is the exception; it charges 15%.

EATING OUT

The local government's desire to keep things quiet has not precluded the establishment of a couple of casinos. Apart from that you'll find nightlife is largely of the 'do-it-yourself' variety—which, with the influence of the local fishermen and visiting scuba-divers, could well be boisterous on occasion. Try the **Zeezicht Bar & Restaurant** in the harbour, once only a haunt of fisherfolk but now providing seafood and Chinese cuisine for visitors too. Chinese food seems quite popular here: the **China Garden** claims excellent Chinese food, and also Indonesian specialities and T-bone steaks. There's a 'French' bistro, a seafood specialist and a Dutch restaurant. The hotel restaurants are generally more in the 'international' mode.

Part III

GREATER ANTILLES

Collecting coconuts

HAITI

My travelling has taken me throughout Europe and Asia, to the Indian subcontinent, North Africa, the United States and Mexico, yet I have never been anywhere like Haiti. Haiti has been described as 'West Africa in the Caribbean', but in truth I feel it must be unique. The history of this country and its people is one of hardship, strife, independence and forced insularity. Haiti's achievement in attaining and keeping independence has been so unusual and contrary to prevailing political philosophy that the people have suffered from misrepresentation ever since.

GETTING TO HAITI
International links with Haiti are regional, and are based on trade rather than tourism, and even then Haiti is more of a stop on a long-haul route than a destination in its own right.

From the USA
Air France, ALM and Eastern call in here from Miami, and ALM, Eastern and

American Airlines from New York. Haiti Air operates 737s daily from both points. Eastern and American may have through connections from elsewhere in the States.

From Canada
Air Canada flies down from Montreal.

From London
Traditionally the best route has been via Miami, which was both convenient and inexpensive when Air Florida was in business. You could try the cheapest possible London–Miami return and then a sector fare. Otherwise perhaps fly in through Kingston in Jamaica on British Airways and take a sector fare on Air Jamaica or ALM from there.

From Europe
Air France operates scheduled services from Paris. Alternatively you could fly from Madrid to San Juan (Avianca or Iberia) or on Iberia from Madrid to Santo Domingo.

Within the Caribbean
Haiti has air links with its near neighbours but few further afield in the Caribbean. Air Jamaica flies here from Kingston and Montego Bay in addition to San Juan, which, along with Martinique, Guadeloupe and Cayenne (in South America) is also served by Air France. ALM flies to Kingston and Curaçao from here, whilst Dominicana flies in from Santo Domingo. There are some links with South America: Avianca comes here from Bogotá and Barranquilla, COPA from Panama and Air Surinam from Paramaribo.

ENTRY REGULATIONS
No visa is required by citizens of the following countries: Austria, Belgium, Canada, Denmark, West Germany, Israel, Liechtenstein, Luxembourg, the Netherlands, Switzerland, the United Kingdom of Great Britain and Northern Ireland (British passport holders from the Commonwealth or British colonies should check with their nearest Haitian Consulate) and the USA. Australian and New Zealand passport holders will need a visa, which costs around US$5. A tourist card is issued on arrival in Haiti.

ELECTRICITY
The supply is 110–120 volts at 60 cycles, about the same as in the US.

CLIMATE
Very much dependent on altitude. The average annual temperature is 80°F in

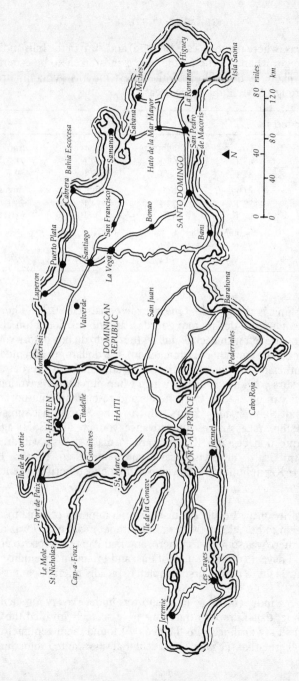

HISPANIOLA: HAITI AND DOMINICAN REPUBLIC

the coastal areas (where the towns are situated) and 76°F in the hills and mountains. It is at night when the cool of the hills is most likely to be experienced. Rain is most likely in the hills, and the driest months generally are from December through March, the tourist season.

Average temperatures

Month	January	February	March	April
Average low	68°F	68°F	69°F	71°F
Average high	87°F	88°F	89°F	89°F
Month	May	June	July	August
Average low	72°F	73°F	74°F	73°F
Average high	90°F	93°F	94°F	93°F
Month	September	October	November	December
Average low	72°F	72°F	71°F	69°F
Average high	91°F	90°F	88°F	87°F

CURRENCY

The currency unit is the gourde. One gourde equals US$0.20. There is no charge for changing US dollars into gourdes, and no restriction on changing any gourdes you are left with back to dollars (but try to do this before you get to the airport in case the bank there is unmanned). US dollars are accepted everywhere at the official rate. Note that prices are quoted in both gourdes and US dollars, so be sure you know which is which when purchasing anything.

Credit cards can be used in many hotels and restaurants, but not in travel agencies (except Southerlands Tours, which is the American Express agent and will therefore take Amex—and advance you up to US$50 against a personal cheque if necessary). If you want to make a cash withdrawal on your Bank-Americard or MasterCard you should go to the Banque Nationale de la République d'Haïti which is the only authorised agent.

POPULATION

The vast majority of the people are black, with a minority of mulattos. Power and wealth seem to be held by the few, but without racial bias. I was told that until recently there was some racism here, and that Papa Doc rose to power on a racist ticket. I have no corroboration of this, and I found no prejudice myself. In fact I found Haiti to be the first completely racially tolerant country I have ever visited.

Haiti has been independent so long, and was under slavery for such a relatively short time, that European traditions have scarcely invaded the African way of life. In all my dealings with the people I found them genuinely helpful and loving. It is true that the poor in particular always wanted something from me, usually money, and if all I had was the shirt on my back they would willingly take that, a trait which can be annoying. But even when no money was forthcoming, people were anxious to help, and one guide, Jacques, even offered to lend me some.

Before I arrived in Haiti, I had been told (in Jamaica) two things about the Haitian people: that they are very cultured and that they live in fear. I found more truth in the former than in the latter. In general I found the people uncowed by authority. I even witnessed occasions when the police were jeered for over-zealousness in the execution of formality. And the police provide food and shelter to the needy on occasion. It should be noted that although visitors need a permit to travel around the country, the native is free to go where he pleases.

Sometimes I found the friendliness of the people a handicap. It means the solo traveller need never be alone, but for me it caused difficulties in working—plenty to write about Haiti, and no time to write it!

LANGUAGE
The official language is French, but only a minority speak it. Everybody speaks Creole. Creole is more than a patois, it is as different from French as Italian is from Spanish. Thus if you speak to the poor people, especially in rural areas, in French, they will be unable to understand you. At the airport some English is spoken, but to a far lesser extent in Port-au-Prince. I found English spoken more in Le Cap than in the capital. There is some Spanish spoken, largely because of the Dominicans here.

FOOD AND DRINK
Haitian food is good but piquant and tough on the teeth. Everything seems to be prepared to be as tough as possible—you even need a hacksaw for the bananas. Maybe the Haitians like a good chew; almost all have perfect teeth. If your teeth are less than perfect be careful what you eat and particularly avoid Tassot Creole.

The other characteristic of the food is the piquant sauces. Although French and 'International' cuisine of a high standard are available, the food is generally Haitian: the ingredients are Caribbean yet prepared in a style to be found nowhere else.

Local dishes are *lambi* (conch), lobster, *steak-au-poivre*, chicken Creole, *riz 'djon djon'* (rice with black mushrooms) and the inevitable *riz et pois*—peas 'n' rice (really rice and beans).

The national drink is Barbancourt rum; the industry was established a little over a hundred years ago. Rum punch is a popular drink and easily available in hotels and tourist haunts. There is a local beer, named 'Prestige', and imported varieties.

203

SHOPPING, BANKING AND OFFICE HOURS

Life begins at dawn in Haiti, and, for many, before that. From 4.30 am the streets become increasingly populated and by 7.30 am they are a hive of activity. Although shops catering for the tourists stay open late, you should note that business hours are generally 8 am to 4 pm; the tourist office at Avenue Marie-Jeanne in Port-au-Prince is open from 8 am to 2 pm and banks from 9 am to 1 pm. So try to get your business done in the morning.

GUIDES

These come in two categories, official and unofficial, although one rarely encounters an official one. Guides can cost you a lot of money, or save you a lot. It depends on the guide.

Wherever you go you will be found by someone wishing to help you. If you want a guide he will assure you that he is the best and can help you save money. If you don't want a guide then he 'understands' and isn't one.

The independent traveller is classed as a tourist, and few Haitians comprehend that you are not in a mad rush to see all the tourist sights, watch a Voodoo ceremony, buy paintings, souvenirs or a woman. But if you are persistent without being offensive you will be alright. A guide can cost you money by taking you to tourist functions and restaurants and by travelling. A cheap restaurant will be expensive if you pay for two people, and all travel costs will be doubled. Because of the discrepancy between native living costs and tourist prices, a guide can save the tourist a lot of money. Yet if you speak Creole or French you can easily find these cheap places yourself and live at perhaps just double native costs.

You may find a guide useful if you can remain in control and perhaps use his services for just the first day or two, until you know your way around. Jacques, who can be found outside the Hotel Beau Rivage, has useful contacts, and will keep a low profile if you prefer just to wander rather than be taken anywhere specific.

THE ARTS

Painting is the most noticeable of the Haitian arts. There are a few painters of real talent, in the primitive style, and many others who have more enthusiasm than ability. But the real volume is in the field of commercial art, whether it be the exuberant decoration of the tap-taps or the hurried daubings produced in vast quantities for the tourist market. More impressive are the mahogany carvings. Here a far greater level of skill is evident, the fine finish of the woodwork proving a strong contrast to the crude work executed in Jamaica. Much of this is also functional, and often a strong inventiveness of design is evident, and it is worth buying something.

Music and dance are surprisingly undeveloped in Haiti. The only real style of music which can be perceived as indigenous is that based on the Voodoo ceremonies; during the day, in restaurants and so on, you are more likely to hear recorded American, French or British music. And dance routines, whilst at least in rhythm to the music, are fairly basic and lack inventiveness, although Haitians appreciate good dancing. In Cap Haïtien I saw three men dancing on a raised platform to a small orchestra; a huge crowd was strongly appreciative of the fine display they were given.

VOODOO

In Haiti there is complete religious tolerance, although Roman Catholicism is the official religion. There are some Protestant churches founded by missionaries from North America. Voodoo is an African religion no more sinister than Christianity, which it exists alongside. Most Haitians attend both Roman Catholic and Voodoo services, particularly in the rural areas. I visited only a tourist Voodoo ceremony, and thus know insufficient about it to be able to give an accurate account. Therefore I quote below an extract from an official explanation of the cult:

'A knowledge, even elementary, of Africa and its peoples is essential if we want to understand and study Voodooism. Haitian Voodooism, according to many ethnologists, cannot claim kinships with all the regions of Black Africa. It has its origins rather in religions practised in Dahomey and Nigeria, and to a somewhat lesser extent in ritual practices in the Congo, Angola, Senegal and Guinea. We find the same organisation of the clergy, the same supernatural world, and the same ritual. The priest is a "houngan" or "mambo", and the servants of the divinity are "hounsis".

Under the supreme God, called the Grand Master and without whose permission nothing can happen, there are groups of spirits, some of them hierarchised, called Loas. They are appointed by God to supervise man and the universe. But in popular Haitian imagination they become personalities endowed with will, intelligence and passions. Hence their anthropomorphism. In Haitian belief, the Loas remain powers to whom they appeal to lavish their benefits on human beings. These divinities are honoured in ceremonies of service, obligation or duty.

The dance is intimately associated with the Voodoo religion and occupies such an essential place in it that we could almost define Voodooism as a religion expressed through the dance. The drum which beats the rhythm of these dances has become the very symbol of Voodooism. Its songs are hymns composed in honour of the divinities. These songs are powerful and original, sometimes slow and nostalgic, sometimes rousing. During the cere-

205

monies, singing is always accompanied by dancing; the actual dances vary from one rite to another. The principal musical instruments played at these ceremonies are drums; they are made of oak, mahogany or pine and covered with ox-hide.

The main symbols employed in Voodoo ceremonies are called veve. They are drawn by hand on the ground with ashes, flour or oatmeal.

The Voodoo temple is called a Houmfort. It contains flags in the national colours, drums, a few pictures of Catholic saints, and certain veve symbols.

It is certain that Voodooism played a large part in the genesis and development of the War of Independence. There is no doubt that certain leaders, Macandal, Boukman, Biassou or Romaine the prophetess, were high priests of Voodooism. All Haitian history books consider the famous ceremony of the Caiman wood as one of the events which originally contributed to the War of Independence. It was one of a number of pacts under which "Dahomians engaged in a perilous enterprise bound themselves with their partners" thereby creating a spirit of solidarity and unlimited confidence between the partners concerned, and absolute discretion. There is no doubt that these African leaders used Voodooism to instil dynamism into the masses under their orders and imbue them with the mystique that is essential to the accomplishment of great tasks.

But just as the Christianity of the Middle Ages is not the Christianity of today, so Voodooism is increasingly losing ground. It is a religion of the night, and the spread of electricity and literacy in country districts is causing it to decline.

Former President François Duvalier said: "I remain convinced that Voodooism, an extremely interesting religious phenomenon, is condemned to disappear sooner or later, and that in the more or less near future it will belong uniquely to our folklore." '

SOME HINTS

Maintain a plentiful supply of small change. Taxis, tap-taps and others rarely appear to have change and will try to get away without giving you any if you thrust a dollar bill at them.

Mosquito coils are essential in Cap Haïtien. They can be bought locally, but it is a good idea to take some with you.

HISTORY

Hayti, populated at the time by Arawak Indians, was discovered by Christopher Columbus in 1492. The name was promptly changed from Hayti—meaning High Land—to Hispaniola, Little Spain. At this time Haiti and Santo Domingo were one, the division of the island into two countries occurring later. As usual, the Arawaks welcomed their European visitors but soon found themselves exploited, being press-ganged into mining for precious metals. Repression, disease and massacres soon wiped out the natives so that, as elsewhere in the Caribbean, slaves were imported from West Africa in shockingly vast numbers (estimates range as high as 50 million) to continue the exploitation of the country.

In 1769 that part of Hispaniola which is now Haiti was ceded to France. The French continued the exploitation of the land and people, increased the rate of human imports from Africa (mortality rates were so high among the slaves that replacement was continually necessary just to maintain the workforce). But they were more successful than the Spanish would probably have been—the Spanish Empire was in decline—so that Sainte-Dominique (as they called it) became the richest jewel in the French Imperial crown.

Like Jamaica, Haiti is a mountainous country, but to a far greater extent. Thus nature provided a haven for those free souls able to escape the drudgery and deprivations of slavery and, as has been seen throughout the world in the past and the present, these same hills provided the perfect base for guerrilla bands, known as 'Marrons', who would institute raids on the colonisers. So the ingredients were there for subsequent events when the French Revolution shocked Europe in 1789.

When the oppressed of France cast off their chains, and equality for all was proclaimed, there was thus a nucleus in Haiti which could take this right. The conditions and times were conducive to an event which has never been repeated before or since: a successful revolt of slaves. That this revolt was ultimately successful was due largely to perhaps the vital ingredient: a great leader. This was Toussaint L'Ouverture, a former slave who had educated himself and worked himself into a position of great power in the colonial infrastructure. He persuaded the guerrilla bands that it would eventually be necessary to work in concert, but that success would only be attained by astute planning, stealth and ruthless action when the time came to strike.

In the summer of 1791 the slaves rose. They massacred most of the whites, burned the farms and committed the atrocities usual when an oppressed people at last has an outlet for its hate. This is when the maturity and wisdom of Toussaint made the crucial difference between eventual success or failure. Rather than relaxing, or trying to accumulate wealth and power for himself, he spent five years travelling the country to educate the people. He taught them that it was necessary to work, and not to hate. He offered their original lands back to those settlers who wished to continue cultivation. He built up an army capable of defending the new-found freedom.

In 1801 Toussaint proclaimed the independence of Haiti with himself as Governor. But Napoleon was at the height of his glory, having conquered most of Europe, where now only England stood against him. He could not tolerate the legalisation of a situation which had been *de facto* for some years, and conse-

207

quently sent an army of 40,000 which included his brother-in-law, Jerome. Toussaint was captured by treachery and imprisoned in France where he was to die less than two years later. But he had able lieutenants, including Generals Christophe, Dessalines and Pétion. So it was that a scorched earth policy, ruthless warfare and yellow fever caused the unconditional surrender of the French army on 18 November 1803. On 1 January 1804 Haiti became the first independent black state, and was to remain the only one for 150 years.

A long period of domestic squabbling and insulation from the rest of the world kept Haiti from developing economically. There was no great leader of the stature of Toussaint, which led Haiti to periods of fragmentation. The country was divided at one time with Henri Christophe holding sway in the north and Pétion controlling the south (from where he gave aid to Simon Bolivar's forces which were, with British help, to liberate South America from the Spanish yoke) and in 1844 the eastern part of the island separated to become the Dominican Republic. The political vacuum was filled with chaos.

In 1915 this led to American intervention. US troops were sent with the ostensible purpose of maintaining order, but soon found themselves victims of the guerrilla bands which quickly formed. They remained for nineteen years, until President Roosevelt withdrew them in 1934.

A degree of political stability was introduced by François Duvalier—Papa Doc—after his election and subsequent presidency beginning in 1957. Duvalier re-introduced the concepts of independence and black power which had slipped away over the years. Before Papa Doc, power rested with a mulatto oligarchy unrepresentative of the people and backed by the army, bourgeoisie and church. Customs and the system of government were in many respects colonial.

Following Papa Doc, his son—Baby Doc—ruled Haiti. Graham Greene, in the introduction to *The Comedians*, claims, 'Poor Haiti itself and the character of [Papa] Doctor Duvalier's rule are not invented, the latter not even blackened for dramatic effect'. Obviously it was quite changed during my visits, and the rather more relaxed atmosphere must have contributed to Baby Doc's downfall. Baby Doc had pledged himself to pursue an economic revolution for Haiti. But he was just a figurehead, largely dominated by his mother and wife. When the iron grip had loosened enough the relaxed and boisterous nature of the Haitians made itself felt first with street demonstrations, then later with a virtual siege of the palace, forcing the army to step in and depose the President to prevent anarchy. Alejo Carpenter's *The Kingdoms of This World* is a fascinating account of the revolution.

Haiti is not a country to be recommended for an average holiday, for there is nothing average here. It is a schizophrenic country, a contrast between rich and poor, cleanliness and filth, kindness and acquisitiveness, *joie de vivre* and low life expectancy. Although the tourist literature claims fine beaches, you have to go out of the towns to find any that are unpolluted: it is not the country for a beach holiday. But it is a must for the traveller who is adaptable enough to assimilate a new lifestyle—and who is prepared to be shocked!

GETTING AROUND

The means of transport vary from colourful to comfortable, but are never mundane. The transport which epitomises Haiti is the **tap-tap,** and there is no better description than that given in a book compiled for travel agents, provided by the Director of Promotion in the tourist office:

> 'A tap-tap is the ultimate in adventurous transportation. It is a prayerful thing, an inter-city gaudily painted truck with such expressions as 'God is my Saviour' and 'Pray for Me' across the front. The name 'tap-tap' is derived from the sound of the vintage engines which emit a tapping sound as they labour over the hills.'

The name 'tap-tap' is also colloquially given to the public transport within and around Port-au-Prince. Actually called **camionettes,** these are Japanese pick-up trucks with wooden, brightly painted bodies and bench seats. They generally carry eight or ten passengers and ply up and down along the main roads in the same way as a bus service. They are far more regular than a bus service, however, and stop to pick up or drop passengers on request. The fare is usually 20 cents or 1 gourde.

Publiques are cheap taxis which collect passengers going to different places around town and drop them off in an order which is convenient to, and decided by, the driver. They can be great for sightseeing but not so good for someone in a hurry. Usually older vehicles than normal taxis, they are identifiable by a letter 'P' prefixing the licence number and a red ribbon tied to the rear-view mirror. The fare anywhere in town is supposed to be 20 cents, but you may be charged more (especially to the airport).

Normal **taxis** with English-speaking drivers carry the 'L' on their licence plates and are much more expensive. The official charge from the airport to any central destination is US$6 per car, and 50 cents for a journey around town.

Haiti now has a domestic **airline**—Haiti Air Inter—with regular services to Cap Haïtien, Jacmel, Jeremie and Les Cayes from Port-au-Prince. Details current at the time of writing are as follows:

Domestic airline schedule

Depart from	At	Arrive	At	Frequency
Port-au-Prince	0700	Cap Haïtien	0735	Daily except Sun
	0800		0835	Daily except Sun

Depart from	At	Arrive	At	Frequency
Port-au-Prince	1015		1130	Mon/Thurs/Sat
	1400		1435	Daily except Sun
	1500		1535	Daily except Sun
Cap Haïtien	0745	Port-au-Prince	0820	Daily except Sun
	0845		0920	Daily except Sun
	1140		1215	Mon/Thurs/Sat
	1445		1520	Daily except Sun
	1545		1620	Daily except Sun
Port-au-Prince	0700	Jacmel	0715	Daily except Sun
	1430		1445	Daily except Sun
Jacmel	0725	Port-au-Prince	0740	Daily except Sun
	1455		1510	Daily except Sun
Port-au-Prince	1000	Jeremie	1050	Daily except Sun
Jeremie	1100	Port-au-Prince	1150	Daily except Sun
Port-au-Prince	0800	Les Cayes	0845	Daily except Sun
Les Cayes	0855	Port-au-Prince	0940	Daily except Sun
Port-au-Prince	not	Port de Paix	not	3 a week
Port de Paix	known	Port-au-Prince	known	3 a week

Port-au-Prince

There can be no place like it; it has echoes of the East, undercurrents of West Africa, a little French chic, a Caribbean climate and friendliness. Whatever opinions one may have of life here, it must be admitted that Port-au-Prince is unique. In what other French-speaking country, for example, can one see, on television, a German football match with commentary in English? Little is known about Haiti throughout the world, yet Haiti remains in touch *with* the world.

Leaving the recorded Voodoo drums and disciplined bustle of the airport behind you, head for the centre of town by taxi or 'tap-tap'. A tap-tap is fine for any centrally located hotel, but you may prefer a taxi or publique until you get your bearings.

Port-au-Prince is located in the Plain of the Cul-de-Sac, guarded by towering mountains. Looking inland from the waterfront, Le Perchoir is reminiscent of the Blue Mountains behind Kingston. But here the resemblance ends, as you will see when you drive into town.

First you are faced with an impossibility: the driving is worse than in Jamaica. There is a word to describe it—crazy. Haitians drive either on the right or down the middle of the road, depending on how much traffic is about. Careering down into the city you are struck by a bustling activity, apparent chaos and a variety in the people which is reflected in the humble architecture. Standing proud above it you will see the new cathedral. Through the haze. For

Port-au-Prince is the first polluted city you will meet in the Caribbean. Nassau is clean enough, as the aquamarine harbour waters prove; the centre of Montego Bay is scruffy but hygienic, whilst central Kingston, although dirty, is being tidied up. But here you will notice a light smog, particularly in the early evening, open sewers along many of the streets, brown water in the harbour and all-pervading smells and aromas. Except in a few of the hotels or a good restaurant you must not drink the water; if the local people don't, then you certainly shouldn't.

But it is a photographer's delight. As everywhere in the Caribbean there are people who will not be photographed and others who insist on it (if your camera is not a Polaroid be sure to advise them it is '*ne pas automatique*'). And when you have finished with the people there is the architecture: the amazing Iron Market (more about that later), decrepit, unpainted or peeling buildings held together by their neighbours, imposing public buildings such as the **Cathedral** and **Presidential Palace** (best seen from the east in the late afternoon when the misty mountains behind imbue it with a regal presence). There is the **Nègre Marron** (or **Le Marron Inconnu,** the Unknown Slave)—one of those rare statues which is a work of art, when most are merely memorials. The sculptor, Albert Mangones, has his subject resting in mid-fight or mid-flight, legs outstretched, a broken chain strung from his left ankle and a massive sword resting in his right hand on the ground. His head is thrown back as he sounds a call to arms through a conch shell.

Going up towards the mountains the squalor is gradually left behind as you pass among modern villas and old *maisons* which are truly *très jolie*.

And things happen. On one visit I was photographing Le Marron Inconnu when I heard behind me, from the Palace, the sound of a bugle. My guide insisted I freeze. I looked up to see that the city had come to a complete standstill. Pedestrians had stopped in their tracks. Motorists had ground to a halt and had left their vehicles to stand at attention. The whole effect was of a three-dimensional mural. The national flag was being lowered. This done, the silence was shattered again and the bustle resumed.

The very next day was a national holiday—2 January, Heroes' Day. On such occasions the President drives among the people distributing money to the poor. Again I saw it happen, twice. Returning from Boutilliers by car we were forced to wait by the roadside. A few minutes later we heard the wail of police sirens and saw the motorcade with police motorcycle escort. Towards the rear of the convoy was the President's official car, and as he swept past and I snapped a photograph, money was flung out of the vehicle to those willing to scramble for it. Two points were noticeable: firstly, that spontaneous applause erupted amongst the excited crowd as the convoy hove into sight; and secondly, it was only a minority that made any attempt to gather the money. The successful ones were happy, yet the unsuccessful ones were not disappointed.

Perhaps fifteen minutes later we stopped in a petrol station and heard approaching sirens again. Quickly I grabbed my camera and ran to the roadside. This time it was the President's mother, Papa Doc's widow. A young-looking woman, she leaned out of the car window and showered notes and coins as she passed me. My guide was a lucky recipient.

Things have changed now and you will have your own experiences.

WHERE TO STAY IN PORT-AU-PRINCE

Unless you're travelling on a tight budget, or prefer the bland anonymity of a large 'international' hotel, you must stay at the **Grand Hotel Oloffson**. This haphazard, wooden, gingerbread edifice was immortalised in Graham Greene's novel *The Comedians* and has since been described as 'the darling of the theatre people and the literary set'. Drenched with character and personality, it is a haven for the jetsetter who has become blasé about travel. Accommodation is certainly not in the luxury category and you shouldn't expect air-conditioning, but you'll not find another hotel in the Caribbean like it. So don't miss the opportunity.

Rooms are named after famous guests who have stayed there (John Gielgud Suite, James Jones Cottage, Anne Bancroft Studio, Marlon Brando Cottage, etc.). Rates include a full breakfast, and a superb dinner is only US$10 to guests. Although centrally situated, its driveway and swimming pool are shaded and surrounded by tropical foliage, thus further enhancing its ambience as a quiet oasis in the middle of the bustle of Port-au-Prince.

Another hotel with character and charm (though not so much), and also a converted mansion, is the **Hotel Prince.** The 20 rooms in the main part of the hotel have been converted and furnished with care, hand-carved wood being a feature throughout. A new wing houses another dozen rooms furnished in more modern style with views of the bay and town. All rooms are air-conditioned. The bar with its foliage, fountain and mirrored ceiling is under the swimming pool, which is well placed for sunbathing. The purified water here can be drunk from the tap.

The **Hotel Castelhaiti** is really for groups and those who like big hotels. Set in an imposing position on the hillside, it is well-furnished in the modern style and affords excellent views. Bedrooms here are air-conditioned and there is a pool.

Villa Bel Soleil is probably the best of the guesthouses. Its surrounding tropical trees and shrubs harmonise well with its bright paintwork, giving a bright, cheerful ambience in a secluded setting. Like all the guesthouses, the different room prices reflect the different facilities available: a US$24 double is without bathroom, a US$35 room has bathroom, and for an extra US$4 you also have air-conditioning. Also like the other guesthouses, there is a swimming pool and prices include breakfast and dinner.

Santos Pacot Guest House can be recommended, although it is further from the central area (at least a 15-minute walk). I was more impressed on my first visit, but, when making a return trip recently, formed the distinct impression that the management had loosened its grip a little. Nevertheless, it is still excellent value for money.

Better situated for excursions into town is **Aux Cosaques Guest House**, which has a good local reputation, and you'll be well looked after here: the management and staff are most courteous and helpful. Further from the town centre is a large guesthouse, **La Griffonne**. I arrived around dinnertime (the food looked excellent) yet the management still had time to show me round. Other guesthouses in Port-au-Prince are **Sendral's**, the **Paulema Hotel**, Route Delmas (tel. 70430), **Thor Auberge Inn**, Thor-le-Volant (tel. 20465), **Hillside Guest House**, 53 Alix Roy (tel. 25419) and the **Pension La Guite**, 5 Avenue Ducoste (tel. 24423).

Cheap accommodation can be found among the squalor and bustle in the centre of town. There are many hotels on Rue du Centre. The **USA** at US$5 per room is poor value as the restaurant prices downstairs are high, although the owners are very pleasant. **Lys Guest House** at 77 Rue du Centre is quite acceptable. The bedrooms are clean and decorated, although toilet facilities are shared and very basic. Over the road is the **Central Hotel**, somewhat

Accommodation in Port-au-Prince
Daily winter rates per room in US$

		Single	Double
Hotels			
Grand Hotel Oloffson, central Port-au-Prince (tel. 20139)	CP:	50, 55 and 60	65, 75, 85, 95 and 120
		(dinner US$10 per person extra)	
Hotel Castelhaiti, hillside overlooking Port-au-Prince (tel. 20624 and 23777)	EP: CP:	31–60 36–65	36–65 46–75
Hotel Prince, central Port-au-Prince (tel. 22765)	EP:	24–35	30–41
Guesthouses			
Aux Cosaques Guesthouse, 62 Avenue Christophe (tel. 54433)	MAP:	12–16	22–28
La Griffonne Guesthouse, Canapé Vert, Zone Jean-Baptiste	MAP:	12–20	20–32
Santos Pacot Guesthouse, Rue Garoute (northwest of Rue Turgeau) (tel. 54417)	MAP:	15–18	20–25
Villa Bel Soleil, 102 Rue Lafleur Duchêne (tel. 55787)	MAP:	14–23	24–39

GREATER ANTILLES

bigger. From what I could make out all rooms appear to have a private bathroom (although the water is not always connected) but toilet facilities and bedrooms are of a spartan nature. What do you expect for US$5?

The Embajadour is also centrally located. Shower and toilet facilities are shared, but there is a lounge, a small kitchen and a helpful honest manager. Both the staff and the clientele are very pleasant.

It is certainly not recommended that you stay in any of the really cheap accommodation here. Guesthouses such as Villa Bel Soleil and Santos Pacot are so superior and, when you consider that these better guesthouses include meals in their prices, you'll find it no advantage to stay in the seedy places in the centre of town.

EATING OUT IN PORT-AU-PRINCE
Three restaurants spring to mind. Almost opposite the Beau Rivage is a small snack bar intended, probably, for members of the Association of Chauffeurs and Guides. Visitors are allowed to eat here. A dinner (example: barbecued chicken with rice, bananas and avocado pear) will cost 7½ gourde or US$1.50 (always check whether prices are in gourdes or dollars). A Coca Cola is one gourde (20 cents) and local 'Cola Champagne' ½ gourde or 10 cents. Liquor prices are listed in US dollars.

On the corner of Boulevard Harry Truman and Rue Paul VI is a large restaurant with modern fittings. For a restaurant that takes credit cards the prices are reasonable, about 1½ times those of the snack bar mentioned above. It does a three-course lunch (until 4 pm) for US$2.95. The clientele are almost entirely tourists. The food is good but the service poor.

The **Tiffany** is expensive by Haitian standards—your guide will catch his breath when you mention it. The prices are about the same as you would expect in a 'good' Jamaican restaurant: US$1 for soup, US$4 for Tassot Creole, US$4.75 for a steak. The food is largely native and genuinely so. Therefore if unused to piquant sauces, or if your teeth are not perfect, avoid the Creole dishes. The service is excellent and the food is very good indeed. The clientele are predominantly tourists with a sprinkling of rich Haitians. I have no hesitation in strongly recommending it for a good meal, but it will be expensive.

There are many cheap snack bars around town with differing standards of hygiene and price ranges. The menus are usually prominently displayed (frequently painted on the wall) but think twice (at least) before drinking the water.

WHAT TO SEE IN PORT-AU-PRINCE
The Iron Market is one of the outstanding sights of Port-au-Prince, along with the Cathedral, the Palace, Le Marron Inconnu and the mountains behind the town. They all stand out because of their colour, size, strength and majesty.

Standing proud among or behind Port-au-Prince's teeming, squalid, noisy streets, all these have 'presence'; and in all cases a presence which is felt most in the late afternoon.

The centre of town is dominated by the **Iron Market,** both in its role as the nucleus of business dealings, and visually. Painted a flamboyant red and green and with a tin roof that gleams in the sun, it can stop you in your tracks at first sight. It boasts minaret-cupolas that could be straight from Agra or Fatehpur Sikri in India! According to legend, a Muslim city in India ordered an iron market to be manufactured in France; at the same time Port-au-Prince required an enclosed market. The French are supposed to have sent the wrong market to each place. However the tourist office states that this story is unlikely to be true (sorry to spoil your fun). Whatever the case, the Muslim influence is strongly represented with an accuracy which suggests that the designer had at least been to Agra. The colour scheme just has to be Haitian. (This colour combination, incidentally, is often used for shop signs and other graphic art throughout Port-au-Prince, consciously or unconsciously derived from the town's centrepiece.)

Inside the market you can buy almost anything you are never likely to need, a wide variety of items you would only dream about, and who knows how many things you don't know the use of—and you may get something you want.

Outside the market, for an area of perhaps half a square mile, the streets have become a large market area. Here more mundane goods, such as food-stuffs, clothes and cigarettes, can be purchased and shoes repaired. The vendors have long since occupied the sidewalk, and on busy days now take up most of the street as well. This forces pedestrians to walk down the middle of the road, cramming to the side every time an impatient horn heralds the approach of a vehicle.

There is another market, dealing principally in foodstuffs, near the oddly named Gare du Nord—the bus station. This is merely a very dirty area with a Texaco petrol station where the inter-city tap-taps terminate. This market is very dirty and smelly. On the other side of the port administration buildings is a good spot to buy local carvings. Workshops line the road and you can see the carvers at work. Nearby, paintings are displayed, many showing by their dupli-cation that they are mass-produced.

Pétionville

Going up into the hills from Port-au-Prince you progressively leave the squa-lor behind. Over the years the rich have done this, and now many of them live in the town of Pétionville, 1,100 feet up and four miles from Port-au-Prince. Many of the plush hotels are here, as are the most expensive restaurants and nightclubs.

Boutilliers

The mountain you see towering over Port-au-Prince is **Le Perchoir**. Boutilliers, at the top, can be reached in two ways: shared station wagon to Pétionville and on up, or the hard way—walking directly up the side of the mountain. The latter is only recommended if you are fit and used to day-hiking. If you doubt your ability don't try it—the sun is very hot and you could choose far better places to get sunstroke. The path itself is fairly easy to find and even easier to negotiate—it has been created by girls walking up all day, every day, carrying several gallons of water on their heads.

This method of progress has its advantages. It obviously affords far better views of the plain, town and bay below, and allows you to take photographs when and where you want to. Also it gives you the opportunity of studying the lifestyle of the poor people in the hills. Although they are faced daily with long walks uphill carrying heavy loads, they have the benefits of peace and serenity, and less squalor and crowds than in the town. They appear to be very industrious.

Kenscoff

Kenscoff is a little further from Port-au-Prince (12 miles) to the south. At an altitude of 4,000 feet, the climate is considerably cooler here than on the coast. Rich Haitians come here in the summer months.

Port-au-Prince to Cap Haïtien and onwards

Assuming you will visit Cap Haïtien (Le Cap), here are three suggested means of travelling between Port-au-Prince and Santo Domingo:

1 Tap-tap to Cap Haïtien, returning to Port-au-Prince by the same means. Fly from Port-au-Prince to Santo Domingo, on the south coast of the Dominican Republic.
2 Tap-tap to Cap Haïtien, fly back to Port-au-Prince, spend about two hours in the airport then fly from Port-au-Prince to Santo Domingo.
3 Tap-tap to Cap Haïtien. Bus across the north of Hispaniola turning south around Santiago for Santo Domingo. A variation is to go back to Port-au-Prince anyway, and take a bus from there to Dominicana (this is probably easier).

If you are taking option 1 or 2, it is a good idea to confirm a reservation on your intended flight to Santo Domingo before you leave Port-au-Prince for the north, as the airline agent in Cap Haïtien will not phone for you if you already have a ticket.

Route option 1: First you will need a permit to take the bus to the north. While you may be told by some people that it is not essential, it is likely to be inspected on both northbound and southbound trips. To obtain one you should go to the tourist office with your passport and tourist card: the permit will be typed out and stamped while you wait. If you ask they will also give you a very good Texaco map of Haiti.

It is strongly advised that you make a reservation on a bus the day before you wish to travel, at about 4 to 5 pm, so that you can be sure of getting a seat (and possibly a good one). To make your reservation, simply go down to the bus terminal (Gare du Nord—see map) and find a truck or bus bound for Le Cap. I paid US$4 fare each way. Northbound, I suspect I was overcharged by perhaps a dollar. I know that the return trip, in a far better vehicle, was genuinely US$4.

Both north- and southbound buses leave at about 6 am, arriving at their destination between 1 and 3 pm. They all make three trips per week in each direction.

Most of the vehicles comprise a truck chassis with handbuilt wooden super-structure custom-made to the owner's requirements. This means that each row of seats is meant to accommodate at least six and more usually seven persons. In terms of discomfort this may well be the worst journey of your life—remember that a truck has a very rudimentary suspension. This discomfort can be alleviated, however. As these tap-taps have no aisle as such, entry and exit is made by scrambling over the passengers sitting in the centre of the bus. When booking, you should request a window seat. This will leave you relatively undisturbed, although pushed against the woodwork and covered in dust (but you get the benefit of the breeze—glazed windows are a rarity). For the best views (north Haiti) get a seat on the right-hand side of the bus going up, or better, on the left-hand side coming down. You have to keep to the seat number allocated to you (it will be marked on your ticket). The numbers are crudely painted on the *back* of the seat.

As well as the trucks there are some old buses, also gaily painted. I found that the best transport was an unromantic, red and white bus called Ebenezer. This was actually built for the purpose of carrying passengers, so that the only discomfort is the overcrowding—39 passengers instead of the 27 it was designed to carry. It even has fans to circulate the air! Ask for seat 39 northbound or 34 southbound.

If the bus leaves with any empty seats it will stop to pick up until the driver thinks he has enough passengers. He is not always in agreement with his original passengers on this question. Two crewmen travel up on the luggage rack.

The journey itself is visually spectacular at times, if you can stay awake. The route begins and ends on good roads, but in between there are stretches with gravel surface or no surface at all and road repairs and construction may well be in operation. At these points the bus lurches off the road and trundles along

217

until it can rejoin the straight and narrow. At one point an iron girder bridge spans a wide river bed. (Ebenezer can buzz across this, while the trucks roar and bump over the riverbed, fording the rivulets with no reduction in speed.)

All along the route small settlements can be seen: thatched mud and wattle huts, the occasional wooden building, usually gaily painted in pastel colours, Caribbean-style. Vendors surround the bus every time it stops, selling cold drinks, fruit, bread, biscuits, nuts and cigarettes. There are more children about than in Port-au-Prince. Most of the population of Haiti is rural, and this is perhaps the best way to observe them. There are also two towns of some size, Saint Marc and Gonaïves. Throughout the journey frequent stops are made at police checkpoints, although your permit will probably be asked for only on entry to Cap Haïtien.

One of the greatest pleasures is the scenery, which is spectacular in the north. Returning to the capital, we left a little after dawn (at 6.45) with me sitting at the back of the bus on the left-hand side. The mountains as seen from Cap Haïtien are an inspiring sight anyway, but when seen from a mountain road in the early morning, they are incomparable.

It had rained in the night, so that the lush foliage and trees on the mountainsides glistened in the rays of sunlight which filtered through gaps in the clouds. The dust had been turned to a fine mud, rich red in parts, creamy beige in others. With the alternate patches of light and shade the full range of greens speckled the mountainsides, from emerald to turquoise. The mountains themselves were most spectacular, plunging into each other in seemingly endless rows with no real valleys in between. The road was simply a snake, carved into the mountainside and winding up and down at a rate which reduced the bus to a speed of 10 mph. At times it would double back on itself, and other vehicles could be seen far away tackling the ascent or descent in bottom gear.

The bus station in Cap Haïtien is at the south end of town, which means a taxi ride into the town centre. Taxis are usually shared, and the fare should be 4 gourde (80 cents). Agree this first and do not pay more. When you make your return reservation you will be without baggage, so it is easy to take a quiet stroll down to the bus station. The next morning you will be up before dawn and with baggage, so you may prefer to order a car in advance. I just walked, and pretty soon a taxi found me.

Back in Port-au-Prince 'publiques' meet the incoming buses. The fare into town is 2 gourde, but you will be charged more if you go direct to the airport. Again agree this first.

It is possible to take a tap-tap to the airport from Grand' Rue (Avenue Jean Jacques Dessalines) at the corner of Rue Macajou. The fare is 1 gourde per person.

Route option 2: As above to Cap Haïtien. The advantage of this option is that the tiring overland trip is halved. You also save taxi fare, time and trouble between Port-au-Prince and the airport, as you can arrange your schedules so that you have only a two-hour wait between planes. You will still need to get to the airport in Cap Haïtien, of course.

It is best to make your air reservations Cap Haïtien–Port-au-Prince and Port-au-Prince–Santo Domingo before you leave Port-au-Prince. Allow at least three days for the journey, although four is better, i.e. a day travelling to Le Cap, a day for a visit to the Citadelle and Sans Souci, a spare day, and a day for your return. Three days can be enough if you take an afternoon flight back to the capital, as this will give you two half days and two nights in Cap Haïtien itself (not counting the excursion). When planning, remember that although the Air Florida flight to Santo Domingo is daily, there are no Sunday domestic flights at the time of writing. It is possible to book with a travel agent or separately with Haiti Air Inter and Air Florida. This will cost you perhaps an extra US$13 but you do save time and energy. Book as soon as possible.

Route option 3: This is the most time-consuming and frustrating of the three suggestions listed here, and is not necessarily any cheaper. Whether you go to Le Cap and try to cross the border up north, or instead return to Port-au-Prince to take the overland route from there, you will find yourself faced with a tough proposition. In either case, for travel to Cape Haïtien see option 1.

Go to the Ministry of the Interior for a permit to leave Haiti by this means. When you have obtained it, telephone or visit the Dominican consulate to check with them (it should be all right for US, Canadian and British citizens).

There is no surfaced road between Cap Haïtien and the border, and next to no traffic takes that route. Your best chance, and that a slim one, is to find a ship leaving Cap Haïtien which is bound for a north-coast Dominican port.

It is more likely that you will be forced to return to Port-au-Prince. Here you will find occasional, but very rare, buses to Santo Domingo. But don't get excited—they are usually arranged months in advance. There is a more regular service of big trucks that make the journey, but to take advantage of this you will need to speak Creole or at least French. Some Spanish would help too. Try down by the harbour. This is also the place for your last alternative to flying. You could try the port which will advise you if any ships are likely to be leaving for Santo Domingo.

Cap Haïtien (Le Cap)

In itself this is a more charming town than Port-au-Prince with less evident squalor. The streets are cleaner and quieter, the buildings less humble and more picturesque, painted in different pastel colours in the Caribbean style. There is a cathedral in the town and a château on the hill, but apart from this no outstanding sights in the town itself. But it has a charming, peaceful atmosphere. The poor part of town, at times unbelievable in its squalor, is to the south, not far from the bus station.

WHERE TO STAY IN CAP HAÏTIEN

I would recommend the **Brise de Mer** guesthouse (tel. (693)2–0821), 'the best according to the guest', situated in the north of Le Cap. Rates are US$18 single, US$30 double, US$42 triple; 5% tax additional. These rates include private bathroom (some rooms with balcony) and two meals per day. American Express, BankAmericard and MasterCard are accepted.

Of the cheaper guesthouses I would suggest you try the **Columb**. There is only one bathroom (albeit a satisfactory one), no fan and no protection against mosquitoes, but then I was charged a mere US$5 per night—expect to pay about US$8 for a double. I ate only once in the café downstairs. A good cheap place to eat is a snack bar nearby. Turn right when leaving the Columb, then right a the corner and left at the Air Haiti office. The snack bar is about two blocks along on the right.

La Ferrière Citadel, Haiti

The Citadelle and the Palace of Sans Souci

The massive Citadelle was built shortly after independence—it took ten years to complete—by King Henri Christophe to repulse a possible French invasion.

220

On top of a mountain, it can be seen with the naked eye from Cap Haïtien, although it is some considerable distance from the town. It could accommodate 10,000 people within its 12-foot thick walls—the Royal Family was allocated 40 rooms. Cannons in various states of disrepair are everywhere and there is a magazine that holds 45,000 cannon balls. Henri Christophe's tomb is in the centre with the inscription 'Here lies Henri Christophe, King of Haiti. I am reborn from my ashes.'

The Citadelle is reached by way of the town of Milot. Take a tap-tap or publique to Milot and register at the police station. Here you organise your entry and transport (which is by horse, as you ascend by means of a mountain track) to the Citadelle. Expect to pay US$1.50 for a ticket, US$1.50 for a horse and the same again for a guide. Allowing for meals (and including something for the guide) you can expect to pay about US$8 for the excursion.

On the way back down you can visit the ruins of the Palais de Sans Souci, which was designed to rival Versailles in France. It would have been splendid in its day, but it was devasted by an earthquake and now remains only as a shattered reminder of colonial extravagance.

Tortuga

This island off Haiti's north coast was discovered first by Columbus and then by the pirates. It is claimed that Henry Morgan, Jean Lafitte, Blackbeard and Captain Kidd used to rendezvous here until the Spanish asked them to move along. That is when they made Port Royal their home base.

The topography of the island is fairly mountainous with numerous caves and coves and white coral sand beaches. Scuba diving is said to be superb here, both in terms of natural wonders, and also because the area abounds in old wrecks. This island alone is bigger than some Caribbean countries.

Jacmel

Jacmel is a quiet town on Haiti's south coast, important for its coffee, orange and tangerine industries. Coffee is Haiti's main export, and you can visit a coffee-sorting plant in Jacmel.

There are many houses with New Orleans-style wrought-iron balconies. These were brought from France and Belgium as ballast for the ships, which were to return laden with coffee and fruit. There are two nearby beaches: **Black Sand Beach,** in the town itself, and **Raymond des Bains,** 20 minutes away.

These cold facts about Jacmel don't even begin to give a feeling of the spirit of the town. To call it a ghost town would be inaccurate because, though it is vastly underpopulated when compared to Port-au-Prince, it is certainly not dead; it is more a living museum. The old colonial architecture with its fading pastel hues affords lovely views, of the town and sea from above, of serene, tree-lined streets in the town itself. There is none of the capital's pollution here, the beaches, though of black sand, being fit for swimming and sunbathing. A visit to the coffee-sorting plant in the small port is in itself an experience: the only machinery is crude and the sorting methods themselves primitive.

Accommodation in Jacmel
Daily winter rates per room in US$

	Single	Double
Hotel Craft, Main Square (tel. 82641)	EP: 18	26
	CP: 22	34
Hotel La Jacmelienne sur Plage, Rue Sainte Anne	EP: 39	58
(tel. 83331/83451/24899)	CP: 44	68

As its name suggests, the **Hotel La Jacmelienne sur Plage** is situated right on the beach. It is an attractive, modern, two-storey building, but with its architecture very strongly influenced by the traditional Haitian style, and flanked with palm trees and tropical shrubs. It has a large pool and open-air terrace bar. Although all the sea-facing rooms are well-furnished and blessed with modern conveniences (though not air-conditioning), this is not a case of an international hotel being plonked in the middle of a rustic setting. It harmonises well with its surroundings.

The **Hotel Craft,** once a private home, is really a guesthouse. You will notice that the prices are higher than can be found in the capital; this may or may not be due to the arrival of the Jacmelienne on the scene. It is cosy, quiet, clean and well-maintained with delicious Creole food—probably a great place to write a book. On the other side of the square, overlooking the lower part of the town, the beach and the bay, is the **Pension Alexandra**. A double room here will cost you US$40 to US$50 with meals. Again, it is slightly overpriced by Haitian standards, and the rooms are inferior to the Craft's, but it may be worth staying here if only because it has the best views.

If you are travelling on a tight budget there are one or two more basic guesthouses in Jacmel; expect to pay about US$15 to US$20 for a double room.

CALENDAR
1 January is Independence Day, and the parades and fireworks continue into 2 January which is Forefathers' Day, the day for celebrating the national heroes. The other big event is Carnival which takes place during the three days preceding Lent.

REPUBLICA DOMINICANA

(Dominican Republic)

Haiti is lovely, but it is always a relief to get back to civilisation. The most incredible feature of the two countries which share Hispaniola is the difficulty one has in travelling between them. Almost equally incredible is the difference. Chalk and cheese are far more similar. Haiti seems out of place because it is West Africa transplanted. The Dominican Republic is the opposite extreme— Latin America in the Caribbean. It has echoes of Mexico, but is cleaner and more prosperous. When I was walking through Santo Domingo unidentifiable chords were struck in my memory but although it is far more international, it remains first and foremost Dominicana.

GETTING TO THE DOMINICAN REPUBLIC
The Airport of the Americas itself contrasts strongly with Port-au-Prince: big, modern and efficient with all the facilities you would expect in such a place. Formalities are straightforward enough, but transport to town can present a problem as the airport is a long way out. The taxi fare is 10 to 15 pesos per car. Everyone will tell you that there is no bus service, but in fact there is (at least from the town to the airport). Ask. The company is Expressos Dominicanos and the fare US$3 per person. Their town terminal is centrally situated, near the recommended accommodation.

From the USA
Dominicana, the national airline, flies in from New York and Miami, as do Pan Am and Eastern. American Airlines provides services from New York.

From Canada
There are no services from Canada, so you should take one of the New York or Miami services.

From London
There is a through fare via Madrid with Iberia on the APEX basis. Otherwise try via Miami, either all the way with Pan Am, or take your preferred transatlantic carrier (Pan Am, British Airways or Virgin Atlantic) and then the Dominicana Caribpass (see below).

From Europe

The only European city with scheduled flights to Santo Domingo is Madrid (Iberia). Probably the best idea is to fly to Miami and take advantage of the Caribpass.

Dominicana's Caribpass

At the time of writing Dominicana has a 'Rover' ticket, valid for up to 30 days and for four flights at a cost of US$180. Points covered include Miami, Puerto Plata, Port-au-Prince, Santo Domingo, San Juan, Curaçao, Caracas, Barranquilla and Panama. So for US$180 you can make a Miami–Santo Domingo round trip and still have two coupons left for a diversion to Haiti, Puerto Rico or wherever takes your fancy. It is also possible, on payment of an extra supplement, to upgrade the ticket, either to have additional coupons or to include flights to/from New York. (Telephone number for Miami: 305–592 3588; toll free elsewhere in the USA: 800–327 7240.) European contacts are as follows:

West Germany: Caribpass Information, Grosse Bockenheimer Strasse 6, D–6000 Frankfurt/M1 (069–287551).

Spain: Dominicana Airlines, Ms Janet Nivar de Melo, Ave de Brasil No. 4, 9 piso 4–D, Madrid 28020 (431–5354).

Italy: Dominicana Airlines, Gateway srl. Via S. Vito 26, 20123 Milano (860901/8053932).

Within the Caribbean and Latin America

There are very few Caribbean countries linked to the Dominican Republic; main trading ties are with Spain and the Spanish-speaking world. Haiti is served by Dominicana; Sint Maarten by ALM; Puerto Rico by Dominicana, ALM and Eastern; and Curaçao by Dominicana, ALM and Viasa. Iberia serves Guatemala exclusively, and shares the honours with COPA and Dominicana on the Panama route. Avianca flies in from Bogotá and Barranquilla, and Viasa from Caracas.

ENTRY REGULATIONS

Citizens of the United States, Canada, Jamaica, Mexico, Puerto Rico and Venezuela need proof of identity, not necessarily a passport. Those without a passport must purchase a tourist card for US$5. British passport holders and citizens of many Western European countries (and some other countries) need a passport but no visa or prepaid tourist card and are allowed to stay for up to three months. All visitors are required to show return tickets. As in almost all countries, there is a departure tax (U$10).

ELECTRICITY

The supply is 110–120 volts at 60 cycles, about the same as in the US.

CLIMATE

It is generally much the same as Haiti's. (During my visit it was substantially cooler, dropping to about 60°F at night in Santo Domingo, but then these were freak conditions—it was snowing at the time in Nassau!)

CURRENCY

During both my visits to the Dominican Republic the peso was officially at par with the US$, though in fact was worth less. As a consequence money-changing took place on the streets (mainly El Conde) rather than in the banks. In fact I once ventured into a bank, an empty, echoing and dusty place, and was promptly ushered back into the street! Recently the government has done the sensible thing and fixed the peso at a realistic rate: at the time of writing US$1 equals 2.80 pesos. US dollars will probably continue to be gladly accepted, but be careful about the exchange rate you are offered.

POPULATION

In ethnic terms, there is the full range from white to ebony black, with the vast majority somewhere in between. A word of warning: the incidence of male tourists being led to prostitutes, particularly in the old part of town, is so high that even the official tourist guide makes an oblique reference to it. So, if you are looking for nocturnal company, accept no offers of help in finding it and keep your money and valuables locked up out of harm's way.

LANGUAGE

Spanish is spoken everywhere, and, except at the airport, little English is spoken. In general, the people seem to find it difficult to understand the average traveller's pidgin Spanish.

FOOD AND DRINK

There is a strong Spanish and Italian influence. The Spanish accent is weaker here than in Puerto Rico, probably because the Dominican Republic became independent before Puerto Rico changed hands, and partly because the country wishes to play down its colonial past whilst Puerto Rico is proud of its cultural heritage.

The Dominican national dish is *sancocho*, a concoction also found in parts of South America. Having no set recipe, it is based on many different meats and vegetables cooked in a broth. You will find the Caribbean favourite of fried chicken with rice (*pollo con arroz*), roast pork and goat, and lots of fresh fish and seafood. Almost every restaurant in central Santo Domingo seems to sell pizza, lasagne is freely available, and there are a number of Italian restaurants of differing standards and prices.

Rum is the national drink.

HISTORY

Discovered like most of the islands by our friend Columbus and rapidly exploited by Spanish imperial interests, Hispaniola was, for much of the 16th century, the centre of Spain's American interests, and Santo Domingo was its headquarters. In 1795 Spain was forced to cede its two-thirds of the island to France. As this event coincided with the revolution in Haiti, Toussaint was forced to pacify Dominicana too, a problem from which the Haitians were freed when this country reverted to the Spanish crown following the downfall of Napoleon. Independence was first declared in 1821 and lasted a full four months before a Haitian army put the country back under its wing. So it is from 1844 that independence is usually dated, although there was a four-year period when Dominicana returned—voluntarily—to Spanish control.

Domestic rule has been turbulent with very many revolutions, presidents and constitutions. The most famous dictator, General Trujillo, ruled from 1930 until his assassination in 1961. Anarchy could well have been the order of the day in the 1960s, but the intervention of the CIA and US Marines helped to establish a stable government which continues today.

GETTING AROUND

There are speedy and regular **bus services** throughout the Dominican Republic at reasonable cost. The terminals are conveniently clustered around Puerta del Conde in Santo Domingo. Some of the main bus companies (with telephone numbers in Santo Domingo) are:

Estrella Blanca (EBL; tel. 682 0523)
Compañia Nacional de Autobuses (CNA; tel. 565 6681)
Metro (MET; tel. 566 3919)
Expresos Dominicanos (EXP; tel. 682 6610 and 687 6313)
La Experiencia (LA; tel. 689 3576 and 689 9242)

Some bus services from Santo Domingo

From Santo Domingo to	Departure times	Bus company
Airport	6.30 am to 4.30 pm	Expresos Dominicanos
Bonao	7 am/1.45 pm/3.30 pm	Expresos Dominicanos
Bonao	6 am to 6 pm (2-hourly)	Compañia Nacional
Jarabacoa	8 am/5 pm (3 a week)	Expresos Dominicanos
La Vega/Santiago	7/8/10.30 am/1.45/5 pm	Expresos Dominicanos
Santiago/Puerto Plata	7.30/10 am/4 pm	Metro
Puerto Plata	8 am/5 pm	Expresos Dominicanos
San Pedro de Macoris	6.30 am to 4.30 pm	Expresos Dominicanos
San Pedro de Macoris	5.40 am to 7.40 pm	La Experiencia
San Pedro/La Romana	2 pm	Metro

From Santo Domingo to	Departure times	Bus company
La Romana	7 am	Metro
Pedernales	6.30 am	Estrella Blanca
Bani/Azua	6.30 am/1 pm/1.30 pm	Estrella Blanca
Bani/Azua/San Juan	6.30 am/1.30 pm	Estrella Blanca
Bani/Azua/San Juan	1.30 pm	La Experiencia
Barahona	2.30 pm	La Experiencia
Barahona	2.30 pm	Estrella Blanca
Hato/Mayor/Seibo/Higuey	7 am/1 pm/4 pm	La Experiencia
Hato/Mayor/Sabana/Miches	6.30 am/3 pm	La Experiencia
Higuey	7 am/1 pm/4 pm	La Experiencia

If you want to do some flying you will be pleased to learn that the **domestic airline,** Alas del Caribe, operates regular services at reasonable fares. Remember that you will have to add taxi fares between town and airport in most cases, and also that this airline operates from Herrera airport in Santo Domingo (more convenient than the Airport of the Americas).

Taxis are called *carros de concho* and operate on a sort of publique system; they follow regular routes picking up and dropping passengers on the way. The fare is 20 or 25 cents. For your own taxi on a specific route or for a specific destination, ask the driver for a *carrera*: the fare will vary between US$3 and US$5 within Santo Domingo, but agree this first. Taxis are painted either blue and white or red and blue. It is possible to telephone for a taxi and be collected anywhere; the number is 565 1313.

There are **buses** within Santo Domingo, called *guaguas*, with a fare of 10 cents.

Santo Domingo

Although the drive into town from the airport is long, it is also pleasant. You will immediately notice a very good, fast, uncrowded road, and thoughtfully laid out gardens between it and the sea. It would be nice to stop and take a short walk. 'New' Santo Domingo has little of interest. Wide highways and boulevards run into and through the town, and apartment blocks and spacious residential areas are in marked contrast to Haiti. There is at least one very large park and most of the big, flashy hotels. To get around and see it you will need transport.

'Old' Santo Domingo is something of a misnomer; most of the city was destroyed in the hurricane of 1930, which perhaps explains why it lacks character and soul. The only really old part of any interest lies south of Calle Mercedes; here there are a few buildings of architectural interest, and a few of historical interest. One of them is the **Cathedral** which houses the tomb of Christopher Columbus. Also, at the end of El Conde, is **Puerta del Conde,** whose bell pealed independence in 1844. Behind here a mausoleum contains giant statues of three national heroes. There is also the restored **Alcázar,** or **Casa** Columbus. Built in 1510, this was the palace of Don Diego Columbus, Christopher's son, who was the first Spanish Viceroy. Across from the Alcázar is **La Atarazana**. Originally a colonial arsenal dating from 1507, it has been restored and now houses restaurants, shops and galleries.

People talk of the 'old town' as if it had some kind of magic, but don't be taken in. You will find yourself being shown this and that, but if you are being guided at night be wary of travelling north of Calle Mercedes. This is not the old town, merely the poor part and the red light district. You will probably be quite safe from attack, but anyone who takes you there is hustling.

WHERE TO STAY IN SANTO DOMINGO

The Dominican Republic is not a tourists' paradise. Santo Domingo itself is not a tourist resort, and Puerto Plata is more a case of a resort being created for the Yankee dollar than somewhere tourists would flock of their own volition. The accommodation guide that follows is thus intended for the traveller, and not the tourist.

Accommodation here is better value for money than in many parts of the Caribbean. In Santo Domingo it is best to find somewhere centrally located, near Puerta del Conde. There you will find restaurants of all prices, bus terminals, money-changing facilities and airline offices, all within walking distance, with the old town and the sea near at hand. The Hostal Nicolás de Ovando, purported to be the oldest hotel in the New World has 60 rooms in the old Spanish-colonial style. It is full of atmosphere and has a small pool. The rates are approximately US$75 for a double room.

You will find it difficult to find better value than at the **Anacaona** (slogan 'the best in the heart of Santo Domingo'). The rates quoted here are year-round and include tax. All rooms have good private bathroom, hot water, telephone and air-conditioning, and there is a good restaurant downstairs. It is a well-run hotel. Try to telephone a reservation from the airport if you speak Spanish.

If the Anacaona is full, which is possible, you could try the **Hotel Aida** at the corner of El Conde and Espaillat. Prices are similar, as are facilities, superficially, but the appearance is more dingy.

If saving money is of prime importance you could try the **Dominicana Hotel** on El Conde—not that I'm recommending it. I was charged $8, but you should treat all quoted prices as negotiable. I got a bed with clean sheets, soap, towel and toilet paper. However, the other four beds in the room were covered in dust, as was the washbasin which had not been cleaned—or indeed used—

228

for some time. The bathroom (*baño*) down the hall had a peculiar water supply system: the only running water came from a spout on the bath and was transferred somehow to two oil drums. The door was not lockable or even properly shuttable, but then I had left all notions of privacy behind in Haiti. My room had a balcony, but there was nothing worth looking at.

Alternatively you could try the **Comercial Hotel,** a large, well-known establishment further down El Conde, or any of the small pensions which can be found with a little searching in the streets running off El Conde.

Accommodation in Santo Domingo
Daily summer rates per room in US$

	Single	Double
Anacaona Hotel, Palo Hincado 303 (tel. 689 0622)	EP: 12	20
Comercial Hotel, El Conde/Hostos	EP: 18	22
Dominicana, El Conde	EP: 8	14
Hotel Aida, Espaillat/El Conde	EP: 12	20

WHERE TO EAT IN SANTO DOMINGO
There are plenty of restaurants but none can be specifically recommended. Try just walking about, observing the prices, food and clientele. Prices in expensive restaurants are higher than in the Haitian equivalent. **El Acázar** has an international menu, as well as local specialities and is attractively designed in a Moorish style by Oscar de la Renta. Expensive (tel. 532–1511). For delicious local seafood try **La Bahía** in Avenida George Washington. Price of a meal is moderate to cheap.

WHERE TO STAY OUTSIDE THE CAPITAL
One of the joys of this country is the splendid scenery. With good roads and a cheap and comprehensive bus service, it is possible to visit other towns easily. Here is a selection of some of the cheaper accommodation in other parts of the country.

Daily winter rates per room in US$

Name	Address	Single	Double
Arienm	Santiago Rodriguez	8	10
Caoba	Valverde, Mao	14	22
Cofresi	Puerto Plata	20	30
El Naranjo	Higuey	9	19
Long Beach	Puerto Plata	18	24

Name	Address	Single	Double
Macorix	San Pedro de Macoris	19	28
Maguana	San Juan	16	22
Mercedes	Santiago	12	20
Mi Cabana	Constanza	10	16
Montana	Jarabacoa	12	20
Montemar	Cabañas, Puerto Plata	20	40
Nueva Suiza	Constanza	10	16
San Cristóbal	San Cristóbal	16	21
Ugarocuya	Barahona	18	22
Villas del Mar	Juan Dolio, San Pedro de Macoris	28	34

CALENDAR

The best time to go to the Dominican Republic is at the end of July, when the ten-day Merengue Festival takes place. This lively dance was invented here and in Santo Domingo the rum flows as everyone joins in. There's outdoor music, a fish fair, performances by the local folklore theatres, and all the hotel chefs present their specialities.

Continental holidays are observed as well as Independence Day (27 February) and if you come over Christmas be sure to book well in advance.

SHOPPING

Amber is an island speciality, but be careful as this is sometimes difficult to distinguish from plastic. Other small gift items are made from Dominican turquoise, a very pretty local stone, and tortoiseshell. Stick to plastic tortoiseshell if you are planning to return home to the States as the tortoise is considered to be an endangered species and may not be imported to the US.

Rocking chairs (self assembly) can be bought in Santo Domingo, but stay away from imported clothes as these are very expensive. There are duty-free shops in the town at the Centro de los Héroes.

NIGHTLIFE

There is nightlife for all tastes in Santo Domingo, Latin American, disco, merengue and for the spectator live shows; some of them folkloric—some of them hot.

Casinos can be found in the major hotels. You must be over 18 and jackets are required for men.

SPORT

Sports are taken more seriously here than in Haiti. There are popular beaches at Playa Grande and Sosua near Puerto Plata (the coast at Santo Domingo is not suitable for swimming).

Other sea based sports are snorkelling, scuba diving, sailing and fishing—and if you are lucky you may be able to reserve a place on the schooner *Merengue* for a day's sailing and snorkelling around Catalina Island's coral. Check with your hotel or the tourist office at Calle Arzobispo Merino 156 in Santo Domingo (or on Gregoria Luperón in Puerto Plata).

Inland sports include tennis, golf, riding and polo. Spectators can watch baseball—very popular here from October to February—or polo.

PUERTO RICO

At 100 miles long by 35 wide, Puerto Rico is about the same size as the Bahamian island of Andros, though with a personality at the opposite end of the spectrum. With the US Virgin Islands, it must be the wealthiest part of the Caribbean, both US Commonwealths benefiting from their association with the world's richest nation. The population is just over 3 million—again a strong contrast with Andros—with a long life-expectancy the norm.

Gold was first sought by the Spanish after their arrival in the first years of the 16th century, but as this was not available in substantial quantities they turned to the growing of sugar and coffee. As with the rest of the Caribbean, these crops were initially lucrative and became less so in the course of time, so that by the early years of this century Puerto Rico's poverty was a byword in the Caribbean. Steps were taken to correct this in the 1940s with an intensive industrialisation programme and the initiation of the tourist industry.

In the meantime Puerto Rico had changed hands. Following the Spanish-American war Spain ceded Puerto Rico to the United States in 1898. Puerto Ricans became US citizens in 1917, elected their governor for the first time in 1948 and became a Commonwealth associated with the United States in 1952.

GETTING TO PUERTO RICO
San Juan is something of a crossroads in the Caribbean. Airline routes spread out like the legs of a spider, covering North, South and Central America, Europe and a scattering of Caribbean islands.

From the USA
There must be more US departure points for San Juan than for any other Caribbean point. Eastern undertakes a large part of the work, flying down here from Atlanta, Baltimore, Boston, Chicago, Los Angeles, Miami, Orlando,

Philadelphia and San Francisco. Delta has links from Atlanta and Chicago. American flies in from Boston, New York, Tulsa, Miami and Dallas. TWA operates from Miami and New York, and World flies from New York and Los Angeles.

From Canada
Take a flight to any of the cities above and get a connection from there.

From London
There used to be direct flights (on British Caledonian) but, sadly, these are no more. Connect either via New York (either a charter or low APEX transatlantic fare) or Miami with connections as above. It is also worth looking at Iberia's through fares via Madrid, and sometimes there are deals available on Avianca via Paris.

From Europe
Lufthansa and Avianca operate services from Frankfurt, Iberia and Avianca from Madrid and Avianca from Paris.

Within the Caribbean
The vast majority of Caribbean services from here are operated by airlines using small aircraft to Puerto Rico's near neighbours. The US Virgin Islands of Saint Thomas and Saint Croix have a host of connections operated almost exclusively by local airlines and from both airports; these include seaplane services (Saint John is connected only by seaplanes). Sint Maarten has frequent services, operated by Dorado Wings, Air BVI, ALM, American Airlines and LIAT. Santo Domingo is linked by Eastern, Dominicana and ALM. Dorado Wings and Air BVI both serve Anguilla, Beef Island (Tortola) and Virgin Gorda. LIAT also serves Beef Island and there are seaplane services to Tortola (West End). Within the immediate area there are services to Saint Kitts operated by Dorado Wings and LIAT and a small plane service to Saint Barthélemy. More important and further-flung Caribbean destinations tend to be served by large jet aircraft; in these cases San Juan is more of a transit stop for long-haul flights. Aruba and Curaçao are both served by ALM; BWIA flies in from Trinidad, Barbados and Antigua (with American and LIAT) and Air France has a flight originating in Cayenne which passes through Martinique and Guadeloupe before reaching San Juan and going on to Haiti (which is also served by Air Jamaica, which goes on to Kingston and Montego Bay). Latin American destinations are dispersed as Barranquilla, Bogotá, Cancún, Caracas, Guayaquil, Lima, Mexico, Panama, Quito and San José are served by their national airlines and the European airlines Iberia and Lufthansa.

ENTRY REGULATIONS

All except US and Canadian citizens will need a USA visa. Multi-entry is recommended in case you retrace your steps (e.g. San Juan–Saint Thomas–Tortola–Saint Thomas). It is always best to apply for a United States visa in your home country; in particular, Australian and New Zealand citizens resident in the United Kingdom can expect difficulties if they apply in London. Onward and homeward tickets should be available for presentation. On arrival US and Canadian citizens should have few problems, but the rest of us get the usual US immigration hassle: long queues and being sent back if forms are not filled out perfectly (when filling them out, press hard). But immigration officials are only doing their jobs, and it is the law of the USA that scrutiny should be strict. The same is true of customs.

ELECTRICITY

The supply is 110 volts at 60 cycles, as in the US.

CLIMATE

Similar to Hispaniola, with an average 80°F in summer and 75°F in winter on the coast. Mountain areas can be cooler. The island benefits from the easterly trade winds, but rainfall is higher here than in Hispaniola. That shouldn't trouble you—you may welcome it.

CURRENCY

The US dollar is the only legal tender. Traveller's cheques and credit cards are widely accepted.

POPULATION

All but one percent of people of Puerto Rico are Caucasian of Spanish descent. Culturally and ethnically the country's soul is from the Mediterranean, economically and politically it is part of the United States. Thus the values and morals of Western 'civilisation' govern the attitudes and personality of the people.

Those very few people who ask you for money are genuinely poor, maimed or both, the casualties of society. But the majority are 'Poor no more'.

LANGUAGE

The Spanish language is preserved, along with other cultural ties. A great deal of English is spoken, particularly of course in tourist areas (although during my stay most tourists seemed to be Spanish-speaking too), but surprisingly little English is used by the younger generation.

233

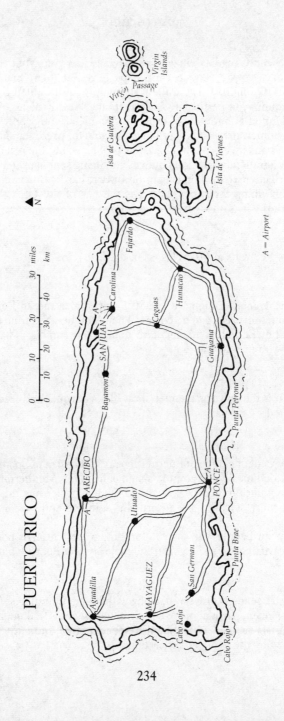

PUERTO RICO

Virgin Islands

Virgin Passage

Isla de Culebra

Isla de Vieques

N

30 miles
km

0 10 20 30 40

0 10 20 30

A — ARECIBO

Aguadilla

Utuado

MAYAGUEZ

Cabo Rojo

San German

Punta Brae

PONCE
A

Punta Petrona

Bayamon

SAN JUAN
A

Carolina

Caguas

Humacao

Guayama

Fajardo

A — Airport

THE CULTURAL HERITAGE
This is seen to best effect in the architecture—not in the tower blocks and urban sprawl of new San Juan of course, but in the preserved and restored buildings to be seen in and around the Old Town. Because the town was attacked so often down the centuries, most of the buildings are actually comparatively recent. But with a large budget available for restoration, and a great civic and national pride in its heritage being evident, San Juan manages to combine cultural authenticity with well-kept and clean streets. Many new buildings (including the outstandingly beautiful Casa de España on Avenida Ponce de León) have been constructed in the colonial style.

All this, with the fort that surrounds it, gives San Juan a Spanish flavour far stronger than that of Santo Domingo, and even than that of Madrid. The Old Town, though admittedly affected by tourism, is very charming, particularly during the day.

GETTING AROUND
Good roads and modern vehicles make getting about the islands less of a trial than in many other countries on this trip. Throughout Puerto Rico, distances are expressed in kilometres but speed in miles per hour. Taxis and limousines stop immediately outside the terminal. A taxi should cost about US$6 per car, and a limousine about US$2.50 per person. For públicos and the bus you walk up the ramp towards the car park; you should take a público if you are going to another town, but if you are staying in San Juan there is little point. The bus stop is easily found, but beware; it is adorned with a large sign which says 'No baggage or large packets allowed'. (I ignored this and in fact was allowed on the bus when it eventually came.)

Note that there are two airports in San Juan: Isla Verde International, at which you almost certainly arrived, and Isla Grande in town, from which you will probably leave.

Car hire: All the big names are here, at the airport and in San Juan. Smaller firms may not take credit cards. Do not be afraid to use the horn, especially on winding roads.

Buses ply the main street of San Juan on regular schedules. The majority terminate in Plaza de Colón (Columbus Square) in the old town, near the entrance of Fort San Cristóbal. Travelling eastwards these buses take Avenida Muñoz Rivera, whilst on the return trip to Old San Juan they use Avenida Ponce de León. Both these roads are one-way streets, and in both cases the buses move *against* the traffic flow. Special bus lanes, identified by a yellow line, exist for this purpose, which is a feature of San Juan. Thus it is important that you look both ways when crossing any street.

Bus stops are identified by yellow posts bearing the legend 'Parada de Guaguas' with shelters often provided. The fare is one quarter on almost all buses, and you must have the exact change as you enter through a coin-operated turn-stile. If taking a bus from the Old Town to the Miramar area note that you can take any except numbers 10 and 41 (although I was told the exact opposite by the tourist information people, whose literature is similarly misleading). If staying on the Atlantic coast (Condado, Ocean Park) you should use number 10. Number 41 serves the Isla Verde hotels. To and from the airport you can take number 17, which also serves Los Angeles.

At the time of writing the only long-distance bus is one which links San Juan with Mayagüez. The company is Puerto Rico Motor Coach, address 327 Recinto Sur, Old San Juan, and fare US$5.50. It departs from Rio Piedras in San Juan, and takes about four hours.

Públicos: Inter-city travel is usually undertaken by public cars displaying 'P' or 'PA' after the numbers on their licence plates. They generally terminate in the main plaza of a town; in the capital they leave from Plaza de Armas, Old San Juan, Stop 15, Santurce, and the airport (Isla Verde). The fare to Mayagüez is about US$6.50/$8, and to Ponce maybe US$5.50.

Taxis are metered. Rates are 40 cents to start and 10 cents every $\frac{1}{5}$ mile. Check that the flag is up when boarding. They also charge 25 cents per suitcase.

Boats: San Juan Bay can be crossed by ferry. These leave the old town (from the pier near the tourist information centre) every 15 minutes. A daily launch also leaves the east coast town of Fajardo bound for the islands of Vieques and Culebra. Departure from Fajardo is at 9.15 am and 4.30 pm, arriving in Vieques 1 hour 20 minutes later. The earlier boat continues to Culebra arriving at about 11.30 am. Return times are: from Vieques 7.30 am and 3 pm, and from Culebra 1.30 pm.

San Juan

The capital is an almost schizophrenic contrast between the charming old town and a modern city as up-to-date and hectic as you are likely to find anywhere. The new city is a featureless concrete jungle of skyscrapers, wide roads and overpriced tourist entertainments built on a naturally beautiful coastline. In contrast, the old town of San Juan was enclosed within a strong city wall and defended by the forts of El Morro and San Cristóbal. The building of these fortifications was a continuous process justified by repeated attacks (mainly by the English) but in the end they were unable to prevent history taking its course. The fort of San Cristóbal itself seems to have been designed mainly with aesthetics in mind, leaving it vulnerable to an attack from its landward side.

WHAT TO SEE IN SAN JUAN

You should visit one of the tourist centres which will give you glossy brochures full of very useful information and advertisements. They can be found at:

Isla Verda Airport (791 1014/3443/1853/5365)
Banco de Ponce building, Hato Rey (headquarters) (764 2390)
La Casita, Old San Juan (behind the post office and near pier one)
(722 1709)
Foyer of City Hall, Calle San Francisco, Old San Juan
Listed here are the outstanding sights in San Juan.

Although **Casa de España** does not appear to be listed in any of the tourist guides, it is a magnificent building; apparently recently built, it specialises in social functions (wedding receptions, etc.) for the wealthy.

San Juan's fortifications, **El Morro** and **San Cristóbal,** although occupied on occasion, seem to have done the job they were designed for most of the time. The Earl of Cumberland led the only invading force to occupy El Morro. He was driven out by dysentery. This was in 1598, three years after Sir Francis Drake failed to secure the harbour. The Dutch also met with failure. San Cristóbal, the fort at the other end of the old town, was built in the 18th century to prevent the town and El Morro being attacked from the landward side. Both forts are open from 8 am to 5 pm. There are many other beautiful and historical buildings in the old town which is well worth at least one long visit.

Metropolitan San Juan also has sights for the architecture buff. **El Capitolio** on Avenida Ponce de León near Casa de España is the home of the Legislature of Puerto Rico. The parallel road of Avenida Muñoz Rivera runs along a coastline that can be dramatic at times, past a statue of John the Baptist, until it arrives at quite a large park. A little further on, near the Caribe Hilton, is the small **Fort San Jerónimo** which the British unsportingly battered in 1797. It was rebuilt two years later. Puerto Rico is the world's largest producer of rum, and you can visit the Bacardi plant near Catano (free samples). Most beaches involve travel as you would expect, but there is a small one in the Miramar/Condado area (see Miramar map). It is crowded and not much good for swimming, but adequate for half a day's sunbathing and getting wet.

WHERE TO STAY IN SAN JUAN

Accommodation in San Juan is spread out from Old San Juan to the Isla Verde airport area, a distance of perhaps some 6 to 10 miles. There are three principal locations (for the purposes of this book): in the Old Town, in the Miramar/Condado area, and along the coast from Condado to Isla Verde.

Old San Juan: The **Hotel San Cristóbal** is opposite the entrance to the fort of the same name. It is an old hotel, about eight storeys high and with signs of decay. It is quite well-known, and many young people stay here. Service is,

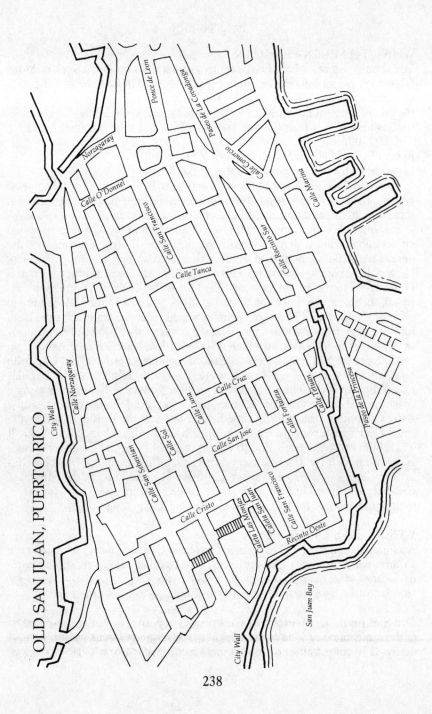

OLD SAN JUAN, PUERTO RICO

from personal observation, slow in coming and curt on arrival. The rooms have fine views, but the hotel is only average, or below average, in terms of value. The **YMCA** is expensive by Y standards. But it is also good by Y standards. Although furnishings and décor have that institutional flavour Ys love (perhaps they believe it is good for you), it is comfortable enough, with good bathroom and toilet facilities. There is cheap accommodation on or near Calle Luna, the poorest part of town. This accommodation is regarded with some humour locally. Expect to pay US$8 or less and regard all quoted prices as negotiable. To find it, use the Spanish method: find a bar (finding a doorway that isn't a bar is more difficult), go in and ask for 'habitaciones'. They will usually answer 'Aquí no' but direct you to the nearest. Good luck.

Miramar/Condado: There are a large number of hotels in this vicinity, many of which are tourist-orientated and overpriced. Most are set along the coast at Condado and will be of little interest to you. The ones you may prefer are in Miramar, further from the beach but on or near the main bus route between Old San Juan and Isla Verde airport. With frequent bus services you will find most of what you want quite accessible. (I used to walk into the Old Town and take the bus back.)

The **Miramar Guesthouse** offers the cheapest rates. The rooms are comfortable yet shabby. No rooms have private facilities but there are plenty of bathrooms. The manager is a Liverpudlian and has retained his Liverpool sense of humour. This must be the best value around for a single room and is worth considering for a double too. However, the **Hotel Toro** represents the best value for two or more people travelling together. It is a small, owner-managed hotel designed in Spanish style with a restaurant next door (details are given in the *Eating out* section below). Besides the normal rooms, some two-bedroom suites are available, comprising one bedroom with two twin beds, the other with a double. All rooms have private facilities, air-conditioning and ice box or refrigerator. The hotel also has a laundromat. This is recommended accommodation for couples and groups.

The **Borinquen Hotel** is a moderate hotel at luxury prices with a casino, cocktail lounges, boutiques, and all that sort of thing. While it would be easy to be critical of it (for a start, service was bad), it is probably typical of the big hotels (it is one of the biggest, its Cloud Room giving magnificent views of San Juan) and reasonable when judged by those standards.

There are three moderately priced hotels in this area (and one slightly outside). At the time of my visit the Iberia Hotel was about to change its name to the **Miramar Laguna**. All rooms have private facilities, including a lounge and kitchenette. American Express cards are accepted. The **Hotel Miramar,** not to be confused with the guesthouse of the same name, and the **Olimpo Court** are the two other reasonably priced hotels in this area. Outside the Miramar area proper, towards Old San Juan, is another small hotel, the **Ocean Side,** close to the towering Caribe Hilton. It is well-sited for buses and beaches. Rooms and facilities are very slightly better than those of the Toro, but then prices are significantly higher. This is probably because they accept all major credit cards.

Most hotels in the **coastal and easterly** group are in the expensive to very expensive bracket, and it is unlikely that you would want to stay in this part of San Juan anyway. Nevertheless, details are given here of the cheapest of them.

Accommodation in San Juan
Daily summer rates per room in US$

	Single	Double
Central Hotel, 202 Calle San José (tel. 722 2741)	EP: 14–18	20–24
El Convento, 100 Calle Cristo (tel. 723 9020)	EP: 65 MAP: 88	75 120
Fortaleza Hotel, 252 Calle Fortaleza (tel. 722 5012)	EP: 22–28	28–34
San Cristóbal Hotel, 450 Calle Norzagaray	EP: 14	24
YMCA, Stop 1, Avenida Ponce de León	EP: 12	
Condado/Miramar area		
Borinquen Hotel, Fernandez Juncos, Miramar	EP: 36–44	56–64
Hotel Miramar, 606 Avenida Ponce de León, Miramar	EP: 18–24	20–28
Hotel Toro, 605 Miramar Avenue, Miramar (tel. 725 5150 and 725 2647)	EP: 15–18 Triple 24–30	18–22
Miramar Guesthouse, 609 Olimpo, Miramar (tel. 724 9610)	EP: from 8, from 50 weekly	from 12, from 70 weekly
Miramar Laguna (ex *Iberia*), 604 Avenida Ponce de León, Miramar (tel. 723 0100)	EP: 20	30
Ocean Side Hotel, 54 Muñoz Rivera, near Hilton (tel. 722 2410)	EP: 20	25–40
Olimpo Court Hotel, 603 Miramar, Miramar	EP: 28–32	30–36
The Coastal and Easterly Hotels		
Bolivar Hotel, 609 Bolivar, Santurce (tel. 724 5023)	EP: 15	20
Interline Guesthouse, 20 Uno Este, Villamar (nearest to airport; tel. 726 5546)	EP: 20	30–34
Lily's Guesthouse, 2064 España, Ocean Park (tel. 725 8964 and 727 0548)	EP: 18–24	24–30
Ocean Breeze Guesthouse, 8 Tapia, Ocean Park (tel. 727 4002)	EP: 14–20	24–34

There is a government tax of 5% on room rates. There is no compulsory service charge, so you should tip according to the standard of service.

EATING OUT IN SAN JUAN

Generally prices are high (Bahamas levels and over), the food good and service bad. Cuisine is generally Puerto Rican, American and Spanish, but ethnic restaurants abound—for example Chinese, French, Argentinian, Italian. Food is generally well cooked from the widest range of meats, fish and vegetables. Service is of the lowest standard in the Caribbean, due probably to a combination of the Spanish influence, the country's recent rise to prosperity, and an uncomplaining tourist clientele. Service is abrupt and intimidatory, dishes being served at a frequency to suit the waiter rather than the diner.

The **D'Arco Restaurant** is on the ground floor of the Hotel Toro, 605 Miramar Avenue. It is open all day and takes BankAmericard and Master-Card. This is one of the best restaurants I found and by local standards gives very good value for money. I ate there twice. The first time was for dinner when I was impressed by the quality of the food (Puerto Rican and American menu). Service was somewhat inefficient, not rude.

El Mediterráneo, 254 San Justo in Old San Juan, is open all day and accepts most credit cards. It serves international cuisine with the accent on Spanish. I tried Paella Valenciana which was very good indeed. Again service was bad. The waiter brought the paella dish to my table then shovelled it out on to my plate as if it was Kat-o-meat (Nine Lives). When the dessert—caramel creme—arrived it hit the table so hard that the creme wobbled as though sinking in a tidal wave of caramel. But when it was time to pay the waiter took time to point out a Spanish print on the wall, helped himself to one of my Haitian cigarettes and suddenly remembered that I was his long-lost brother. I had to laugh: ten minutes after my arrival a group of four tourists entered and seated themselves at the table next to mine. This waiter then intimidated them all into having exactly the same as I had ordered!

Fornos in the Hotel Iberia (now Hotel Miramar Laguna), 604 Avenida Ponce de León, serves dinner and cocktails only. The food is predominantly Spanish with Puerto Rican and international dishes. American Express, Bank Americard, and MasterCard are accepted here. Although the *à la carte* menu is expensive, a daily menu with six or seven choices is also offered—a three-course meal (four including coffee) for anything from US$6 to $9.50. I chose the most expensive: superb Spanish soup, delicious sirloin steak with french fries and salad, flan and coffee. It is very strongly recommended, especially if you choose from the set menu. Don't go in jeans. Service tended towards the abrupt, but is certainly not rude or overbearing.

Puerto Rican snack bars, bar/restaurants and cafeterias are to be found all over town, but are particularly thick on the ground in the old part. Prices vary, but are generally at about Bahamian levels. Liquor is reasonably priced, 80 cents for local beer, 85 cents for Cuba Libre, but beware of the Puerto Rican coffee! This concoction—hopefully unique—is a brew made of milk as an

241

intrinsic element, the result being a sort of coffee-flavoured hot milk. Fortunately there is also Expresso coffee, and if you want something that approximates to real coffee ask for American Express—expresso with hot water added.

WHAT TO SEE ON PUERTO RICO
If you have time to make a visit outside the capital, or perhaps a trip round the island, you are unlikely to be disappointed. The mountains run almost the length of the island, through the centre. Whilst the northern side is green and fertile, the southern side is dry. These mountains, named the **Cordillera Central,** carry a spectacularly scenic road, the Routa Panoramica. You are likely to see sugar-cane plantations in the lowlands and coffee at higher altitudes. There are many rivers and 23 man-made lakes (no natural ones).

WHERE TO STAY OUTSIDE SAN JUAN
A selection of moderate- and budget-priced tourist accommodation follows. You can also expect some guesthouse accommodation in some of the towns.

San Juan, Puerto Rico

Daily summer rates per room in US$

	Single	Double
Hacienda Gripinas, Rte 527, Jayuya (tel. 763 8855)	EP: 28–35	35–40
Hacienda Rosas (on coffee plantation), Rte. 140, Utuado (tel. 894 2374)	MAP: 26–28	36–44
Hotel Delicias, (facing wharf), Fajardo (tel. 863 1818)	EP: 25	35
Hotel El Coche, La Rambla, Ponce (tel. 842 9607)	EP: 22	30–35

	Single	Double
Hotel El Sol, Calle El Sol, Mayagüez (tel. 833 0303)	EP: 28–40	40–50
Hotel La Palma, Mayagüez (tel. 832 0230)	EP: 15–24	35–40
Hotel Villa Parguera, Ocean Front, Rte 304, Parguera (tel. 892 9588)	EP: 16–40	40
Hotel Vivi, Rte 111, Utuado (tel. 894 2376)	EP: 15–25	25–35
La Casa Roig Guesthouse, 10 Betances, Yauco	EP: 8–18	12–20
Parador El Verde (edge of rain forest), Rte 186, El Verde (tel. 786 5325)	EP: 24–30	34–40
Posada Porlamar, Ocean Front, Rte 304, Parguera	EP: 20–26	26–34
Punta Borinquen, Aguadilla (2- and 3-bedroom villas at former Air Force Base; tel. 891 1510)	EP: 60–70 per villa	
Ranchos Guayama, Bo. Cimarrona, Guayama	EP: 25	25–50
San José Guesthouse, 47 Calle Cristina, two blocks from plaza (tel. 842 0281)	EP: 26	34–48
Villa Antonio (on beach), Rte 115, Rincón (tel. 823 2645)	EP: 20–28	34
	Cabins 65–80	

WHERE TO EAT OUTSIDE SAN JUAN

Although the best restaurants are located in San Juan, there are others which are worth trying: **Bolo's Place** in Mayagüez, **Restaurante Tito** in Ponce, or **El Conquistador** in Arecibo for example. If you are driving along the south coast, you may well find some of the little local places are worth a look.

CALENDAR

There are so many special events in Puerto Rico that you would be very unlucky indeed if your holiday dates missed one. The best plan is to get a copy of *Qué pasa* ('What's happening') or ask the Tourist Board before you go. Apart from local festivities Puerto Ricans celebrate both US holidays and Spanish saints' days. There's even a year-long festival, called LeLoLai, of island culture with some events included in package tours.

SHOPPING

Local handicrafts abound in Puerto Rico. Visit the Folk Arts Center in the 16th-century Dominican Convent in Old San Juan which has an exhibition room as well as items for sale. A shopping trip to the old town is well combined with a historical tour of this once-walled peninsula. (Music lovers should take in the Pablo Casals Museum nearby.) There are many little shops in the old part of town selling jewellery, lace or rum.

Puerto Rico is not a duty-free port so prices are no cheaper than in the US for imported goods. Rum is cheaper of course; this merely means you have to pay your own duty if you bring home more than your allowance.

As well as handicrafts and clothes there is a lively industry in original art, of every form, and almost everything else you could think of from personally rolled cigars to collectors' butterflies.

NIGHTLIFE

San Juan is not the holiday centre for the shy and retiring. Casinos are in the larger hotels (dress well); Latin American, French and flamenco floor shows can be found, as can classical and folk music concerts, Spanish theatre and the predictable discos. Quieter evenings should be sought outside the town—at Catano, a romantic ferry ride from Old San Juan, or further along the coast.

SPORT

Record-breaking wins have been reported in deep-sea angling tournaments from Puerto Rico, and exotic species are best fished from May to November. Boats can be chartered for fishing or sailing from various centres (ask your hotel or the tourist office). There are also snorkelling and scuba-diving opportunities, golf, tennis and riding. The dozen or so public beaches are well-organised with lockers, showers and picnic tables but remember that swimming is rougher on the Atlantic side. Surfing is particularly popular at Rincón, where the Professional Surfing Contest takes place, and good surfing can be found on several beaches.

Spectators can find baseball and horse racing, while those with a strong stomach can watch cock fighting.

TURKS AND CAICOS ISLANDS

The Turks and Caicos Islands are a Crown Colony, and the majority of the islanders seem to prefer their colonial status. In 1980 discussions between the British government and the islands' government on the subject of independence reached an advanced stage, and independence seemed to be close. In that same year however—in November—an election was held, and the opposition, which ran on an anti-independence ticket, was elected with a substantial majority. The upshot of this was a shelving of plans, and new tactics from the British government to encourage the islanders to welcome independence.

The key to this apparently strange reluctance to assume complete control of their affairs lies in the islands' nickname—'The Forgotten Islands'. Very few people have heard of the Turks and Caicos Islands. Tourism is the main industry, and is increasing daily. One is repeatedly told: 'There's no industry here; if we were independent we would starve.' Even the salt industry is currently non-existent.

Thus the British government is investing large sums of money in developing tourism in the islands. Providenciales, the island which is furthest from the capital on Grand Turk, is the centre of most development, which includes an airport capable of handling large jets: perhaps it is intended to be another Grand Bahama.

All this will take time of course, so if you want a quiet backwater with excellent diving, some lovely beaches and regular inter-island connections, come here soon.

GETTING TO THE TURKS AND CAICOS ISLANDS

There are three airports capable of handling jet aircraft: Grand Turk, Providenciales and South Caicos, although the airstrip at the latter is not really up to the job. Currently the gateways are therefore Grand Turk (the capital) and Providenciales (at present being developed for tourism).

From the USA
Atlantic Gulf flies in from Miami and Tallahassee and Pan Am from Miami. Pan Am has connections from some other US cities.

From Canada
Make your way to Miami, from where you can take connections as shown above, or alternatively there are flights from Montreal and Toronto to Nassau (on Air Canada) from where you can connect with Turks and Caicos Airways.

From London
This used to be relatively easy in the good old days of Air Florida, but became very difficult with its demise. Now that Pan Am operates the route it should be fairly straightforward to connect through Miami, though an overnight stop there may be necessary. You will need a visa if you travel via the US.

From Europe
Again, through Miami, which can be reached direct from Berlin, Hamburg, Madrid and Paris (all on Pan Am), Oslo (Northwest Orient) and Madrid (Iberia and Aeromexico). Aeromexico and Delta also fly from Paris, and Lufthansa serves Miami from Düsseldorf and Frankfurt.

Within the Caribbean
International and domestic services are operated by Turks and Caicos Airlines. Cap Haïtien, Freeport and Nassau are linked with both Grand Turk and Provo, whilst there is also a service from Grand Turk to Puerto Plata. The

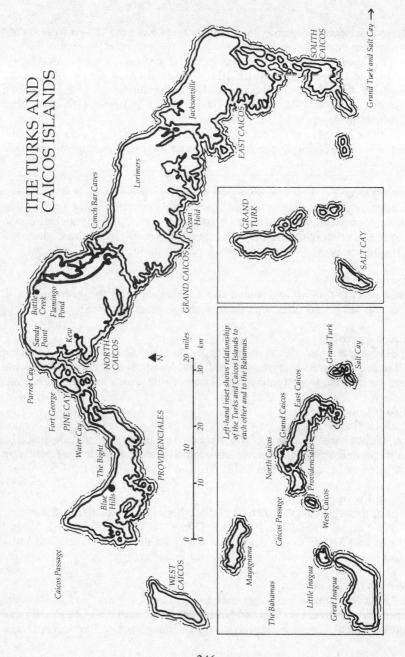

THE TURKS AND
CAICOS ISLANDS

Caicos Passage

WEST
CAICOS

Parrot Cay

Fort George

PINE CAY

Water Cay

Sandy
Point

Bottle
Creek

Flamingo
Pond

Kew

NORTH
CAICOS

Conch Bar Caves

Lorimers

Jacksonville

Ocean
Hold

EAST CAICOS

SOUTH
CAICOS

Grand Turk and Salt Cay →

The Bight

Blue
Hills

PROVIDENCIALES

GRAND CAICOS

N

0   10   20   miles

0   10   20   30   km

Left-hand inset shows relationship
of the Turks and Caicos Islands to
each other and to the Bahamas.

GRAND
TURK

SALT CAY

The Bahamas

Mayaguana

Caicos Passage

North Caicos

Grand Caicos

East Caicos

Providenciales

West Caicos

Little Inagua

Great Inagua

Grand Turk

Salt Cay

national airline links up all the islands with an airstrip on its domestic services—Mid Caicos, North Caicos, South Caicos and Salt Cay.

ENTRY REGULATIONS

Visas are normally required only by citizens of Communist bloc countries. It is absolutely necessary for you to have an onward or return ticket and adequate funds to cover the period you intend to stay.

ELECTRICITY

The supply is 110 volts at 60 cycles, the same as in the US.

CLIMATE

The temperature range is between 77°F and 83°F, and the climate generally is very similar to the Bahamas. There is little rainfall in the most easterly islands. Because of this the Tourist Board asks visitors to conserve water as much as possible during their stay.

CURRENCY

The US dollar and Turks and Caicos crown, which are at par, are both legal tender. US$ traveller's cheques are widely accepted, but there are currently few places which honour credit cards.

POPULATION

The total population numbers around 7,500 of whom about 4,000 live on Grand Turk, mainly in and around Cockburn Town, the capital. Salt Cay is home to about 400, whilst 1,200 live on South Caicos, 500 on Middle Caicos, 1,200 on North Caicos and 700 on Providenciales; 95% of the people are black. East Caicos and West Caicos are currently uninhabited, though they once had industrial and plantation settlements. A quick glance at the map will show that the population figures do not correlate with the land masses within the island chain.

The Caicos Islands, separated from the Bahamas by 30 miles of water, comprise the majority of the land area in the group. They are separated from Grand Turk and Salt Cay by the 22-mile-wide Turks Island Passage.

LANGUAGE

English.

HISTORY

Geographically these islands are part of the Bahamas group, and at times in their history they have also been so politically. Control of the islands has been fought over by Bahamian interests, the French, Spanish and British. At the end of the 18th century the islands became part of the Bahamas, separating in 1848. In 1874 they became a dependency of Jamaica from whom they finally separated on Jamaican independence in 1962.

GETTING AROUND
All the islands are fairly small and your hotel should be able to arrange a tour by taxi for a moderate sum. If you feel the need to hire a car Hertz are on Grand Turk and Provo, and local firms operate on most of the islands. (Drive *on the left*.) You can also charter a small plane for an aerial tour.

WHAT TO SEE
Here is a brief summary of the islands, starting in the west:

West Caicos
It is uninhabited, a sanctuary for wild birds, and bordered by a fine fishing ground; rarely visited.

Providenciales
Although it boasts only a small native population, Provo (as it is colloquially called) has been designated as the main island for tourist development. There has been substantial American investment here, with most facilities being provided around the narrow middle of the island, at Turtle Cove. There is some excellent wall diving off North West Point and some good shallow dives: there are two dive operations. Also on this island are the ruins of a great house, Stubbs Hall

The Cays
Linking Providenciales with the main Caicos Island group are a number of small cays, of which Pine Cay, Fort George Cay and Parrot Cay are notable. Pine Cay is one of the few islands in the group with no fresh-water problem. Its main claim to fame is its superb beaches, but it also offers the visitor some of the best diving to be experienced in the Caribbean. 'Serious' divers are welcomed, and the accent here is on conservation and education. The operators' slogan is 'Take only pictures, leave only bubbles'. Fort George Cay, as you would expect from the name, has a fort, established in 1798. Now in ruins, it is nevertheless an interesting sight, surrounded by a National Park

North Caicos
Sparsely populated, until recently this island was undeveloped. As this book goes to press the luxurious Prospect of Whitby Hotel is being refurbished but this need not prevent you from visiting this garden island with its unspoilt six-mile beach, where you can scuba dive, snorkel or beachcomb for glass floats.

Middle (or Grand) Caicos

There is no tourist development here, though there is a small government-run guesthouse in the main settlement of Conch Bar. There is no telephone. Wild cotton plants are evidence of past development by Loyalists at the end of the 18th century, and there was a thriving guano industry in the 1880s. The island also boasts fine seascapes of limestone cliffs sheltering sandy coves along its north coast, and cathedral-sized caves in which have been found primitive artefacts.

East Caicos

Now uninhabited, this was once the centre for sisal growing and cattle breeding. A few wild cattle still roam as living proof.

South Caicos

The Air Florida jets used to come in here, but the service was discontinued because loose stones around the runway caused damage to the jet engines. The airport is now home to a requisitioned DC3, impounded whilst being used for smuggling. Cockburn Harbour is the best natural port in the island chain, still thriving as the centre of the fishing industry. Lobster, conch and gamefish are caught in profusion. There are both hotels and guesthouses here.

Wild ponies and donkeys roam parts of the island, and the beachcombing and diving are both considered excellent. There was some salt production here, and Cockburn Harbour was the port from which the majority of the islands' salt was exported. There is a well-established dive operation at the Admiral's Arms.

Grand Turk

Although the most densely populated of the islands, this is a favourite. Whilst retaining the 'laid back' feeling of all these islands, it presents far more opportunities for human contact. There is an easy mixture of native, expatriate and tourist; there are few bars and hotels so it is difficult to avoid meeting an interesting cross-section of people. Most of the tourists are divers anyway, and some excellent dives are only about ten minutes' boat ride from the beach which fronts the three hotels. In fact almost everything is beside the beach: the road winds in from the Airport, finding its way to the beach at the earliest opportunity, and then runs alongside it through the town and beyond. The seat of government, two wooden buildings protected by 18th-century cannon and sheltered by palm trees, is only separated from the beach by this road.

One can walk everywhere one would want to go (even to the airport, if necessary). One can stroll around with camera in hand during the hours of daylight, photographing the buildings so obviously influenced by both Loyalist and Haitian styles, or take a moonlit walk without needing to go far for serenity.

Dawn breaks gently over the salt pits and the sun sets spectacularly over the small jetty.

One has the feeling that when, in a few years' time, Provo has become a thriving, major tourist resort, Grand Turk will still be a sleepy village of wooden buildings with fishermen playing dominoes in the sun.

Salt Cay

I was told I could see all of Salt Cay in a day. In the event it took about four hours, and only so long because I was considerably slowed down by the friendliness of the local people. Although I was travelling in the high season, I was the only passenger on the early morning flight and there was not a single tourist on the island. The disused salt pits, White House, beaches and a herd of wild donkeys all came my way, punctuated by short chats with passers-by, sometimes on an upturned boat and sometimes on the road. Tourist accommodation is limited to Mount Pleasant Guest House (owned by James Morgan, formerly manager of the salt-producing operation) and Balfour Beach Cottages, which were closed, locked up and patronised only by two cows lying in their shade. Salt Cay may be the ultimate antidote to city life.

CALENDAR

The only events of note on these sleepy islands are the Annual South Caicos Regatta at the end of May and the Carnival in late August.

WHERE TO STAY

Grand Turk: Both of the islands which have international air links have ample tourist accommodation. On Grand Turk I stayed at the **Turk's Head Inn**, attracted both by its price and by a suspicion that it would be a wooden guesthouse type of place. My suspicions were well-founded: Turk's Head has all the charm and character of a well-managed guesthouse, plus an extremely congenial atmosphere. It is owned and managed by Californian expatriate H. R. (Russell) and serves (I was told) the best food on the island. I can certainly vouch for the excellence of the food: I had all my meals here, afraid to dine elsewhere in case I missed something.

There are seven rooms, including one cubbyhole of a single which is sometimes rented for less than the advertised price. All other rooms have bathrooms *en suite*, and at least one is furnished with a large four-poster bed. The main restaurant is inside, but breakfast and lunch are usually served in the tree-shaded garden outside.

In addition to the main white and green inn building across the road from an excellent beach, H. R. has two cottages on the beach itself. He also has a barbecue and bar facility on the beach, though this has fallen into disuse.

There are two other small hotels on Grand Turk. The **Salt Raker Inn,** which, like the Turk's Head, is a converted wooden balconied home, has eight rooms and a cottage in its delightful gardens. This too is across the road from the beach, on which small boats are invariably drawn up. **Kittina Hotel, a** little further along, appears to be purpose-built. It specialises far more than the other two in dive packages (one of the island's two dive operations—Underwater Research Ltd—is resident here), is better appointed and more suitable for small groups (there are 24 rooms).

South Caicos: The island is well-provided with tourist accommodation, most of which is concentrated in and around Cockburn Harbour, a short taxi ride from the airport.

Admiral's Arms, the oldest tourist hotel, sits high on a cliff overlooking the fishing village itself. Some of the best diving in the islands can be experienced from here, including a wall 10 minutes from shore, and there are excellent chances of encountering sharks, barracuda and turtles.

Caicos Reef Lodge is a pastel-painted collection of small wooden cottage units set on a large sandy beach. Accompanying them is the main hotel building

Accommodation in the Turks and Caicos Islands
Daily summer rates per room in US$

	Single	Double
Kittina Hotel, Front Street, Grand Turk (tel. 2232)	EP: 65	75–85
Salt Raker Inn, Front Street, Grand Turk (tel. 2260)	EP: 30–70	50–80
Turk's Head Inn, Cockburn Town, Grand Turk (tel. 2466)	EP: 40	80
Balfour Beach Cottages, Salt Cay	approx. EP: 20–30, extra person 10	
Mount Pleasant Guest House, Salt Cay	AP: 60	80
Admiral's Arms, Cockburn Harbour, South Caicos (tel. 3223)	EP: 75	100–160
Corean's Cottages, Cockburn Harbour, South Caicos	EP: 30	38
Caicos Reef Lodge, Cockburn Harbour, South Caicos	approx. EP: S or D 30–50	
Prospect of Whitby, North Caicos (tel. 4250)	Closed	
Meridian Club, Pine Cay (tel. USA (813) 263 2327)	EP: 140	200
Leeward Marina and Villas, Providenciales (tel. 4216)	EP: 55	65
Third Turtle Inn, Providenciales (tel. USA (305) 276 7372)	EP: 90	115
Treasure Beach Apartments, Providenciales (tel. 4211/4214)	EP: 80	110

with restaurant and bar. At the time of my visit it had recently been taken over by the previous Minister of Tourism, Mr C. W. Maguire, and thus was not really open for business. Further development can be expected to have taken place, so it's certainly worth a try when you remember that most accommodation in the Cockburn Harbour area is not on a beach. I found the staff very helpful and friendly.

I stayed at **Corean's Cottages,** a small, solidly constructed building of around a dozen rooms. They were fairly simply but adequately furnished, with fans, though bathrooms are shared. Corean lives about 100 yards away in the village itself. You may have trouble finding her; when you have found her, she may have trouble finding the right keys. There is also another guesthouse here, the **Village Inn,** and **Bassett Apartments** between the airport and the village. Both will cost you about $45 for a double room.

Salt Cay: Mount Pleasant Guest House is the only accommodation which can be relied upon to be open. It is a large, red-roofed building in a large, walled garden. The owner, James Morgan, is generally regarded as a mine of information on the islands, and I certainly saw more reading matter about here than anywhere. It is about 15 minutes' walk from an excellent beach.

EATING OUT
This is a very expensive occupation as virtually everything is imported at high cost. Specialities include lobster, turtle steak, and conch fritters. Most restaurants are found in the hotels; in particular, try **Papillon** or **Amanda's** on Grand Turk, and **Henry's Road Runner** on Provo.

DIVE OPERATORS

Name and address	Type of diving
Phil Pruss, Pepcor, Front Street, Cockburn Harbour, Grand Turk	Drop-off (to 7,000 ft) quarter mile offshore, begins at 40 ft; coral reefs and gardens, black coral at 60 ft; canyons; night dives; abundant tropical fish, bottlenose dolphin.
Mike Spillar, Underwater Research Ltd, Hotel Kittina, Cockburn Town, Grand Turk (tel. 2386)	Drop-off, coral reefs and gardens, night dives, tropical fish. Compressors: RIX 15 cfm and Mako 8 cfm; Tanks: 50 steel. 32' Flat top (28 divers), 26' Stapleton (8 divers) dive boats. Sample dive packages (accommodation at Kittina): 4 nights (6 dives) $348, 7 nights (12 dives) $585. PADI certification course (1 week, 1 beach dive and 4 boat dives) $200.
Turk-Cai Watersports, Admiral's Arms Inn, Cockburn Harbour, South Caicos	Drop-off, shallow reefs, large sponges and abundant marine life.

Name and address	Type of diving
Seaquatic Divers, Prospect of Whitby Hotel, South Caicos	Coral hills, canyons, mini-walls. Tiny marine life. Wrecks.
Pride Divers, Meridian Club, Pine Cay	'Second Phase' diving (for pleasure and education); marine ecology courses; serious divers only (no groups).
Provo Turtle Divers, Third Turtle Inn, Providenciales	Excellent wall diving, coral reefs, coral gardens.

Notwithstanding the above, it is important to remember two salient points about diving in these islands: first, the government and the dive operations are most concerned with preserving the ecology of the sea, and there are dire penalties for scavenging; second, the main pleasure of diving here is its pioneer aspect. Very few sites out of the vast potential have been established and properly recorded, so there is always the possibility of something unexpected being seen.

Remember that these islands are undeveloped, so you will find film, batteries, etc. very hard (if not impossible) to get locally. Also bring your own fins, snorkel, regulator and buoyancy compensator. Spearguns are not permitted.

NB: There are mosquitoes in the islands so be sure to bring a repellent. On the other hand, be sure to leave any illicit substances at home, as being found in possession of these will result in instant imprisonment.

JAMAICA

Until Columbus arrived, Arawak Indians were quite happily living in Xaymaca, 'Land of Wood and Water'. He renamed it Saint Jago. The island remained under Spanish control until 1655 when a force of Cromwell's soldiers, who should have gone to Haiti instead, landed and despatched the Spaniards. It was some time after this that the island was rechristened Jamaica.

The island is 144 miles long and 49 miles wide and a complete contrast to the Bahamas. It is very mountainous; the highest peak, Blue Mountain Peak in the eastern parish of Saint Thomas, rising to 7,402 feet. Roughly speaking, the mountains run along the spine of the country, with other hilly areas too. The fairly large town of Mandeville is 2,000 feet above sea level. There is a hilly area with few roads between Falmouth and Mandeville which is known as the Cockpit Country. This is the home of the first independent Jamaicans, the Maroons, runaway slaves who established independent villages during the Spanish and British colonial periods. Their name is an anglicised version of the Spanish word 'Cimarrones'. They harassed the planters to such an extent

Reggae vocalist

that various treaties were signed granting them extensive rights of self-government. I am given to understand that even today the Maroons have almost complete control over their own affairs.

The rest of the country is politically divided up into three counties: from left to right, Cornwall, Middlesex and Surrey. These are subdivided into parishes. Government of the country is based on the British system with a two-chambered legislature, Prime Minister and Cabinet, and official opposition.

There are two main political parties, the Jamaica Labour Party which is nationalist, and the People's National Party, which is socialist. Rivalry between these two parties over recent years has sometimes even led to bloodshed, particularly at election times. The two most recent elections have seen governments elected with 'landslide' majorities: in 1976 Michael Manley's PNP was decisively re-elected and in 1981 the JLP led by Edward Seaga stormed to power.

Jamaica's main industries are bauxite (for aluminium), tourism and agriculture. Tourism is the main foreign exchange earner and has risen nearly 30% in the last six years (the Tourist Board tells me). Bauxite mining has declined due to the slump in the international market and although competition has been tough for the banana and sugar markets there is a healthy and growing trade in winter vegetables and exotic fruits.

Jamaicans in the towns seem to live better than their Bahamian counterparts, largely because Jamaica is self-sufficient to a great degree. But there is a great difference here between what the native pays and what the visitor is expected to pay.

Jamaica used to be one of the more expensive Caribbean islands for tourists, but that was way back in 1976. At that time the Jamaican dollar was worth *more*

254

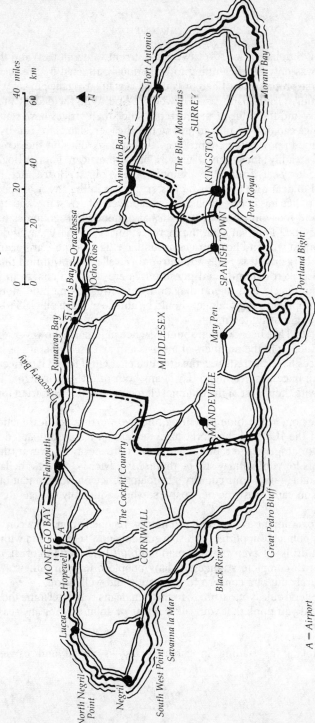

than the US dollar (it was over twice its current value, in fact) and the tourist industry was only just beginning to be seriously affected by the scare stories and adverse propaganda. There was thus a certain arrogance in some quarters towards tourists and many cases of overcharging. With the decline of the tourist industry and the value of the currency since then, prices have stabilised, so that Jamaica can now be ranked among the cheaper islands to visit. By the time Seaga came to power the country was almost bankrupt, but the economy has improved steadily since then. The work of the Jamaican Tourist Board is now beginning to bear fruit. For example, the Tourist Board Act has been enhanced to deal with people who pester tourists in the street. A special force of tourist police has been established, with powers of arrest for 'anti-tourist activities', and those involved in tourism have attended programmes on putting the visitor first. Tourism is on the increase, but prices have stayed down.

The tourist will find hotel prices around average for the Caribbean, though there are bargains. It is really the intrepid traveller who will find the greatest savings. Local restaurants and guesthouses are likely to charge in Jamaican dollars (but check) and so you may find yourselves paying little more than in Haiti. A couple on a tight budget should be able to manage on US$40–50 a day without economising too much.

A great deal has been written about violence in Jamaica; however, the consequent reduction in the numbers of tourists and extensive operations by the security forces have cleared away the criminal element. I found it perfectly safe to walk about in central Montego Bay at any hour of the day or night. The tourists, and with them part of the criminal element, have now departed for greener pastures.

In Kingston, at the time of writing, the two warring political factions, supporters of the JLP and the PNP, have declared a truce, and stated that they want to work together to rebuild the nation's prosperity. However, the volatile ingredients for conflict may still be there. My advice is to check the latest situation at home—with your country's Foreign Office or Department of Foreign Affairs. You can't trust the newspapers, who continually exaggerate the 'violence'.

The government is actively promoting reconciliation between different groups of political supporters. Most arguments now seem to end with an apology and a drink—I even saw one man jump off his bicycle to break up a fight between two complete strangers. Many people offered me their services as guides purely out of a concern for my safety and well-being.

As a general rule, your attitude to the Jamaicans will determine the way they treat you. If you think that you will feel fear or animosity for any reason, then don't come!

NB: Smoking or trading in ganja—grass—is illegal and carries severe penalties. Firearms are prohibited and customs search almost everyone on arrival.

Be careful but not paranoid with your baggage.

When venturing out at night leave your valuables safely locked away and carry no more money than you will need.

GETTING TO JAMAICA

Jamaica is important within the Caribbean both commercially and as a tourist destination, and this is reflected in the airline routes which pass through or terminate here. Most of the commercial traffic is to Kingston, the capital, whilst most tourists will disembark at Montego Bay. Some flights serve both cities.

From the USA

There are six US cities which are joined to both Kingston and Montego Bay by the same airlines: Atlanta, Baltimore, Los Angeles, New York, Philadelphia and Tampa. Air Jamaica flies down from all these points; American serves both destinations from New York, Eastern shares the honours on the Atlanta run and also serves Kingston from Detroit. Three airlines, Air Jamaica, Eastern and Challenge International, link both points with Miami.

From Canada

Air Canada and Air Jamaica connect both Kingston and Montego Bay with Toronto. Halifax, Montreal and Winnipeg are linked with Montego Bay by Air Canada. It is also worth checking whether there are charters.

From London

British Airways and Air Jamaica have a 'shared service' (British Airways aircraft) three times a week to both of Jamaica's jet airports, stopping on the way. On other days of the week they will route you, for the same through fares, via Miami: British Airways to Miami and Air Jamaica onwards. Between late December and early March there is a joint Concorde operation from London via New York to Montego Bay. Sometimes the cheapest fares, particularly if you want an open ticket and don't mind roughing it, are via Moscow(!) on Aeroflot.

From Europe

There are no direct services on Air Jamaica from Frankfurt or Paris. Good connections are available from France, Italy and Germany through New York or Miami. You need a visa if you transit the US.

Within the Caribbean

Four Caribbean points are linked to both Montego Bay and Kingston: Grand Cayman (Air Jamaica and Cayman Airways), Nassau (British Airways), Haiti

(Air Jamaica) and Puerto Rico (Air Jamaica on both routes and BWIA on the Kingston route only). In addition there are flights to Kingston only from Antigua, Barbados, Trinidad and Sint Maarten (BWIA); Curaçao (ALM); and Cuba (Cubana).

ENTRY REGULATIONS

Citizens of the USA, UK, Canada, the Commonwealth and most of Western Europe do not need a visa, although French citizens do. Onward or return tickets and evidence of adequate funds are required. If you have recently come from or transited a yellow fever endemic area you will need an appropriate inoculation certificate.

ELECTRICITY

The supply is not standardised; 110 volts predominates, but some hotels use 220 volts. So check with reception before plugging anything in.

CLIMATE

It is very dependent on altitude. As elsewhere in the Caribbean, sea breezes keep beach and coastal temperatures below the 90°F mark in summer and around the 80°F level in winter, so there is rarely what I would call oppressive heat (though this means you can underestimate the power of the sun and burn instead of tanning if you are not careful). Up in the mountains you can expect cooler weather; winter temperatures in Mandeville often drop to 50°F at night. You may be glad of it. The months of heaviest rain are generally May and October.

CURRENCY

The Jamaican dollar (J$) is now the only legal tender. As you cannot import or export this currency you will need to get some at the airport bank. Be very careful about changing money in Jamaica. When you exchange cash or traveller's cheques be sure to get a receipt from the bank. You will need it to change your Jamaican dollars back into US dollars when you leave the country. No bank gave me one of these slips, although I changed in excess of US$200, so that when I tried to change a paltry J$12 back into real money on leaving, the clerk in the airport bank refused. For $12! This was probably deliberate, as Jamaican currency is worth only half its face value outside the country. A Jamaican lady in the queue before me was forced to take J$100 out of the country illegally for the same reason.

I found Jamaican banks amongst the world's worst, particularly First National City Bank (although I found this bank pretty bad throughout the Caribbean). Service is poor for Jamaicans and visitors alike.

It is therefore important always to get a receipt when you change money. Currently the rate of exchange is US$1 = J$5.48 (subject to fluctuation).

POPULATION

'Out of many, one people.' This is the national motto, which is printed on some of the banknotes. It is certainly true. Jamaica has been a melting pot for all the world's races, and although the negro strain predominates there is a wide variety of physiognomy. Among Jamaicans themselves there is no racism; a man may hate another illogically because of his politics, but not because of his colour. What little racism there is has been introduced by the tourists, and is mainly due to a lack of understanding on both sides.

The Jamaicans are outgoing, colourful, cheerful, excitable, loving and gentle if shown respect, and vicious when upset. One of the unique points about Jamaicans is that a gentle man can become violent if he thinks he, or Jamaica, is being insulted, whilst a potentially dangerous hustler will be kind and helpful if shown respect.

Jamaicans are colourful in their dress, mannerisms, music and most of all in their speech, a unique patois—perhaps vibrant is a better word. When spoken fast, as it usually is, and with strong accentuation, this patois sounds like a foreign language. This is one of the strengths of the reggae music, where a good vocalist can add excitement to what would otherwise be mundane lyrics.

The total population of Jamaica is around two million.

LANGUAGE

Officially English, but Creole is widely spoken.

FOOD AND DRINK

For me, Jamaican food is not as good as Bahamian. But then restaurant food in the Bahamas is usually of a very high standard, probably because Bahamian food is generally cooked to order, and therefore always fresh.

In Jamaica one can eat in a good restaurant yet find the food bland: international cuisine, with few native dishes on the menu. Also, because it is patronised by tourists, expatriates and (to a lesser extent) the native bourgeoisie, prices will be high.

Fortunately Jamaica has many more of the cheap native restaurants than can be found in the Bahamas. This is largely because Jamaica is fairly self-sufficient in food; the goat is the national animal and the hen the national bird. Cattle are reared for both milk and meat, rice is grown (in Westmoreland), bananas are seemingly limitless, and the yam (not dissimilar to the potato when on your plate) is just one of the incredible range of vegetables cultivated. Fruits you may never have heard of include *sweetsop*, *soursop*, mango, pawpaw, *sapodilla*, *ortanique* and *otaheiti* apple. Milk and orange juice can be bought cheaply and excellent coffee is grown here (in the Blue Mountains), not to mention sugar.

In the cheap restaurants the menu is generally fried chicken, stewed beef, curried goat and boiled fish. There are of course many variations. Prices will vary widely according to where you are and, in some localities, may be higher in winter. Expect to pay between J$5 and J$8 for lunch or dinner. The quality and quantity will not vary according to price in this range.

Jamaican native restaurants and bars seem unwelcoming and hazardous to the wary tourist. They are usually shabby outside, dark within and often feature locals framing the doorway. They can sometimes be difficult to find too—round the back of a house or up some stairs. But all are safe for the traveller, with the possible exception of those in some parts of Kingston.

The standard accompaniment to the meat/fish/fowl dishes mentioned above is peas 'n' rice, or boiled rice, with tomato and possibly lettuce or banana. In better restaurants you should be served a wide variety of Jamaican vegetables. Often rice is served in a separate bowl.

The impecunious traveller will be glad to know that saving money by economising on food is more easily done in Jamaica. A good breakfast can cost between J$3 and J$5, depending on whether you use a native restaurant or your hotel for the purpose. Lunch can easily consist of a spiced bun or beef patty, and soft drink, fruit juice or milk. This leaves you free for a good dinner in the evening. Local dishes include ackee and salt fish, suckling pig, jerk pork, stamp-and-go mackerel, pepperpot soup and curried goat (which I often found hard to get).

The local beer, 'Red Stripe', is very good and available everywhere. Prices will depend on where you are. The Jamaican rum is very fine, superb mixed with a little ginger ale.

MUSIC

This is where it comes from: reggae, the best modern dance music. Now firmly established worldwide as one of the principal forms of rock music, it is based on a hypnotic, eminently danceable beat with lyrics telling of everyday life in Jamaica, particularly in the shanty towns, love songs and many numbers with strong sexual undertones or overtones. But don't worry—only a Jamaican can understand the words!

Its beginnings were in the early 1960s, a development from North American rhythm and blues and jazz blended with Caribbean calypso. At this stage it was known as bluebeat. Later progressions took it through ska and rock steady to reggae, the beat which has made Jamaican musicians internationally famous.

The music has always enjoyed some popularity in England (largely because the sizeable Jamaican community there ensures a large market), from the early days of Prince Buster's 'Al Capone'. Desmond Dekker and others enjoyed much success in the 1960s, and the mid 1970s saw the music mushroom in popularity in the United States, principally through Bob Marley and the Wailers. British and American big-name artists now regularly record reggae music.

Bob Marley's songs were centred principally upon the Rastafarian cult. His success led to Rastafarian philosophy and references becoming one of the most important themes of late 1970s reggae, with artists like Tapper Zukie building almost all their material around the religion, in itself the strongest rallying point of West Indian youth.

THE RASTAFARIANS
This cult is becoming better known all the time as its adherents grow in number throughout the world. Rastafarians are easily recognised by their beards and braided hair. The terms 'Rastaman' and 'Natty Dread' (the hair style is often referred to as 'dread locks') are used to describe sect members of differing outlook. A Rastaman is usually a reserved, peace-loving hippy, whilst the Natty Dread conveys heavy political and violent overtones (as far as I can tell there is no visual difference between the two).

The beliefs of the cult are both religious and political. Rastafarians draw a parallel between their own history and that of the Jews in the Old Testament. They regard Ethiopia both as their home and their promised land; the New World to which their ancestors were transported they believe to be Babylon. Jamaicans are more itinerant than most Caribbean peoples, and have spread throughout the world in large numbers. Many Rastafarians in other parts of the world (e.g. England) regard their current country of residence as Babylon.

Although the cult originated in Jamaica, it has spread to the extent that many young people in other Caribbean countries—the Bahamas and Saint Lucia are two examples—have adopted the dread locks and subculture. One of the chief vehicles for the dissemination of the cult is reggae music.

GETTING AROUND
You can get almost anywhere in Jamaica by **bus** or **minibus.** Country buses are very old and crowded, slow and cheap. You can learn much about the country by travelling on them. Theoretically they run to schedules, but nobody knows what these schedules are. Minibuses run when they feel like it, providing a very fast and efficient service at a slightly higher price than country buses, but are very dangerous. Jamaican drivers must be high in the Top Ten of the World's Worst Drivers, and the more reckless become minibus drivers. There are city buses in Kingston and Montego Bay. Shared **taxis** are also available, though at a high price and without any advantage to be gained from using them. As far as normal taxis are concerned, you should note that by no means all are metered and you should therefore always confirm the fare before jumping aboard.

There are two cross-country **railway** routes, both of which start in Kingston. The longer of the two runs through Spanish Town, May Pen, Mandeville and such places as Balaclava, Kendal, Ipswich and Cambridge to Montego

Bay. The second major route skirts the Blue Mountains then passes along the coast to Port Antonio. Both routes afford splendid views of Jamaica's spectacular scenery.

There is also a domestic airline, Trans-Jamaican, serving five airfields. This is only really of interest if you are short of time, as you will miss too much by flying. The airports served are Kingston (Tinson Pen), Montego Bay, Ocho Rios, Port Antonio and Mandeville. Jamaica Air Taxi will fly just about anywhere you can land a plane, but this is charter of course and therefore only suitable for groups unless you can get an empty seat. Bookings with both these lines can be made with Air Jamaica offices in North America or Europe.

Car hire is difficult and expensive, but not impossible. Cars can be in short supply so it may be best to rent one in writing from one of the bigger names like Hertz or Avis before you arrive and bring along the agreement when you come to claim the car. You need to be 21 years old with a valid driving licence and may well have to fork out a hefty deposit as well as paying dear for petrol. And drive *on the left*.

CALENDAR
Independence Day is the big celebration of the year on the first Monday in August when absolutely everyone takes part. But there are also special Christmas festivities when masked dancers in weird costumes parade through the streets.

Montego Bay

The main, big hotels start at the north end of town and follow the coast, roughly, up to the airport, with the odd one or two (like the Half Moon and Wyndham Rosehall) as far away as Rose Hall. This is where you find the shopping arcades, tourist trade restaurants, wayside vendors selling wood carvings, etc.—and the beaches. And of course the tourists, and most (though there are few anyway, less than in Nassau) of the hustlers.

The centre of town is full of real life. During the day there are a few tourists, but I saw none at night. Away from the centre of town it is difficult to walk down the street without being spoken to by people who want something. Here, you are ignored as people go about their business. But ask a question, or for directions, and you will be helped most courteously. Similarly if you extend a greeting it will be returned with warmth and interest. The centre's narrow streets pulse with hustle and bustle occasionally punctuated by the pounding of reggae from a record shop; but it is at night that it swings.

One of my best evenings out on the whole trip was here, with free Christmas celebrations, Jamaican-style. A stage had been set up in the main square outside the town hall and different reggae musicians and vocalists performed most of the night. Young and old were there, and whole family groups with little children running about. People danced. I watched two-foot-long lengths of sugar cane being shaved of the skin, or bark, and sold for immediate consumption. There were small boys selling peanuts, oranges and corn on the cob. I was the only tourist enjoying the show and the people seemed pleasantly surprised that I was there.

WHERE TO STAY IN MONTEGO BAY

Montego Bay has never struck me as particularly appealing to the one-centre-holiday vacationer, who will find more congenial surroundings at Negril or Ocho Rios. This section is thus aimed mainly at the traveller, who will be visiting different parts of the country and comparing the different towns and resort areas. The accommodation I inspected closely has these needs in mind.

You can walk easily from the airport to the **Ocean View Hotel,** which is among the lowest-priced accommodation listed by the Tourist Board in Montego Bay. You can easily avoid tiring yourself, however, by asking the Tourist Board desk at the airport to telephone Mr Mathews for you; he will then send his minibus down to pick you up. The Ocean View is clean, the rooms are well-furnished with two entrances (one direct to the outside of the building) and maid service is good. Breakfast costs US$3, and the excellent dinner (which has to be ordered before 2 pm) only $6. I was served a three-course meal, the main course being T-bone steak accompanied by too many different kinds of vegetables to count and a separate bowl of rice which I couldn't even touch. There was certainly no stinting on quantity, and it was as good as any other meal I had in Montego Bay.

Another place worth trying is the **Chiltern Apartments,** which are air-conditioned and within walking distance of Doctor's Cave Beach. Apartments cost US$25, whilst single rooms cost from US$9 to US$12 and doubles US$20.

In the centre of town you could try the **YMCA** on Humber Avenue, which costs US$5 per person per day or US$18 per week; it is thus extremely good value for stays of four nights to a week. This is also available for couples, as there are some double rooms. Spartan washing facilities are of the communal variety, and the rooms are starkly furnished, but then what do you expect? Millie, who runs the place, is very friendly, and has some tourist guests, though the majority are local people. Staying here also solves another problem, that of laundry. There are no laundromats in Montego Bay, and the only way you can get washing done—apart from doing it yourself—is by using the laundry in the centre of town. The YMCA is also conveniently situated for the bus to Negril.

Ladies could try the **YWCA** in Church Street. The building is not labelled, so ask for directions when you get near to it. In the heart of the central town

263

area are some guesthouses, usually situated over a bar or restaurant. **The Walpole** in Union Street could be a good bet for couples at US$8 per room daily. Very centrally located, it provides a better standard of furnishing than the YMCA, and has two adequate bathrooms. Another place is at the **MaComba Club** (principally a bar and discotheque) on Church Lane. The price here is US$6 per room. These last two places are for those who want to hear the non-stop rhythm of reggae when at the hotel.

Accommodation in Montego Bay
Daily summer rates per room in US$

Name and address	Single	Double
Doctor's Cave Beach Hotel	EP: 50–60	68–75
	MAP: 70–80	108–115
Harmony House	CP: 30	48
	MAP: 40	68
Ocean View Hotel, Sunset Avenue	EP: 17	26
The Upper Deck	EP: 50–55	55–56
YMCA, Humber Avenue, Central Montego Bay	EP: $5 per person per day	
YWCA, Church Street, Central Montego Bay	EP: $5 per person per day	

EATING OUT IN MONTEGO BAY
A patty and soft drink for lunch can be bought for J60 cents at any of the little snack bars (look out for them, as they are so small and dimly lit you could easily walk straight past) and I found that J$2 bought me breakfast of spice cake, orange juice and a pack of cigarettes. Of course you cannot live on this fare, and you will want a proper meal at least once a day. If you want native food the central restaurants are best. The standard of cuisine is not as high as in the Bahamas, but besides being the cheapest way of trying native dishes (lunch is usually J$5 or less) you will find that the choice of native dishes offered in the restaurants further out is small (whatever they tell the folks back home, the tourists seem to prefer the food they are used to). I tried the **Dome House,** where I had ackee with cod fish, and the **Little Delicious,** where I had fried chicken in sauce with salad, peas 'n' rice and yams.

For a fairly good meal in pleasant surroundings you could try the **Town House** in Church Street. The extensive menu includes some native dishes with French, American and 'International' cuisine. It is in the basement of an old house, cool with brick walls, thoughtful decor and a slightly rustic atmosphere. It is fairly expensive, though you would only need one meal the day you eat here, and take credit cards. I paid J$9 for a three-course meal with beer, but you could pay half or twice as much and anything in between. It claims to be Montego Bay's first and most popular restaurant.

The nearest fairly cheap food place to the Ocean View is the **Pelican Grill,** a walk of a little over a mile. Food is mainly American type with a few local dishes such as curried goat (about J$4). A hamburger meal will cost you about J$3, including french fries, etc. The **Front Porch,** next to the Pelican Grill, was also recommended to me.

Back in the centre of town, **Uncle Vic's** was suggested by a knowledgeable native as being good and cheap. The **Walpole** also has a restaurant.

Bus services
The number one bus runs between central Montego Bay and Rose Hall every 40 minutes and every 30 minutes in the rush hour. Bus stops are clearly marked between the town centre and the start of Sunset Avenue, and from there on the bus will stop when and where requested. There are other services too. These municipal buses are green.

Hall's Transport and others operate ancient country buses for lower prices and longer distances.

TOURIST INFORMATION
You should visit the Cage, a small, squat brick building in the centre of town. Originally constructed to keep runaway slaves until they could be returned and/or punished, it now houses the tourist information office which is staffed by a charming and very helpful lady.

BEACHES
The best-known beach, and the one which brought tourism to Montego Bay, is Doctor's Cave. During my stay there I saw few tourists in Montego Bay, so the beach was relatively uncrowded. But get used to the idea of paying to use it (50 cents). There are other beaches along the coast, but these very often belong to the big hotels.

WHAT TO SEE AROUND MONTEGO BAY
The Jamaican Tourist Board provides a multiplicity of colourful brochures full of useful information to help you spend your money. Here is just a brief selection.

Rafting on the Martha Brae: You can take a one-and-a-half hour trip down the Martha Brae near Falmouth. A boatman takes you down the river at a cost of J$12 per raft. For transport to Falmouth, expect to pay around a dollar, round trip, on the country bus, and maybe twice that by minibus. If you take a bathing suit you can swim from the raft.

Rose Hall: Annie Palmer was known as 'The White Witch of Rose Hall'. In fact she was not a white witch (one who uses her powers for good, usually healing, purposes) or even a witch at all. She was called the White Witch because of the colour of her skin, and the story, as I was told it (in the Bahamas) runs as follows:

In the days of slavery Annie Palmer would be seen, by the servants and slaves, at first on her balcony and then a short time later on the beach (perhaps 500 yards away). But nobody ever saw her walk down to the beach. So she was presumed to have gone there by the exercise of evil powers. In fact she had a number of slaves who built a tunnel from the house to the beach; these slaves were kept in leg irons and dungeons until the job was completed, when they were killed, so only she knew about the tunnel. When not engaged on this she found the time to murder six husbands; it was the seventh who found out what was going on.

This is the story I was told. If it is not true please write and tell me.

Rose Hall can be seen from the main road. It is between 300 and 500 yards from the beach, on the right-hand side as you travel from town to the Intercontinental Hotel. Guided tours are available from 9.30 am until 5.30 pm.

South of Montego Bay, past Reading, is the **Rocklands Feeding Station,** a bird sanctuary. It is open from 3.30 pm until dusk.

The Governor's Coach Tour leaves Montego Bay railway station at 10 am every Tuesday, Thursday and Friday, returning at 4 pm; the tour includes a snack lunch. It will take you 40 miles inland, features a calypso band and a visit to Appleton's rum distillery and is full of tourists. Book (two days in advance if possible) with Jamaica Tours (952 2887).

The Maroons are best visited from Montego Bay or Mandeville. Descended from runaway slaves who formed guerrilla bands and harassed the planters, they still live under military order and it is recommended that you have a guide if you wish to visit them. They form an almost separate state within Jamaica, as they have a constitution affording them a large measure of self-government. They charge for photographs, so check the price before using your camera.

Montego Bay to Negril

You can go by taxi, minibus or country bus. The country buses are slow, noisy, old, uncomfortable and cheap. They are also probably the safest way to go—if you hit anything, then God bless the anything! I was told by the tourist office that buses leave at 9.30, 12 noon and 2.30, but they seem to be more frequent than that. They leave from south of town, but drive right through it—because of the one-way system—before commencing their journey proper. The fare to Negril is J$2, and there are two routes: along the coast road to Hopewell, then south through Chigwell, Chichester, etc. to Savanna la Mar, then west to Negril; or along the coast road for the whole trip.

My bus (Hall's Transport) took the inland route. The beginning and end of the trip were along roads recognisable as such, although potholed, particularly in the latter stages. But for most of the journey (timewise) we bounced along unsurfaced roads which petered out into little better than cart tracks, and at one point was a cart track. The thought of a big bus thundering along a cart track no wider than the vehicle, cut between sugar-cane fields (growing right up to the road) sounds incredible, but I was in it. Progress was slow on these sections owing to the inadequate roads, uphill gradients (we sometimes climbed up hill at less than 2 miles an hour) and frequent stops. We would often stop between sugar-cane fields with no sign of habitation. Someone would get off, and disappear heavily laden, or someone would emerge from the crop and climb aboard. Our progress was further slowed by a flat tyre and arguments with passengers complaining about broken items in their baggage. You will have plenty of time to observe village life. My bus left at 1.45 and got to Negril at about 7.30.

Minibuses are more frequent, more expensive and more dangerous. They buzz along at high speed slamming on the brakes to pick up or drop passengers. Expect to pay J$2 to J$2.50 but negotiate this before boarding. Taxis are more expensive again and the fare should definitely be agreed before acceptance.

Exploring the streams of Jamaica

Negril

Negril is usually described as 'unspoilt' (though I found it very much spoilt) and according to the tourist board 'will remain unspoilt'. By this they mean an

absence of high-rise hotels, flashy boutiques and restaurants, and ersatz disco-
theques. But there are too many tourists already, of the trendy type who tell the
folks back home that they go to an away-from-it-all place. Prior to my visit a
new 250-room hotel had just been opened. In this 'away from it all' place I
saw more tourists than I had seen in the Bahamas and Montego Bay combined!

The seven-mile beach is in itself superb. Protected by a reef, the bottom
barely shelves at all and you can walk out a fair way and still be only waist deep.
When the sea is calm it is perfect for poor swimmers (like me) and children.
The sea is warm and there are plenty of shady spots on the beach.

The older generation tend to stay on the beach itself, or at the west end of
Negril where the coastline is rocky and more suitable for strong swimmers and
for diving. The centre of Negril is the new Mecca for the young, mainly American (Jamaicans were constantly asking me which State I came from). All these
tourists go down to the beach regularly, so that it is, in my opinion, crowded.
This means that vendors ply up and down selling arts and crafts, and heavy
dudes stroll by, eyes popping out of their heads at the sight of expensive-
looking cameras. I was told in Montego Bay that the hustlers and thieves had
been run out of town; this is where many of them have come to.

To summarise: the beach is beautiful but crowded, so come out of season. It
is more dangerous here than in Montego Bay, but if you are careful you should
be all right. I made a point of speaking to anyone who spoke to me, but it is what
you say and how you say it that matters.

WHERE TO STAY IN NEGRIL

I wouldn't particularly recommend where I stayed. The bus dropped me off at
a roundabout, where a small boy offered to take me to his mother's house. 'It is
very clean with two bathrooms' (which wasn't strictly true). It was dark, I didn't
know the place, so I thought, what the hell, why not. I was taken to Red Ground
at the back of town. Marion was the proprietor. The cost is US$6 per bed (the
original figure I was quoted by the boy, which Marion tried to raise to $8 and
which was only reduced again by hard bargaining). It would be all right for a
couple, but the facilities are inferior to those at the YMCA in Montego Bay.

There are in fact a large number of houses in Red Ground taking in guests,
at prices between US$6 and US$12 per bed (or per room). They usually have
no identification. The best advice I can give if you want to stay up here is to
arrive in daylight and take one of the more expensive places, where towels, soap
and toilet paper, etc. are normally provided.

If you want to stay nearer the beach and the action, try the **Rocky Edge,**
which is centrally situated. This is primarily a restaurant and bar with reasonable meals at fair prices and drinks at about Montego Bay non-tourist levels.
Mary also has a small number of presentable rooms, with two bathrooms.

Further along the same road you will come to a minor junction, and a sign advertising **The Delicatessen**. It is embellished with a picture of a cat. On the left is Papa Lawrence's establishment, the **Tigress Cottages**. This comprises a large number of cottages and apartments set in spacious grounds. There is a restaurant near the road, and self-catering facilities up the hill. The clientele is exclusively tourist.

Out west there is no beach but also no shortage of rocky coves. If you prefer diving and snorkelling you could try **Tensing Pen**. It is built in a very attractive rustic style with thatched roofs and is very well laid out with winding paths and flowering shrubs. It is about three miles from the Negril roundabout, however, so you will need to organise some form of transport. Over the road is a Rastafarian vegetarian restaurant.

Accommodation in Negril
Daily summer rates per room in US$

Name and address	
Negril Beach Village, Seven Mile Beach	AP: 650 per person per week
Rocky Edge, Main Road, Negril Centre	EP: S or D 10
Tensing Pen, West Negril	EP: S 18, D 36
Tigress Cottages, Main Road, Negril Centre	EP: S or D 14–25
Villas Negril, Negril	EP: S 40, D 50

EATING OUT IN NEGRIL
It is possible to eat at the **Rocky Edge**. The food and drink are quite reasonable, as described earlier, and there is the perennial juke box. The company, mainly local, is good too. Up in Red Ground there are restaurants and snack bars, again with reasonable prices for what you get, not to mention the **Delicatessen** and **Papa Lawrence's**.

Leaving Negril
The difficult part is getting to Savanna la Mar, from where services to Mandeville and straight through to Kingston are readily available. A bus leaves Negril, from the roundabout, at about 9.30 am bound for Kingston. The fare to Mandeville is about J$2. Minibuses leave at intervals, at a higher fare, although most will be going as far as Savanna la Mar only. Hitch-hiking is possible but not recommended; it is far more difficult than in the Bahamas, and here there are regular cheap bus services. The wisest thing to do is to make an early start and be prepared to change at Savanna. A minibus from Savanna to Mandeville should cost you J$3, but agree the fares first.

Mandeville

I'm not one to welcome cool weather generally, but I was glad of the relief from the heat. In the colonial days, Mandeville was where the administrators' families escaped for the summer; it was also Jamaica's main tourist centre, as it was believed in those days that a sub-tropical climate caused degeneracy.

The town is larger than I imagined, and somewhat spread out. One always seems to be walking up or down a hill, and the roads are rarely straight. The old colonial atmosphere is prevalent in the architecture and the way the town is laid out. The parish church looks very English, the small courthouse has Georgian overtones, whilst many buildings feature sash windows rather than those designed for a sub-tropical climate. Jamaicans in Montego Bay and Negril told me that Mandeville is a wealthy town, but all the people I spoke to complained of poverty. The town looks well off, with many neat, well-kept houses, so perhaps the people have fallen on hard times recently. Mandeville is cool in all senses of the word; besides the weather the people are extremely pleasant. There are no tourists here which perhaps explains it.

Manchester is the most recent of Jamaica's fourteen parishes. It was formed in 1814 with Mandeville as its administrative centre. More recently the discovery of bauxite in the hills around has brought prosperity and expatriates. There is an Alcan plant just north of the town. Staff members, largely American, live in Mandeville and are provided with a Kentucky Fried Chicken restaurant.

I found that Mandeville had the advantages of a big town without the disadvantages. It is packed with banks; besides the Bank of Jamaica and Workers' Bank, there are the foreign banks: Barclays, First National City, Nova Scotia, etc. They are in two areas; most are in or around the centre of town, whilst some, including First National City, are near the Belair Hotel.

Ironically, the birthplace of Norman Manley, who led Jamaica to independence, is nearby, although in 1976 the town voted for the opposition Jamaica Labour Party.

WHERE TO STAY IN MANDEVILLE

The **Mandeville Hotel** is the best in town and very well situated, just off the main square. It is also the most expensive, but only by a small margin, and there is no saving if you take a taxi to one of the other hotels. Rates include a bathroom of course, and breakfast. There is no service charge, but there is a government tax of 5% on room rates. The hotel will only take cash or traveller's cheques and prefers foreign currency. Its main drawback is its size—it has 66 rooms.

The **Belair** is further from the centre of town and could be expensive for a single person, at US$22 plus 5% tax. I ate at the Belair and found it acceptable, but I suspect that what you choose is important. I had pepper steak at J$8.50. There is no native food on the menu, although the clientele appeared to be local bourgeoisie and businessmen. Credit cards are accepted. Both the Belair and the Mandeville have swimming pools.

The **Astra** is a long way out of town and you will definitely need a taxi. The higher-priced rooms have carpets on the floor. All rooms have private facilities, telephone, etc. Credit cards are accepted.

I stayed at the **Mayfair Guest House,** about three-quarters of a mile from the town centre on Newleigh Road. The rooms, costing US$18, include a private bathroom. Cash (Jamaican dollars) is preferred for payment. The management is very suspicious of traveller's cheques. I would say US$18 is a good price for a double, but a lot for a single.

There is cheaper guesthouse accommodation available. One is apparently located on Caledonia Road past the Belair, and there are others on Wards Avenue, above restaurants there. Wards Avenue is your best bet as there is more of it and it is centrally located. Inquire at the police station.

Accommodation in Mandeville
Daily summer rates per room in US$

Name and address	Single	Double
Astra Hotel (far end of Wards Avenue)	EP: 18–22	32–40
Belair Hotel, Caledonia Road	EP: 22	30
Mandeville Hotel (near Main Square)	CP: 15–23	26–42
Mayfair Guest House, Newleigh Road	EP: S or D 12–18	

EATING OUT IN MANDEVILLE
Native restaurants, bars and betting shops abound here. Food is cheaper than in Montego Bay and Negril. A pork chop dinner with peas 'n' rice, yams, tomato, lettuce and chicken soup costs J$2.80 at the bar/restaurant at the junction of Manchester and Newleigh, and this seems to be the standard price. Chicken dinners cost the same.

Manchester Road has a number of restaurants, but the main area is Wards Avenue, just across from the traffic lights. Soft drinks sell for J40 cents and a shot of rum is the same price. I found the **Esquire** restaurant/bar upstairs on Wards Avenue (before you get to the Tudor Theatre) good and cheap. The only trouble was there was no reggae; they were playing old American rock 'n' roll (unless it was misguidedly for my benefit).

271

Mandeville to Spanish Town
Spanish Town was the capital of Jamaica until 1872, although Kingston had been the commercial capital, chief port of entry and most important centre for some time. The square is said to be one of the finest examples of Georgian architecture in the western hemisphere. There is a memorial to the British Admiral Rodney and a cathedral—to Saint Jago de la Vega—which is supposed to be the oldest in the West Indies. There is also a folk museum. In the short time I was there I found the people amongst the most friendly in Jamaica. Unfortunately, although everyone was helpful, no one knew of any accommodation in town (there are hotels outside the town), so I did not stay very long.

My recommendation is as follows: leave Mandeville early. Walk or take a taxi to the bus terminal in the centre of town. You will soon be hustled into a bus or minibus bound for Kingston. Ask to be put out at Spanish Town (I was charged J$2.50, but I was told later that this is on the cheap side). If you are there before 12 you will have plenty of time to look around before taking a regular bus into Kingston (fare 40 or 60 cents).

Kingston

Kingston was founded at the end of the 17th century as a planned city subsequent to the collapse of Port Royal. The town centre is laid out in blocks, with Victoria Park five blocks from the waterfront and George VI Memorial Park further north.

You are strongly recommended to arrive in Kingston before dark. The best place to stay is probably mid-town, closer than the outskirts to the action and probably cheaper and safer than the centre of town. Many accounts have been given concerning the risks to personal safety in Kingston, and the bars on the windows tell their own story.

GETTING AROUND KINGSTON
Buses run down to the centre of town along Half Way Tree Road, Trafalgar Road (number 14) and Old Hope Road. Most of them (the exception is number 14) terminate in King Street. Buses to Port Antonio and other parts of Jamaica go from the corner of Pechon Street and Beckford Street. Note that after dark, buses at the King Street terminus are parked higher up the street.

The town centre
The centre of Kingston is pleasant in the daytime. A bus ride into town provides interesting sights—try to get a window seat—and I found Kingston and its people more cordial than I expected. Old dilapidated buildings alternate with new skyscrapers, but I found the streets wider and less crowded than a

272

glance at the Esso map and casual conversation intimated. Vendors dot the pavements, and those with business to attend to hurry past those with nothing to do. I was not hassled, either for a handout or to buy dope. On the contrary, I found myself either ignored or, if caught looking at a map, helped. I think this is because tourists are a rarity here.

During the late afternoon you will see the heavy dudes begin to arrive. After dusk decent citizens hurry to finish their business and the buses turn around in a more brightly lit and populated part of King Street (nearer the Parade). But during the day the centre has all the facilities you will need—banks, cheap restaurants, bars, the new harbour development, supermarkets—and a day in the area, perhaps including a ferry trip to Port Royal, would be well spent.

Down by the waterfront, redevelopment has produced an attractive area, aimed at tourists but not yet filled with them. The area is well laid out with flowers and bushes, and shopping/office plazas with apartments above at intervals. The **Tourist Information Office** is at one end, and the **Victoria Crafts Market** at the other. Nearby is the ferryboat pier for **Port Royal**. The boat leaves here at 8, 9, and 10 am and on the hour from 1 to 7 pm and returns from Port Royal on the corresponding half-hour; the journey takes 20 minutes. The railway station is also near here.

Half-day closing in central Kingston is Wednesday (Thursday in the Cross Roads area).

Port Royal

In its day the 'Wickedest City on Earth', Port Royal was built by the English in 1655, immediately after they had captured Jamaica from the Spanish. Brandy was imported from England ostensibly with the intention of providing revenue for constructing fortifications—though no doubt some of the income derived from its sale found its way into the royal purse. It didn't take long before the Caribbean pirates made this their base. Here they unloaded their loot captured from Spanish galleons and settlements; merchants came from Europe to bargain for the goods and gold. With an economy based on brandy and piracy it is not surprising that public morality was reputedly lower than anywhere else. Whorehouses alternated with warehouses. Perhaps a third of the population were pirates (or buccaneers as their apologists prefer to call them). Others were tradesmen and artisans who, although often mediocre in their standard of work at home, were able to make a good living here.

The most famous pirate was Henry Morgan. Accounts differ as to whether he was merely greedy for loot and action, or whether he had any patriotic motive. His operations, including the famous sacking of Panama, were carried out against the Spaniards; he was knighted, and did become Governor of Jamaica. But then intelligent and cunning men with great wealth at their disposal have a way of finding favour with the authorities.

In 1692, four years after Henry Morgan had died, Port Royal was hit by an earthquake. About a quarter of the population was killed and most of the town fell into the sea, leaving only Fort Charles and a few houses standing. Lewis Galdy was a celebrated survivor of the disaster. First swallowed up by the land, he was then, in a succeeding spasm, flung into the sea; he survived by swimming until he was picked up. Half of the remaining residents died through disease in the following weeks, most of the survivors eventually moving over to the mainland to found Kingston.

Nowadays there is little to see in Port Royal. There is the Quarterdeck in Fort Charles—upon which Nelson is said to have paced impatiently—the police training academy, a small museum with excavated submarine remains, and Lewis Galdy's tombstone—upon which his experience is engraved. But it is worth the trip for the atmosphere. Now a small fishing settlement of humble dwellings, with a disused Anglers' Club building (starkly magnificent when seen from the pier), and a hotel with something about Henry Morgan in the title, it is worth a visit in the late afternoon. On a clear or slightly cloudy day the views of Kingston and the mountains behind can be beautiful. As it sinks, the sun casts a pink glow over the capital, whilst even more dramatic views can be observed by turning west. There is a small fishermen's bar near the pier where the beer is 60 cents and the reggae continuous.

WHAT TO SEE AROUND KINGSTON
The cheapest is free—the superb views of the mountains and coast. As stated before, these can be seen to best advantage from Port Royal and its ferry in the late afternoon. The new central **harbour development** is also free until you start buying things, and it has been constructed largely with the visitor in mind. Time spent there can be rewarding. **Devon House,** near Half Way Tree, is always quoted as one of Jamaica's great houses still maintained in colonial splendour. Its restaurant employs waiters dressed up as pirates and serving wenches (but cleaner), and many tourists to Kingston go there. At the eastern end of Old Hope Road is a **botanical garden** and small **zoo.** A trip to the **Blue Mountains** by whatever means you choose could be rewarding.

WHERE TO STAY IN KINGSTON
The **Green Gables,** run by a Scottish lady, represents fairly good value and may be your best bet on arrival in Kingston. It is well situated for convenience in the Half Way Tree area and is close to a bus route. Depending on which road your bus from Spanish Town takes into Kingston, you may be able to get off before the central terminus, very close to the guesthouse—keep half an eye on your map and half an eye on the road. Occupants of the cheapest rooms share a bathroom with one other room. Rooms with private facilities are available at slightly higher cost. There is a restaurant, cheap by hotel standards but

more expensive than local restaurants (about US$5 for a chicken dinner), and a bar, called the London Tavern.

I stayed at the **Indies Hotel,** not having discovered the cheaper accommodation at the time. The rooms here are all standard with twin beds, good wardrobe facilities, plenty of drawer space, air-conditioning, hot water in the shower, glasses—and everything worked. After difficulties elsewhere with the plumbing, it was good to have superior accommodation which, besides having essentials like toilet paper, also had nice little touches like book matches and tourist newspapers. The hotel seems to cater for businessmen rather than tourists (of whom there are few in Kingston anyway).

Guests at the Indies Hotel are able to use, free of charge, the swimming pool at the nearby Courtleigh Manor Hotel. There is also a laundry service—allow two days for items to be returned. While you shouldn't expect food to be cheap here, at least it's good. Breakfast ranges from US$2 (juice, toast, coffee) to US$4.50 for 'the works', six choices in all. The lunch and dinner menu includes fillet steak at US$9, chicken at US$5, pizzas from US$4.50, hamburger US$2—a very wide choice in all, at reasonable prices, but with no local food. The breakfast includes a pot of coffee, not just a cup.

If you are looking for cheap accommodation and find the Green Gables full, try **Peter's Motel** at 7 Richmond Avenue. Note, however, that the facilities are quite basic, and in value-for-money terms both the above are better.

The **Green Lantern** at 5½ Ripon Road charges US$12 per room, whether occupied by one or two persons. This is nearer to the centre of town than the other suggested accommodation, and is thus more convenient during the day but may inhibit your night-time walking. This establishment is run and patronised by Jamaicans and has about eight rooms. Bathroom facilities are shared. Very loud reggae pounds from the juke box. The building is single-storey, and I was impressed by the cleanliness of the rooms, most of which have washbasins.

I was able to visit but not inspect the **Retreat Guesthouse** at 19 Seaview Avenue, run by Mrs Miller. Security is very tight; entrance was barred (literally) and no way was Mrs Miller going to open up if I wasn't staying there. So all I can say is that it is very quiet and lives up to its name.

I will mention one cheap hotel situated downtown which cannot be recommended, on account of its location. The hotel is upstairs from **Duke's,** mentioned below under *Eating out*, and under the same management. I actually stayed here on my last night, so as to be near the airport bus stop. The very spartan shower/toilet facilities are of course shared. Although there is nothing intrinsically wrong with the place, I cannot recommend it. I was treated as a curiosity, being the first white man to stay there. I suspect that if hordes of young travellers started using the place some resentment would set in, and of course the criminal element would soon be attracted—definitely not for couples or women, and you should not go out at night.

Accommodation in Kingston
Daily winter rates per room in US$

Name and address	Single	Double
Green Gables, Cargill Road	EP: from 14	from 24
Green Lantern, 5½ Ripon Road (Cross Roads area)	EP: S or D 12	
Indies Hotel, Holborn Road	EP: 16	19
Peter's Motel, 7 Richmond Avenue	EP: S or D 14–20	
Retreat Guesthouse, 19 Seaview Avenue	CP: 15	24

EATING OUT IN KINGSTON

On Half Way Tree Road is a cheap eating place, **MacDonalds** (it has no connection with the American chain of similar name). Curried goat is J$3 here—the cheapest I have seen it—and all meals are cheap by Kingston standards (Kingston prices are a little higher than Mandeville's). The quality was very poor, but you are unlikely to get food poisoning.

Beer seems to be a standard US80 cents at the Indies, Green Gables and **Take 5 Club.** This last is next to Peter's Motel, and is a nightclub with native entertainment and clientele. Over the road from the Indies Hotel is the **Pub and Grill,** under the same management as the Indies. I was unimpressed by the food and the service, which was very slow, and it was too much like an English pub. It is frequented by expatriates, businessmen staying at the Indies, and the native bourgeoisie.

In the centre of town you could try **Duke's** restaurant at the corner of Duke and Queen Streets. Chicken is J$3, stewed beef J$3.10, curried goat J$3.10. I tried the chicken, with pepper strips, tomato, peas and rice, and found it very good.

Two restaurants in New Kingston were recommended to me for their cleanliness and economy. Both are in Knutsford Boulevard, opposite the British High Commission (which is appropriately on Trafalgar Road). One is the **Victoria Grill,** next to the Citibank building, the other is the pharmacy attached to the Imperial Life over the road. Both are patronised at lunchtime by the local office staffs.

Port Antonio

Port Antonio has perhaps the most beautiful scenery in Jamaica. Wide river valleys flanked by thick, lush vegetation meander down from the towering Blue Mountains to a sleepy, friendly town. Although it is being promoted as a tourist spot, I will be very surprised if you find many tourists there.

Trade is largely based on the export of bananas, but there is some fishing, for sport as well as for food. There are fine views over the town and bay from the hills, and nearby is the famous **Blue Hole,** an almost land-locked lagoon so deep that the water is cobalt blue, surrounded by lush green vegetation. Rafting down the Rio Grande is also possible—similar to the Martha Brae experience. The site of Mitchell's Folly is in Port Antonio. This was a stately mansion, built on classical Roman lines in 1905 by a rich New Yorker for his bride. However, on their arrival, it collapsed; sea water had been mixed in with the concrete used for its construction.

Port Antonio's easterly position makes it a possible departure point for Haiti, though this may be more difficult than you imagine.

Arrive early in the day if you want to find cheaper accommodation than that advertised by the Tourist Board. One good tip is to try the police station: all places offering rooms for rent have to register, so the police generally know about the cheap ones.

On the shores of the Blue Hole is a new restaurant, the **Blue Lagoon,** which features vegetarian and native seafood dishes. The proprietor is Horatio Spencer, whom you should ask to speak to. Expect to pay around US$8.50 for a meal.

Dunns River Falls, Jamaica

Ocho Rios

Literally, from the Spanish, it means 'Eight Rivers'. This is the new tourist Mecca. Unlike Negril, however, which has a centre from which the tourist areas spread, the hotels here extend along some 40 miles of coastline. These hotels are mainly of the villa or cottage variety, though I am advised that guesthouse accommodation does exist. **Dunns River Falls,** one of Jamaica's foremost tourist attractions, are about four miles west of Ocho Rios' centre and Fern Gully. You can climb to the top in your swimming gear assisted by a surefooted local guide.

Ian Fleming lived near here, in its unspoilt days, and drew much inspiration for his James Bond novels from the area. The bauxite plant at Ocho Rios was used in the film *Dr No*, although in the book it had a more sinister purpose and was ostensibly blown up. 'Boonoonoonoos', a patois word meaning something like 'groovy baby', is the title the local Tourist Board has given to its events programme.

Another famous name associated with Ocho Rios is that of Noel Coward, who lived at Port Maria towards the end of his life. The house is run by the National Trust and contains original music scores, paintings and memorabilia. Noel Coward himself is buried in the grounds overlooking the bay which inspired the song 'Room with a View'.

Travelling west you arrive at Runaway Bay and Falmouth. Again, these are very touristy, although Discovery Bay, the site of Columbus' landing, may be of historical interest. To the non-tourist this area's greatest attraction probably lies in the splendid views that the coastal road affords.

Accommodation in Ocho Rios
Daily summer rates per room in US$

Name	Single	Double
Hibiscus Lodge Hotel (tel. 974 2676)	EP: 30	40
Jamaica Hilton (tel. 972 2382)	EP: 90–110	93–114
	MAP: 117–135	147–168
Jamaica Inn (tel. 974 2514)	EP: 145	170–220
Plantation Inn (tel. 974 2501)	EP: 100	170–215
Sans Souci (tel. 974 2353)	EP: S or D 90–150	
	EP: Apartments 190–210	
Shaw Park Beach Hotel (tel. 974 2552)	CP: S or D 120–130	

SHOPPING
Everything is available, from chic and sophisticated fashions—with matching prices—to wood carvings worked by humble artisans. Rum is a speciality (or did you guess?) and so is Tia Maria, along with Rumona—a rum liqueur. Other gift items unique to Jamaica are original paintings and carvings, island-made fashions and gemstones mined locally.

SPORTS

The sportsman—and woman—can find activity of almost every kind in Jamaica, even parasailing (at Negril). Experienced divers are welcome at all centres and waterskiing is available at Negril, The Blue Hole and Ocho Rios.

The beaches are pretty good, but can get crowded in some of the more popular places. There is nude swimming and sunbathing on some private beaches.

Fishing is good in Port Antonio and for the more adventurous inland there is riding and waterfall climbing (see above, *Ocho Rios*).

Tennis and jogging trails are offered by some hotels and spectators can watch cricket, football, polo and horse racing in Kingston.

CAYMAN ISLANDS

The Cayman Islands group consists of three islands—Grand Cayman, Cayman Brac and Little Cayman—and lies 480 miles south of Miami. Cayman Brac and Little Cayman are about 80 miles east-north-east of Grand Cayman, on which is located the capital, Georgetown. This is also the commercial centre.

Tourism is a flourishing industry and is very important to the island's economy. Facilities provided are of an up-market standard and are inevitably centred around the beaches: excellent diving and yachting and, of course, fishing. Informality is nevertheless the keynote. Both the standard and the cost of living are high (the latter due to the fact that most food and other necessities have to be imported).

In 1670 the islands were ceded to the British Crown (from Spain) and the first natives included 'mixed groups of shipwrecked sailors, marooned mariners [which I would have thought were the same thing], debtors, buccaneers and beachcombers'. The group is a British colony and the head of government a Governor appointed by Queen Elizabeth II. He is assisted by an Executive Council made up of three appointed and four elected members. There is also a Legislative Assembly, most of whose members are elected.

GETTING TO THE CAYMAN ISLANDS

Grand Cayman's importance is far greater than its small size or tiny population (18,000) would suggest: as a tax haven it has attracted 500 banks, and tourism is a very significant industry. (Although the tourists rarely impose on the island's informal way of life, there is more tourism here than you might think.) This all means that the islands have their own airline (Cayman Airways, which has three aircraft, two of them 727–200 jets) and excellent links with the USA. Ask your travel agent specifically to check with the airline for fares: I bought my ticket in Miami from a travel agent in Miami Beach who insisted there was no excursion fare valid for my duration of stay. I insisted he phone the airline, and there was a fare which saved me $60 (then he started grumbling that 'these airlines will do anything to fill their planes'!).

From the USA
Almost all flights to the Caymans are from the USA. Even if you live in a relatively obscure place you can be pretty sure that Republic Airlines will find a way to get you to Grand Cayman; it flies from Chicago, Detroit, Indianapolis, Memphis and Miami. Cayman Airways connects with Houston and Miami.

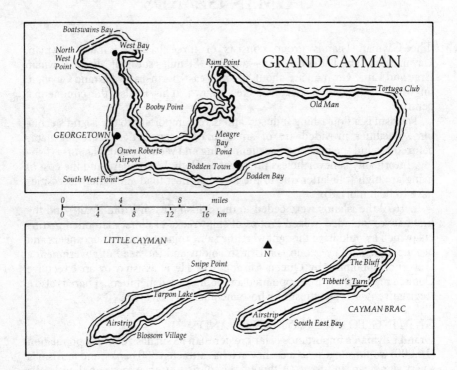

From Canada
Depending where you are coming from, you'll probably find it most convenient to connect via Miami.

From London
Grand Cayman is reached almost exclusively from London via Miami. There are same-day connections. If you are using British Airways to Miami and Cayman Airways onward there is an arrangement whereby you can transit Miami without needing a visa and being pestered by immigration. Note that there is no through fare at the time of writing unless you are booking a package; Grand Cayman is consequently a destination where booking a package can show substantial savings.

From Europe
Via Miami. Pan Am has flights from Berlin, Hamburg, Madrid and Paris, and Northwest Orient flies here from Oslo. Aeromexico flies from Paris (as does Delta) and Madrid (which is also served by Iberia), and Lufthansa from Düsseldorf and Frankfurt.

Within the Caribbean
Cayman Airways and Air Jamaica fly in from both Kingston and Montego Bay.

ENTRY REGULATIONS
No visa is required for citizens of most countries, nationals of Communist bloc countries being the main exception.

ELECTRICITY
The supply is 110 volts at 60 cycles, the same as in the US.

CLIMATE
It is similar to that of other small Caribbean islands: average 80°F in summer and 75°F in winter.

CURRENCY
The legal tender here is the Cayman Islands dollar (CI$) which currently equals US$1.25 approximately. US$1 = CI$0.80. US currency is accepted in the islands.

POPULATION
About 27,000 people live on the two larger islands, while only 27 live permanently on Little Cayman.

LANGUAGE
English is spoken here, liberally spattered with nautical terms and pronunciation, which in itself shows Cornish, Welsh, Irish, Scottish and English regional variations, not to mention echoes of the American south.

GETTING AROUND
There are flights using small aircraft from Grand Cayman to Little Cayman on Mondays, Wednesdays, Fridays and Sundays; these same flights go on to Cayman Brac and return to Grand Cayman, via Little Cayman, on the same days. There is a daily Trilander service between Grand Cayman and Cayman Brac.

The natives of the Cayman Islands are very much a seafaring people, whether it be by luxury yacht or humble fishing boat. You thus stand a good chance of visiting the two smaller islands by sea.

There is a bus service on Grand Cayman from the capital, Georgetown, to Turtle Farm, passing West Bay and Seven Mile Beach. Taxi fares are fixed by the local cab drivers' association; some (approximate) specimen rates from the airport to other points are: Georgetown CI$5, South Cove CI$7, Le Club CI$9, Bodden Town CI$16, Rum Point CI$28.

Diving on the coral reefs

Car hire rates begin at around US$16 for a small car to US$41.25 for a Datsun Venette. The car hire firm will issue a driving permit providing you have a valid driving licence. It is also possible to rent a moped or bicycle, ideal when considering that the size of the island is comparable with New Providence in the Bahamas in length, although in area somewhat smaller. A Honda

C50 can be obtained from Caribbean Motors in Grand Cayman for CI$11 per day, or CI$30 for three days (at the time of writing) and cycles can be rented from Cayman Cycle Rentals from around CI$6 per day, or on Cayman Brac from Cayman Brac Cycle Rentals at CI$12 per day (CI$64 per week). Drive *on the left*.

Excursions by sea and air are also available, even under the sea in a chartered submarine. One of these, *Atlantis*, tours the sea bottom from Georgetown Harbour illuminating the coral and multicoloured fish for the passengers to view from the large portholes. This offers under-sea experiences to untrained aquanauts

WHAT TO SEE

Georgetown

This is the capital and seat of government of the Cayman Islands as well as being a busy harbour for cruise ships. This tends to shift the emphasis from sightseeing to shopping to cater for the short-stay visitor. The main shops are along the habour front, or very nearby, with a large supply of handily transportable duty-free goods to tempt the luxury goods buyer. Black coral is the island speciality and there are turtle shell products made—but note that these cannot be imported into the US.

The sightseer won't see any skyrise hotels in Georgetown; all the buildings are no higher than the trees, and although many buildings are new they mainly represent the most attractive of modern architectural styles. Some older-style wooden houses can still be seen with their verandahs near the harbour.

Elsewhere on the island
The turtle farm is Cayman's main land attraction in the village of West Bay. It has a gift shop where, if you wish, you can buy a four-foot polished shell of a mature turtle, not an easy trophy to smuggle home to the US!

Alternatively you can go to **Hell**, if only to buy a postcard to send home from this rocky outcrop on the west of the island. It was once a snow-white rock formation but now, one and a half million years later, has become black with algae. It possibly received its sinister name from the jagged spikes of black limestone that are such a feature of the place.

Cayman Brac

This was formerly supposed to be the lair of Blackbeard the pirate. Now it has the appearance of a tropical garden and bird reserve surrounded by good diving locations.

If you spend some time in tiny Cayman Brac you could take in the museum with its display of shipbuilding tools and other local craft-tools and artefacts from the early days of the century.

CALENDAR
June and October are the best times to catch the action in the Cayman Islands. In June, apart from celebrating the Queen's birthday with a full dress uniform parade and a 21-gun salute, the month is taken up with a massive fishing competition called Million Dollar Month.

In October there is Pirates' Week, where everyone dresses as a pirate or his wench and captures the Governor in a mock battle.

WHERE TO STAY

South Cove and **Sunset House,** which are quite close together, have an ultra-informal, sporty, young people's feel to them. They are set up primarily as diving operations and are not really suitable if your idea of an ideal vacation is just lazing on the beach. For a start, they are not on the beach (though they are both right on the seafront). Both are excellent for serious divers, and offer other facilities such as a gift shop and car hire facilities. Rooms are air-conditioned.

There are surprisingly few hotels considering the large amount of accommodation available on the island (apartments predominate, though I have only listed a selection here). I stayed at the **Galleon Beach Hotel,** which is right in the middle of the fabulous Seven Mile Beach (originally named West Bay Beach, but apparently renamed with the opening of the Holiday Inn). This 33-roomed hotel is set back from the beach proper, so there is a sandy, tree-shaded expanse which hosts weekend evening barbecues. Sailing, watersports and diving can be conducted right off the beach, and there are tennis courts, a disco and a good restaurant.

The apartments I particularly liked were **Cocoplum,** now merged with **Grapetree.** Externally Cocoplum's wooden construction is attractive, and internally these two-bedroom, two-bathroom units are lovely. Not luxurious, they offer a complete contrast to the normal squared-off rooms one is used to—definitely for eccentrics and artists. Grapetree is built in a more conventional, stucco, style. There are two swimming pools and a tennis court.

Reef House Apartments may be the answer for a mixed group of divers and non-divers although they are five miles from the beach.

EATING OUT

Local specialities are, of course, based on seafood. Try the following: turtle steak, turtle soup, cod fish and ackee, conch stew and Seafood Newburg. The island chefs also prepare an excellent Steak Diane. Unfortunately eating out in the Cayman Islands is extremely expensive, and small local cafés are often the best value for money. If you are looking for something more glamorous, try the **Grand Old House** (but note that they won't accept credit cards), the **Lobster Pot**, or the **Periwinkle**.

Accommodation in the Cayman Islands
Daily summer rates per room in US$ (1986 rates)

Name and address	*Single*	*Double*
Dive Lodges		
Cayman Diving Lodge, East End, Grand Cayman (tel. 1–800–262–7686)	MAP: 95	90
South Cove, PO Box 637, Grand Cayman (tel. 1–809–949–2514)	EP: 65	90
Spanish Cove, Conch Point, Grand Cayman (tel. 1–809–949–3765)	EP: 95	95
Sunset House, Georgetown, Grand Cayman, (tel. 1–809–949–5966)	STD: 45	55
Hotels		
Brac Reef, Cayman Brac (tel. 1–800–327–3835)	EP: 59	59
Cayman Kai, North Side, Grand Cayman. 1–800–223–5427)	beach villas, 1-bedroom/1 bath 2-bedroom/2 bath EP150	
Holiday Inn, Grand Cayman (tel. 1–800–421–9999)	STD: 102	106
Apartments, Cottages and Guesthouses		
Grapetree/Cocoplum, Seven Mile Beach, Grand Cayman (tel. 1–809–949–5640) (no credit cards)	EP: 1-bedroom (2) 75	
London House, Seven Mile Beach, Grand Cayman (tel. 1–809–947–4060)	EP: 1-bedroom (2) 155 EP: 2-bedroom (4) 195 (deluxe)	
Plantana, Seven Mile Beach, Grand Cayman (tel. 1–809–947–4430) (no credit cards)	EP: 1-bedroom (2) 90 EP: 2-bedroom (4) 175 (penthouse)	
Reef House Apartments, Georgetown, Grand Cayman (tel. 1–809–949–7093)	EP: 2-bedroom (min 2) 25 per person	
Victoria House, Seven Mile Beach, Grand Cayman (tel. 1–809–947–4233) (no credit cards)	EP: studio (2) 64 EP: 2-bedroom (4) 98 EP: 3-bedroom (6) 129 (penthouse)	
West Indian Club, Seven Mile Beach, Grand Cayman (tel: 1–809–949–2494) (no credit cards)	EP: 1-bedroom (2) 135 No rental less than five days	

Government tax on all accommodation is 6%. Most hotels charge 10–15% gratuity and there is a departure tax of US$5.

NIGHTLIFE
Hotel-centred, particularly at the **Cayman Islander** supper-club, **Holiday Inn** or the pool-side barbecue and dancing under the stars at the **Royal Palms**. Otherwise there is a cinema and the Cayman National Theatre.

DIVE PACKAGES
It is not necessary for me to describe the kind of diving that can be experienced in the Caymans. Even non-divers know that these islands offer some of the best diving in the world. Here are details of some dive packages (all rates high-season):

South Cove: 4 days/3 nights CI$300 single, CI$280 double: includes 2 half-day boat trips with unlimited offshore diving, tanks, back pack, weights and tax.

8 days/7 nights CI$715 single, CI$680 double: 6 half-day boat trips with unlimited diving.

Learn to Dive Package (7 nights) CI$775 single, CI$724 double: accommodation, meals, transfers, etc. plus 7 full days scuba certification, all diving equipment, one half-day boat trip.

Cayman Diving Lodge: 7 nights CI$630/CI$714 single, CI$490–630 double: two one-tank boat dives daily; tank, back pack, weights, belt, guide; film and slide shows; breakfast and dinner.

Sunset House: 4 days/3 nights CI$300–330 single, CI$250–255 double: includes 2 half-day two-tank boat dives and unlimited offshore diving, tanks, back packs, weights, belt, guide; breakfast and dinner daily (service charge and tax not included), airport transfers.

8 day/7 nights CI$720–800 single, CI$580–620 double: 6 half-day boat trips.

SPORT
Apart from the diving every other kind of sport is on hand. Golfers might like to try the new 9- or 18-hole course and there are also facilities for rugby, cricket, football, volleyball, basketball, tennis, darts, squash, hockey, sailing, windsurfing, snorkelling and fishing, as well as a gym.

CUBA

Obtaining a visa to get into Cuba is such an exhausting occupation that if you succeed you will feel you have earned your holiday. I have built up a cordial relationship with the Consul and his staff at the Consulate in London, and have even received a 'Best Wishes for the New Year' card from them, but getting them to issue a visa is still an uphill task. But don't give up, as it will grant you entry to one of the most interesting parts of the Caribbean.

GETTING TO CUBA
Flights to Cuba from most places are irregular and often unreliable. Probably the best thing to do is to book an inclusive tour and leave the headaches to the tour operator.

From the USA
It is possible to get to Cuba from the USA providing a visa is obtained beforehand. Charter flights operate from Miami.

From Canada
Cubana operates flights from Montreal.

From London
The most reliable way is Iberia via Madrid. Otherwise there are Cubana flights via points such as East Berlin, Brussels, Madrid, Paris and Prague, sometimes at competitive fares, but, believe me, organising these will give you a headache. A marginally better alternative is to use Aeroflot via Moscow, Interflug via East Berlin or CSA via Prague.

From Europe
Either take Iberia from Madrid, Cubana from Madrid or Paris, or Aeroflot from Luxembourg or via Moscow.

Within the Caribbean
As Cuba's trading ties are with Communist and/or Spanish-speaking countries you would expect very few services within the Caribbean. In fact there is a fortnightly Cubana service to Georgetown, Guyana via Barbados, and a weekly service to Kingston. That's it. Occasional connections with Latin America include Lima (Cubana and Aeroflot), Managua (Cubana), Mérida, Mexico (Mexicana), Mexico City (Mexicana and Cubana), Panama (Cubana and Iberia) and San José, Costa Rica (Iberia).

A Bohio, in the style built by the Cuban Indians

ENTRY REGULATIONS
Visas are required in almost all cases. If you are travelling independently you may find yourself experiencing the same unfortunate delays as I, but if you have booked an inclusive holiday the tour operator can normally organise it for you. If you recently visited or transited a yellow fever endemic zone you will require proof of inoculation.

ELECTRICITY
The supply is 110 volts at 60 cycles, as in the US.

CLIMATE
The average winter temperature in the coastal and lowland areas is about 75°F rising to around 80°F in the summer. You can expect some slightly cooler weather, especially at night, up in the mountains.

CURRENCY
The currency unit is the Cuban peso, which is exchanged (in Cuba) at a rate of US$1.20 = 1 peso. All money has to be changed into pesos on arrival, any unspent pesos being changed back into the original currency on departure. On no account use a black-market moneychanger; if caught, you could end up in jail and will certainly have to forfeit your funds.

POPULATION
Of Cuba's 9,800,000 people, only a quarter are of African descent—less than in almost every other Caribbean country. Most of the remaining 75% are

288

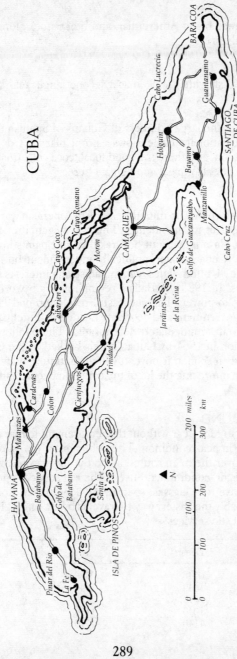

CUBA

Pinar del Rio
La Fe
ISLA DE PINOS
Santa Fe
Golfo de Batabano
Batabano
HAVANA
Matanzas
Cardenas
Colon
Cienfuegos
Trinidad
Caibarien
Cayo Coco
Cayo Romano
Moron
CAMAGUEY
Jardines de la Reina
Cabo Cruz
Golfo de Guacanayabo
Manzanillo
Bayamo
Holguin
Cabo Lucrecia
Guantanamo
SANTIAGO DE CUBA
BARACOA

N

0   100   200   300   km
0   100   200 miles

289

Spanish, the balance being Amerindian and other stock along with some interesting racial mixtures.

LANGUAGE

Spanish, with English widely spoken as a second language.

FOOD AND DRINK

When you consider the large numbers of Cubans of Spanish descent, it is not surprising that the national cuisine shows a strong bias towards Spanish dishes. The rum is very good, and there is a good local 'coca cola' (maybe they left the recipe behind). They also make good cigars here.

HISTORY

Cuba was a Spanish colony up until the Spanish-American war, although there were many attempts at independence. This war began after the US warship *Maine* blew up in Havana harbour and resulted in Spain's loss of both Cuba and Puerto Rico. Cuba became politically independent but was dominated economically by the United States, which had strong interests in the sugar and tourism industries. In 1933 the Batista regime, now a byword for corruption and cruelty, came to power. The successful revolution of 1959 established a socialist form of government and economy headed by Fidel Castro. Relations with the United States immediately deteriorated. There followed the abortive Bay of Pigs invasion in 1961 by Cuban rebels backed by the CIA, the missile crisis of 1962, and an economic boycott which continues today. Yet Castro has been successful in improving the lot of the common people and he enjoys great popularity.

GETTING AROUND

It is now possible to rent a car without the requirement to hire a chauffeur, but it is unlikely to be in peak condition. The public buses (*guaguas*) in Havana are very cheap and cover the main routes, as do the more expensive but infinitely more comfortable air-conditioned buses. The rail services operated by *Ferrocarriles de Cuba* have four classes: special, air-conditioned first, ordinary first and second. Probably the easiest way to travel is by air, and I give below details of Cubana's domestic services:

From Havana to	Depart	Arrive	Frequency
Camagüey	0740	0850	Daily
Camagüey	1940	2040	Daily
Camagüey	2010	2210	Daily
Cienfuegos	1040	1130	Fri/Sun
Holguín	1140	1310	Daily

From Havana to	Depart	Arrive	Frequency
Nueva Gerona	0630	0700	Daily
Nueva Gerona	0840	0915	Daily
Nueva Gerona	1230	1305	Daily
Nueva Gerona	1430	1505	Daily
Nueva Gerona	1630	1705	Daily
Santa Clara	1015	1105	Daily
Santiago	0640	0810	Daily
Santiago	1500	1630	Daily
Santiago	1915	2115	Wed/Thurs/Sun
Santiago	2010	2350	Daily

WHAT TO SEE

From the 1920s to the 1950s, Havana was the glamour spot of the Caribbean; now it seems to be in a state of permanent revolution. A good place to start exploring is the Malecón, the road which runs along parallel with the sea. From here you can visit several of the most interesting 16th and 17th-century fortifications; look out particularly for **El Morro**, first a castle, then a prison, now a restaurant. Also worth exploring is the **Plaza de Armas**, traditionally the place where Havana first began; the **Temple** and the **City Museum** are worth a visit if you like that kind of thing. Otherwise stroll on, taking in the **Cathedral** and the **Central Park**, a good place to stop and soak up the atmosphere.

CALENDAR
July is the time to catch the carnival spirit in Cuba, climaxing on 26 July, National Rebellion Day. Religious festivals are no longer celebrated.

WHERE TO STAY

Cuba is a fairly well-developed country, with some large towns and many long straight roads, dissecting great cultivated areas. You should have a fair chance of finding suitable lodgings of the native type, though a knowledge of Spanish will help. If you decide to visit Havana only, you should find abundant hotels of varying sizes and prices but mainly of a fair age and showing signs of dilapidation. This is not meant as a criticism; it seems to me that the government has achieved a great deal just in maintaining Cuba's solvency and integrity as an independent nation, when one considers the difficulties it has had to face.

SPORT

Watersports and beaches are just as popular here as elsewhere in the Caribbean, sport fishing being perhaps the best known. The Cubatur desk at your hotel should have details or contact the official tourist agency in Havana, at Calle 23 #156, Vedado (tel. 32–4709).

NB: Tipping is not permitted.

Part IV

THE BAHAMAS

A beach view

On reaching the Bahamas, Columbus wrote as follows:

'This country excels all others as far as the day surpasses the night in splendour: the natives love their neighbours as themselves; their conservation is the sweetest imaginable; their faces always smiling; and so gentle and affectionate are they that I swear to Your Highness there is not a better people in all the World.'

Columbus soon changed all that.

The natives—gentle Arawak Indians—were transported as slaves to the colonies of Cuba and Hispaniola and officially became extinct in the Bahamas. It is indeed unlikely that any pure-blooded Arawaks remain, but it is pretty certain (though not official) that some Bahamians can claim Arawak forefathers. Today the majority of Bahamians are black, descendants of slaves brought from Africa, with a scattering of whites (both native—descended from pirates, sailors, etc.—and immigrants) and Creoles.

The ethnic background, however, does not tell the full story. If you are able to spend some time in the Bahamas you will soon notice differences between the people on different islands. In and around the capital of Nassau you will find much of the hustle and bustle always evident in large towns; yet on many of the Out Islands (or Family Islands, as Bahamians call them) you will find that Columbus could, if he returned, write the above quotation again, word for word.

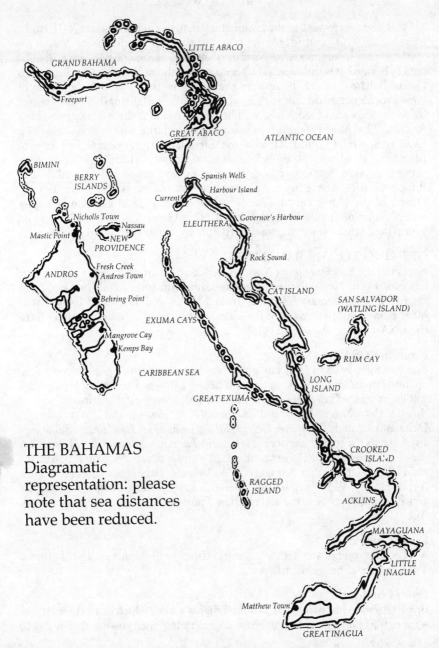

LITTLE ABACO

GRAND BAHAMA

Freeport

GREAT ABACO

ATLANTIC OCEAN

BIMINI

BERRY
ISLANDS

Spanish Wells

Harbour Island

Current

Nicholls Town

Mastic Point

Nassau

NEW
PROVIDENCE

ELEUTHERA

Governor's Harbour

Rock Sound

ANDROS

Fresh Creek
Andros Town

Behring Point

CAT ISLAND

SAN SALVADOR
(WATLING ISLAND)

EXUMA CAYS

Mangrove Cay

Kemps Bay

RUM CAY

CARIBBEAN SEA

LONG
ISLAND

GREAT EXUMA

THE BAHAMAS
Diagramatic
representation: please
note that sea distances
have been reduced.

CROOKED
ISLAND

RAGGED
ISLAND

ACKLINS

MAYAGUANA

LITTLE
INAGUA

Matthew Town

GREAT INAGUA

293

Counting every speck in the group, the Bahamas comprise some 700 islands. Fewer than 30 are considered important in terms of population or size.

Many people suppose that Nassau is situated on one of the larger islands, merely because it is the capital. Others presume the capital must be situated on Grand Bahama, merely because of the name. In fact, although the island of New Providence is the home of more than half the Bahamas' 230,000 population, it ranks about tenth in size. The largest island is the sparsely populated Andros. The Abaco group, fast becoming a favourite with tourists, covers a large area, whilst Grand Bahama and Eleuthera are nowadays well-known. Eleuthera, an island with three international airports, which is 100 miles long yet only as wide as the road at its narrowest point, has already played host to Prince Charles and Princess Diana (they stayed at Windermere Island). Others of the better known islands are the Exuma Cays (excellent yachting waters), Bimini (home of Hemingway, 'The Game Fishing Capital of the World' and site of some supposedly Atlantean remains) and San Salvador.

GETTING TO THE BAHAMAS
Access to the Bahamas from North America and Europe is easier now than it has ever been. Not only have communications to the capital, Nassau, been improved with increased services from Florida and additional flights from other points, but now many of the Family Islands can be reached direct from the USA.

From the USA
You can fly to Nassau from any one of seventeen departure points on services operated predominantly by 'household name' airlines. The choice is so great I will list routes and carriers in alphabetical order for greater clarity:
Atlanta: Bahamasair, Delta and Eastern; *Boston:* Eastern and TWA; *Chicago:* Delta and United; *Cleveland:* Delta; *Dallas:* Delta; *Fort Lauderdale:* Bahamasair, Chalk's (seaplane service), Delta and Eastern; *Kansas City:* TWA; *Los Angeles:* TWA; *Miami:* Bahamasair, Chalk's and Eastern; *New York:* Bahamasair, Delta, Eastern, Pan Am and TWA; *Orlando:* Bahamasair and New York Air; *St Louis:* TWA; *San Francisco:* Delta; *Seattle:* Eastern; *Tampa:* Bahamasair and Eastern; *Washington:* Eastern; *West Palm Beach:* Chalk's and New York Air.

From Canada
Air Canada operates scheduled services from both Montreal and Toronto. There may also be some charters.

From London
British Airways has two Jamaica-bound flights a week which call in here. If you want to travel on a day when they are not operating, then you can fly any day of

the week via Miami (Pan Am, British Airways, and Virgin Atlantic). Indeed, on occasion it is cheaper to fly via Miami, as there are often discounted fares on this route and often special bargains available (such as Virgin's inaugural fare of £99 one way). You need a US visa if passing through Miami.

From Europe
Via London, Miami or New York. Pan Am has flights from Berlin, Hamburg, Madrid and Paris, and Northwest flies to Miami from Oslo. Aeromexico flies from Paris (as does Delta) and Madrid (as does Iberia), and Lufthansa operates from Düsseldorf and Frankfurt.

Within the Caribbean
British Airways flies in twice a week from Kingston and Montego Bay, and Turks and Caicos Airways from Providenciales.

Direct to the Family Islands
Those of the Family Islands which can be reached direct from the USA are Abaco, Bimini, Cat Cay, Eleuthera, Exuma and Grand Bahama. Although many flights are by jet aircraft, generally you will find (as you would expect) that these flights are operated by small, piston-engined aircraft. Chalk's flights are by seaplane (and therefore worth trying just for the experience).

Airfares
At the time of writing airfares are extremely volatile; you must therefore check with your travel agent or the airlines for the latest information. Don't forget to ask them about special excursion fares. You should also bear in mind that although there are direct flights from as far away as Boston or Chicago, because of the airfare tariff war it may be cheaper to buy a domestic ticket to Miami and an international ticket from there. On the other hand, sometimes it may be cheaper to use a through fare from a point which doesn't actually have a through service (such as Seattle). To give an idea of costs I list below some sample fares from Miami (round trip).

From Miami to	Round trip fare in US$	Airline(s)
Bimini	90	Chalk's
Cat Cay	120	Chalk's
Freeport	92–158	Bahamasair and Eastern
Georgetown	230	AeroCoach Aviation
Governor's Harbour	160–190	Proair, Caribbean Express
Marsh Harbour	158–170	Proair, Caribbean Express
Nassau	80–158	Bahamasair, Eastern and Chalk's
North Eleuthera	178–190	Proair, Caribbean Express
Rock Sound	178–190	Proair, Caribbean Express
Treasure Cay	158–170	Proair, Caribbean Express

ENTRY REGULATIONS

No visa is required of United States, Canadian, British or most other Western European passport holders, or citizens of Commonwealth countries. All nationalities, except residents of the Bahamas, will be expected to show an air ticket out of the Bahamas and a return ticket to their country of domicile (boat tickets may be accepted, but check). You may also be required to show that you have adequate funds.

If you have come from or transited a yellow fever endemic zone within the last fourteen days you will be required to show proof of inoculation.

CUSTOMS

The usual allowances with regard to smokes and drinks apply. In fact it is a good idea to take advantage of them if you indulge, as cigarettes particularly are expensive in the Bahamas. There are no problems over introducing cameras, personal sports equipment, etc., but young people should note this official regulation:

'The possession of marijuana or other narcotic drugs is a serious offence in the Bahamas. Offenders can expect quick and severe punishment, with normal time of about three days between apprehension and conviction.'

ELECTRICITY

The supply is 120 volts at 60 cycles, about the same as in the US.

CLIMATE

The Bahama islands are principally—sometimes entirely—made of coral. This is largely the reason for the beautiful turquoise colour of the sea. But it also means that there are no highlands here (Mount Alvernia on Cat Island is the highest point at 200 feet). Consequently temperatures are uniformly sub-tropical.

	Jan	Feb	Mar	Apr	May	Jun	Jul	Aug	Sep	Oct	Nov	Dec
Maximum daily temperature °F	83	83	82	87	88	90	92	92	90	90	88	86
Minimum daily temperature °F	52	46	51	61	61	61	70	69	60	60	60	50
Average daily temperature °F	70	68	70	75	78	80	82	81	81	78	76	71
Total monthly rainfall in inches	2.3	1	0.5	1.2	3	7	6	9	13	12	7	2
Number of rainy days	9	5	5	6	11	12	15	17	19	16	15	9
Average daily sunshine hours	6	7	9	9	10	9	9	8	7	7	7	6

CURRENCY

The Bahamas dollar, divided into 100 cents, is at par with the US dollar. Both currencies are used, but you should make sure that you have changed your Bahamas dollars into American before you leave the country.

The Bahamas are very expensive, for the native as well as the tourist. In fact the Bahamas are unusual by Caribbean standards in so far as the traveller can live for the same sort of cost as the itinerant native, who suffers the same high prices. These prices are due mainly to two influences: firstly the tourist boom of the 1960s which only began to subside in the mid 1970s when worldwide recession set in (this coincided with independence in 1973); secondly, the Bahamas' dependence on imports, particularly from the United States. Do not lose heart, however: on the credit side it should be noted that over the last five years hotel prices have risen less rapidly than in some other Caribbean countries.

POPULATION

As a generalisation it is true to say that the people are very friendly. This is largely natural to them, though there are those who make a special effort.

As in any country it is best not to wander the back streets of the capital at night. Elsewhere you should certainly be safe.

The population is around 230,000, of whom 130,000 live on New Providence. I noticed an abundance of young children, particularly on Andros.

LANGUAGE

English, heavily accented by blacks and whites alike.

FOOD AND DRINK

On my first trip I thought there was no such thing as bad Bahamian food, but then on a subsequent visit I had a meal that was mediocre. Generally it is true to say that you will find native dishes to be of a high standard (and you can also get European and American food—even including McDonalds, Burger King and Kentucky Fried Chicken if you really insist).

As you would expect, seafood dishes are prominent, particularly conch (pronounced 'conk'), snapper and crayfish (similar to lobster). Grouper is a particularly delicious fish. Chicken, generally fried with peas and rice, is another mainstay on native menus. The traditional breakfast features boiled fish, but if this is too much for you first thing in the morning you'll have little trouble getting a conventional breakfast. In Nassau and Freeport it is extremely easy to find restaurants serving American and/or European meals.

Locals prefer German beer to American, and there is usually a small price difference which reflects this. The Caribbean drink of rum is popular here, and there is a Bacardi plant on New Providence. Milk is sometimes difficult to get.

HISTORY

San Salvador (known as Watling Island in British colonial days) is thought to be the island first spotted by Columbus and thus has the distinction of being the first part of the New World to be discovered by Europeans.

The Bahamas were never developed as a colony in the same way as, for example, Cuba, Hispaniola and Barbados. This is because the islands had few natural, exploitable, resources—only the sea and the beaches, which were of no use to the early colonists. They could find fertile land and better naval bases elsewhere, fairly close at hand.

The Spanish, who at this time were by far the most powerful people represented in the New World, thus had no interest in the Bahamas once they had transported the inhabitants to work elsewhere. The islands then seemed to fall under British influence by default. Religious dissenters and pirates became the two main groups settling there, the former to avoid persecution in the North American colonies as well as at home, and the latter because it gave them a base perfectly distanced from the Spanish shipping lanes. The best known group of religious dissenters chose Eleuthera for their home; the pirates chose Nassau.

In 1703 a joint Franco-Spanish expedition destroyed Nassau. This action provided the spur to Nassau's inauguration as a pirates' republic: they reasoned that if Nassau, with its magnificent harbour, became the base for all the pirates, they would then be sufficient in number to repel future attacks. By 1716 there were apparently some 2,000 pirates here. They were led by the notorious Edward Teach—better known as Blackbeard—who was the model for Stevenson's Flint. Among his constituents were the two women pirates, Anne Bonny and Mag Read, who, when subsequently brought to trial in Jamaica in 1720, escaped hanging by announcing that they were pregnant.

The reality of pirate life was very different to its romantic image. At this time Nassau was a shanty town with houses and shops made of palm fronds and worn-out sails. Grog shops and brothels predominated among its commercial institutions, and it was said that you could smell New Providence before you could see it.

During the 16th and 17th centuries British governments tacitly supported the pirates so long as they preyed upon Spanish shipping and settlements and just as long as Spanish power and influence in the area was supreme. But the situation had changed by 1718: Spain's power and empire had declined substantially and the other European seafaring nations—Britain, France and the Netherlands—all had their own colonies in the New World. The pirates had served their purpose and could now be dispensed with.

A governor was thus sent out to bring Nassau formally under British jurisdiction and with the principal task of stamping out piracy. Woodes Rogers was himself an ex-privateer, but, having switched allegiances, he energetically initiated a campaign to clean up the islands. An amnesty was announced for those who gave up piracy immediately, whilst at the same time it was made clear that those who maintained their way of life would be hunted down and hanged. Many who accepted the amnesty turned to the legitimate business of salvaging, whilst others changed sides from poacher to gamekeeper.

Through able administration, the summoning of the Representative Assembly in 1729 and the suppression of piracy, Woodes Rogers brought some form of law and order to the islands. Vagrancy and drunkenness became illegal, sanitation was introduced and ex-pirates were involved in the building of houses and churches. By the time he died in 1732 Woodes Rogers had played an important role in establishing a stable society in the Bahamas. The islands now entered a peaceful period.

Even without the pirates, the prosperity of the Bahamas remained tied to events abroad. The American Revolution and Civil War, European powers' colonial wars and Prohibition were all events which brought prosperity to the Bahamas. The American War of Independence brought an influx of refugee Loyalists and their slaves who attempted to introduce some agricultural industry to the islands; the Civil War introduced a period of unparalleled prosperity as a direct result of smuggling. From Nassau the blockade runners transported food and guns across the Florida Strait to the Confederate ports, returning with cheap cotton which would then be sold at ten times its cost. The profits this generated were spent on paved, gas-lit streets and a police force in the capital. In between these American wars there had been a brief return to piracy, as privateers were encouraged to prey upon enemy shipping during the wars of the colonial powers.

Economic stagnation was once again interrupted by events in America, this time the imposition of Prohibition. The number of vessels using Bahamian ports quadrupled as rum-running became established as a quick way to make money.

Tourism began to develop just before the last war. Strictly speaking, its beginnings could be traced back to 1859 when Samuel Cunard set up a regular New York to Nassau steamship service, but development of the islands themselves really began in the 1930s when Canadian millionaire Harry Oakes poured money into developing a large tract of land he had bought in New Providence; he built the island's first airport, a golf course and hotels. Tourism is now the main industry. It is still mainly centred around Nassau and Freeport (which was developed as a glittering gaming resort after the revolution in Cuba terminated Havana's pre-eminence) but the more relaxed Family Islands—principally Abaco, Eleuthera, Exuma and the Berry Islands—are proving a great attraction for those tourists who want something out of the ordinary.

Politically the Bahamas have been quite stable. With brief interruptions by a short spell of Spanish occupation and an even shorter American invasion, the Bahamas remained a Crown Colony until independence in 1973. There was, however, a period of unrest in the 1950s, mainly due to feelings of resentment against an oligarchic clique that dominated Bahamian affairs. These people—'The Bay Street Boys'—had made their money and acquired their power from their rum-running activities in the Prohibition years.

The political system is based on the British model, with two Houses of Parliament, a Government headed by a Prime Minister and an official opposition. Queen Elizabeth II is the Head of State.

The Bahamas still retain much of their historical heritage. Grog shops—now known as liquor stores—proliferate in Nassau on Bay Street (which is supposed to have more liquor stores in one mile than anywhere else in the world), and fine colonial buildings still represent the islands' best architecture. Offshore banking thrives as the main industry apart from tourism.

CALENDAR
The most colourful of the public holidays are Boxing Day and New Year's Day, when there are exuberant street parades.

NEW PROVIDENCE

The earliest settlers, a group of Loyalists, arrived around 1666 and named it Sayle's Island. The settlement they established was called Charles Towne, it being the practice of the time to name places in the colonies after a monarch; in 1695 it was renamed Nassau after Prince William of Orange Nassau.

Although the island is only 21 miles long by 7 wide there is much to see and it is worth while hiring a car, motorscooter or bicycle. Most of the hotels are in and around Nassau or across the bridge on Paradise Island, though there are others further from the action, in particular to the west of town on Cable Beach.

The first tourists, in the 1930s and just after the last war, were the rich and famous. They still come, and the Bahamas are still regarded as an up-market holiday destination, but New Providence and Nassau itself tend to be the hosts for the less rich. Americans are of course the largest group; fairly inexpensive excursions can be made by plane or cruise ship from Miami, and many cruise liners call here.

GETTING AROUND
Car hire is of course available here, minimokes (minicars) as well as internationally popular models. A rough idea of car hire rates (correct at time of writing) is:

NEW PROVIDENCE

PARADISE ISLAND

NASSAU

Harbour

Sea Gardens

Winton Highway

Bernard Road

Village Road

Prince Charles Avenue

East Street

Nassau Street

Baillou Hill Road

Independence Drive

Wulff Road

The Grove

Harold Road

Carmichael Road

Carmichael Village

Cable Beach

West Bay Street

South Beach

Blake Road

John F Kennedy Drive

Lake Killarney

Love Beach

Gambier Village

Coral Harbour Road

Windsor Field Road

Nassau International Airport

Sea Gardens

Southwest Road/Adelaide Road

Adelaide

CORAL HARBOUR

Mount Pleasant

Golf Course

N

0   2   4   6   km
0   2   4   miles

Volkswagen 1300 $44 per day, $308 per week; Plymouth Reliant K or Olds-mobile Omega, both automatic and air-conditioned $62 per day, $434 per week. Minimum driver age 25; collision damage waiver $6 per day.

Any valid driving licence is accepted. In the Bahamas you drive on the left, and speed limits are in the range of 30–40 mph.

Bicycles can be hired outside the Sheraton British Colonial Hotel; the cost is $5 a day plus a $5 deposit, expensive considering the fact that they are in bad condition, but an enjoyable way to get around the island if you are fit. A couple may prefer to hire a **scooter;** at $16 a day it works out very little more than a bi-cycle per person (although petrol is extra of course) and allows longer trips to be made. These can be hired from the same place, but I suggest you shop around (there are a number of places on West Bay Street and Paradise Island). The machines are generally Yamahas and Hondas, and the law requires you to wear a helmet.

Jitney bus services ply the main roads out of Nassau, east, west, north (Paradise Island) and south. The fare is 50 cents, unless you are going to the far west of the island, when it is $1. They do not run to the airport. To take a bus you can either walk out along the road in the direction you wish to travel and find a bus stop (marked on the road or by a stand or post), or go down to Frederick Street from where many buses leave.

Some of the Jitney bus routes are indirect, zipping through residential areas covering the whole range from wooden cabins to luxury villas. This is particu-larly true of the Fox Hill Jitney service. If you are not hiring a bicycle or scooter you should thus take the opportunity of seeing something of New Providence and the outskirts of Nassau by Jitney.

WHAT TO SEE

If staying more than a day in Nassau, you'll probably want to explore New Pro-vidence Island. The best way to do this is to hire one of those expensive and inefficient bicycles. Allow two days—I did the 30-odd miles in one and really felt the pace. A suggested itinerary is to take the coast road (West Bay Street) out of Nassau, passing miles of fine, sandy, deserted beaches. Cross the island at its west end and return along South West Road.

The **Oasis** is a convenient stop for lunch. It is a bar with restaurant, pool table and juke box. Food and clientele are local. Fried chicken, peas, and rice and salad cost $6—not a knockout but not unreasonable either.

Note that this itinerary is arduous, covering over 30 miles. It is simple by scooter, and in theory should present no difficulty by bike, but I found that neither my body nor the cycle were in good condition. It took me nearly 6½ hours, including stops (total cycling time about 4 hours). The route can be shortened considerably by taking Blake Road and Coral Harbour Road past the airport. This also passes Lake Killarney.

There's also plenty to see east of Nassau. You can walk, but it is fairly arduous in the heat; you can cycle or scooter easily, or alternatively you can take a bus either to Montagu Heights or Paradise Bridge. The Jitney buses run along Shirley Street and will cost you 40–50 cents. These buses generally stop only at recognised bus stops.

Fort Montagu is in a relaxing setting, on the headland guarding the eastern approaches to Nassau harbour, but is in itself really only a gun emplacement with a grandiose name. A handful of rusty cannon remain to remind one of a turbulent past. Continuing down Eastern Road (it's quite a walk) you will eventually come to **Blackbeard's Tower**. A small sign marks the path up the hill. From here Blackbeard used to keep a lookout for anyone trespassing in his waters.

From the tower walk back along the main road to Fox Hill Road and walk up the hill into Sandlands (Fox Hill). Here in the main square you will find a bar/restaurant which serves native food, and is recommended. Here is a pool table, usually occupied. I found the fried fish with peas and rice and a small side salad very good. **Saint Augustine's Monastery,** though of no great antiquity, may be of interest if you are in the area.

Beaches on New Providence: The nearest beach is actually in Nassau. It begins in front of the Sheraton British Colonial Hotel and runs westward to Arawak City. Considering it is within the harbour waters it is surprisingly clean. The only problem is that although sandy, it is rocky in places, and steeply shelving at times. Travelling along the north coast in a westerly direction you will see other, fairly empty, beaches: Saunders Beach, Cable Beach, Delaporte Beach, Love Beach and others. More beaches are situated at the west of the island, principally Pleasant Bay, and in the southwest Adelaide Beach is a stretch some three miles long. Elsewhere on the island there is only one other principal beach, South Beach, which, as its name implies, is due south of Nassau.

Other attractions include **Ardastra Gardens,** west of town. Here, twice a day—at 11 am and 4 pm—a flock of pink flamingos is paraded military-style; admission is $5. **Fort Charlotte** is the largest of the forts here and the only one worthy of the name. Built in 1788, it has a moat, dungeons and battlements. Guides are dressed in the uniform of the British West Indies Regiment. Another fort, **Fincastle,** was built in the centre of Nassau on high ground; it is of less interest to the tourist than the steps hewn out of the rock to reach it, the **Queen's Staircase**. A waterfall runs alongside this.

If you are staying in Nassau long, you should take the opportunity to go on a boat cruise. Glass-bottomed boats to the Sea Gardens have already been mentioned, but there is also a catamaran cruise on the *Tropic Bird.* Described as 'one of the largest catamarans in the Atlantic' and big enough to carry a band as well as passengers and crew, she sails six days a week from Prince George

Dock (at 10.15 am returning at 1.15 pm). The price of $20 covers a cruise to 'one of the most beautiful beaches in the Bahamas' where a picnic lunch is served.

There are of course local companies that operate sightseeing tours; here are some of them:

B and B Tours	Nassau Street, Nassau (tel. 34350)
Calypso Taxi Tours	Sheraton British Colonial Hotel, Nassau (tel. 24116)
Happy Tours	Taxi Union Building, Nassau Street, Nassau (tel. 35818)
Howard Johnson Tours	Shirley Street, Nassau (tel. 28181)
Island Sun Tours	Charlotte Street North, Nassau (tel. 56959)
Majestic Tours	Charlotte Street, Nassau (tel. 22606)
Playtours	Shirley Street, Nassau (tel. 22931)
Tropical Travel Bureau	Myers House, Bay and Victoria Streets, Nassau (tel. 24091)

Medium-sized and large hotels will be able to organise any excursions, car hire, flight arrangements, etc. for you in the usual way.

Nassau

Arrival in Nassau: Jet flights arrive at Nassau International Airport, in the western part of the island. Taxis are metered; if you are staying in Nassau itself the cost should be about $10. It will cost you about $6 if you intend staying in the Cable Beach area and about $14 if you will be holidaying on Paradise Island (if you are staying on Paradise Island you may be interested to know that Chalk's seaplane base is there). Note that there is no bus service from the airport. If you arrive on an evening flight money-changing facilities may be closed, so make sure you have some US dollars in cash with you.

It is certainly possible to take a holiday in the Bahamas without visiting Nassau, but in practice it is only old hands who will do this. The capital has a style and bustle not to be found on the Family Islands, yet it is also quite different from other Caribbean capitals.

Nassau is a fascinating blend of old and new. The mock Gothic architecture of the Cathedral, shyly tucked away in the centre, contrasts with the brash shops and restaurants of Bay Street; on Paradise Island the Cloisters, built in France in the 12th century, and subsequently exported first to the USA and then to the Bahamas, are barely a stone's throw from skyscraper hotels and casino gambling. Old cannon point out to sea along West Bay Street, colourful artillery pieces guard Parliament and Queen Victoria's statue, forts such as Montagu and Charlotte are reminiscent (in name at least) of a turbulent past. Imposing pink-and-white painted public buildings and tree-shaded wooden mansions recall a leisured age which is echoed by the multi-masted sailing ships in the harbour. Amongst this is the mushrooming new Nassau: nuclear-age paper-bag eating houses, modern hotels, ocean-going luxury liners, the concrete arc of Paradise Bridge, all screaming modernity. Yet somehow they blend—it feels right. Only the sight and sound of jet aircraft seem out of place.

WHAT TO SEE IN NASSAU
Nassau has plenty to offer. Paradise Island, which can be reached by ferry from Prince George Wharf (50 cents) or Paradise Bridge (25 cents), features the casino where you can gamble or just walk around. At the end of the bridge, on Paradise Island, is Hurricane Hole, the yacht marina.

Potter's Cay is under the bridge, almost halfway between Nassau and the island. Here is the Produce Exchange, where the incoming boats from the Family Islands bring in cargo, mainly foodstuffs. Along the lower road under the bridge running into Nassau you will see where the small fishing boats tie up. Here you can buy from the wide variety of fish and conch or just watch the fishermen preparing their catch. Here also you can see a small artificial island, made up entirely of discarded conch shells. Potter's Cay dock is where the majority of mail boats to the islands leave from.

The **Sea Gardens** (at the east end of Paradise Island and opposite Love Beach) are underwater coral reefs of great natural beauty. A glass-bottomed boat can be taken from Nassau (Prince George Wharf) or Paradise Island (ferry point) to view those at the eastern end of the harbour. One of the amazing sights of the Bahamas, even today, is the clarity of the blue-green water. Even in the harbour, where rubbish is continually casually tipped into the sea, the water remains clear.

Horse-drawn surreys are more traditional taxis which ply the streets of Nassau. Usually pink or red, they generally depart from Rawson Square (opposite Parliament Square). There is a straw market on Bay Street stretching back to Woodes Rogers Walk housed in a new building specially built for straw goods.

WHERE TO STAY
The range of accommodation encompasses everything from luxury hotels with golf, tennis and watersports to lowly guesthouses providing accommodation only. A full list is available from any Bahamas tourist office, but here is a selection.

Hotels: As you would expect from a hotel in the price range of the **Ambassador Beach Hotel,** the rooms are all luxuriously furnished with two double beds and air-conditioning. The facilities of boutiques, barber, beauty salon, coffee shop, beachfront bar and grill, French and Bahamian cuisine and dancing are also provided by the hotel. There is a new hotel and casino complex, The **Cable Beach Resort and Casino,** one of two casinos on New Providence, the other, on Paradise Island, being the longer established. When you consider that sporting activities such as golf, scuba diving, fishing, sailing and tennis are available, allied with the fact that the hotel is right on Cable Beach, it is not surprising that many guests rarely wander far from the hotel for their entire vacation.

The **Cable Beach Inn, Royal Bahamian, Emerald Beach** and **Nassau Beach** hotels are the other places right on Cable Beach. All can be classed in the luxury category and therefore provide the excellent standards of accommodation and facilities expected, but there are slight differences which give each an identity. The Emerald Beach Hotel is the oldest. The accent here is on organised sporting and social activities. The Royal Bahamian Hotel, on the other hand, is geared more to the rich European's idea of a holiday, with a 'club' atmosphere, marble courtyards with fountains, a gourmet restaurant and a ballroom.

The largest group of hotels is situated in Nassau itself. West Bay Street is a continuation of Bay Street (as you would expect) which becomes the main road out of town to Cable Beach and the airport. Sauntering in this general direction, the first hotel you would encounter is one of the oldest in the Bahamas, the **Sheraton British Colonial**. From its name you would expect it to be a distinguished building; from its Sheraton connections you would not be surprised to find a McDonalds on site. The beach which lies in front is the first you encounter when walking out of town, but it's really a private beach and is difficult to get to without going through the hotel. Large rooms, tradition and modern facilities enable this hotel to maintain its claim to be *the* hotel of Nassau.

Continuing your casual sunlit stroll you'll notice a little kink in the road as it bears right towards the sea and then bends left again to run parallel with the coast. On this corner is the **New Olympia Hotel**. There is nothing special about this medium-priced hotel, patronised as you would expect by young couples. 'Nothing special' is also a tag I would have to attach to most of the next clutch of hotels: **Ocean Spray, Dolphin** and **Lighthouse Beach Hotel**. Like the New Olympia, the Ocean Spray lacks a swimming pool. Don't think however that this will ruin your holiday—there is a good beach opposite all these establishments. If you're under 35, half of a couple and without children, you may find the Ocean Spray to your liking; room rates and restaurant prices are reasonable and there is spontaneous (rather than organised) lively social intercourse.

The Dolphin is something of an unknown quantity to me. The last time I was there it was being refurbished (necessary) and so it is difficult for me to give an accurate assessment. The new owner impressed me however with his commitment to spend the necessary money on improvements, so the rates being reasonable, it could be worth a try.

Nestling among this group of hotels, like a pearl in an oyster, is **El Greco**.

This lovely hotel is quite different from any other hotel on the island. A two-storey building with Spanish-style decor and period furnishings, it boasts what is generally regarded as one of Nassau's better restaurants, Del Prado, a regular (unpackaged) clientele (apparently the British High Commission accommodates visitors here), secluded freshwater swimming-pool, and is just across the road from the beach. At US$75 for a double room it must be first choice of anyone looking for traditional values and service in a hotel. If you must stay in Nassau itself this is the hotel I would unhesitatingly recommend.

Paradise Island has the advantage of a small island's ambience without the usual disadvantages—a dearth of things to do. With its own casino and Nassau just over the bridge there's plenty of action. Most of the hotels are of the multi-storey multi-facilities type, but for the rich and discerning there is the **Ocean Club**. This estate with its golf course, tropical water gardens, tennis court, luxury rooms, suites and villas on Two Mile Beach is the home of the 12th-century cloisters mentioned earlier. There's no bingo, but plenty of other entertainment nearby.

Hotels
Daily winter rate per room in US$

Name	Address	Single	Double
Britannia Towers	Paradise Island (tel. 63000)	EP: S or D 165–200	
		MAP: 145–230	185–270
Cable Beach Inn	Cable Beach (tel. 77341)	EP: S or D 80–105	
Dolphin	West Bay Street, Nassau (tel. 28666)	EP: 63–78	63–78
El Greco	West Bay Street, Nassau (tel. 51121)	EP: 65	75
Emerald Beach	Cable Beach (tel. 78001)	EP: 110–120	110–120
		MAP: 135–155	180–190
Grand Central	Charlotte Street, Nassau (tel. 28356)	EP: 57–65	65–70
Graycliff	West Hill Street, Nassau (tel. 22796/54832)	CP: 100	140–180
Holiday Inn	Paradise Island (tel. 62101)	EP: 105–165	115–175
Lighthouse Beach	West Bay Street, Nassau (tel. 24474)	EP: 70	70
		MAP: 80	74
Loews Harbour Cove	Paradise Island (tel. 55561)	EP: 130–170	130–170
		MAP: 157–197	157–197
Nassau Beach	Cable Beach (tel. 77711)	EP: S or D 165–210	
		MAP: 196–241	196–241
Nassau Harbour Club	East Bay Street, Nassau (tel. 33771)	EP: 64–79	60–84
New Olympia	West Bay Street, Nassau (tel. 24971)	EP: 63	67–70

307

Name	Address	Daily winter rate per room in US$	
		Single	Double
Ocean Club	Paradise Island (tel. 62501)	EP. S or D 115 225	
		MAP: 194–274	243–324
Ocean Spray	West Bay Street, Nassau (tel. 28032)	EP: 45	58
Paradise Towers	Paradise Island (tel. 62000)	EP: S or D 145–225	
Pilot House Hotel	East Bay Street, Nassau (tel. 28431)	EP: S or D 85	
Royal Bahamian	Cable Beach (tel. 76400)	EP: 155	155
		MAP: 205	255
Sheraton British Colonial	Bay and Marlborough Streets, Nassau (tel. 23301)	EP: 106–170	136–190
		MAP: 103–123	124–144 approx.
South Ocean Beach	South West Road (tel. 64391)	EP: 90–125	95–135
Wyndham Ambassador Beach	Cable Beach (tel. 78231)	EP: 115	115
		MAP: 139	168

Apartments: Apartment holidays have not yet become quite as established in the Bahamas as they have in the Eastern Caribbean (Barbados particularly springs to mind), probably because of the greater number of American, rather than European, tourists. It seems to be catching on though, and there are some other apartments and villas besides those listed here.

Cable Beach Manor is the longest established and you certainly gain that impression when walking through the grounds. Much thought obviously went into designing the layout of the apartments, which are of three different types and are situated in one- or two-storey buildings. A free-form swimming pool with sunbathing area is surrounded by random palm trees and shrubs which encourage a haphazard feeling and homely look. During my visit the Manor was full and I gained the clear impression that many families were regular guests. It's beginning to show its age, but it is well-managed and feels comfortable.

Casuarinas Apartment Hotel is much newer and further away from town along Cable Beach. Building hadn't been completed during my visit, but I liked the apartments which I was able to view. Some of the two-bedroomed apartments are split level, and all are tastefully furnished. Much thought has gone into all aspects of the design and facilities, and Casuarinas does not suffer from the modern malaise of corner-cutting. Facilities include a restaurant, cocktail lounge, swimming pool, whirlpool, mini swimming pool, bar and recreation room. It is also right on the beach (though the beach just here is nothing special).

Club Land'Or is also a relatively new establishment, and one which impressed me far less. Situated on Paradise Island, it is well placed for evening entertainment, and its own facilities include swimming pool and bar.

Grosvenor Court Apartments, also on Paradise Island, are probably the best value in all-round terms. Not surprisingly, they were full during my visit, and were already booked up well ahead for most of the year. The main block will not win prizes for originality of design, though the apartments themselves are comfortable and well-maintained. Small clusters of sparse, Spanish-style cottages nearby are very attractive to those seeking a more distinctive yet not necessarily more luxurious ambience. Apartments are air-conditioned with telephones, and facilities include swimming pool and bar.

Apartments
Daily winter rates per apartment in US$

Name	Address	
Cable Beach Manor	Cable Beach (tel. 77784)	EP: studio 95–115; 1-bedroom apt. 135; 2-bedroom apt. 180–210
Casuarinas	Cable Beach (tel. 77921)	EP: studio 75–124; 1-bedroom apt. 110–120; 2-bedroom apt. 160
Club Land'Or	Paradise Island (tel. 51457)	EP: 1-bedroom apt. 95–115
Grosvenor Court	Paradise Island (tel. 55924)	EP: studio 90; 1-bedroom apt. 100; 2-bedroom apt. 150

Guesthouses: Whenever I'm in Nassau I try to stay at the **Mignon Guesthouse**. There are only eight rooms, with air-conditioning or large fans, and two bathrooms, so it may be difficult to get in. Telephone a reservation from the airport. Although not the cheapest accommodation, this is strongly recommended to those on a budget as a perfect base for exploring Nassau: its location—in Market Street, a few yards from Bay Street in the very centre of town—is superb, and I have always found fellow guests (youngish travellers and holidaymakers) friendly and interesting. Mary and Steve Antonas, the owners, keep the place spick and span and are mainly responsible for the excellent rapport which always seems to develop among the guests.

Olive's Guesthouse, though quite a walk from the centre of Nassau, is an acceptable alternative if the Mignon is full. It is larger, having 21 rooms, and has a different clientele, mainly West Indian. The **Yoga Retreat** on Paradise Island is not a guesthouse at all; I have only classified it in this section for convenience. Prices include (vegetarian) breakfast and dinner and you will be expected to participate in yoga sessions (there would hardly be much point in staying there otherwise). Facilities include a private beach, snorkelling and tennis.

309

Guesthouses
Daily summer rates per room in US$

Name	Address	Single	Double
Family	Delancey Street, Nassau (tel. 54147)	EP: 25	35
Klonaris	West Bay Street, Nassau (tel. 23888)	EP: S or D	35
Mandingo Inn	Nassau Village (tel. 43333)	EP: 35–50	40–50
Mignon	Market Street, Nassau (tel. 24771)	EP: 20	24
Mitchell Cottages	West Street, Nassau (tel. 24365)	EP: 26	28–30
Morris	Davis Street, Nassau (tel. 36013)	EP: 15	20–25
Olive	Blue Hill Road, Nassau (tel. 35298)	EP: 20	20
Pearl Cox	Augusta Street, Nassau (tel. 52627)	EP: 10	14–22
Poinciana Inn	Bernard Road, Nassau (tel. 31720/31897)	EP: 45–50	60
Wooden Shoe	Delancey Street, Nassau (tel. 50794)	EP: 16	20–25
Yoga Retreat	Paradise Island (tel. 55902)	MAP: 40	80

EATING OUT
Restaurants

Name	Address	Cuisine
Expensive/Formal dining		
The Boat House	Paradise Island (tel. 63000)	Steaks and seafood
Buena Vista	Delancey Street, Nassau (tel. 22881)	American/Bahamian/Continental
Café De La Mer	West Bay Street, Nassau (tel. 52020)	American/Bahamian
Café Martinique	Paradise Island (tel. 63000)	French
Courtyard Terrace	Ocean Club, Paradise Island (tel. 62501)	French
Del Prado	El Greco Hotel, Bay Street, Nassau (tel. 50324)	American/Bahamian
Graycliff	West Hill and Blue Hill Roads, Nassau (tel. 22796)	Bahamian/French
Mai Tai	Waterloo Lodge Hotel, East Bay Street, Nassau (tel. 31106)	Chinese/Polynesian
Moderate prices/Casual dress		
Bridge Inn	East Bay Street (opposite the bridge), Nassau (tel. 32077)	Bahamian/seafood/European
Cellar	Charlotte Street, Nassau (tel. 28877)	Continental
Chinese Village Rice House	Bay Street, Nassau (tel. 21179)	American/Chinese
El Toro	Bay Street, Nassau (tel. 24729)	American/Bahamian/European
Grand Central	Charlotte Street, Nassau (tel. 52108)	American/Bahamian/seafood
Green Shutters	Parliament Street, Nassau (tel. 55702)	Bahamian/English
Le Papillon	Bay Street, Nassau (tel. 22522)	Bahamian/Greek/Italian
Lums	Bay Street, Nassau (tel. 23119)	American/Bahamian
Poop Deck	Nassau Yacht Haven, East Bay Street, Nassau (tel. 28173)	American/Bahamian/seafood
Bahamian/Casual dress		
Bahamian Kitchen	Trinity Place, Nassau (tel. 50702)	
Basil's	Blue Hill Road, Nassau	
Big Al's	Shirley Street, Nassau (tel. 54635)	

Name	Address	Cuisine
Expensive/Formal dining		
Marietta's	Marietta's Hotel, Okra Hill, Nassau (tel. 28395)	
Poinciana	Poinciana Inn, Bernard Road, Nassau (tel. 31720)	
Skan's Cafeteria	Bay Street, Nassau	
Three Queens	Wulff Road, Nassau	
Tiffany's	Oakes Field Shopping Plaza, Nassau (tel. 36980)	
Traveller's Rest	West Bay Street, Gambier (tel. 77633)	

This is not intended to be a comprehensive list. In particular I have omitted most of the restaurants located in hotels; although most hotels have at least one restaurant, in practice you will only eat there if you're staying there.

Generally you get what you expect in the Bahamas, so all the restaurants at the top of the price scale are a safe bet. Even in the mid-price range you are unlikely to be disappointed; suggestions in this section are the **El Toro** and **Grand Central**. The latter is a Greek establishment on the ground floor of the hotel of the same name, just off Bay Street. If price concerns you, have lunch rather than dinner here. I found the food very good; I tried soup, warm rolls and butter, and conch fritters in sauce, which was very satisfying and delicious, though only a very light meal. Dinners come in large portions and are superbly prepared, but prices are accordingly higher. Prices at the El Toro are similar to Grand Central's; the decor is better but the food not quite as good.

Both these restaurants are situated in the centre of Nassau, and so you would expect a price premium. That philosophy doesn't cover all establishments however, and there are two places at the cheap end of the scale situated right on Bay Street: **Lum's** and **Skan's Cafeteria**. Lum's has an American feel to it in its style and service, yet has many native dishes on the menu (including turtle steak). Skan's is a very cheap eating place popular with locals and tourists alike. I couldn't figure out the prices here: I ordered veal escalope, priced at $4.50. With it I had french fries, dressing and milk, yet I was charged no extra. Then I went back again and got coffee, for which payment was refused. When I tried a variation of this at breakfast the following day it didn't work.

The American-oriented fast-food eating places, **McDonald's, Kentucky Fried Chicken** and **Burger King**, are the cheapest.

NIGHTLIFE

Nightspots in Nassau are not only numerous but usually obvious. A local suggested the **King and Knights,** out on West Bay Street. There is no admission charge (though of course drinks are expensive) and reputedly a good floor show. The bigger hotels have nightclubs, lounges and casinos.

311

SPORTING ACTIVITIES

Diving

Even though resort diving began on New Providence about 30 years ago many people do not realise that there is some excellent diving in this area. Because the most sophisticated tourists tend to visit the Family Islands, and because of the emphasis in Nassau on tourist-style dive trips, it is assumed that diving in this area is limited to shallow reefs. This is not so: there are some excellent dive sites including wrecks, deep drop-offs and ocean blue holes. Whether your aim is a day or two's diving whilst on holiday, or a more serious involvement in the sport, you are unlikely to be disappointed here.

Dive operators

Name and address	Type of diving	Equipment and facilities
Bahamas Divers Ltd, Nassau (tel. 28431)	Drop-offs, wrecks, coral reefs, coral gardens, ocean blue holes.	Compressors: 2 Worthington 16 cfm; Tanks: 50 aluminium and steel; 42' Custom dive boat (50 divers); Novice divers $40, Experienced $30; PADI Certification.
Nassau Dive Supply, Nassau (tel. 24869)	Various.	Compressors: Mako 22 cfm, Mako 3 cfm; Tanks: 12 steel, 2 aluminium; 23' Formula dive boat (8 divers); Resort Certification; PADI affiliated.
Omorka International Watersports, South Ocean Beach Hotel and Golf Club, South West Road (tel. 74391)	Drop-offs, coral gardens, shallow reefs.	Compressors: 2 Bauer 17 cfm; Tanks: 100 aluminium; 44' Burns dive boat (25 divers) and 24' Delta (8 divers); PADI Certification; Equipment repairs; Equipment rentals.
Sun Divers, Nassau (tel. 23301)	Shallow reef, deep reef, drop-offs.	Compressors: Mako 16 cfm, Mako Purus; 20 sets Scuba equipment; 25' Bertram dive boat (16 divers) and 28' Bertram (19 divers); Camera hire.
Underwater Tours Ltd, Divers Haven, Nassau (tel. 23285 and 24869)	Reef diving (drop-offs, wrecks, coral reefs, coral gardens, ocean blue hole by charter.	Compressors: 2 Worthington 15 cfm, Mako 4 cfm, Cornelius 3 cfm; Tanks: 100 steel; 65' Custom dive boat (50 divers), 23' Formula (6 divers) and 26' Formula (8 divers); Equipment rental, Air fills.

Fishing and boating

New Providence is not considered the best base for the hardened fisherman; Bimini is. Yet whether you have your own boat, or wish to charter one, there are excellent facilities here.

Before commencing fishing, a fisherman must clear customs and immigration at the first port of entry and obtain a valid permit. Throughout the Bahamas as a whole you can expect to find the following fishing:

Name of fish	Season	Where found
Allison (Yellowfin tuna)	Most of the year (best months June, July and August).	All deep water areas.
Amberjack	November to May.	Reefy areas.
Barracuda	All year.	All areas.
Blackfin tuna, Bonita	May to September.	All deep water areas.
Blue marlin	Most of the year (best months June and July).	Western Bahamas, from Bimini to Walkers Cay, in the Tongue of the Ocean off Andros, the Berry Islands, Exuma Sound, the Atlantic Ocean from Eleuthera to Green Turtle Cay.
Bluefin tuna	Early May to mid June.	Bimini, Cat Cay, West End (Grand Bahama).
Bonefish	All year.	All areas.
Dolphin	Winter and spring.	All deep water areas.
Grouper	All year.	All reefy areas.
Kingfish	Mainly May, June and July.	All areas.
Sailfish	Summer and autumn.	From Bimini to Eleuthera and from Walkers Cay to Exuma Sound in deep water.
White marlin	Winter and spring.	As for Sailfish.

Marina rates

Name and address	Facilities	Rates
Bayshore Marina Ltd, East Bay Street, Nassau (tel. 28232)	186 slips. Fuel, water, ice, electricity. Yacht repair. Tami-life to 40 tons. Yacht brokerage.	Dockage: transients 50 cents per ft per day. Residents from 12 cents per ft per day.
East Bay Yacht Basin, East Bay Street, Nassau (tel. 23754)	25 slips. Fuel, water, ice, electricity, showers, washers, dryers. Bareboat charter (sailboats).	Dockage: 35 cents per ft per day (includes water and electricity).
Hurricane Hole, Paradise Island (tel. 55441)	82 slips. Fuel, water, ice, electricity, showers. Sport-fishing charter boats available.	
Lyford Cay, western end of New Providence (tel. 74267)	75 slips. Fuel, water, ice, electricity, showers. Complete shopping centre. Private club. Cruising yachtsmen welcome for up to 5 days.	Dockage: 42 cents per ft per day. Water: $3/$5 per day. Electricity: 15 cents per ft per day.
Nassau Harbour Club, East Bay Street, Nassau (tel. 31771)	66 slips. Fuel, water, ice, electricity, showers, pool. Repairs available. Commissary, liquor store, restaurants. Sport-fishing charter boats available.	Dockage: 45 cents per ft per day. Water: $2 per day. Electricity by voltage.
Nassau Yacht Haven, East Bay Street, Nassau (tel. 28173)	82 slips. Fuel, water, ice, electricity, showers. Ship's store and liquor store. Restaurant. Sport-fishing charter boats.	Dockage: 45 cents per ft per day. Water: $4 per day. Electricity by boat.

313

Tennis

Most tennis courts available to visitors are part of hotel facilities. Guests are therefore able to use them free (although there is sometimes a charge for night play) whilst non-guests will pay between $2 and $4 per hour during the day and between $3 and $10 per hour for night play. Details of locations with type and number of courts follow:

Nassau
Nassau Squash and Racquet Club
Independence Drive, Nassau (Har-Tru, 3)
Sheraton British Colonial Hotel (Hard, 3)

Cable Beach
Cable Beach Inn (Hard, 2)
Royal Bahamian (Flexipave, 2)
Nassau Beach Hotel (Flexipave, 9)
Wyndham Ambassador Beach Hotel (Asphalt, 8)

South West Road
South Ocean Beach Hotel and Golf Club
(Asphalt, 4)

Paradise Island
Britannia Towers (Hard, 3)
Club Méditerranée (Har-Tru, 20)
Holiday Inn (Asphalt, 4)
Loews Harbour Cove (Asphalt, 2)
Ocean Club (Har-Tru, 9)
Paradise Towers (Asphalt, 3)

Golf

There are four 18-hole golf courses, three of which are affiliated to hotels:

South Ocean Beach Hotel and Golf Club (64391) has, as you would expect, the most established reputation. Green fees are waived for guests whose only costs should be electric cart hire ($20). Visitors should expect green fees of $20 in the winter and $10 summer, $12 for club hire and $4 for shoe rental. Lessons cost $20 per half hour or $40 per nine holes. The course is 6,707 yards and the clubhouse has a lounge, bars, restaurant, locker room and pro shop.

Coral Harbour Golf Club (61144) in the south of the island is much cheaper—green fees and club hire are half the price for visitors; **Ambassador Beach Golf Club** (78231) is priced between these two. The fourth course is situated on Paradise Island, the **Paradise Island Golf Club** (63000). This appears to be available to guests/members only.

Parasailing

Whether parasailing counts as a sport or not is a matter of opinion. For those of you unfamiliar with it, here is a brief description: take a sandy beach, preferably with no palm trees. Add a brightly coloured parachute and harness, which is strapped around the intrepid gambler. Connect this to a speedboat and take off, launching the happy holidaymaker into the air.

Apparently there were many accidents in the early days of parasailing, but the activity seems to be safe nowadays. There are two locations on New Providence, both on Cable Beach. At the **Ambassador Beach Hotel** it costs $15 for 3/4 minutes and $25 for 6/8 minutes; at the **Nassau Beach Hotel** the rate is $18 for 5 minutes and $30 for 8 minutes. This sport is also now available on Paradise Island.

THE FAMILY ISLANDS

GETTING TO THE FAMILY ISLANDS

The chances are you will want to visit the Family Islands by mail boat. The tourist office on Bay Street will be glad to furnish you with schedules and fares on application. Few of these boats run on schedule, however. So the best way to find out which boats are leaving and where they are going is to go along to the Mail Boat Office on Potter's Cay (where most of them leave from) and ask. Please note that this office is only open from Monday to Friday, and not all day Friday. If it is shut on your arrival ask any of the boat crews.

Mail boats are of course mainly intended for the carriage of cargo, so besides being irregular they tend to provide accommodation of a basic standard. The following table will give you an idea of the regularity of services and tariffs applicable:

Name of Vessel	Destination	Arr. Nassau	Dept. Nassau	Fare
Bahama Daybreak	NORTH ELEUTHERA Spanish Wells Harbour Island	Monday 5.00 pm	Thursday 6.00 am	$17.00
Captain Moxey	SOUTH ANDROS Kemps Bay Drigg's Hill Bluff etc.	Wednesday 11.30 pm	Monday 12 midnight	$16.00
Lady Blanche	EXUMA CAYS Staniel Cay Black Point Rolleville Barraterre	Saturday 6.00 am	Thursday 12 noon	$16.00 & $20.00
Killaurie	SOUTH CAT ISLAND The Bight Rum Cay San Salvador Old Bight Devil's Point	Saturday 10.00 am	Tuesday 2.00 pm	$25.00

Name of Vessel	Destination	Arr. Nassau	Dept. Nassau	Fare
Arley & Charley	CENTRAL ELEUTHERA Hatchet Bay Governor's Harbour South Palmetto Point Tarpum Bay	Tuesday 7 30 pm	Monday 12 midnight	$16.00
Grand Master	GREAT EXUMA George Town Mt Thompson Moss Town	Friday 3.00 pm	Tuesday 2.00 pm	from $25
Lady Eula	NORTH CAT ISLAND Arthur's Town Bennett's Harbour Orange Creek Industry Hill	Saturday 10.00 am	Thursday 12 noon	$20.00
Captain Dean V	ABACO I Sandy Point Moore's Island Berry Island	Wednesday 3.00 pm	Monday 12 noon	from $17.00
Bimini Mack	CAT CAY & BIMINI	Monday 8.00 am Thursday 8.00 am–6.00 pm	Thursday 1.00 pm	$25.00
Deborah K II	ABACO II Cherokee Sound Marsh Harbour Hope Town Man o' War Cay Green Turtle Cay Treasure Cay Great Guana Cay	Monday 9.30 pm	Wednesday 4.00 pm	$20.00
Marcella III	GRAND BAHAMA Freeport High Rock Sweeting Cay Eight Mile Rock West End Water Cay	Saturday 10.00 am	Wednesday 6.00 pm	$30.00
Miss Juanita	SOUTH ELEUTHERA Davis Harbour Rock Sound Green Castle Wemyss Bight Deep Creek	Thursday 1.30 pm	Monday 12 noon	$20.00
Lisa J II	NORTH ANDROS Lowe Sound Nicholl's Town Mastic Point San Andros Morgan's Bluff	Tuesday 12.15 pm	Thursday 6.30 am	$18.00

Name of Vessel	Destination	Arr. Nassau	Dept. Nassau	Fare
Nay Dean	NORTH LONG ISLAND	Friday	Tuesday	$25.00
	Seymour's	6.00 am	12 noon	
	Burnt Ground			
	Scrub Hill			
	Salt Pond			
	Simms			
	Deadman's Cay			
Central Andros Exp.	CENTRAL ANDROS	Sunday	Wednesday	$12.00
	Fresh Creek	1.30 pm	10.00 am	
	Berring Point			
	Bowen Sound			
	Blanket Sound			
	Standard Creek			
Big Yard Exp.	NORTH ANDROS	Sunday	Wednesday	–
	Fresh Creek	12 noon	10.00 am	
	Mangrove Cay			

Generally the bigger boats are more likely to sail on schedule, and are more comfortable but may cost more. Night travel saves you time and money. You may have the opportunity to travel by private yacht quite cheaply. At The Current, Eleuthera, I was offered a free trip to Bimini, the Berry Islands and Miami on a sailing yacht owned by two young Frenchmen. I couldn't accept, but the opportunities are there.

If time is more important to you, and you want to see as many islands as possible in a short time, then you may consider flying between the islands (it is sometimes possible to hop from island to island by plane, but this is not a practical proposition on the mail boats; in practice you have to keep returning to Nassau). I therefore give Bahamasair fares current at the time of writing. You should add the cost of getting to and from airports (usually by taxi) to the fares to give a realistic idea of the cost differential.

Bahamasair fares
Domestic Fares
(One-way economy US$)

Nassau to:	Fare
Andros Town	28
Arthurs Town	45
Chub Cay	34
Gt Harbour Cay	34
Mangrove Cay	28
San Andros	28
South Andros	28

Nassau to:	Fare in $
North Eleuthera	34
Governor's Harbour	34
Rock Sound	34
Freeport	48
Marsh Harbour	45
Treasure Cay	45
Georgetown	45
San Salvador	49
Deadman's Cay	49
Stella Maris	49
Inagua	74
Mayaguana	74
Crooked Island	67

Another possibility in terms of inter-island travel is cruise ships. Prices are much higher than mail boat fares of course, and also higher than airfares.

American Canadian Line operates a 'mini cruise liner' which takes a maximum 64 passengers on a choice of two itineraries around the Bahamas, one tour north of Nassau, and one southbound. Fares start at $230 for a six-day trip. This and other cruise ship accommodation can be booked at R. H. Curry & Company in Bay Street. There is also a company, **Windjammer**, operating six-day cruises (Tuesday morning to Sunday evening—five nights) within the Bahamas by sailing vessels. An itinerary beginning in Freeport and finishing in Nassau alternates with another in the opposite direction. Anyone taking both trips earns a discount and is able to utilise accommodation on board ship between the trips. Prices range from US$350 to US$500. Details available from Windjammer 'Barefoot' Cruises, 824 South Miami Avenue, Miami Beach, FL 33119 (305–327 2600) or TransAtlantic Wings Ltd, London (01–602 4021).

GRAND BAHAMA

This is one island I have no inclination to revisit. Formerly one of the least developed of the islands, it became important some time after Dr Castro's successful revolution in Cuba terminated Havana's position as the rich Americans' playground in the Caribbean. Chosen partly because of its proximity to Miami, Freeport was built speculatively as a tourist and gaming centre. Thus there are six 18-hole golf courses, the International Bazaar stocked with goods from all over the world, red London buses, all the tourist paraphernalia and high prices to boot.

GETTING AROUND

This is mainly done by taxi, though there is a bus service from the International Bazaar to the centre of town and from The Pub on The Mall to the Lucaya area. Car hire costs are similar to those in Nassau. Hitch-hiking seems quite acceptable and is very easy.

Car hire companies

Avis: International Airport (tel. 352 7666), International Bazaar (tel. 352 7675) and opposite Atlantic Beach Hotel, Lucaya (tel. 373 1102).
Eddie's Auto Rentals: Islander Hotel (opposite International Bazaar (tel. 352 8821).
Budget: International Airport (tel. 352 8844).
Hertz: International Airport (tel. 352 9308) and Royal Palm Way, Lucaya (tel. 373 4957).
Holiday Rent-A-Car: International Airport (tel. 352 9325).

WHERE TO STAY

Sometime during my first trip in the Caribbean—I forget where—I was talking to an American girl when the subject of the Bahamas cropped up. 'I didn't like the Bahamas,' she said. This amazed me, as the girl was obviously not undiscerning. 'Where did you go?' I asked. 'Freeport.'

Nevertheless, we try to please all tastes in this book, so I include this short section and maps. The Tourist Board produces a good brochure on the island which, with the Board's accommodation brochure, should supply all the information you need if you are that way inclined.

I have selected the hotels listed here as a reasonable cross-section of the available tourist accommodation on Grand Bahama. Large, luxury hotels (which are in the majority here), usually with the extensive facilities taken for granted in this type of resort, are the **Atlantik Beach** (175 rooms), **Princess Country Club Resort and Casino** (565 rooms), **Castaways Resort** (138 rooms), **Lucayan Beach Resort and Casino** (200 rooms), **Princess Tower** (400 rooms), **Xanadu Beach Hotel** (184 rooms), all located in Freeport/Lucaya, and **Grand Bahama Hotel and Country Club** (416 rooms) at West End. The cheaper hotels, **Coral Beach**, **Channel House** and **New Victoria Inn**, all have between 11 and 40 rooms, which are air-conditioned. All these hotels have swimming pools.

Deep Water Cay Club is on its own island half a mile offshore, with its own airstrip. Guests in this ten-room resort have come mainly to unwind in an exclusive atmosphere, and activities are limited to fishing and boating.

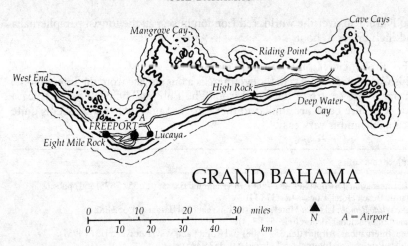

GRAND BAHAMA

0		10		20		30	*miles*	▲ N	A = Airport
0	10		20		30	40	*km*		

Accommodation on Grand Bahama
Daily winter rates per room in US$

Name and address	*Single*	*Double*
Atlantik Beach, Freeport/Lucaya (tel. 31444)	EP: 69–95	85–120
	EP: apartments	106–204
Princess Country Club Resort and Casino (tel. 26721)	EP: S or D	100–115
	MAP: 135–150	170–185
	EP: suites and villas	150–250
Castaways Resort, Freeport/Lucaya (tel. 26682)	EP: S or D	54
Coral Beach Hotel, Freeport/Lucaya (tel. 32468)	EP: 69	89
Lucayan Beach Resort and Casino (tel. 31667)	EP: S or D	105–120
Princess Tower, Freeport/Lucaya (tel. 29661)	EP: S or D	100–115
Xanadu Beach Hotel, Freeport/Lucaya (tel. 26782)	EP: S or D	95–125
	MAP: 137–167	179–209
Deepwater Cay Club, Deepwater Cay	FAP: 160	210
Grand Bahama Hotel and Country Club, West End	FAP: 130–150	230–250

EATING OUT
Grand Bahama has a tremendous number of restaurants, and a comprehensive range. There seem to be examples of every country's cuisine, as well as 'gourmet' restaurants, Bahamian restaurants and, inevitably, American and fast-food restaurants.

320

The gourmet restaurants are principally located in the large luxury hotels; all three Princess group hotels have a gourmet restaurant, as does the Grand Bahama Hotel and Country Club at West End. Other restaurants in this category are **Lucayan Steak and Lobster House** in Midshipman Road (373 5101) and the **Oasis** in El Casino (352 7811).

Name and address	Type of cuisine
International restaurants	
Bavarian, International Bazaar (tel. 352 5050)	Bavarian
Bonanza Sirloin Pit, Midshipman Road, Lucaya (tel. 373 5100)	American/Greek
Café Michel, International Bazaar (tel. 352 2191)	American/French/Italian
Café Valencia, International Bazaar (tel. 352 8717)	French/Italian
China Temple, International Bazaar (tel. 352 5610)	Chinese
El Morocco, El Casino (tel. 352 7811)	American/Continental
Japanese Steak House, International Bazaar (tel. 352 7096)	Kobe steak
Marcella's Italian Restaurant, East Mall and Kipling (tel. 352 5085)	American/Italian
Pub on the Mall, The Mall (tel. 352 5110)	American/English
Sir Winston Churchill Pub, The Mall (tel. 352 8866)	American/Bahamian/English
Bahamian restaurants	
Bahama Reef Club, Royal Palm Way (tel. 373 1056)	
Captain's Charthouse, East Sunrise and Beachway Drive, Lucaya (tel. 373 3900)	
Ruby Swiss Restaurant, John Wentworth Avenue (tel. 352 5809)	
Spanish Main Restaurant, Atlantik Beach Hotel (tel. 373 1444)	
Britannia Pub, King's Road (tel. 373 5919)	
Buccaneer Club, Deadman's Reef (tel. 348 3794)	
Café Valencia, International Bazaar (tel. 352 8717)	
Freeport Inn Steak House and Bar, Freeport Inn (tel. 352 6648)	
Island Lobster House, East Mall (tel. 352 9429)	
American/Fast food	
Burger King, West Mall (tel. 352 6551)	
Howard Johnsons, Castaway Hotel, The Mall (tel. 352 6682)	
Kentucky Fried Chicken, The Mall and Queen's Highway (tel. 352 6531)	
Zanzibar, International Bazaar (tel. 352 5050): snacks and pizzas	

NIGHTLIFE

Whilst it could not be said to have more nightlife than Nassau, Freeport certainly has more nightclubs, tourist lounges and discos than the other Family Islands. Most of the large hotels have some form of evening entertainment, and there are several discos.

Other nightspots include **The Backroom**, Logwood Road (352 8997), **Studio 69**, Midshipman Road (373 2158), or for native entertainment try the **Yellow Bird**, Castaways Resort (352 6682).

321

SHOPPING

One of the most advertised facets of a holiday in Freeport is the shopping. You are not restricted to local handicrafts (though these are also available in profusion), the International Bazaar prides itself on bringing the best of the world to the Bahamas. Obviously there is a lot of gimmickry, such as the Moorish architecture of El Casino, but the Bazaar itself has nearly 80 shops with goods from all over the world at free-port prices.

SPORT

Diving

Name and address	Type of diving	Equipment	Boat details
Freeport/Lucaya Underwater Explorers Club, Lucayan Bay Hotel (tel. 809–373 1244)	Coral reefs, inland blue holes, coral gardens, night dives and the wall.	Compressor: twin 21 cfm, Ingersoll-Rand; scuba tank: 120 steel.	42' Thomas, 24 divers; 32' Prowler, 18 divers.
Xanadu Beach Marina, Xanadu Beach Hotel (tel. 809–352 6782)	Medium dives $25 one tank & equipment, Wall dives $35 two tanks, Night dives $55 three tanks, Wreck dives $100 six tanks, Inland blue holes $38 for lessons and dive with instructor. Certificate course available on request.	Compressor: twin 21 cfm, Ingersoll-Rand; scuba tank: 120 steel.	41' Thomas, 24 divers; 32' Prowler, 18 divers.
West End Jack Tar Village (tel. 809–346 6211) Mailing address: 158 Port Road, West Palm Beach, FL 33404 (tel. 305–848 3478)	Coral reefs, coral gardens.	Compressor: (2) Ingersoll 12.5 cfm; scuba tank: 20 steel.	28' Crestliner, 4 divers.

All centres have air fills and full line of equipment.

Fishing and boating

Name of marina	Facilities and rates
Freeport/Lucaya Lucayan Harbour Inn (tel. 809–373 1667)	15 slips. Fuel, water, ice, electricity. Tami-lift to 30 tons. Restaurants, bar, showers, laundry, taxidermist's agency. Liquor store, gift shop. Dockage: transients $.40 per ft per day; water $4 per day; 110 electricity $5 per day; 220 electricity $10 per day. Dry storage available.

Name of marina	Facilities and rates
Running Man Marina (tel. 809–352 6834)	110 and 220 electricity. Water, fuel, ice. Tami-lift to 40 tons. Complete marina service. Shower, taxidermist's agency. 6 sport fishing charter boats. Tackle shop with bait. Dockage: transients $.75 per ft per day. Dry storage available. Deep-sea fishing half day $210, full day $480. Shark fishing nightly. Six persons capacity.
Xanadu Beach Hotel (tel. 809–352 6780)	36 slips. Fuel and showers. Bahamas Air Sea Rescue base. Water, telephone service, cable TV, restaurant, liquor store. Arrangements can be made for boat repairs. 28′ and 46′ sports fishing boats, 6′ draft at high tide. Dockage: transients $.75 per ft per day. Deep-sea fishing $40 per person per half day, $80 per full day. Charters available.
West End Jack Tar Village (tel. 809–346 6211) Mailing address: 158 Port Road, West Palm Beach, FL 33404 (tel. 305–848 3478)	98 slips. Fuel, water, ice, electricity. Minor repairs available. Sport fishing, reef drift. Liquor store. Dockage: Transients up to 30′ $20 per day, $.50 per additional foot. Electricity $5 per day. Drift fishing free to hotel guests. Bone fishing available.

Tennis

This is available at some of the larger hotels, five of which have at least some courts lighted for night play. The main difference here is that guests often have to pay, as well as non-guests. Details, with number and type of courts and cost per hour, are given here.

Hotel	Type and number of courts	Cost
Freeport/Lucaya		
Bahamas Princess Resort & Casino (tel. 809–352 6721 & 809–352 9661)	12 courts. 3 clay, 9 flexipave surface. 5 lighted for night play.	Guests and non-guests $5 per hour daytime. $10 per hour at night. Lessons available: $10 per half hour.
Holiday Inn (tel. 809–373 1333	4 courts. Hard surface. No playing at night.	Guests and non-guests $5 per hour. $10 per half hour.
Lucayan Bay Hotel (tel. 809–373 1555)	2 courts. Hard surface.	Hotel guests free. Non-guests $16 full day. With pro. – $8 half day.
Princess Tower (tel. 809–352 9661)	6 courts. 3 clay, 3 hard surface. All lighted for night play.	Guests and non-guests $5 per hour daytime, $10 per hour at night.
Shalimar Hotel (tel. 809–352 9631)	2 courts. Asphalt surface.	Courts free. Racquets $1.50 per hour.
Silver Sands Hotel (tel. 809–373 5700)	2 courts. Hard surface.	Guests free, non-guests $3 per hour. Racquets $3 per hour.

323

Hotel	Type and number of courts	Cost
Xanadu Beach Hotel (tel. 809–352 6702)	4 courts. Hard surface. 2 lighted for night play.	Guests and non-guests $4 per hour daytime. $10 per hour at night. Racquets $2 per hour.
West End Jack Tar Village (tel. 809–346 6211) Mailing address: 158 Port Road, West Palm Beach, FL 33404 (tel. 305–848 3478)	16 courts. 10 cushion, 6 clay surface. All lighted for night play. Pro shop.	Guests only.

Golf

Name	Green fees	Par	General information
Freeport/Lucaya Bahamas Princess Resort & Casino (tel. 809–352 6721)	Guests: $15 (9 or 18 holes) Non-guests: $20 (9 or 18 holes)	72	Yardage—7,005. Lessons. Annual membership fee—guests: $98, non-guests: $125 with storage. Restaurant, pro. shop.
Bahama Reef Golf & Country Club (tel. 809–373 1055)	$14 (18 holes), $10 (9 holes)	72	Yardage—6,768. Lessons. Annual membership $150. Family membership $250. Junior membership $50. Snack bar, pro. shop.
Fortune Hill Golf & Country Club (tel. 809–373 4500)	$7 (9 holes), $12 (18 holes)	72 (m) 74 (w)	Yardage—6,916. Annual membership $150. Family membership $225. Restaurant, bar, pro. shop.
Lucayan Golf & Country Club (tel. 809–373 1066)	$14 (18 holes) $11 (9 holes)	72	Yardage—6,916. Annual membership $550. Family membership $850. Lunch only is served at Clubhouse. Lessons. Cocktail lounge, pro. shop.
West End Jack Tar Village (tel. 809–346 6211) Mailing address: 158 Port Road, West Palm Beach, FL 33404 (tel. 305–848 3478) (18 hole)	$9	36	Yardage—6,800. Lessons. 18 holes in morning only on Saturdays and Sundays. 9 holes afternoons only. Clubhouse.

Charges are fairly consistent: club hire costs from $6 to $7.50 for 18 holes, and electric carts $14 to $18 for the full course. Shoe rental, where available, costs from $2 to $8.

ELEUTHERA

The name of this island group is derived from the Greek word meaning freedom, so named by dissenters who first left England and then Bermuda in search of somewhere for men to be free from religious persecution. As can be seen from the map, it is a long, thin, awkwardly-shaped island, some 100 miles in length, with a few smaller islands clustered around its northern end. Main industries are agriculture and tourism. The main settlements are Cape Eleuthera, Rock Sound, Tarpum Bay, Governor's Harbour, Hatchet Bay, Harbour Island, Spanish Wells and The Current, but there are other smaller settlements as well. At its narrowest (Glass Window) the island is only as wide as the road.

From the first days agriculture was difficult, because the topsoil, though fertile, was thin, and in many places soon exhausted. Sugar and cotton have been cultivated here in the past, but the crops are no longer economic. Now fruit is grown: tomatoes (many of which are exported direct to the USA), mandarin oranges, mangoes, bananas, custard apples, papaya and the best pineapples in the world, so sweet and soft you can eat the core. These crops are mainly produced however for domestic consumption. Rock Sound once had a fishing industry, but this has died and fishing is now conducted only on a small scale. The exception is at Spanish Wells, where fishing and spongeing are the main industries.

There are three airports on Eleuthera: North Eleuthera, near Upper Bogue, Governor's Harbour near the US Naval Base (10 miles north of Governor's Harbour settlement) and Rock Sound, a little to the north of Rock Sound.

GETTING AROUND
There is no bus service on Eleuthera, except for children, so that the only means of travelling is taxi, hired car or hitch-hiking. If you are travelling far (remember the island is 100 miles long) a taxi will be out of the question. To hire a car costs approx. $40 a day plus refundable deposit; cars can be hired at airports, the petrol (gas) station in Rock Sound and in other major settlements. A hired car, however, has to be returned to the place it was hired from, so the only practical way of travelling from one end of the island to the other is by hitch-hiking. As you would expect, there is little traffic, but what there is will be quite likely to stop for you. Thus it is possible to travel to the north of Eleuthera, Spanish Wells or The Current, in a day, if you start early enough.

WHAT TO SEE
Current Island
This isle, about six miles long opposite the headland at The Current, is in-

habited by a people, fairly poor, who live from the land and the sea. Their usual contact with civilisation is by means of the weekly mail boat, which means they are cut off when the weather is inclement.

Banana harvest

Spanish Wells

Nassau was the main base for pirates, yet a little of this business was also carried out from north Eleuthera. Many pirates, when offered the choice of the hangman or an amnesty if they turned to peaceful ways, settled in and around Spanish Wells. As these shores were—and can still be—hazardous to shipping, salvaging became a popular profession. In inclement weather, men with storm lanterns would guide ships onto the reefs.

Nowadays the community is very industrious—and also the only segregationalist settlement in the Bahamas. Until recently blacks were not allowed to sleep on the island unless involved in a special project. This attitude is now being relaxed, through, I was told, the intervention of the Queen.

The people work very hard, their main industries being fishing and diving for sponges. Traditionally they intermarry so that there are few family names here and the people tend to look alike—no wonder that they are clannish.

Although usually referred to as an island, Spanish Wells is actually a picturesque town with narrow winding streets, good harbour facilities and effective 'hurricane holes' (safe refuges for the small boats when hurricanes hit the island) cut into the mangrove swamps. The island itself, reached from the mainland by a ferry, is called Saint George's Cay.

Other settlements in Eleuthera

Hatchet Bay was originally a salt-water lake separated from the sea by a narrow strip of land. A man-made cut has dissected this, providing ideal harbour conditions. There is now a marina and yacht club. There is also a regular mail boat service which means Hatchet Bay has many imported goods available for sale. It is also a centre for packing orange juice, icecream and other foods. This makes Hatchet Bay one of the foremost shopping centres on Eleuthera.

Gregory Town is notable for its surfing facilities. One spot here is said to be one of the finest places for surfing in the world.

Harbour Island is one of the oldest resorts in the Bahamas; its tourist life began at the end of the 19th century. Most accommodation is expensive here, however; the cheapest listed is the **Trigum Village International** ($35 single and $50 double).

Shortly before Harbour Island the road crosses Glass Window. This is the narrowest part of Eleuthera, little wider than the road, where the Atlantic meets the Caribbean. When I passed through there was a strong easterly wind, making the Atlantic very rough and throwing huge foaming breakers against the rock and over the road; in contrast, the turquoise Caribbean was as smooth as a mirror.

WHERE TO STAY

The lack of transport on Eleuthera means it is important to choose the right accommodation. If you book into the wrong place, you may have to go 50 miles to find somewhere you like in your price bracket. The island group does have a full range of accommodation: from exclusive resorts such as Windermere Island to fairly cheap and basic guesthouse and cottage accommodation. Eleuthera is one of my favourite islands largely because of its low level of 'tourist pollution': although it is the most developed of the Family Islands, I have never had anyone try to bum a cigarette or money off me, and I have never seen the 'beach bums' here (so common nowadays in heavily touristed parts). There is so little crime in Eleuthera that many hotels do not have locks on their doors.

Moving north we come to **Cotton Bay Club**. There really would be little point in staying here if you didn't intend playing golf, as the hotel boasts an excellent Robert Trent Jones championship golf course. Described as 'unquestionably the finest golf course in the Bahamas and one of the greatest in the world', this 7,068-yard course has a par of 72.

The hotel itself is one of the longest-established on the island and has an international reputation going back many years and a satisfactory level of repeat business. Again my inspection was a fleeting one: on the plus side I very much liked the layout— meandering drive through lovely well-kept gardens to the main building with its courtyard, lounge, restaurant, bar and patio. I loved the fabulous, almost deserted beach on which it is situated. My only criticism was that some of the cottages seemed a little run down, but I understand that since my visit these have been refurbished.

Edwina's Place was formerly known by the unfortunate title of Nu-View Motel. I say 'unfortunate' because motels have acquired a somewhat seedy reputation, and thus this name must have lost Edwina much potential business. The new name is not a great improvement: it makes Edwina's sound like a wooden shack without the compensating low prices to match.

In fact it's my favourite accommodation on the island. Not the most luxurious, nor the cheapest, but really excellent mid-range accommodation, particularly for the under 40s. The accommodation is laid out motel-style: six or eight rooms, air-conditioned. There is a swimming pool and tree-shaded private beach with jetty, a dining room and bar. But this cold description of facilities doesn't really explain why Edwina's is such a nice place to stay. Edwina herself, a charming local lady, now getting on in years but giving no indication that she might be thinking of retirement, runs her place and prepares the food herself. Obviously she had a lot to do with the choice of site, design of the buildings and gardens, and selection of facilities. That is why the rooms are bigger than necessary and well-carpeted, and why there is plenty of lighting and furniture.

Eleuthera's best beaches are on the Atlantic side. One of the most beautiful, a pristine pure white gentle curve of soft sand, is home to **Winding Bay Beach Resort**. Making the most of the surrounding lush gardens, the 36 cottages are spread facing the sea. Watersports and dive shop facilities are here, as well as tennis (lit for night play).

Cheap accommodation is hard to find on Eleuthera. As the table shows, most of it is to be found in Tarpum Bay. This settlement is not the most idyllic part of Eleuthera, however, and I found its beach left much to be desired.

On my first trip I did find cheap guesthouse accommodation (unlisted by the Tourist Board) in Rock Sound itself. I had left the mail boat *Captain Moxey* and, walking into the settlement, discovered the **Flamingo Bar and Restaurant**. A single room cost $10 a night in the guesthouse above it, so you would expect to pay about $15 for a single and $20 for a double now. Recently I called into the Flamingo, where I was advised that the guesthouse—managed by the proprietors of Kemp's store, next door—was still in business. Incidentally, food at the Flamingo (a mixture of native and hamburgers) is reasonably priced and good.

Governor's Harbour is the major settlement on Eleuthera. Although there is a beach in the village itself—a wide, sweeping curve alongside the road—this is not ideal for sunbathing and swimming. The beach over on the Atlantic side, on which the **Club Méditerranée** is situated, is the one usually used by tourists.

Just five minutes' walk up from this beach is the **Cigatoo Inn**. This 24-roomed, fairly new hotel has swimming pool, dining room, bar, lounge and sometimes evening entertainment. Its atmosphere is informal. The management is looking for increased business all the time and so is very happy to arrange any activities you may require, including boating, fishing, diving and tennis.

The Current is perhaps my favourite settlement on Eleuthera. On my first visit, five years ago, I was stranded here for four days and had ample opportunity to meet people, make friends and develop an affection for the place. I also had ample opportunity for writing and for taking sunset photographs. At that time I stayed at **The Rock**, an establishment no longer listed by the Tourist Board, although it is still there. Mrs Sue Williams, the dear old American lady who owned and managed the place at the time of that first visit, has since died, and now the property is cared for by an even older couple. Sadly I cannot be sure that The Rock will continue to be available, but nevertheless, if you are stuck, it is worth a try. Expect to pay $20 to $30 per efficiency unit.

On the way into The Current you will pass the **Sea Raider**, unless you decide to stop and stay there, which I recommend. This is now the best choice of accommodation in the settlement, the only drawback being the lack of a beach here. All the apartments face the sea and are spacious, well-maintained and all have the necessary facilities. You should note, however, that Sea Raider is really just a collection of cottages: there is no bar, swimming pool, games room or restaurant.

Of the two stores in The Current, **Durham's** seems to have lower prices and a wider range than **Arthur's**. Although frozen meat is available, mainly frankfurters, hamburgers and bacon, fresh or indeed frozen fish is difficult to get. Fresh-baked bread is available in two places; at **Monica's Spot** or from **Dolly**, in the turquoise house opposite Arthur's. Burge, Dolly's husband, often goes out to catch fish, but usually needs a day's or several days' notice. Dolly also needs to be given notice for the bread, so it is best to put in your order when you first arrive.

There are beaches all round The Current, situated as it is on a headland, but the best by far is the one nearest The Rock (known as North Beach). For those who like to plunge in it is best at high tide, when it shelves steeply. Those who prefer shallower waters should pop down at low tide, when they can walk out for 25 yards before being immersed. Trees behind the beach provide shelter when the sun gets too hot. During my stay the water was placid, but of course this is not always the case. This beach also provides the best spot for observing the sunset. Near the Equator the sun drops quite quickly into the sea, and on a clear day you can actually see the orange ball of fire dropping behind the horizon.

Bicycles and cars can be hired at The Current, but not scooters. It is a difficult place to get to or leave by land, and its mail boat service is only weekly. Even if flying into North Eleuthera, you would need a taxi to get to The Cur-

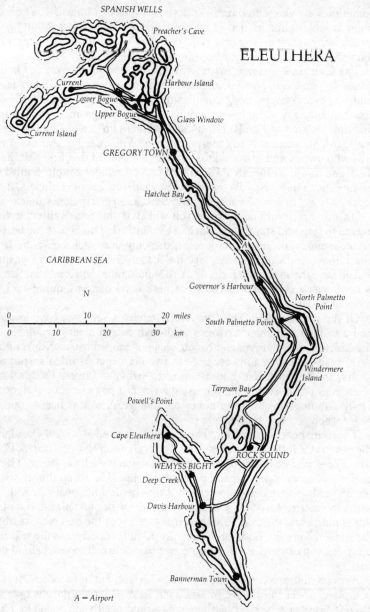

SPANISH WELLS

Preacher's Cave

ELEUTHERA

Current
Lower Bogue
Upper Bogue
Current Island
Harbour Island
Glass Window

GREGORY TOWN

Hatchet Bay

CARIBBEAN SEA

N

Governor's Harbour

North Palmetto
Point

South Palmetto Point

0   10   20 miles
0   10   20   30   km

Windermere
Island

Tarpum Bay

Powell's Point

Cape Eleuthera

ROCK SOUND

WEMYSS BIGHT

Deep Creek

Davis Harbour

Bannerman Town

A = Airport

330

rent. But these difficulties in themselves make it a perfect get-away-from-it-all spot.

Accommodation on Eleuthera (inc. Harbour Island and Spanish Wells)
Daily winter rates per room in US$

Name	Location	Single	Double
Nearest airport: Rock Sound			
Cartwrights Ocean View Cottages	Tarpum Bay (tel. 42054 ext. 215)	EP: Up to six persons 110	
Cotton Bay Club	Rock Sound (tel. 42101/42156)	MAP: S or D 195–240; suite 185; cottage 150–275	
Edwina's Place	Rock Sound (tel. 42094)	EP: 42	60
Ethel's Cottages	Tarpum Bay	EP: 25 per cottage	
Hilton's Haven	Tarpum Bay (tel. 42131)	EP: 30	50
Windermere Island Club	Windermere Island (tel. 22566)	AP: 245–705	300–775
		1-bedroom suite 465; 2-bedroom suite 605–660	
		EP: 3-bedroom cottage 825	
Winding Bay Beach Resort	Winding Bay, Rock Sound (tel. 42020)	MAP: 155–190	175–210
Nearest airport: Governor's Harbour			
Cigatoo Inn	Governor's Harbour (tel. 22343)	EP: 48	55
Palmetto Beach Inn	South Palmetto Point (tel. 22533)	EP: 1-bedroom apt. 30; 2-bedroom 60; 3-bedroom 90	
Palmetto Shores Vacation Villas	South Palmetto Point (tel. 22305)	EP: 1-bedroom villa 60; 2-bedroom 60; 3-bedroom 120	
Nearest airport: North Eleuthera			
Cambridge Villas	Gregory Town (tel. 22212)	EP: 35	45
		EP: efficiency 60–80	
Sea Raider	The Current (tel. 32290)	EP: studio 35; efficiency unit 40; 1-bedroom studio 65	
Harbour Island			
Coral Sands Hotel	Harbour Island (tel. 32350)	EP: 50	60–75
		MAP: 78	116–121
Ocean View Club	Harbour Island (tel. 32276)	EP: 80	95
Rock House	Harbour Island (tel. 32053)	EP: 40	50
Romora Bay Club	Harbour Island (tel. 32325)	EP: 94–120	116–146
Valentine's Yacht Club	Harbour Island (tel. 32142)	EP: 60	70
Spanish Wells			
Spanish Wells Beach Resort	Spanish Wells (tel. 299)	EP: 65	78
		EP: apts. 122	
Spanish Wells Harbour Club	Spanish Wells (tel. 297)	EP: apt. 80–100	

SPORT

Diving
The best diving off Eleuthera lies off the very north and very south of the

331

island. The Current Cut, a drift dive between The Current and Current Island, has been described as 'one of the most thrilling undersea phenomena' and 'shooting the cut is probably the closest thing to skydiving that a scuba-diver is likely to experience'. There are also some excellent reef dives and wrecks in the area. Off the Cape, at the south end of Eleuthera, are 'some of the most spectacular drop-offs to be found anywhere in the Caribbean'.

Dive operators

Name and address	Type of diving	Equipment and facilities
Rock Sound area Winding Bay Dive Centre (tel. 42020)	Coral gardens, coral reefs.	Compressor: Mako 15 cfm; Tanks: 15 aluminium; 28' Flat top dive boat (10 divers); Air fills and equipment. One tank dive from $15.
Harbour Island Romora Bay Club (tel. 32324)	Drop-offs, coral gardens, wrecks, coral reefs.	Compressor: Mako 10 cfm, Worthington 12 cfm; Tanks: 55 cf steel; 30' Custom (16 divers) and 25' Delta (10 divers) dive boats.
Valentine's Yacht Club (tel. 32142)	Coral reefs, coral gardens, wrecks, drop-offs, drift, cave.	Compressors: Mako, Worthington 18 cfm; Tanks: 90 aluminium, 10 steel; 38' Thompson (30 divers), 36' Stuart Angler (20 divers), 36' Custom Thompson (20 divers), 22' Aqua Sport (6 divers) and 20' Custom open (4 divers) dive boats. Air fills, full dive shop.
Spanish Wells Spanish Wells Beach Resort/Harbour Club (tel. 297 or 371)	Wrecks, coral gardens, drop-offs, coral reefs, drift, cave.	Compressors: Joy 15 cfm; Tanks: 40 aluminium; 28' Bertram (15 divers), 14' Boston Whaler (2 divers), dive boats. Air fills, equipment rentals, dive shop.

Tennis

As on New Providence, you will find that tennis courts are provided as part of hotel facilities. Therefore guests can usually play free of charge, whilst non-guests will have to pay between $2 and $6 per hour (the higher figure is for night play).

Governor's Harbour	Club Méditerranée (Asphalt, 8)
Harbour Island	Coral Sands Hotel (Fibreglass, 1) Dunmore Beach Club (Plexicrome, 1) Pinks Sands Lodge (Cork, 3) Romora Bay Club (Hard, 1) Valentine's Yacht Club (Hard, 1)
Spanish Wells	Spanish Wells Beach Resort (Hard, 1)

Fishing and boating

Name	Facilities and rates	
Harbour Island		
Coral Sands Hotel (tel. 32320)	Bone and bottom fishing. Deep-sea fishing.	Deep-sea fishing $250 per day. Bottom and bone fishing $60 per half day.
Romora Bay Club (tel. 32325)	Bone fishing. Sunfish for hire. Deep-sea fishing.	Bone fishing at $60 per half day. Deep-sea fishing arranged at $275 per day.
Valentine's Yacht Club (tel. 32142)	15 slips. 174 ft dock. Water, electricity. Showers, laundry, bar, restaurant. Small boat rental.	Dockage: transients 35 cents per ft per day.
Spanish Wells		
Sawyer's Marina (tel. 225)	Slips and dock. Fuel, water, ice, electricity. Boat charter and fishing trips available.	
Spanish Wells Beach Resort	Dock. Fuel, water, electricity.	Deep-sea fishing from $250 per half day.

Golf
There are two golf courses here, both par 72. The 7,068-yard Robert Trent Jones course at **Cotton Bay** (42101) is the longer-established of the two and a reason in itself why many visit Eleuthera. It is expensive, even for guests. **Cape Eleuthera** (42152) has a 7,200-yard Dick Wilson-designed course.

THE ABACOS

This island group is another natural for tourism. It comprises the large island of Great Abaco, Little Abaco Island and innumerable cays. It has not been forgotten that the islands were settled by Loyalists after the American Revolution 200 years ago: at the southern tip of Green Turtle Cay stands New Plymouth, its brightly painted wooden houses very reminiscent of New England. One island is covered with forest, offering a wild haven for boar and ponies. There are 130 miles of variety and beautiful beaches.

WHERE TO STAY
Resort hotels are rare in Abacos, but two are worthy of mention: **Treasure Cay Beach Hotel** and **Walker's Cay Hotel**. The former is the larger by far, with 178 rooms and villas, four swimming pools, two restaurants, three bars, evening entertainment, beauty shop, gift shops, marina, etc. Walker's Cay, with 62 rooms, only has one of each—swimming pool, restaurant, bar, disco— but it is, at least, a private island.

Two medium-sized, medium-priced hotels, both on Green Turtle Cay, are **Bluff House** and **Green Turtle Cay Club**. Bluff House is tucked away on a wooded hillside, its eighteen rooms surrounding the pool and its villas standing proud and apart. Below lie a superb beach and the hotel's own marina. Green Turtle Cay Club with 37 rooms is twice as big, with perhaps a greater emphasis on the boating and fishing.

Those looking for cheaper accommodation will have noticed from the prices given here that they will be best advised to work on a self-catering basis. **Linton's Beach Cottages** on Green Turtle Cay work out at about $60 a day for each of four sharing.

Accommodation in The Abacos
Daily winter rates per room in US$

Name and address	*Single*	*Double*
Nearest airport: Marsh Harbour		
Ambassador Inn, Marsh Harbour (tel. 72022)	EP: 46	52
Conch Inn, Marsh Harbour (tel. 72800/72233)	EP: 60–65	75
Great Abaco Beach Hotel, Marsh Harbour (tel. 72158)	EP: 66	81
Abaco Inn, Hope Town, Elbow Cay (tel. 72666)	EP: 90	95–105
Elbow Cay Beach Inn (Elbow Cay Club) (tel. 72748)	EP: 64–74	74–94
Hope Town Harbour Lodge, Hope Town, Elbow Cay (tel. 72277)	EP: 62	70
Nearest airport: Treasure Cay		
Treasure Cay Beach Hotel and Villas, Treasure Cay (tel. 72847)	EP: 98–116	118–136
	MAP: 147–157	203–213
	villa 150–176	
	2-bedroom 225, 3 persons 275, 4 persons 250–300	
Bluff House, Green Turtle Cay (tel. 75211)	EP: S or D 90	
	suite 1-bedroom 106	
	deluxe villa 1-bedroom 128	
Coco Bay Club, Green Turtle Cay (tel. 75933)	EP: 2-bedroom cottage 570 per week	
Green Turtle Cay Club, Green Turtle Cay (tel. 72572)	EP: 70	87
	MAP: 93	133
Linton's Beach Cottages, Green Turtle Cay	EP: 2-bedroom cottage (up to 4 persons) 300 per week	
New Plymouth Club and Inn, New Plymouth, Green Turtle Cay (tel. 75211)	MAP: 55	80
Sea Star Beach Cottages, New Plymouth, Green Turtle Cay (tel. 75444/75177)	EP: 50–55	60
	cottage 450 per week	
Nearest airport: Walker's Cay		
Walker's Cay Hotel and Marina, Walker's Cay (USA tel. 305–522 1469 or 800–327 3714)	EP: S or D 90–125	

SPORT

The Abacos have been described as 'the sailing capital of the world'. There is thus a wider range and greater number of marinas than anywhere else in the Bahamas (including New Providence). There are four dive operations.

Dive Operators

Name and address	Type of diving	Equipment and facilities
Chambered Nautilus Dive Center, Marsh Harbour (tel. 72846)	Coral reefs, wrecks, marine preserves, current cut, inland blue hole.	Compressors: Mako 9.2 cfm, Ingersoll-Rand 5 cfm; Tanks: 54 aluminium, 10 steel; 31' Pacemaker (10 divers), 16' Novurana (8 divers), 13' Avon (4 divers), 2 × 10' Semperit (3 divers) dive boats. Air fills, full line of equipment.
Dave Gale's Island Marine, Abaco Inn, Hope Town, Elbow Cay (tel. 72666)	Coral reefs, wrecks, marine preserves.	Compressors: Mako 8 cfm, Mako 2.5 cfm; Tanks: 50 steel; 25' Bertram (6 divers) and 20' Bertram (4 divers) dive boats. Air fills, full line of equipment.
Treasure Cay Diving Center (UNEXSO), Treasure Cay (tel. 72570)	Coral reefs, wrecks, caverns, inland blue hole.	Compressor: RIX 17.5 cfm: Tanks: 60 steel. 30' Island Hopper (20 divers). Air fills, full line of equipment.
Walker's Cay Dive Shop, Walker's Cay (tel. USA 305–522 1469)	Coral reefs, wrecks, marine preserves, night dives, cavern.	Compressors: Worthington 14 cfm, Bauer 17 cfm; Tanks: 44 aluminium, 80 steel; 38' Ensign (24 divers) and 22' Custom (6 divers) dive boats. Air fills and equipment. Windsurfing, waterskiing, surfing.

Golf

One course only, at the **Treasure Cay Golf Club** (part of Treasure Cay Beach Hotel); this is a 6,985-yard, par 72, Dick Wilson-designed course. Green fees are $15 to visitors (free to guests); club hire is $8, electric cart hire $15 (all prices for 18 holes).

Tennis

As you would expect, tennis is not particularly well catered for. As you would also expect, the largest resort hotel—**Treasure Cay Beach Hotel**—has most courts. These are Har-Tru surfaced, and 4 of the 10 are lit for night play. There is a bar and pro. shop at the courts, and guests play free. **Walker's Cay** has two courts with all facilities free to guests. On Green Turtle Cay two of the hotels have a hard-surfaced court: **Bluff House** (free to guests) and **Green Turtle Club** (guests $5 per hour).

Fishing and boating

Marina	Facilities and rates
Nearest airport: Marsh Harbour	
Bahamas Yachting Service Ltd, Marsh Harbour (tel. 72214)	No dockage for private yachts; 48 boats for charter. Bareboat rates: 30' to 44' from $695 to $1,795 per week. Provisions at $14.50 per person per day, skipper at $55 per day.
Conch Inn Marina, Marsh Harbour (tel. 72800)	45 slips. Fuel, water, ice, electricity, showers, laundry. Small boat rentals. Dockage: transients 35 cents per ft per day.
Abaco Bahamas Charter Ltd, Hope Town, Elbow Cay (tel. 72277)	Mooring facilities. 15 CSY 44' Walk-throughs and cutters for bareboat and provisioned charters (from $595 per week).
Elbow Cay Club, Hope Town, Elbow Cay (tel. 72748)	No slips – 200' dock. Water, ice, electricity, showers, laundry, liquor store. Dockage: transients 10 cents per ft per day. Deep-sea fishing in 38' cruiser $150 per half day, $250 per day.
Guana Beach Resort, Great Guana Cay	200' straight dock (5 yachts). No electricity or ice. Dockage: 35 cents per ft per day. Deep-sea fishing with captain available.
Pinders Cottages, Great Guana Cay	No slips. Moorings for 6 boats. Dockage: transients $10 per night. Deep-sea fishing in 25' Bertram $175 per half day, $275 per day. Bareboat charter: 26' $400 per week, 23' $350 per week.
Nearest airport: Treasure Cay	
Bluff House Club and Marina, Green Turtle Cay (tel. 75211)	Moorings. Water, ice, electricity. Dockage: 35 cents per ft per night, $1.40 per ft per week, $4.50 per ft per month.
Green Turtle Club and Marina, Green Turtle Cay (tel. 72572)	22 slips. Fuel, water, ice, electricity, showers, laundry. Dockage: transients 35 cents per ft per day. Electricity: 110 $3 per day, 220 $5 per day. 25' sport fishing boat at $100 per half day, $180 per day. 14' Whaler.
Treasure Cay Beach Hotel, Treasure Cay (tel. 72570)	44 slips. Fuel, water, ice, electricity. Dockage: transients 40 cents per ft per day. Bone fishing $100 half day, $140 full day. Reef fishing $40 per person. 22' sport fishing boat $200 half day, $250 full day. Sunfish, sailfish, hobie cats and windsurfers.
Nearest airport: Walker's Cay	
Sea Lion Marina, Walker's Cay (tel. USA 305–522 1469)	75 slips. Fuel, water, ice, electricity, showers, ships' stores, liquor store, taxidermist agency. Dockage: 25 cents per ft per day for first 30' and 40 cents each additional ft. Boston Whaler $70 per day bareboat, $115 per day with guide, bait, tackle. Reef fishing in Mako $145 full day.

ANDROS

This is the largest Bahama island, 104 miles long by 40 wide, yet very sparsely populated. The interior, which is unexplored, is inhabited mainly by the Chickcharnies, little people who may be related to the Irish leprechauns. They are little red-eyed pixies with three fingers and three toes, and have been known to hang by their tails from cottonwood trees.

In the middle of the 19th century a group of about 50 Seminole Indians, fearing enslavement, left the Florida Everglades and canoed to the northwest coast of Andros. Their descendants still live at Red Bay Village with their own administration and traditions.

The west coast of Andros shelves gradually into shallow water. There are 80 miles of mud flats in all shades of sand, brown and green. The east coast is paralleled by the world's third-largest underwater reef, some 120 miles long. Inside it is 12 feet deep; outside—The Tongue of the Ocean—it is 6,000 feet deep. Nearby are the Andros Blue Holes (seemingly bottomless holes in the ocean floor).

The main settlements are on the east coast: Congo Town, Drigg's Hill, Mangrove Cay, Fresh Creek (Andros Town), Staniard Creek, Mastic Point and Nicholl's Town.

WHAT TO SEE

Fresh Creek and Andros Town

Fresh Creek is about halfway along the east coast. The atmosphere on stepping ashore is quite unlike any part of New Providence or Eleuthera. The layout of the settlement is along both sides of an inlet which serves as a natural harbour. A causeway juts out from the south shore, and a bridge joins this to the north. It is on the north side of town, at Fresh Creek proper, that the boat berths, and here the Chickcharnie, the cheaper of the two hotels, is situated.

The most noticeable aspect right from the start is the children. They come in a variety of sizes and ages, and are evident in large numbers. Chasing them in the population stakes are our canine friends. I noticed dogs around the homes and farms in New Providence and suburban Nassau where they were largely introduced as guard dogs. But here, and at the hotel in particular, they are just around, sometimes in packs. They are harmless.

Fresh Creek is a small settlement which the romantic writer would describe as a shanty town. This is not an accurate description, although many buildings are wooden and the people obviously poor, for a shanty town is usually part of a big city and consists of temporary dwellings made from whatever materials come to hand. Rusting, stripped bodies of car wrecks are here in profusion, as elsewhere in the Bahamas. There is a shortage of mechanics to service vehicles regularly, and spare parts have to be imported at high prices and with great difficulty from Nassau or Miami. Cars are very rarely garaged, and often parked under trees, where they collect drips from the overhead foliage, and the salt air is a killer. They are very rarely waxed. In addition, there are no wrecking yards, as are found all over North America and Europe. Thus the number of abandoned cars is disproportionate to the number of vehicles operating.

Tourism is a fringe industry here. During my stay the more expensive of the two hotels, the Lighthouse Club, was closed due to 'electrical difficulties', and I seemed to be the only guest at the Chickcharnie. There are no tourist comforts here, no beaches and no swimming. Boating and fishing can be worth-

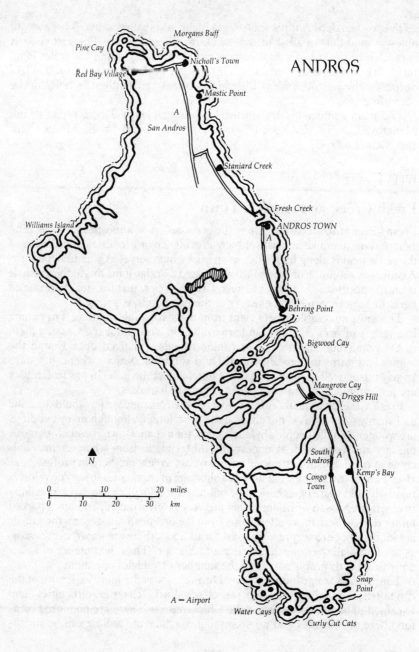

ANDROS

Morgans Buff
Pine Cay
Nicholl's Town
Red Bay Village
Mastic Point

A
San Andros

Staniard Creek

Fresh Creek
Williams Island
ANDROS TOWN
A

Behring Point

Bigwood Cay

Mangrove Cay
Driggs Hill

N

0   10   20 miles
0   10   20   30   km

South
Andros   A

Congo
Town   Kemp's Bay

Snap
Point

A = Airport

Water Cays
Curly Cut Cats

while activities, however. I arrived from Nassau on the first day of the winter season, when the streets of the capital were thronged with tourists and natives from the Family Islands.

Mastic Point

Mastic Point comprises two main settlements, north and south, separated by a road junction. This is officially the case anyway, although some of the local people are unsure which is which. In fact the inhabitants populate both sides of a road winding north to south more or less along the coast. The houses bunch into small settlements in perhaps four or five places, whilst elsewhere single houses, or groups of three or four, straggle along the road. Other stretches of road are either bordered by mangrove swamps or thick undergrowth, with no habitation. At one point in the south end of town the road runs by a small cemetery. Here small, simply carved tombstones alternate with the crudest of wooden crosses. This contrast of moderate wealth with abject poverty is echoed throughout, and seen to best advantage by just walking up the road.

In the south part of town there are three stores. Noah's Family Fare, Tinker's and Fowler's. The houses here are predominantly crude wooden shacks, apparently with few facilities. In the far south, the road tapers out to a track running along the coast. Here at low tide are extensive mud flats. The northern settlement begins about half a mile from the San Andros road junction and boasts a larger number of stone buildings, many with gigantic TV aerials towering over them. There are two stores here—the larger of the two is the second one you come to. At the far north end of the town is a small jetty, where a large ship is being built of wood in traditional style. To the west of the jetty is Bahama Harbour—the grandiose title given to the charming little inlet where the *Miss Beverley* docks. This is a natural miniature marina, where the channel has been widened and perhaps deepened. There is a small rocky headland from which some of the natives fish. Flotsam and jetsam dot the beaches, which are not recommended for swimming.

Walking up the road I felt like Dr Livingstone. People would stop and stare, though often only after I had passed them. Silence would fall upon the children as if I were a Martian, although some of the braver (or ruder) ones would call out 'Hey white man, give me a dollar'. I would turn round and say 'My name is Frank.' Some would then reply, 'Hey Frank, give me a dollar,' but the majority were stopped in their tracks.

Other settlements in Andros

Travelling between the settlements is difficult, as again there is no bus service. Hitching a ride is the only possible means of travel, but this is harder than on Eleuthera, with less traffic going shorter distances. All the settlements, such as

339

Blanket Sound, Love Hill, Stafford Creek, are small and it may be impossible to find accommodation—or a cooked meal. One place that does serve food—very good food too—is **Emily's,** a little yellow shack on the way into Stafford Creek. If you get a chance to eat here, and you are not in a hurry, do.

The road from Mastic Point northwards is in poor condition and paved for only a short part of the way. But it is an interesting ride, as the road is bordered on both sides by young pine trees. Farms can be seen, both for crop-growing and for cattle rearing. There is an increasing incidence of joint Bahamian-American agricultural development here. As elsewhere in the Bahamas, the soil can be shallow, but where it is deep it is rich and fertile. This entire area was once the property of Neville Chamberlain, before he was summoned to the United Kingdom by his family to enter British political life. The natives in these parts (though few, if any, can have known him) all speak highly of him.

WHERE TO STAY
The following summary of economic accommodation in Andros illustrates one interesting fact: the only guesthouse named below but not listed by the Tourist Board (Fowler's) is of poor value. This highlights my opinion that the Tourist Board does a good job here, listing all accommodation (when the proprietors supply them with details), and not just the expensive stuff, as many Caribbean countries do. So get the official brochure.

The **Chickcharnie Hotel** was my first disappointment in terms of accommodation. The price for a double room is $40.00 and up, but a single person has to pay almost the same. This price does not include bathroom, but as that was next door to my room it caused no discomfort. There also appeared to be some problem with the water supply (to be fair, this can be experienced almost anywhere in the Bahamas). When I came down at 8.10 for breakfast, using the outside staircase, I found all doors locked and had to wait for perhaps 30 minutes. Little hiccups like that, caused by the novelty of tourism to the management (I presume), are common. Perhaps they add to the charm of the place. The hotel can only keep going because its bar and restaurant are open to the public, and it also features a well-stocked village store. The food here is not too good.

Everyone in Fresh Creek was friendly, with the exception of the hotel management who were, however, courteous. I was treated with some reserve on my arrival, though the manager can be forgiven for this. My hair was long, unkempt and knotted from my nightmare voyage and my clothes filthy from sprawling on the deck amongst the cargo (most of it, ironically, destined for the Chickcharnie) trying to die.

Andros Town, across the inlet from Fresh Creek, is almost a ghost town. The Andros Yacht Club, liquor store, bank and customs office make up the main part of the settlement. During my visit the hotel complex of the Lighthouse Club, which can take up to a hundred guests, was closed but in good repair and scheduled to re-open shortly. Rates would be about $45 per double room, MAP.

The effect of the hotel's closure can be seen on the way out of town; there are specially constructed buildings for the hotel staff, many now obviously unoccupied. Some do still house families, whose poverty is evident.

There appears to be no accommodation in the north part of Mastic Point, although there is one bar/restaurant, the **Desert Inn.** The best value for accommodation is probably **Oliver's Guesthouse,** a clean, small single-storey building situated just south of the junction. Further south is **Fowler's,** where I stayed. This is run by the *Miss Beverley*'s Captain (his daughter is called Beverley). Although the room itself was adequate, the bathroom facilities could be improved. Mrs Fowler told me that her prices were $12 single and $24 double (EP). I was charged $10 a night, so you can perhaps regard these figures as negotiable. Mastic Point is not used to tourist traffic, the regular clientele being entirely native and no doubt paying substantially less. If Oliver's is full, try **Tinker's** (near the cemetery).

Accommodation in Andros
Daily winter rates per room in US$

Name, address and nearest airport	*Single*	*Double*
Nearest airport: Andros Town		
Charlie's Haven, Behring Point	AP: 30	60
Chickcharnie Hotel, Fresh Creek (tel. 83025)	EP: S or D 40–59	
Small Hope Bay Lodge, Love Hill (tel. 82014)	FAP: 87–125	174
Nearest airport: San Andros		
Andros Beach Hotel, Nicholl's Town (tel. 92012)	EP: S or D 65 approx.	
	MAP: 80	95
*San Andros Inn and Tennis Club, San Andros	EP: 42	45
	AP: 64	89
Tradewinds Villas, Nicholl's Town (tel. 92040)	EP: villas 65 to 80 for 2 to	
	6 persons	
*Fowler's Guesthouse, South Mastic Point	EP: 28	
*Oliver's Guesthouse, Main Street, South Mastic Point	EP: 20	28
*Tinker's Guesthouse, Main Street, South Mastic Point	EP: 24	
Nearest airport: Mangrove Cay		
Bannister's Guesthouse, Mangrove Cay	AP: 45	60
Longley Guesthouse, Lisbon Cay	EP: 25	25
*Diana's Guesthouse, Little Harbour	EP: 16	17
	AP: 27	39
*King's Guesthouse, Little Harbour	EP: S or D 18	
Moxey's Guesthouse, Little Harbour	EP: S or D 25–40	

Name, address and nearest airport	*Single*	*Double*
Nearest airport: South Andros		
Congo Beach Guesthouse, Kemp's Bay	EP: 20	40
Las Palmas Hotel, Congo Town	EP: S or D 30	
	MAP: 50	70

* Rates approximate. Not listed by Tourist Board.

SPORT

I think the above will have given you an insight into the character of Andros: though the largest island, it has no developed tourist infrastructure and most facilities are only suitable for the traveller intending to stay in guesthouses and mix with the locals.

Although the island lacks development, its surrounding waters are some of the richest in the Bahamas. The barrier reef and The Tongue of the Ocean make the east coast waters both a superb area for bone fishing and also an excellent diving area. Near Fresh Creek is a long-established and well-organised dive operation, **Small Hope Bay Lodge**, specifically located here to take advantage of the superb diving.

Fishing and boating

There are no proper marinas here. The **Chickcharnie Hotel** at Fresh Creek has a small dock, but no slips. The cost for deep-sea fishing is $85 per half day, or $150 per day. Bone fishing costs $40 for half a day ($60 a day) and a Boston Whaler $60 per day with guide. The **Andros Beach Hotel** at Nicholl's Town also has a dock (no slips). Fuel and water are available, and sport fishing boats and sunfish can be rented. Sunfish and Boston Whalers are also available at **Las Palmas Hotel**, Congo Town.

Tennis is available only at the **San Andros Inn and Tennis Club**, a somewhat pretentious name for an establishment with only two courts (both lit for night play). You don't go to Andros to play tennis.

Dive operators

Name and address	Type of diving	Equipment and facilities
Small Hope Bay Lodge, Fresh Creek (tel. 82014)	Drop-offs, walls, wreck, coral gardens, drift, night dives.	Compressors: 2 Joy 15 cfm; Tanks: 60 steel; 34' Flat top (24 divers), 31' Flat top (18 divers), and 28' Flat top (18 divers) dive boats. Air fills, equipment rentals. Also Whirlpool. Redwood hot tub on beach, windsurfing, games room, sailboats.
Andros Beach Hotel and Villas, Nicholl's Town (tel. 92012)	Reefs, drop-offs, wreck, blue hole.	Compressor: Mako 3 cfm; Tanks: 40 steel; 18' Boston Whaler (15 divers) dive boat.

BIMINI

Two main islands comprise Bimini: North and South Bimini. North Bimini has most of the tourist accommodation and most of the native population, with two settlements, Alice Town and Bailey Town.

I didn't like Bimini at all. Prior to my visit I had heard good reports of the islands, so I was very surprised to find that they lacked the charm and friendliness usually associated with the Bahamas.

I think the problem originates from Bimini's location as the nearest part of the Bahamas to the United States, being about 50 miles due east of Miami. The islands have thus become a haven for smugglers who, for obvious reasons, have no desire to encourage tourism. It seems that South Bimini is more heavily used than the main island for smuggling (besides being quieter, it has an airstrip) though the smugglers go over to North Bimini for rest and recreation. I was advised not to go over to the South Island because it was plagued by mosquitoes.

Sometimes known as 'the game fishing capital of the world', Bimini certainly has much to offer the sport fisherman, notwithstanding my grumbles. All hotels will arrange fishing boat hire. There is also a dive operation here (based at Brown's Hotel). Most dive sites are wrecks—this area is rich in them—but of particular interest to those who are familiar with the legend of Atlantis are the Bimini Walls. This not yet fully excavated structure appears to be a wall, or pavement, made up of 16-ft square blocks of stone set tightly together.

Deep-sea fishing in the Bahamas

343

Because the stones have straight edges, are the same size and set flush, they must be man-made. The total structure is at least 300 ft long and is thought to be at least 6,000 years old. All we really know is that it is prehistoric, unless the Atlantis legend is regarded as history.

If we remember that Troy was discovered by an archaeologist who traced the site through Homer's writings, and also that many Biblical stories have been proved true by excavation, then we must consider the possibility that Atlantis did exist and is under the Bahamas. This would certainly explain various odd occurrences in The Tongue of the Ocean area (otherwise associated with the so-called Bermuda Triangle theories) and also why pyramids are found in two distinctly different parts of the world—Mexico and Central America, and Egypt (whence came the Atlantis legend).

WHERE TO STAY

The most noticeable point about the list given here is the reasonable cost of accommodation compared with other Bahamian islands. Each of the three most expensive hotels has a swimming-pool, but there are no resort hotels as such. The largest, **Bimini Big Game Fishing Club** (51 rooms), has a hard-surfaced tennis court, lighted for night play and complementary to guests.

I was not impressed with either of the cheaper hotels. **Brown's** was decidedly tacky and gave a strong impression that guests were not welcome. It had very obviously seen much better days: antiquated newspaper clippings and other dusty bric-à-brac hanging on the wall behind the bar imply that this was once, a long time ago, a favoured watering hole. Nowadays the bar is staffed at the owner's rather than the customer's pleasure and the highspot of the evening seems to be watching fourth-rate quiz shows on the TV. The rooms were acceptable and probably worth the money. If you are determined to use Brown's marina and/or dive operation I suggest you stay elsewhere.

The Compleat Angler was also a great disappointment. This former home of Hemingway looks superb in its colour brochure: the real thing is a let-down. Perhaps its best feature is the display of photographs and information concerning the Atlantis legend, with special emphasis on the finds off Bimini. The bar too is fine, air-conditioned, comfortable and far more lively than Brown's. However, nobody was interested in showing me a room (though this was never actually refused) and the communal toilet was in a disgusting state.

On the plus side, Bimini has a comprehensive selection of restaurants, mainly providing Bahamian food and with a good price spread. And there are more nightclubs than you would expect on an island this size (five, including The Compleat Angler) and souvenir-type shopping is in evidence.

In spite of my generally negative attitude to Bimini I wouldn't want to deter you completely. If you are Nassau-bound on Chalk's seaplane service it is worth noting that for a small surcharge you can stop off at Bimini; the seaplane ramp is at Alice Town, a short walk from the hotels (unlicensed porters are readily available to help you with your baggage).

Accommodation in Bimini
Daily winter rates per room in US$

Name and address	Single	Double
Bimini Big Game Fishing Club and Hotel, Alice Town, North Bimini (tel. 72391)	EP: S or D 92 EP: cottage 112; suite 215	
Bimini Blue Waters Marina, Alice Town, North Bimini (tel. 72166)	EP: S or D 95–110 EP: cottage 169	
Brown's Hotel, Alice Town, North Bimini	EP: 35	40
The Compleat Angler Hotel, Alice Town, North Bimini (tel. 72122)	EP: 50	60–65

SPORT

Dive operator

Name and address	Type of diving	Equipment and facilities
Bimini Undersea Adventures, Brown's Hotel, Alice Town, North Bimini (tel. 72227)	Coral gardens, wrecks, coral reefs, drop-off, drift dive, night dives.	Compressors: Mako 15 cfm, 10,000 cf air storage; Tanks: 150 steel; 40' Custom diesel (24 divers), 28' T Craft (20 divers) and 30' T Craft (16 divers) dive boats. Air fills and snorkel rental.

Fishing and boating

Marina	Facilities and rates
Bimini Big Game Fishing Club, Alice Town, North Bimini (tel. 72391)	60 slips. Fuel, water, ice, electricity, showers, liquor store. Dockage: 55 cents per ft per day. Electricity $10 per night. Deep-sea fishing ($200 per half day) can be arranged.
Bimini Blue Waters, Alice Town, North Bimini (tel. 72166)	42 slips. Fuel, water, ice, electricity, showers, lockers, deep freeze. Dockage: transients 50 cents per ft per day. 28' Bertram $250 per half day, $375 per day. 13' Boston Whalers $40 per half day, $70 per day.
Brown's Marina, Alice Town, North Bimini (tel. 72227)	22 slips. Fuel, water, ice, electricity, showers. Dockage: transients 55 cents per ft per day. Deep-sea fishing $225 per half day, $350 per day.

345

SAN SALVADOR

This is the supposed site of Columbus' first landfall in the Americas, though there is some doubt in the matter. I have even seen a map on which the nearby, much larger, Cat Island is named San Salvador—presumably in error! The British renamed San Salvador 'Watling Island', but in 1926 officially gave it back the title of San Salvador, apparently in deference to the great explorer. The island, which is about the same size as New Providence, and the nearest of the Bahamas to Europe, now boasts a monument to Columbus and an important airfield.

WHERE TO STAY

Accommodation in San Salvador
Daily winter rates per room in US$

Name and address	
Riding Rock Inn, Cockburn Town (recently refurbished. Current rates not available.)	EP: S or D 58 AP: S 81, D 104 EP: 1-bedroom villa 80; 2-bedroom 120

As you can see from the table, San Salvador is hardly developed at all, with no real tourist infrastructure. So this is certainly the place to come to get away from it all. The island's population of 1,200 is scattered liberally in ten settlements. There are many miles of beautiful beaches. It is ironic, when one considers the current development and population of the Americas, that the site of Columbus' first landfall has remained much the same.

In one respect though, the tourist infrastructure has become well developed: scuba diving. **Island Divers Ltd,** based at Riding Rock Inn, is a sophisticated and go-ahead dive operation that guarantees plenty of underwater time at four sites on the west and southern coasts. Dives include drop-offs, wrecks, coral reefs and coral gardens. Facilities are comprehensive: compressors—3 × Ingersoll 15 cfm, Poseidon 15 cfm and Mako 7.5 cfm; 218 steel tanks; 4 dive boats, each a 34' Flat top taking 18 divers. There is also a marina at Riding Rock Inn, with six slips but no repair facilities.

LONG ISLAND

As you can see from the table, San Salvador is hardly developed at all, with no real tourist infrastructure. So this is certainly the place to come to get away from it all. The island's population of 1,200 is scattered liberally in ten settlements. There are many miles of beautiful beaches. It is ironic, when one considers the current development and population of the Americas, that the site of Columbus' first landfall has remained much the same.

In one respect though, the tourist infrastructure has become well developed: scuba diving. **Island Divers Ltd,** based at Riding Rock Inn, is a sophisticated and go-ahead dive operation that guarantees plenty of underwater time at four sites on the west and southern coasts. Dives include drop-offs, wrecks, coral reefs and coral gardens. Facilities are comprehensive: compressors—3 × Ingersoll 15 cfm, Poseidon 15 cfm and Mako 7.5 cfm; 218 steel tanks; 4 dive boats, each a 34′ Flat top taking 18 divers. There is also a marina at Riding Rock Inn, with six slips but no repair facilities.

One of the first crops to be grown here with success was sea island cotton. Crops today are corn, bananas, mangoes, peas and other vegetables and fruit. Long Island leads the Bahamas in stock rearing; sheep, hogs, goats and horses are raised here. The total population is only a few thousand.

WHERE TO STAY

Accommodation on Long Island
Daily winter rates per room in US$

Name and address	Single	Double
Stella Maris Inn, Stella Maris	EP: 65	96
	EP: apts. 85–134	
	2-bedroom villa 128–198	
Thompson Bay Inn Apartments, Salt Pond (Deadman's Cay Airport)	EP: 40	45

Stella Maris Inn is the only large establishment in the above list, boasting in all some 42 rooms (the others all have less than ten) and the only one with a swimming pool. There is a comprehensively equipped dive operation. **Stella Maris Divers Ltd** (62106), has four dive boats and extensive facilities.

347

THE EXUMAS

The gentle Arawak Indians, who made such an impression upon Columbus, named these islands 'Yuma'. Today's population of 3,000 is an interesting mix; besides those of African origin, there are the descendants of loyalists from Carolina who remained patriotic to Britain and settled in Great and Little Exuma in the 1870s. Of the blacks, over half bear the surname Rolle. This does not indicate inbreeding on a massive scale, rather, when the slaves were voluntarily emancipated by their landowner Lord Rolle in the nineteenth century, most took his name along with their slice of his land.

Between the mid-seventeenth and mid-eighteenth centuries, the Exumas were highly popular among pirates and it is said that even today stolen treasure lies hidden in the depths of long-forgotten coves. A new breed of twentieth-century buccaneer is reputedly in action today: these unromantic pirates do not fly the Jolly Roger, and prey upon the private yachts which sail down the Exuma Cays. Nevertheless, sailing is certainly the best way to see this scenic string of coral outcrops, part of which is a National Park. The sea is so clear that the ocean floor can be seen at a depth of 60 feet. One can set a course with the accent on enjoying the natural beauty, and take time over it. The same cannot be said about the poor man's alternative of taking the mail boat.

Aero Coach and Bahamasair operate direct flights between Miami and George Town.

WHERE TO STAY

Daily winter rates per room in US$

Name and address	Single	Double
Exuma Supplies, George Town (tel. 62506)	EP: apt. 48	
Hotel Peace and Plenty, George Town (tel. 62511)	EP: 56–90	56–90
Marshall's Guesthouse, George Town (tel. 62571/62081)	EP: 24	42
Out Island Inn, George Town (tel. 62171)	FAP: 108–112	
Pieces of Eight, George Town (tel. 62600)	EP: S or D 60	
Regatta Point, George Town (tel. 62206)	EP: apt. 60	
Sand Dollar Beach Hotel, George Town (tel. 62522)	EP: S or D 80	
Two Turtles Inn, George Town (tel. 62545)	EP: S or D 60–65	
Happy People Marina, Staniel Cay (tel. 42217)	EP: 25	35 approx.
Staniel Cay Yacht Club, Staniel Cay	FAP: 95–150–460 DBL EP: 2-bedroom 125	

SPORT

These are indeed fabulous yachting waters—some say the best in the world. There are also some interesting dive sites, notably **Thunderball Grotto** on Compass Cay (so called because it was used in the James Bond movie of that title) which can actually be snorkelled into, the **Mystery Cave** on **Stocking Island** and the beautiful sea gardens of the **Exuma National Park.**

Dive operators

Name and address	Type of diving	Equipment and facilities
Exuma Dive Company, George Town (tel. 62170/62030)	Coral reefs, coral gardens, ocean blue hole, caves.	Compressor: Mako 5 cfm; Tanks: 36 steel; 38′ Houseboat (18 divers) and 23′ Thunderbird Formula (8 divers) dive boats. Air fills, complete dive shop.
Staniel Cay Yacht Club, Staniel Cay	Charter groups only: drop-off, coral reefs, coral heads.	Compressor: Mako 8.3 cfm; Tanks: 35 steel; 4 × 13′ Whalers (4 divers each). No regular dive trips, rentals and air only. Windsurfing and sailboats.

Fishing and boating

Marina	Facilities and rates
Exuma Docking Services, George Town (tel. 62578)	Fuel, water, ice, electricity, showers, laundry. Marine accessories. Bottom and bone fishing.
Minn's Watersports, George Town (tel. 62604)	No slips, small dock. Marine store and light repairs. 16′ Boston Whalers $45 per day. Other boats available.
Happy People Marina, Staniel Cay (tel. 42217)	6 slips. Fuel, water, electricity, showers. Repairs. Sport fishing arranged. Dockage: 40 cents per ft per day. Electricity per size of boat.
Staniel Cay Yacht Club, Staniel Cay	12 slips. Fuel, water, ice, electricity, laundry. Full repair service including electronics. Sport fishing arranged with local guides. Dockage: 40 cents per ft per day. Electricity from $10 per day.

Tennis is available only at the **Out Island Inn,** which has two courts (Flexi-pave) at $10 per hour, pro. shop and lessons. Most of the social life revolves around the hotel **Peace and Plenty.**

The Berry Islands

A large number of small cays with a total area of 12 square miles comprise the Berry Islands. Tourism is confined to one of the islands, **Chub Cay,** right at the south of the group. Here the **Chub Cay Club** provides the only accommodation (double rooms from $125), marina (74 slips with all facilities including repairs, but only one boat for charter) and dive operation.

Thus the Berry Islands are really best for those who have their own yacht.

Cat Island

If it's a really quiet island with miles of virgin beaches you're looking for, then maybe Cat Island is for you. The population of around 4,000 still makes a living from agriculture, and ruins of old plantation buildings peep out from insurgent vegetation. Cat Island can also claim the highest point in the Bahamas, the 206-ft Mount Alvernia. Caves containing Arawak Indian pre-Columbian artefacts can be seen near Port Howe.

WHERE TO STAY

Name and address	Daily winter rates per room in US$
Cutlass Bay Yacht Club, Cutlass Bay	AP: S 45, D 80 approx.
Fernandez Bay Village, Fernandez Bay, The Bight	EP: 95 (villas)
	cottages for 2 persons 50
Greenwood Inn, Port Howe	AP: S 60, D 80 approx.

Cutlass Bay and **Greenwood Inn** are not totally dissimilar developments, with swimming-pools but no air-conditioning. The greatest difference is in size—Cutlass Bay has fourteen rooms and Greenwood Inn twenty. There is a small dive operation and marina at Cutlass Bay (dock but no slips; Boston Whaler for charter). **Fernandez Bay Village** gives the freedom of apartments and cottages and has, like the other two, the basic hotel facilities of bar and restaurant. Bicycles, cars and scooters can be hired on the island.

Crooked Island/Acklins

These two hooked islands, joined by a ferry, seem as natural as the day Columbus discovered them. By comparison, in terms of tourism, Cat Island is a thriving metropolis. There is one foreign-owned hotel (Pittstown Point Landings) which has a reasonable range of facilities (it has a private airstrip, small dive operation and may be able to arrange boating).

The smaller of the two islands, with an area of 70 square miles, is Crooked Island. Nevertheless the airport is here, as is most of the accommodation for visitors. The much longer Acklins (120 square miles) does seem to have reasonably priced car hire—a necessity.

You'll not find much evening entertainment here. As the official information quaintly words it: 'Juke box music is provided in most eating places.'

WHERE TO STAY

Guesthouses to the rescue. Not only can one 'get away from it all' here, but one can do so for a reasonable price. There are no air-conditioning or swimming-pools at the guesthouses of course, and you can expect accommodation to be fairly spartan.

Accommodation in Great Inagua
Daily winter rates per room in US$

Name and address	*Single*	*Double*
Pittstown Point Landings Ltd Inn, Landrail Point, Crooked Island	FAP: 40	49
Sunny Lea Guesthouse, Colonel Hill, Crooked Island	EP: 30	55
T and S Guesthouse, Church Grove, Cabbage Hill, Crooked Island	EP: 22	32
Williamson's Hilltop View, Pinefield, Acklins	EP: 14	20 approx.

Great Inagua

You will almost certainly visit this island if you intend to try to reach Haiti from the Bahamas by way of the Turks and Caicos Islands, whether travelling by sea or air. There are two points of great interest here: first, it is home to one of the largest flamingo colonies in the world (sometimes numbering up to 50,000) and also provides shelter for an extremely comprehensive collection of wild birdlife. Secondly, it has a large salt lake, which provides sea salt for Mortons (the factory, which can be visited, is in Matthew Town).

WHERE TO STAY
There are two five-roomed guesthouses, one of which at least (**Ford's Inagua Inn**) is closed four months of the year. It seems to charge $30 per room (EP), whilst **Main House** charges $25 per person (EP). Both are situated in Matthew Town.

351

INDEX

Page numbers shown in *italics* refer to maps.

353

INDEX